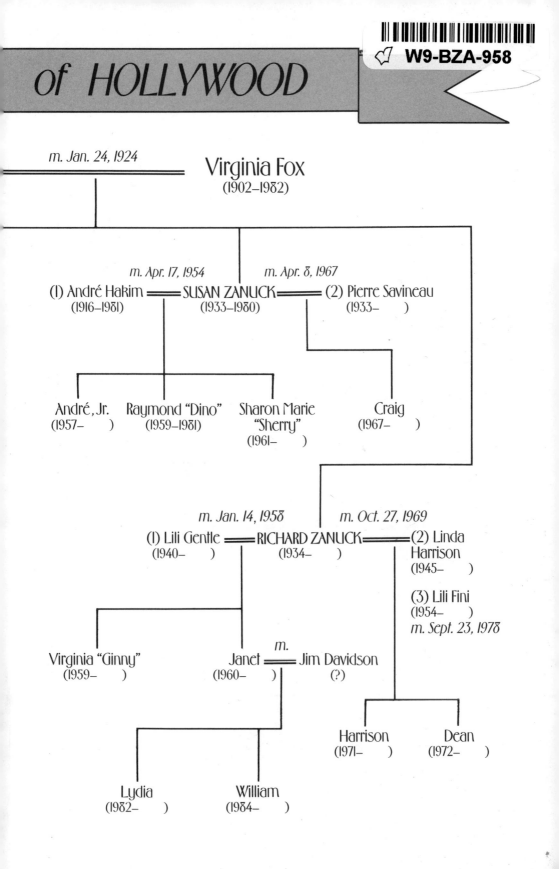

m. Jan. 24, 1924

Virginia Fox
(1902–1982)

m. Apr. 17, 1954   *m. Apr. 8, 1967*

(1) André Hakim ═══ SUSAN ZANUCK ═══ (2) Pierre Savineau
(1916–1981)   (1933–1980)   (1933–   )

André, Jr.   Raymond "Dino"   Sharon Marie   Craig
(1957–   )   (1959–1981)   "Sherry"   (1967–   )
                     (1961–   )

m. Jan. 14, 1958   *m. Oct. 27, 1969*

(1) Lili Gentle ═══ RICHARD ZANUCK ═══ (2) Linda
(1940–   )   (1934–   )   Harrison
                                (1945–   )

(3) Lili Fini
(1954–   )
m. Sept. 23, 1978

Virginia "Ginny"   Janet ═══ Jim Davidson
(1959–   )   (1960–   )   (?)
                       m.

Harrison   Dean
(1971–   )   (1972–   )

Lydia   William
(1982–   )   (1984–   )

THE ZANUCKS OF
HOLLYWOOD

■

THE ZANUCKS OF HOLLYWOOD

THE DARK LEGACY OF
AN AMERICAN DYNASTY

·

MARLYS J. HARRIS

CROWN PUBLISHERS, INC., NEW YORK

For the Harrises of Hollis Hills—
Norman, Max, and Ezra

Published by Crown Publishers, Inc.,
225 Park Avenue South, New York, New York 10003

CROWN is a trademark of Crown Publishers, Inc.

Grateful acknowledgment is made to Delacorte Press, a
division of Bantam, Doubleday, Dell Publishing Group, Inc.,
for permission to reprint an excerpt from *The Happy Hooker*
by Robin Moore, Xaviera Hollander, and Yvonne Dunleavy.
Copyright © 1972 by Robin Moore and Xaviera de Vries.

Manufactured in the United States of America

Book design by Linda Kocur

Library of Congress Cataloging-in-Publication Data

Harris, Marlys J.
  The Zanucks of Hollywood.

  Includes bibliography, index.
  1. Zanuck, Darryl Francis, 1902–1979.
2. Zanuck family.
3. Motion picture producers and directors—United States—
Biography.
I. Title.
PN1998.3.Z36H37 1989
791.43'0232'0924 [B] 88-35220

ISBN 0-517-57020-3

10 9 8 7 6 5 4 3 2 1

First Edition

CONTENTS

■

Prologue
HOMECOMING
1

One
THE PRODUCER
11

Two
HOLLYWOOD WIFE
51

Three
STUDIO BRAT
90

Four
SA SEULE AMIE
136

Five
TWENTIETH CENTURY PRINCESSES
176

Six
TOGETHER AGAIN
206

Seven
ALL THE LITTLE FOXES
241

Eight

THE WAR OF THE WILLS

258

Epilogue

A FAMILY DIVIDED

290

Notes

297

Bibliography

332

Acknowledgments

334

Index

337

PROLOGUE
HOMECOMING

∎

N either those on board the plane nor those waiting on the ground in the sweltering Palm Springs heat knew exactly what to expect when the aircraft touched down late in the afternoon of April 7, 1973. The unfolding drama in which they played depended on the jet's most important first-class passenger, Darryl F. Zanuck—but then, everything always had.

Zanuck, as head of production at Twentieth Century-Fox studios, had once been a ruling monarch of Hollywood. His career spanned half a century. He had supervised more than six hundred motion pictures, among them some of the industry's most memorable and important, including *The Grapes of Wrath, Gentleman's Agreement, All About Eve,* and *The Longest Day.* Armies of writers, directors, technicians, and actors had labored under his command. Careers had flourished and withered at his direction. For years, he ran Twentieth Century-Fox like a proprietary company, awarding jobs to family members, hiring skiing buddies and polo-playing companions as producers, and ordering up contract actresses like malted milks for afternoon trysts in his office. Reporters had once flocked to hear and note down his every action and utterance. He told them that, no matter what they heard, all he ever cared about was making movies.

Now, however, Zanuck was seventy years old and ailing, and his activities went almost unnoted by the press. That morning, he had checked out of a New York City hospital after a ten-day stay for a multitude of illnesses. Accompanied by his twenty-seven-year-old Parisian girlfriend, Genevieve Gillaizeau; his two married daughters, Darrylin de Pineda and Susan Savineau; a grandchild, André Hakim, Jr.; his secretary, Vinnie Argentino; and his two beloved Yorkies, Tina and Lisa, Zanuck had flown home to be reunited with his wife after a separation of seventeen years.

On the ground awaiting Zanuck was his thirty-eight-year-old son, Richard, a notable producer whose success would eventually rival his father's. *The Sting*, one of the movies he co-produced that year with his partner David Brown, would win the Academy Award for best picture, and in 1975, he and Brown would bring to the screen the saga of the giant shark, *Jaws*, a legendary money-maker. Relations between Richard and his father had been cool since 1970 when Zanuck had made headlines by presiding over his son's firing from Twentieth Century-Fox.

At Richard's side stood a tiny elderly woman—Zanuck's estranged wife, Virginia. She had remained obsessively devoted to her husband since 1957 when he walked out on her, on the studio, and on Hollywood to take up a free-wheeling Bohemian life in Europe and New York. The two had separated but never divorced. For years Virginia had kept track of her husband's various affairs with young actresses and models, including his enduring eight-year attachment to tall, blond Genevieve.

Zanuck's poor health had forced his homecoming. Only a few days earlier, his New York doctor had informed Darrylin, Susan, and Richard that their father was becoming senile. Zanuck's forgetfulness made a continued solo existence in his seven-room suite at the Plaza Hotel impossible. He would need constant care and supervision. Zanuck owned Ric-Su-Dar, a luxurious compound in Palm Springs, named for his three children. In the late forties and early fifties, the Zanucks had played weekend hosts at the estate to Joseph Cotten, David Niven, Judy Garland, Elsa Maxwell, Moss Hart, and other prominent members of the movie colony. The gracious estate with its two houses, enormous swimming pool, and fragrant, well-manicured lawns seemed an ideal place for Zanuck to regain his health.

None of the children had been certain that Zanuck would agree to go to Palm Springs. For nearly two decades he had shown no inclination to return home. When his children broached the subject to him at the hospital, however, he was surprisingly agreeable. Zanuck's secretary, Vinnie Argentino, later recalled, "It was suggested to him . . . that . . . it would be good if he got into the sun; and if he would go to Palm Springs . . . it would be a great place for him to recuperate. His first reaction was, 'They'll never let me in,' very jokingly. He was a very humorous person. . . . He wasn't going to do it alone, and if he would go, his daughters would go, his grandson would go, I would go, and Genevieve would go."

Richard, who was already back in Los Angeles, was notified of his father's acceptance of the Palm Springs plan. He called his mother and asked if Zanuck could use the estate. Virginia agreed immediately and enthusiastically. Although this was a moment she had dreamed of for years, Zanuck had caught her unprepared. When the call came, she was living at the Wilshire Holmby in Los Angeles with her companion Alma Diehl. Her driver was on vacation, and the Palm Springs caretaker had been hospitalized. She called Ed Meena, a close friend, and he and another friend, Tom Shirley, drove her up to Palm Springs to help her buy groceries and get organized.

The children had hoped that Zanuck's girlfriend, Genevieve, would stay behind in New York. Darrylin was later to say that her father had lost interest in Genevieve, but that she insisted on coming along. Zanuck instructed Darrylin to order another ticket for her. "I can't take the strain. She wants to go, and that's that," Darrylin recalled him saying. Genevieve had never doubted that she was to be part of Zanuck's group. She, too, had had a talk with Zanuck's doctor. She learned, she later said, "that we were going to Palm Springs because [Zanuck] had a house, which I had been in before, invited by Virginia. That we were going to spend some time in Palm Springs just to rest, so he can recover." Virginia knew that Genevieve was coming, but what would Genevieve say when she saw Virginia?

So Zanuck's daughters and Genevieve, locked in a superficial truce, traveled together. The entire party boarded the first-class section. The flight was fraught with strain and disruption. At one point, Genevieve recalled, Zanuck became confused and anxious. He wanted to jump out of the plane. Genevieve confided to Darrylin that Zanuck was driving her crazy. She opened Zanuck's briefcase to get him a tranquilizer. When Darrylin spotted the array of pills, she exploded. *She* was to be the only one allowed to give Daddy any drugs. The pills Genevieve had been giving him were what got Zanuck in trouble in the first place, Darrylin insisted. She instructed Genevieve to dump all the medications down the toilet in the airplane lavatory. Genevieve complied, and Darrylin gave her father a sedative that his doctor had prescribed.

By the time the plane finally set down in Palm Springs, Zanuck's mood had improved. Wearing the dark glasses that had become his trademark, he grabbed his dogs and sailed to the door of the plane in order to be the first to disembark. He was already down the boarding steps and yards across the tarmac by the time Genevieve got to the door of the airplane. She was astounded. There, right on the airfield, three cars awaited. Virginia stood by the first. "It was like in a movie," said Genevieve. "The car arrived at the plane, and they grabbed him, put him in the car. And Virginia was there, and the doctor [had] told me she was not supposed to be there." Before Zanuck was stashed in the car, however, he greeted his wife with unexpected warmth. Said Argentino, "He walked with his wife. He took her arm. They went arm in arm. They walked away."

Everyone was astonished. It seemed clear from the very first moment that Zanuck meant to stay with his estranged wife; he scarcely seemed aware of Genevieve. He had come back to Virginia as though he had never been absent. In mapping out his plan of action for his father's homecoming, Richard had not anticipated this turn of events. He had originally planned to drive his father and Genevieve to Ric-Su-Dar while everybody else, including his mother, rode in two other cars. Richard had, in fact, asked his mother to wait for them at Ric-Su-Dar in the hope of sparing her a public humiliation—her husband's return with his French girlfriend. Virginia was off in her own orbit, however. "I wouldn't miss it for the world," she insisted. Richard, Susan, and Darrylin had to fight back tears when their father took Virginia's arm. Maybe, just maybe, the family could once again be whole and normal—or at least appear so.

Moving quickly, Richard had whisked his parents into his car before Genevieve could say a word. She was enraged. She had stayed by Zanuck's side when his family wouldn't even look at him. Now they were trying to pretend that she didn't exist, shutting her out, taking him away. She ran across the tarmac and hurled Zanuck's heavy briefcase at him through the open car window. Richard got the car into gear and sped away, leaving Genevieve to ride with Darrylin and Ed Meena. Genevieve curtly ordered Meena to load the luggage, to get going, and to drive faster; at one point he became so incensed at her pushiness that he stopped the car and threatened to throw her out. He was not a servant, he informed her, and she had better behave herself. Knowing the surly Genevieve was desperate to follow Zanuck, he gave his two passengers a Cook's tour of Palm Springs, delaying their arrival at the great gates of Ric-Su-Dar.

When they finally reached the Zanuck family compound, desert darkness was falling with its usual suddenness. Inside the guest house the lights had already been turned on and Zanuck was sitting in the living room. He acted as though his family life had flowed un-interrupted since 1957. When he arrived at the main house that evening, he headed immediately for his old bedroom, which hadn't been used in years. Zanuck ignored his mistress for the most part. Virginia was happily passing around cheese and crackers, and her husband was munching them and drinking a beer. Genevieve's fury had not abated. Guests heard her say of Virginia under her breath, "I'd like to knock down that seventy-year-old hag." Genevieve was miffed that Darryl had eased back into his family circle without a thought for her. Only hours before, in New York, she had been saying that there was absolutely nothing wrong with Zanuck. Now she had changed her mind: he was sick, she reasoned, and he ought to be tucked into bed immediately.

Genevieve was not going to allow the sweet domestic denouement to continue. The family seemed to want her to blend into the scene quietly, like a friend or a houseguest. Instead she crashed through the warmth of Zanuck's homecoming by frostily staking out her claim. People recall her demanding coldly, "Where are Darryl and I going to sleep?" The room went dead with shock, and Richard told Genevieve to shut up—an instruction that produced the opposite effect. She started screaming at him. How dare he talk to her like that? "I could kill you," she yelled. "You are at the bottom of this."

Zanuck finally intervened. "Calm down," he told her. "Calm down." But she couldn't calm down. His injunction merely infuriated her. Why should she calm down? Nothing was as it should be. Virginia wasn't supposed to be here, and Richard had no right to order her around. She grabbed Zanuck's cane, which was propped against a chair, threw it at him, and ran from the room sobbing.

Outside by the pool, Genevieve wept angrily. The Zanuck daughters came out, and Susan tried to comfort her. Genevieve later said that she had already decided to leave. Richard told her that Meena would drive her wherever she wanted to go, but she refused the offer. She saw conspiracy on all sides. Tom Shirley and Ed Meena, Virginia's friends, were acting as bodyguards and if she went with them, some harm would come to her. Let them call her a taxi.

She wanted to bid Zanuck good-bye before she left. When she approached the screen door to the guest house, however, Richard stood in her way. "I am leaving," she told him. "Let me say good-bye." No, Richard firmly responded. The confrontation quickly escalated from softly spoken words to yelling and shoving. According to Meena, "Richard was threatening her. He was going to throw her in the pool. He was going to drown her, he said." Susan held Richard back while Genevieve scuffled with Darrylin. She was trying to push Darrylin in the pool, but managed only to kick her in the leg. The two were yanking each other's hair. Vinnie Argentino tried to intervene and received a sharp kick in the ankle from Genevieve. Richard was screaming that he would kill Genevieve. Virginia watched the battle from a window. She knew her son's temper and she ordered, "Don't strike her! Don't strike her!"

Even when the noise filtered in from the patio, however, an unfazed Zanuck sat contentedly in an armchair eating cheese and crackers. He didn't notice when Genevieve left in a taxi.

It was not back to the airport that she fled, however. Instead she commanded the driver to take her to the Palm Springs police station. By the time she arrived, she had a story ready. Zanuck, she told the cops, had been kidnapped. She had been evicted from the house, she added. "I tried to tell the police what happened to me, and they sent a cop to the house. And I was waiting in the station, and the police said that the cop said, 'I have been told that he went back with his wife.' " The policeman had brought back the fur coat she had left at Ric-Su-Dar. "I don't remember how I got back to Los Angeles, because I believe it was early evening, and this is it, and I left," said Genevieve. "I don't know how I got back."

*   *   *

The confrontation between the Zanucks and Genevieve had lasted only a few minutes, but the ugly scene would be played and replayed in excruciatingly slow motion for years after Zanuck's death in 1979. The major characters argued that his behavior on the night of April 7 clearly revealed his intentions and thus should determine the outcome of an eight-year court battle over his estate. Genevieve came to believe that, after that night, Zanuck was held a virtual prisoner by his relatives until his death. In his previous wills—the last written just two months before his April 1973 reunion with his family—Zanuck had left Genevieve nearly half of his estate, about $2 million. After he returned home, declining in health and mental competence, she claimed, he was prodded by his relatives to cut her out cold. When that effort failed, she charged, Darrylin forged her father's signature on a new will.

Darrylin adamantly denied having forged her father's signature. She and Richard maintained that Zanuck's mind was only temporarily enfeebled by anemia, malnutrition, and unsupervised intake of prescription drugs. Only weeks after he returned to Palm Springs, he became his old self again. It was Zanuck's idea to write Genevieve out of his will. He had tired of her and wanted nothing more than to go back to the wife to whom he had always remained secretly devoted. His romance with Virginia was one of the greatest love stories ever, Darrylin insisted.

That illusory notion of family harmony became ever more difficult to maintain as time went on, however. The battle between Genevieve and the family quickly spawned a flurry of lawsuits, including a bitter legal battle waged by Richard's young sons in an effort to reclaim Virginia's money after her death in 1982. When the Zanucks went to court, private disputes—between mother and son, and sister and brother—went embarrassingly public. A family that had enjoyed all the fruits of boundless success and Hollywood glamour—limousines, polo ponies, celebrity, wealth, and a healthy dose of scandal—was engulfed in enmity. Few consoling fragments of family peace survived.

The grievances addressed in the court cases only partly explained the breaches in the family. For the most part, they simply aggravated the antagonism that had festered just under the surface for years. In their resentment and anger, the Zanucks are not that different from millions of other families. What makes their particular tale worth telling is the extraordinary Darryl Zanuck himself, and the collective memory passed on through his progeny of a life lived outside the commonplace.

✳   ✳   ✳

From the time he was very little, Darryl Zanuck seemed to have a tremendous flair for grandiosity. He was determined to be a great man—indeed, a hero. He rose to power in Hollywood in the late 1920s by devoting himself energetically and tirelessly to one goal: making movies. His power allowed him to give free rein to his vanity. He performed astounding feats—dodging elephants on safari, riding horses like a daredevil, filming under fire in World War II, and partying with Parisian intelligentsia in the 1950s. Only his well-grounded sense of humor kept his arrogance from utterly alienating those who had to live or work with him.

His family regarded him as remarkable and grand. His superiority bound them to him more than to the average patriarch. They needed his approval and his attention not only because he was husband and father but because he was so special. Zanuck loved his family—he probably would have said that he would die for his family—but in some ways they were no more real to him than flickering images on the silver screen. He often treated his wife and children with much the same offhand inattention he directed toward his minions at Twentieth Century-Fox.

To bind themselves to the remote and contradictory figure, his wife and children tried to merge and lose themselves in his commanding personality. Their sense of self came largely from him. Virginia overlooked his constant infidelity. Richard scrambled desperately to please his imperious father, only to be slapped down when he became too successful. Darrylin and Susan designed their lives to parallel their father's, leaving and returning to their California roots when he did.

Even Genevieve remained Zanuck's captive for years after his death. She fought bitterly with his family over his money to prove the importance of her attachment to him.

The mogul's grandchildren played out their own dramas in the darkness of his overwhelming shadow. The most important fact of their lives has been their proud connection to his genius and fame. Their parents' involvement with Zanuck sapped many of the grandchildren of their own drive to achieve. Their legacy should have been wealth, accomplishment, and recognition. Instead, some of them were endowed with a grand sense of entitlement, a small bequest from their grandfather's estate, and little practical training for the real world.

Zanuck was way ahead of his time, not just as a producer but as a man who thought he could have it all. Actress Corinne Calvet, who, against her wishes, almost came to know Zanuck on the casting couch, observed, "In 1950, he was doing what people are doing in the 1980s. Zanuck was a genius; you can't expect him to live a normal life." His sense of entitlement to an extraordinary life free of restraints or obligations has become a twentieth-century disease. Like so many people today, Zanuck wanted to be producer, director, and star of a fantasy that provided him limitless wealth and hours in the spotlight. His wife, his daughters, his son, and his girlfriend were expendable supporting players.

Zanuck's return to Ric-Su-Dar should have signaled a triumphal coming-together of his family, and for a while that appeared to be the case. Yet only a few years later, the Zanucks were hardly on speaking terms with one another. Weak and mentally incapacitated, Zanuck himself could no longer play a central role in their lives. Without him to direct their destiny, they collapsed in on themselves with explosive results. Accusations of neglect, inattention, theft, and greed were flung back and forth. In the supercharged atmosphere even banal family disputes seemed to attain the high seriousness of Greek tragedy.

The battle over Zanuck's will itself took on an epic quality. It became the only way for his wife and children to gain something they'd never had: a sense of themselves as a real family. The struggle over the diminishing fortune lasted for eight years. Those who had loved Zanuck could not give up what they hoped to win—even if the prize was only symbolic.

Had Darryl Zanuck lived to witness the bitter fight that was waged over his money, he might have clicked his tongue in exasperation. He would have taken his family and his girlfriend in hand and prodded them into polite accord, much as he bullied directors, writers, and producers into uneasy agreement during his marathon story conferences. He would have run up against a wall, however. He had set the family's scenario in motion long ago, and by the time he at last returned home in 1973, it was already too late to edit or cut.

It was a wrap.

ONE
THE PRODUCER
■

Darryl Zanuck was tiny and rather unattractive, but he threw off the glow of a 500-watt light bulb. His energy and dynamism animated everyone around him—particularly his family, who felt the magic in his presence. Nobody was more affected by that magic than his wife, Virginia. Even though she sat yards and yards away from him amid the spangled audience at the Academy Awards presentations to watch him receive three Irving Thalberg awards for best producer, she was warmed by his incandescence. His daughters' faces always brightened when he turned his attention on them—to take them horseback riding at a Pasadena country club, for example, or swimming in the pool at the family's Santa Monica beach house. In cutting rooms at Twentieth Century-Fox, his son, Richard, was stunned by his father's brilliance at transforming a batch of flickering images into a bold movie with a tight plot and a fast pace. Zanuck was usually busy and only rarely glimpsed by his family. Still, they felt animated by his light.

His brightness never seemed more extraordinary than it did in late April of 1935 when he adventurously flew cross-country from Los Angeles to New York. The trip took twenty hours, including six stops. A dust storm in the Midwest delayed the flight by nearly a day, but his arrival was triumphant nonetheless. He had made the trip to attend the New York openings of two of his movies, *Les Misérables* and *Cardinal*

Richelieu, and to celebrate the second anniversary of Twentieth Century Pictures, a production company he had founded with Joseph Schenck, president of United Artists.

Zanuck's presence at New York headquarters created a storm of its own. As soon as he was installed in an office, the switchboard lit up and his minions plunged into feverish activity. They labored to match the energy of the dynamo who was churning box-office successes out of the United Artists lot at an impressive rate. His fledgling company had produced eighteen pictures, and all but one had been moneymakers. Though Zanuck was only thirty-three years old, *The New Yorker* had proclaimed him "one of the biggest figures in Hollywood." Somewhat less restrained, *Variety* declared Zanuck "the greatest piece of motion picture property living today." As a producer, he had been a trendsetter, introducing realism into a cycle of gangster movies, taking crews on location, and mining history for scenarios. Legend had it that it was his idea to have James Cagney smash a grapefruit into Mae Clarke's face in *Public Enemy*. After that, every producer in Hollywood felt obliged to have film gangsters belt their sweethearts.

Observing the flurry of activity at the United Artists headquarters, Frank Nugent, the *New York Times* reporter who waited to interview Zanuck that April day, was understandably apprehensive. He wrote, "If an eight-footer with a long black beard, a bull whip, and the mannerisms of the Red Queen had come through the door [I] would have arisen promptly and said, 'Hello, Mr. Zanuck.' " Instead, out popped "a slim, dapper, youngish man with light hair, a blond mustache, an incisive voice, a cigar, and pin-striped, broad-lapelled, gray flannel suit."

Zanuck, one of the first baby moguls, looked like an accountant; he talked like one, too. He complained bitterly to Nugent about a proposed California tax that he predicted would force the film industry to relocate to Florida or South Carolina. A man earning a salary of $200,000 would be left with only about $66,000 in disposable income, he said. It would be impossible for, say, an actor to live on such a meager income. "He must have two cars and two chauffeurs for day and night trips to the studio. Then add the cost of a home, family, life insurance—and an actor's crazy if he doesn't carry at least $500,000— county and city taxes, personal property taxes, charity and—why that leaves only $320 a week for living. It can't be done!" he exclaimed.

Nugent wrote sardonically that he "pondered for a moment the impossibility of anyone getting along on a net income of $320 a week." Zanuck certainly knew that few people in 1935 earned that much. He had a keen eye for budgets and paid his own script readers only about $35 a week. Outside the office where Zanuck and his subordinates bustled, the nation was mired in one of the most desperate years of the Great Depression.

When he complained about the proposed tax, however, Zanuck wasn't particularly concerned about the sufferings of the masses. He was more worried about himself and his family—his wife and their three children, Darrylin, three and a half; Susan, two; and Richard, five months. Though many actors earned more than he, Zanuck's $4,500 a week salary allowed him to hire servants, buy a ranch in Encino where he kept a string of polo ponies, travel to Europe first class, and go on safari in Africa. In England recently, he and his wife had acquired so many eighteenth-century antiques that their house could not accommodate them. The furniture collected dust in storage for years.

Hollywood was and still is a place where economic rules never apply in quite the same way as they do in the rest of the country. Of course there were breadlines and soup kitchens in Los Angeles, too; but in 1935 the job of the film industry headquartered there was to waltz people's minds and spirits away from poverty, dreary jobs, secondhand clothing, and dispiriting reality in general. For whenever Americans could afford to lay out ten cents for a movie ticket, they could sit in a darkened theater and escape to deserts, palaces, elegant hotels, jungles, nightclubs, and mansions. Hollywood created a dreamland, and as a reward for having accomplished this marvelous feat, its denizens—actors, directors, writers, and producers—were insulated from hard times.

That suited Darryl Francis Zanuck just fine, because he viewed himself as exempt from rules, regulations, taxes—applied or implied— and other petty infringements on his freedom. When he was a child, he could not be held in check by parents, grandparents, or teachers. Later, when he was a young man, people scorned his efforts to break into Hollywood. But he smashed through the gates with self-confidence and gall. He styled himself as a writer, a producer, a man of action, a soldier, a ground breaker, a leader, a creative genius. He felt compelled to shatter all molds. Nearly twenty years later, when he was honored by the Screen Producers Guild, he declared that, early on, "I decided to become a genius. . . . And being a genius, I had to live that way. I took up polo, big game hunting, and skiing."

As a self-styled superman, Zanuck liked to feel that he didn't need anybody. But he loved and needed his wife, Virginia, and had wooed her during their courtship like a general waging battle. Almost from the start of their marriage, however, he punished her for her importance to him, by sleeping with other women. He doted on his son, Richard, and brought him into the business, only to fire him when he began to get in the way of Zanuck's own sense of grandness. He showered affection on his daughters, but saw them as peripheral. His concentration was so tightly focused on himself that other people came to life only when they played important roles in his heroic adventures.

Years later, after Zanuck had left his wife and children, lost his film empire, and faded mentally, his glow dimmed until only its memory touched their lives. Even that seemed enough for them, however. Everything he touched was charged with an electricity of its own that defied nature and made it special, just as Zanuck had once been to them. After his death, Darrylin found that her father had carried in his wallet a pressed red rose she had given him as a child. The rose startled her because, she said, it was the same bright red it had been when she handed it to him years before.

*   *   *

In those early days, Zanuck got a kick out of passing himself off as a "rube" from Wahoo, Nebraska, a town about thirty miles west of Omaha. He was born there on September 5, 1902, but most of his growing up was done with his wealthy grandparents in Oakdale, a tiny farm town about one hundred miles to the north, or with his mother and stepfather in Glendale, California. As an adult, Zanuck remembered only a few things about Wahoo. He recalled sliding down the long banister of the little hotel his parents once ran there—a ride more thrilling than a roller coaster. His most significant recollection, he once admitted to reporters, was falling in a cesspool. His mother had warned him not to go near it, but characteristically, he had played right on its rim.

14

Zanuck always liked to play on the edge. His certainty that nothing terrible could happen to him probably had its roots in his childhood. Life with his family was not always smooth, but no matter how bad it got, he grew up with a safety net—provided by his wealthy grandfather Henry Torpin, a rancher who operated grain elevators and flour mills in fifteen Nebraska towns. Torpin's daughter Louise was a willowy blue-eyed platinum blonde, who was somewhat spoiled and who didn't have particularly good taste in men. She met Darryl's father, Frank Zanuck, son of a much less prestigious family of Swiss-German descent, at a Methodist church picnic and married him after a brief courtship. The match was most advantageous to Frank, who had a reputation as a heavy drinker and gambler. Torpin gave the couple the Storrs Hotel in Oakdale as a wedding present and sent them off to Omaha for a lavish honeymoon. In 1893 Louise gave birth to the couple's first child, a boy named Donald. Nearly nine years went by before Louise again became pregnant, this time with Darryl. By that time, the young Zanuck family had moved to Wahoo, where Frank ran the LeGrand Hotel. There, in a corner room on the second floor, Darryl Zanuck was born.

Only a few months after Darryl's birth, his older brother Donald, only nine years old, died after being kicked in the chest by a horse. Whatever harmony Louise and Frank had previously enjoyed may have been lost with the death of their first boy; virtually all Zanuck could remember of his parents from his early years was fighting and more fighting, about his father's drinking and the couple's chronic lack of money. If it hadn't been for Henry Torpin's financial help, they would never have gotten by.

Torpin helped his daughter ease her way out of the unhappy marriage after Louise developed tuberculosis when Darryl was six and was sent to Arizona for a cure. Her father decided that she and Darryl, who seemed small and frail, would be better off living permanently in the warm, dry climate of Los Angeles. Away from Frank, she determined to divorce, and a short time after she did so, Torpin fired his former son-in-law, who later made his way to California where he ran the Hargrave Apartment Hotel in downtown Los Angeles.

Darryl's home life did not improve, however. Louise immediately found and married an even less desirable man, an accountant named C. C. Norton. He drank heavily and regularly beat Louise and her

15

son. A minister's child, Norton always had a ready quote from the Bible to justify his harshness. There was little Darryl could do to protect himself or his mother from his stepfather's rampages. Even trying to speak his mind became a problem. By the time he was eight, he had developed a stutter. And his teeth, which protruded like a rabbit's, made his heroic challenges to Norton seem laughable. The laws his stepfather laid down at home were so harsh and irrational that Darryl began to doubt if any rules and regulations made sense. He saw no need to attend classes and regularly played hooky from his public elementary school in suburban Glendale, where the Nortons lived. He made his film debut as an Indian maiden during one of his many truancies, but his mother spotted him from a passing streetcar and promptly returned him to school. Darryl did no better at the Page Military Academy, a strict Los Angeles boarding school. After a few months, he began running away to visit shops, look in store windows, and wander the city streets aimlessly. During the summer months, his mother and stepfather sent him back to Oakdale to visit his grandparents.

As an adult, Zanuck insisted that he had always had a flair for drama and claimed that he wrote fantastical made-up accounts of wonderful but untrue adventures on his many solo trips by train back and forth between California and Nebraska. In fact, his jottings, some of which his grandfather had published in the local newspaper in 1914, were straight journalism that gave evidence of an eye for detail and abrupt dismissal of the extraneous. "We have two engines and are making forty miles an hour," he wrote. "It is so hot the [writer] is compelled to stop writing. It is now three o'clock and I can write again. All we see now is desert with sagebrush every few inches. The porter says it will be like this the rest of the day so there is no more to write today."

In 1915, when he was thirteen years old, his mother and stepfather, unable to keep Darryl in boarding school or to get along with him at home, sent him to live permanently in Nebraska with his grandparents. Now, nestled in the bosom of the adoring and rich Torpins, he seemed to settle down at school. Darryl was not an outstanding student, though friends recall that his grades were fairly high. He had more important items on his personal agenda than schoolwork and had perfected a gift for gab that tended to cover any lack of effort in geography or math. Irven Wagner, who attended junior high school with Zanuck, remembered, "Darryl was the type of a boy that had a very vivid imagination. He would talk whether it pertained to the subject that the teacher asked the question on or not." His teachers sometimes called his bluff. Added Wagner, "I remember Mrs. Leith saying, 'Darryl, sit down! That doesn't pertain to the question at all.' "

Early on, Zanuck displayed a special gift for leadership. He formed his own boys' club. Part of Darryl's magnetism as a leader, however, was financial. Recalled Wagner, "Grandpa Torpin had money, so Darryl had money and he could finance [the group's] activities. Grandpa Torpin shelled out freely to him." Darryl began his career as a producer then, staging shows with friends for townspeople in his grandfather's barn and charging a penny for admission. The young troupers, whom he had assembled for the shows, would parade through Oakdale's streets in flapping swallowtail coats to publicize the theatricals. They played to capacity crowds.

Some townspeople considered Darryl a little too energetic and exciting. Once he accidentally shot a friend in the hip with a .22 caliber rifle when they were playing cops and robbers. Other high jinks prompted some parents to warn their children not to play with "that Zanuck kid."

His reputation as a troublemaker didn't bother him a bit. By the time he was fourteen years old, Oakdale already seemed too small and narrow for his ambitions. Dreams of glory and derring-do, which might have satisfied other boys, were not enough for Darryl. He yearned to do things immediately, without waiting to be "grown-up" or "old enough." War fever was sweeping the country during those years. Europe was embroiled in hellish trench warfare, and from Mexico, Pancho Villa had launched raids on U.S. territory. Darryl felt he had to get in on the action—or else. He tried to enlist in every branch of the armed services, though he weighed only 107 pounds—3 pounds short of the minimum. By September 4, 1917, the day before his fifteenth birthday, he managed to gain enough weight to pass the physical and to con the recruiting officer into believing he was eighteen. That night he was inducted into the Omaha National Guard. Henry Torpin was at first angry but eventually grew sympathetic to his grandson's desires. He agreed to write his daughter and persuade her not to report the underage soldier to authorities.

After a seemingly endless stay in New Mexico that found him waiting on tables in the officers' mess and clearing sagebrush, his unit was shipped to Brest, France, where he caught his first frightening sight of war casualties. It immediately dawned on him that he could be entering a bloodbath—in fact, his company had been sent to relieve an Ohio division that had been all but wiped out. Any other sixteen-year-old might then have confessed his age and begged to be sent home, but not Darryl Zanuck. He was going to fight.

By the time the troops entered Belgium, he was a private first class. He worked as an orderly with a hospital group and sometimes served as a runner delivering messages to forward positions. At last his ideals of high adventure seemed to have come true. Once, he narrowly escaped getting his feet blown off. More often, he modestly asserted later, his wounds resulted from his own clumsiness. His worst was a large cut on his head, which he sustained when he ignominiously fell on a rock. Many of his adventures and misadventures were described in letters he sent to his grandfather, who enthusiastically had them published in the Oakdale newspaper. They were not the stuff of which movies are made but rather flat accounts of delousing and other minor military tribulations. One of Zanuck's commanding officers was so impressed with a letter the private showed him that he sent it to *Stars and Stripes*, which printed it.

In August of 1919, when he was mustered out of the army, he returned to Oakdale but found nothing to keep him there. Only days later, he took off for his parents' home and more schooling in California. His adventures as a teenage soldier made him even more intolerant of the slow pace and petty rules of school. After a few weeks at Manual Arts High, he dropped out. He later said: "I just couldn't get my mind back into it. The whole thing seemed so silly—so hopeless."

School wasn't hopeless—it just wasn't leading him anywhere special. Darryl Zanuck wanted to be special.

*   *   *

In 1919 Los Angeles was full of bright, adventurous young people who were riding high on the burgeoning film industry and its stunning salaries. While Zanuck lived humbly with his parents, other men only a few years older than he were riding in chauffeur-driven Packards and building palatial estates in Bel Air and Santa Monica. Darryl was determined to break into that world. His few literary successes—small though they were—convinced him that he could make his mark as a writer. He wrote a few short stories and sold his first to *Argosy* just before his eighteenth birthday in 1920. Another, called "Mad Desire," was bought by *Physical Culture*. The story was a shameless potboiler about an adventurer named Malcolm Dale who had fled London in favor of a locale with the exotic name of Papal, after killing two men he thought were his wife's lovers. Subtitled "Determined to die in a futile effort to make amends, love points him a better way and rekindles his desire to live," the tale established Zanuck—in his own mind, at least—as a writer.

He tried to crash the studios to sell his screenplays, but met with little success. In the early 1920s, screenwriting did not require terribly artful writing. Most scenarists simply had to pull together a plot and write "intertitles"—dialogue and narrative that interrupted silent-screen action. Zanuck was certainly capable of crafting an action-packed plot. The movies had changed a great deal since he dressed up as an Indian maiden in Glendale nearly a decade earlier, however. Melodrama was on the way out in the early 1920s; longer, more sophisticated dramas were in vogue. American moviemakers had sopped up inspiration from European counterparts such as Ernst Lubitsch and Fritz Lang, who used the close-up to explore the psychology of their characters.

Zanuck scrambled desperately to start a career. He took on a series of unrewarding jobs—eighteen of them in a year's time. He worked for a drug company, then took a job as a salesman in a shirt store. He sold subscriptions to a Los Angeles magazine, wearing his military uniform to elicit sympathy from his prospects. At one point he took a brutalizing job as a rivet-catcher at the shipyards in Los Angeles Harbor. He lasted only a few weeks. Belatedly, he began to regret having quit school and took some correspondence courses in commercial art. With this dubious background as an artist, he got a job tinting posters in the lobby of the Orpheum Theater in downtown Los Angeles. In his spare time he operated the Darryl Poster Service, and walked from shop to shop in Los Angeles soliciting orders for posters, which he painted at night. The company promptly failed. Had it not been for a continuous flow of checks from his grandfather, he would have been completely broke.

It looked as though he was going nowhere. One day while trying to hawk his posters in a beauty parlor, however, he met A. F. Foster, a wealthy Canadian who was marketing a hair tonic made from the yucca plant. The hair goop was called Yuccatone. Together the two men cooked up the idea of making a movie about the virtues of Foster's product. They would show the film at state fairs to stampede all the rubes into buying pots of Yuccatone. Zanuck couldn't believe his good fortune in winning the backing to make a feature on his own. He devised the plot of a one-reel feature that was little more than a long-winded commercial. According to Zanuck, "It started out in the beauty parlor where it showed a woman getting a wonderful shampoo, and then, in a series of dissolves, we see a bottle or a jar of Yuccatone . . . and then, dissolve to the desert where we showed a tribe of Indians making the stuff . . . we flashed back to the beauty parlor, and we showed the woman very satisfied with the shampoo she got with Yuccatone." The title was unforgettable: *You've Never Seen a Bald Indian*—a verity Zanuck believed wholeheartedly. He peddled the movie everywhere and finally got it shown at the California state fair, where it was a popular if not a critical success, and the clay bottles of Yuccatone sold rapidly. About a month later, however, the hair goop started fermenting in its jars. Bottles of Yuccatone began exploding in communities all over California.

The dubious cinematic achievement refueled Zanuck's dream of breaking into the movies. He never for a moment entertained the thought that he might lack the necessary talent. His problem, he decided, was that he had no contacts, no relatives in the movie business. Hollywood was no longer the open city it had once been. In the first two decades of the twentieth century, most film production companies had been fly-by-night operations that needed little capital or management; almost any newcomer to Los Angeles could get a job in the business. Power was then concentrated in the hands of owners of theater chains and distribution exchanges. As the years rolled by, however, the public appetite for movies proved insatiable, and theater owners didn't have enough "product" to shove at them. By the end of World War I, many of the most powerful theater magnates—Carl

Laemmle, Adolph Zukor, and William Fox—had founded their own studios. The weather drew them to Los Angeles where they could shoot outdoors year round.

The up-and-coming titans of the movie business were nearly all European-born Jews. Los Angeles appealed to their immigrant yearnings to belong to American life; there was as yet no firmly entrenched society that would snub them. Indeed, the town still had the look of a frontier outpost. There were few paved roads, and scattered houses were almost unnoticeable among the groves of orange and lemon trees. Yet, soon after the Jewish magnates arrived, they established an exclusionary social and professional structure of their own. They employed their children, sons-in-law, uncles, and brothers in the business. Failing that, they looked to other Jews as reliable employees—people they could trust. Of course, the Jewish moguls also hired gentiles; had they recruited only other Jews, they would quickly have run out of prospective employees. As a midwestern Methodist, however, Zanuck felt that he was out.

His strategy was to ally himself with the movie industry's WASPs. The Los Angeles Athletic Club—located in an austere building on Seventh and Olive, which housed residential accommodations, a gym, a swimming pool, and a restaurant—had become a social center for Charlie Chaplin, Roscoe "Fatty" Arbuckle, Mack Sennett, comedian Ray Griffith, Jack Pickford, and dozens of other film notables. Zanuck begged his grandfather to underwrite a membership that would help him mingle with the great and near-great. Ironically, Zanuck was initially rejected because club members mistakenly believed he was Jewish. Torpin almost withdrew his support when he learned of the club's anti-Semitic membership policy. His grandson, who later produced *Gentleman's Agreement*, Hollywood's first and only attack on anti-Semitism, wasn't concerned about high-minded principles back then. "Everybody has prejudices," he told his grandfather. To move his career forward, he had to belong.

The club's sound-mind-in-a-sound-body philosophy appealed to young Zanuck, who had always made up for his small stature with fervent athleticism. He had boxed for a spell in the army, but at the club, he began running, swimming, working out with weights, and following other body-toning pursuits. If Zanuck hoped to develop a coterie of flunkies at the athletic club, as he had during his childhood in Oakdale, he was initially to be disappointed. The young boy with all the teeth did not quite fit in. Ray Griffith, one of the few who befriended him, declared years later that hardly anybody there believed Zanuck's stories about having served with the army in Belgium; Zanuck simply looked too young. To many at the club, he seemed like a social-climbing upstart. When club members threw a Christmas party his first year there, they left him out. Practically everyone played a joke on him at one time or another. One favorite pastime was to send him rushing across town where a fabulous but nonexistent job awaited. Once, when he confided to a few men that he was eager to sell a story, they introduced him to an Italian film producer—actually a club hanger-on. The "producer" pretended great enthusiasm for the script. Zanuck danced attendance on the man, desperately spending the money his grandfather sent him on elegant meals for the phony Italian mogul, who strung him along with promises but never signed a check for the script.

For the Hollywood brat pack of the 1920s, the athletic club functioned like a college fraternity house. Its residents kept themselves busy exercising, getting drunk, "making" women, exchanging locker-room jokes, and making nuisances of themselves. Zanuck's zest for pranks and high jinks eventually won over his fellow club members, and it wasn't long before he, too, was part of the practical-joking in-group. He often bragged later about one night at the ballet when he egged on a drunken friend to throw a potted plant from the balcony at a dancer bouncing across the stage in swooping jetés. It missed its mark but hit the conductor square in the back of the head, dislodging his toupee.

The back-slapping paid off. William Russell one day handed his friend a play called *The Storm*. The action took place on one set, and Zanuck was sure he could turn it into a screenplay. He borrowed some money to purchase the property, rewrote it into a scenario, and sold it to Universal Pictures for $525. In 1923, at the age of twenty-one, he thought he had made it in Hollywood.

His success was crushingly brief. His newfound glory went smash up against a change in producers' tastes. Increasingly aware of movies as an art medium, filmmakers were in the market for "literature." They wanted authors with big names. Movie magnates competed furiously to buy the works of writers like Somerset Maugham, J. M. Barrie, and Elinor Glyn. Zanuck scarcely knew how to market himself in light of

Hollywood's rage for published authors. One day, Zanuck bemoaned his stalled career to Raymond Griffith, while the older man was shaving. Without paying too much attention, Griffith responded, "So write a book." So Zanuck did—kind of. In two weeks' time, he patched up two of his rejected scenarios to look more like stories than screenplays, added a new yarn, and wrote a one-hundred-page testimonial to Yuccatone, which he disguised as fiction. A. F. Foster, the manufacturer of the hair tonic, agreed to finance the publication of the book. The novel, which should have been called *Yuccatone Redux*, was entitled *Habit*.

The hair-tonic novelette began with a murder in a New York nightclub, moved on to kidnappings and conflagrations, and wound up with the unlikely arrival of the U.S. cavalry and the historic discovery of Yuccatone. Zanuck sent the studios engraved announcements of the publication of *Habit* and even managed to get the collection reviewed in the *New York Times*, where it was praised for its "ingenuity of plot" and "great variety of invention"—no kidding—but Zanuck's stylistic overkill would probably have made his junior high school teacher, Mrs. Leith, squirm. The book's first sentence was "Ling Foo Gow riveted his jet orbs on the burly figure that advanced on the narrow sidewalk of cracked asphalt, and with an excessive display of facial contortion, brought the aged lines of his poppy-hued countenance to an intensified scowl." To the unliterary producers and executives Zanuck sought to impress, however, *Habit* could have been *David Copperfield* or *The Red Badge of Courage*. A book was a book. Now that he, too, was an author, Zanuck sold every one of the stories and earned $11,000.

He was now in steady demand. His outrageous sense of humor won him jobs as a gag writer and later a position as a scenario editor for Mack Sennett, one of his L.A. Athletic Club friends. He never cared much for Sennett, who ruled his studio roost like a nineteenth-century straw boss, always on the alert for writers who slacked off playing cards—an activity Zanuck and his fellow writers could scarcely resist. Later, Zanuck switched to a job as a gag writer for Charlie Chaplin but moved on again to work for H. C. Witwer, a popular short-story writer. Zanuck adapted Witwer's comedies to screenplays, and Mal St. Clair, a pal from the Sennett studios, directed the productions. Zanuck was earning $150 a week—a tremendous salary at the time.

Darryl Zanuck was an unquestionable success, and he was only twenty-one years old—though he looked more like seventeen with his slight build and downy cheeks. He could live the life of a Hollywood playboy, getting drunk with his friends, shrieking over the pranks they constantly played on one another, dining and dancing at the Sunset Inn, the Vernon Country Club, or some other night spot with an eager and willing starlet on his arm. He looked like anything but the answer to female yearnings. A physical culturalist, he was wiry and strong. Five feet six was as tall as he ever got, however, and then only when he stretched his spine straight. A high, square forehead seemed to squash his nose and mouth into the lower half of his face, and his teeth snaggled out of his mouth when he let his lips go slack.

His manners *were* questionable, and his grammar was not always grammatical. He sometimes made up words as he went along. He was still a very rough diamond—maybe just a piece of coal in transition. Yet he had a ready wit, a zest for action, and limitless—some would say unjustified—self-confidence. He already had a bit of power and money, which often count more than looks with Hollywood women. And he had experience—some in the army at bordellos and plenty of adventures with women in his days at the athletic club—that made him believe he was something of a lady-killer. He hardly seemed like marriage material, but he was—or, at least, he became—a good prospect when he met Virginia Fox in 1923.

*   *   *

Virginia, six months older than her future husband (though she would usually tell people she was the same age or a year younger), had already won Hollywood success in her own right. She was tiny—only four feet eleven inches—and lovely, with perfect teeth, glossy dark brown hair, and a porcelain complexion. For a while, she was a Mack Sennett bathing beauty, described by the *Hollywood News* as a "pocket Venus." Later she played opposite comedian Buster Keaton in *Cops*, *The Blacksmith*, and *The Playhouse*. She didn't really think she could act. By her lights, she simply followed directions. "If I was hanging from an elk's head and they said, 'Hold it,' I held it—even if they went to lunch, I did whatever I was told."

and, worse yet, not even in a church. Virginia's father and her brother Freddie did turn up, however. So scant was the attendance at the early-morning ceremony that the couple had to recruit a janitor in the building to serve as a witness. Zanuck proudly bestowed on Virginia a platinum wedding band with three large diamonds, but he looked frightened. Virginia joked that he was as gray as the coat he was wearing. Her father gave them a brand-new Hudson, his mother a year's free rent for a bungalow in the motel complex she owned.

The groom was able to wangle only a long weekend away from his work on the Witwer series for his honeymoon, and he booked a room at the castlelike Coronado Hotel in San Diego. A group of Virginia's girlfriends—Mary Pickford, ZaSu Pitts, and Mildred Lloyd among them—bade the couple a raucous farewell at the train station. Their derision was ill-concealed. Several of Virginia's bathing-beauty pals had also dated Darryl Zanuck and had endured his adventurous paw-ings. When the girls learned that John Philip Sousa's marching band was on the same train, they determined to get back a little of their own from Zanuck. Just as the bride and groom were settled cozily in their compartment, they were blasted by strains of "The Stars and Stripes Forever" as the entire band trooped into their car. In no time at all, the entire trainload of people knew the couple had just married. Zanuck was mortified, but he was stuck until the train arrived a few hours later.

Virginia gave up acting soon after they returned to Los Angeles. "When I met Darryl Zanuck, all thoughts of a career left my mind," she later told an interviewer. Soon after, her husband got his first big break, writing a script for one of the decade's biggest stars: Rin Tin Tin. The dog had been "discovered" as a puppy on the Western Front in World War I by American fliers who named him Rin Tin Tin after a yarn doll they hung for luck in the cockpits of their airplanes. After the war—and some training—Rin Tin Tin became a sensation as a night-club performer. The dog could pick up a coin with his nose and deposit it in a cup, jump up and down on a stool, and count to ten with his paws. Producer Jack Warner signed the dog and determined to make him a star.

Jack Warner asked Zanuck if he could put together a screenplay for the dog after the two men were introduced at a restaurant one night by Mal St. Clair. Warner recalled Zanuck as a "down-cheeked youngster who looked as though he had just had the bands removed from his teeth so he could go to the high school prom." "Oh sure, give me a couple of days," replied Zanuck with characteristic chutzpah. Four days later, the three men met in Warner's office. Zanuck and St. Clair had a story called *Find Your Man* with a North Woods setting. St. Clair played the man, and Zanuck acted out the role of Rin Tin Tin by getting down on all fours, scratching, snarling, and running through the "North Woods" of Warner's studio office. Warner laughed at Zanuck's antics but hired him on the spot.

Zanuck did not consider the pooch a joke at all. Rin Tin Tin got him a job—writing scenarios for the dog's adventures. "He was the most brilliant bloody animal that ever lived," Zanuck declared years later. Rin Tin Tin provided Zanuck and the studio with steady profits and taught him a valuable lesson in filmmaking: when you have a good idea, copy it and do it again and again until you find a new idea. Later he was to copy and recopy gangster movies, musicals, historical dramas, and movies with preachy themes of social concern in a similar fashion.

Zanuck began haunting the cutting room, where he learned how to streamline his often overblown story lines by splicing and looping. People at Warners found his energy daunting. Zanuck could devise a screenplay in a matter of days or edit someone else's in a matter of hours and make it work. Soon he was grinding out scenarios for humans, too. In 1926 he was asked to write the screenplay for *The Better 'Ole,* the very first picture in which sound effects were used.

Supposedly Zanuck was a mature married man, but he and Virginia behaved more like a footloose comedy team. She was reputedly a terrible cook, so they dined out every night, usually at the Los Angeles Athletic Club. There Zanuck could jaw about business with other writers and indulge in one of his favorite hobbies—back-slapping. Virginia could gaze on admiringly, joining when she could get a word in. The Zanucks were slim, trim, smart, and stylish—a snazzy little Hollywood couple.

At home, though, things were not so smooth. Zanuck still felt as though he wasn't making it big enough and fast enough. He chronically suffered from nightmares that kept Virginia from sleeping. He was competitive at work and competitive at athletics and competitive with his bride for control of their household. In 1926, two years after their marriage, he came home one evening and happily announced that he had bought—on his own—a big house for them, complete with pots and pans and furniture, on Gardner Street. Virginia was annoyed that her husband would deprive her of a say in choosing her own home. He couldn't understand why she was furious with him. In the Hollywood scheme of things, the house was not particularly grand; but Virginia worried that they couldn't afford it. She obediently packed and moved—but icily. She won the point. Though many more difficult domestic battles with her husband lay ahead of her, that was the last time Zanuck played autocrat on the home front.

*　　*　　*

In the mid-1920s, Zanuck was working on the Warner Brothers studio lot with other writers—and behaving like an adolescent. He didn't seem to worry about hurting other people's feelings or causing them unnecessary grief or stress. Zanuck and Roy Del Ruth, the director, shared an office, and they delighted in drilling holes in the wall to peer at and unsettle their next-door neighbor writer Bess Meredyth, who was later to marry director Michael Curtiz. Zanuck and Del Ruth also bought electric gadgets, which they carefully placed in some stooge's chair. When they heard the resulting "bzzzzz," they screamed with laughter. The two delighted in installing fake telephones in new staffers' offices. When directors Henry Blanke and Ernst Lubitsch joined Warner's, their English was so fractured that they were terrified of speaking on the phone. Yet the Zanuck-inspired prop phones rang every few minutes. When the two finally got up the courage to answer, they found nobody on the line. "It was a big joke on us," recalled Blanke years later.

Zanuck became the most prolific writer at Warner Brothers. In 1926 he wrote so many scripts—he totted up nineteen—that an exhibitor got up at a sales convention and protested that the company was charging too much to overhead. "You're only paying this one writer—Zanuck," he yelled. So the Warners instructed Zanuck to keep a lower profile. He began to write under several other names and reserved the use of his own name for productions he really cared about. Cagily, he copyrighted his pseudonyms—Melville Crossman, Mark Canfield, and Gregory Rogers. He liked to joke that MGM actually tried to hire Crossman.

Few of his efforts scored points with critics. They dismissed *The Social Highwayman* and *Footloose Widows* as "hokum" or an "old wheeze." *The Better 'Ole*, however, became one of the biggest comedy hits of 1926. Almost every story idea Zanuck turned his hand to wound up a box-office smash. He seemed to possess an uncanny ability to make a story work on the screen, and he began to see himself as a genius. Directors were dismayed when he invaded the sets of Warners' "class" productions to declaim in a shrill voice, illustrated with exuberant horseplay, exactly what they were doing wrong. A few disgruntled directors petitioned the head office and had him barred from their sets. Gradually, however, the Warners decided his ideas made sense; on some features they asked him to "supervise"—to produce, in today's parlance. His capacity for overwork led him to take over the supervision of more and more pictures. It wasn't long before he was producing half of Warners' output.

The studio was constantly in upheaval. The Warners ditched general managers more often than banana republics overturned governments. Some studio bosses lasted no more than a few months. Late in 1927, Jack Warner summoned Zanuck to his office. The very next day, Warner announced, general manager Raymond Schrock would be gone. Zanuck was to take over production at a salary of $1,000 a week. He had better buy himself some glasses and grow a mustache, Warner joked, because no one would take orders from someone who looked like a kid. Warner also laid down the law. He wanted Zanuck to turn out twenty productions in the next year on a budget of $1.3 million—only $65,000 a picture, a small amount even then.

Zanuck later remarked he was so excited that "I almost wet my pants." As he stood in front of the doors to the main office, breathing in the night air and feeling as if he had taken over all of Hollywood, the doorman called to him. "Psst, psst," he hissed. In Zanuck's ear, he whispered gossip that Schrock was on his way out. He speculated who would get the top job. "Me," Zanuck told him. The old man thought that idea was so funny he couldn't speak. Said Zanuck, "I was only twenty-five years old, and I looked less."

Hal Wallis, then a rising producer at Warner Brothers, didn't find Zanuck's elevation funny at all. At the Burbank lot, where he had been responsible for half of all Warners' productions, he arrived at work one morning to find that his young colleague was now his boss.

Zanuck moved quickly to make his status felt. He had sent a workman to Wallis's office to paint in Wallis's new, less important title. Wallis later wrote that he sat down on the stairs in front of his freshly painted door and laughed.

Producers then rarely received screen credit, but Zanuck wanted it known that Warner Brothers' many successes were his responsibility. And not the least of his great, self-ascribed credits was the unprecedented use of sound. Warners bought rights to Vitaphone, a new technique for producing sound—a kind of record player that moved in sync with film. The studio had already used the system on two earlier movies for sound effects and music. To exploit the gimmick further, Warners bought the rights to *The Jazz Singer*, the Broadway stage play about a cantor's son who breaks away from his family. Zanuck supervised the production, which starred Al Jolson. Originally, Zanuck planned to record only the songs and to use titles for dialogue, but one day, he later told Mel Gussow, his biographer, "We were all standing around waiting for the music to be played. Suddenly it dawned on me, why don't they have a conversation? The mike was on! I said, 'Why doesn't Jolson turn to his mother and say, "Mama, I wanna sing a song for you." ' Then the guy turned the sound machine on early. When they played it back, there was Jolson's voice as clear as a bell. That was when the talking thing started." Wallis, his rival, didn't remember Zanuck's participation at all, and Jack Warner, of course, declared that *he* was the one who directed Jolson to speak. The critics panned the movie, but the public made it a runaway hit.

Thereafter, Zanuck presided over a relentless wave of sound. *The Lights of New York,* his next picture, featured screeching taxis, whistles, bells, dialogue, and crashing doors that practically obliterated the drive of the plot; it cost only $21,000 but grossed over $3 million. In 1929, Zanuck determined to make the very first sound spectacle, and he chose Noah's Ark for his subject. Animals growled, barked, twittered, and squeaked, waves crashed, thunder boomed, and thousands of extras screamed into concealed microphones. For years, critics considered it a bellwether—the worst movie ever made. Some time after the production appeared, Zanuck ran into writer Arthur Caesar in a bar in Tijuana. Without ceremony, Caesar gave Zanuck a hard kick in the pants. "That's for taking a book that was a hit for nineteen hundred years and making a flop out of it," yelled the writer. Zanuck characteristically refused to admit that the disaster epic was a disaster. "*Noah's Ark* was *not* the worst picture in the world. . . . It went okay in Europe," Zanuck argued.

Sound for sound's sake quickly staled for him. By 1930 he was already riding the crest of a wave of gritty gangster movies. Again he was looking to copy and recycle a popular subject, in this case, the frightening world of mobsters. The urban terrorism of bootleggers and gangsters was then on virtually every front page in America. Zanuck's one-time partner A. F. Foster, the Yuccatone magnate, had turned bootlegger and died in a gangland murder. "It's a war out there," declared Zanuck like a tenacious city-room editor. The stories had to be told to the public. The public, after all, wanted to know. After the success of his first gangster effort, *Doorway to Hell* (1930), Zanuck produced the now classic *Little Caesar* (1930), the violent saga of a gangster, starring Edward G. Robinson. The story was based on a novel by W. R. Burnett about a gangster whose career closely resembled that of Al Capone. Jack Warner claimed to have been the one to read it, acquire it, and cast Edward G. Robinson as the antihero. Zanuck supervised the picture but didn't take much of a creative role in its production. He merely let it happen. Although he was later to admit that he really was only 10 percent responsible for the picture (he gave director Mervyn LeRoy the balance of the credit, omitting Jack Warner), he willingly took credit for the hit for years. Warner bitterly complained, "If there are any regrets about the [*Little Caesar*] blockbuster—and it was all of that as Hollywood went into the gangster cycle—it is that Darryl Zanuck has recently taken credit for his pioneering exposé of the Chicago underworld. Mervyn LeRoy and I put *Little Caesar* together, and Zanuck had nothing to do with its success."

Public Enemy, in 1931, however, was a Darryl F. Zanuck production all the way. It broke more ground than the earlier movies, revealing the criminal character with broad—some would say obvious—cinematic gestures: Jimmy Cagney shooting the horse that killed his buddy, for example, shoving his mother around, and calling his upstanding brother a sucker for working hard. Of course, the most memorable scene—when Jimmy Cagney, bored with the prattling of his wife played by Mae Clarke, rams a grapefruit into her face and twists it around—Zanuck inaccurately claimed as his own idea. "I thought of it in a script conference," he said. In fact, the episode appeared in *Beer and Blood*, the unpublished book on which the movie was based.

Zanuck's involvement with work was intense. He would arrive at the studio at ten, dictate letters, story ideas, and memos, lunch with his executives, and hold story conferences until late in the afternoon. Hefting a sawed-off polo mallet—to strengthen his arm and to punctuate his points—he would lunge around his office, acting out roles, making up dialogue, speaking first in a high, squeaky voice to impersonate a woman and then a low voice for a man. A secretary scribbled shorthand notes, which were later transcribed and dispatched to writers, producers, and directors. Authoritarian he might have seemed, but he listened to his employees. Once, when pacing his office while thrashing out a story, he declared, "And then his love turned to hate." Screenwriter Kathryn Scola asked, "But, sir, why does his love turn to hate?" Zanuck left for the adjoining bathroom. The toilet flushed noisily, and a moment later he returned. "All right," he declared. "So his love doesn't turn to hate."

He cared about every part of every movie being made on the Warners lot. No detail was too small for him to note. When he viewed rushes, he would remember different camera setups. "That was better in the number two shot," he would declare. The director would argue that there had been no number two shot, but when the dispute was sorted out, Zanuck was more often right than wrong. He was ready to fight to get what he wanted—even with his boss, Jack Warner. At a sneak preview of *Public Enemy* in 1931 at the Forum Theater in Los Angeles, Warner decided that the movie's ending—when Cagney's trussed-up body is delivered to his family's doorway—was much too raw for moviegoers. He ordered Zanuck to change it, and Zanuck blew his top. He would quit rather than change the ending, he told Warner. William Wellman agreed with Zanuck, but the unfortunate Michael Curtiz sided with Warner. With a roar, Zanuck hauled off and socked Curtiz right in the mouth, forcing a cigar halfway down his throat. It is not clear whether Warner was intimidated by this display, but the ending stood.

Zanuck would often work deep into the night, cutting and shaping pictures. To spend any time with her husband, Virginia would have to join him at his nightly movie-editing sessions. He valued her opinions;

if she didn't like a scene, he would have it changed—much to the chagrin of his writers and directors.

Despite his attachment to his wife, however, he cheated on her constantly. Everybody at the studio knew about his affairs because he was so busy he carried them on at the office. Invariably, he chose ingenues and minor starlets for these sexual liaisons. Actress Myrna Loy recalled that "I opened the wrong door at the studio once and caught a sort of half-star at Warners sitting on his lap. I quickly closed the door, but maybe he never forgave me for that. I used to tease him about it, which didn't help matters."

While Zanuck could take revenge on the redheaded, fair-skinned Myrna Loy by making her play inappropriate roles as Creoles and Mexicans, he trembled with anxiety to think that his wife might learn of his romantic intrigues—which she did. When he felt he had done something that would displease her—like getting drunk with his friends or gambling all night at a poker game or turning up with lipstick on his collar—"he would get in quite a stew," remarked Curtiz. "Then he was like a little boy trying to think up an alibi." And no wonder. When Virginia learned of his flirtations, she blew up and usually threatened to leave him. He didn't want to lose her; he would patch things up with apologies and jewelry.

Zanuck's expanding responsibilities squeezed Virginia into a small corner of his life. Only when she gave birth to their first child, Darrylin, on August 13, 1931, did she spring back into primacy in his life. When she went into labor, Zanuck appeared at the last minute to supervise the birth in the delivery room. He stood alongside the doctor and nurses, telling them what to do as though they were his employees at the studio.

His new role as a father did not lure him home to his family, however. His true family became a group of flunkies he gathered around to yes him. "I guess he needed the group to bolster his confidence—he was so young he barely knew what he was doing," observed Philip Dunne, who later worked for Zanuck at Twentieth Century-Fox. The group held story conferences together, ate lunch together, and played together—at whatever game or sport Zanuck chose.

He organized a duck-hunting club so everybody in Zanuck's coterie—even Jack Warner himself—had to go duck hunting. The group

traveled in lavish Hollywood style—in private railroad cars with cater-
ers and servants. Still, Michael Curtiz later recalled the trips as dreary
exercises in follow-the-leadership. "I had no idea about duck hunting
and neither did anybody else at the studio. But we all had to go. The
casting director almost blew my head off. He had no idea how to use a
gun. There we were—sitting in those damn trenches in the rain one
morning at three or four o'clock—but that was the order from
Zanuck."

Zanuck continued to get into fights—he never had been able to shy
away since his military school days. In Seattle, the jumping-off point
for a Canadian hunting trip with some of his buddies, Zanuck picked a
fight with director William Wellman one night in a speakeasy. Wellman thought the pushy little producer was "acting too high and uppity,
bossing everybody around." They were drunk—Wellman more so
than Zanuck—and Wellman punched Zanuck in the nose. The director, who was tall enough to gaze down on Zanuck's pate, was
surprised when Zanuck began punching him back. Wellman retired to
his room the worse for wear, and all night long, two other hunting
buddies tried to engineer a reconciliation between the two men. It was
finally Zanuck who went to Wellman's room to shake hands and
declare a truce.

This gentlemanly behavior, however, was belied by his needling of
Wellman on the rest of the trip. An extravagant expedition, consisting
of fifty-three packhorses, wound its way up the rough terrain of Mount
Robson. One morning, as Wellman sat on his horse, suffering from a
violent hangover, he turned to a friend and remarked, "I think I'll go
on the wagon." A voice behind him cut in sarcastically, "You haven't
got the guts." It was Zanuck, sneering as he rode past. For the rest of
the trip, Wellman was too proud to take a drink. He began to have
some hope a day later when Zanuck announced that the party would
split in two—he and one man would look for grizzlies on the "bad," or
cloudy, side of the mountain while the rest of the group would
navigate the sunny side. Improbably, however, since the two men
hadn't spoken for days, Zanuck turned to Wellman and declared,
"Bill, I want you to come with me." Wellman was miserable. Not only
couldn't he go back to the bottle, but, he recalled, "What a trip! You
had to shake the porcupines down out of the trees at night and get rid
of them. Otherwise they'd eat your shoes or your leather jacket off by

morning. It snowed. We had to break trail for the horses. We were snowbound for three days. Zanuck chased a grizzly for thirty hours and came back with a sprained ankle. We made twenty separate fords. We lost the horse carrying our medicine. I got blood poisoning. It was the damnedest trip I've ever seen, but *Zanuck loved it*."

In 1932 Virginia Zanuck became friendly with the wife of Juan Reynal, a famous Argentinian polo player. The Zanucks began attending polo matches at the exclusive Midwick Country Club in Pasadena, and Zanuck became an enthusiast almost overnight. The game embodied everything he wanted—thundering action and noise, fierce competition, beautiful animals, and cachet. Almost every producer of note in Hollywood then indulged in the exotic and expensive pastime in an effort to belong to the crème de la crème of Los Angeles society who played at the Midwick Country Club. Incongruously, first-generation Jews from Brooklyn and Chicago, wallowing in their new-found wealth, began building stables and worrying about goal levels like South American playboys—a development that led mogul Louis B. Mayer to comment acidly about his hard-riding friends, "From Poland to polo in one generation."

Zanuck began practicing polo with Reynal on the Warner-owned Hudkins Ranch which was used for locations. Soon they were joined by Sam Engel, a Santa Cruz druggist; Aidan Roarke, an Irish polo player and scriptwriter; Will Rogers; and an old friend, Ray Griffith, whom Zanuck had hired to produce at Warners. Zanuck, who led the team, called it Los Indios, and one of Los Angeles's more high-toned players, who looked down on the arrivistes, remarked, "It was the only polo team where the horses were better bred than the men." Zanuck worked hard at the sport, at one point achieving a three-goal rating, but eventually settling back to two. His courage as a horseman was unmatched. "He would ride right into a wall," remarked a friend.

The good polo players eventually joined Warner Brothers as permanent staffers, and Zanuck's group of directors and writers soon learned that they had better play polo if they wanted to be on their boss's A-list. He could easily dominate the men who depended on him for jobs and assignments. The men Zanuck regarded as his flunkies—Curtiz in particular—were treated thoughtlessly. Zanuck convinced the Hungarian-born director that two things were necessary to make him a true American—learning how to eat steak and knowing how to play poker. So, every Friday night, Zanuck would "invite"—in truth, command—Curtiz to accompany him to a posh suite at the Roosevelt Hotel where the biggest magnates in Hollywood—theater owner Sid Grauman and producers Carl Laemmle, Sr., Joseph Schenck, Jack Warner, and Harry Cohn—played poker. "With one pocket, these guys could pay my salary for ten years," said Curtiz. He lost his entire paycheck every Friday night, and Zanuck would give him fifty dollars to live on for the rest of the week. Zanuck himself did not like to lose. If someone else was ahead, he would play all night to get even.

He continued his practical jokes. Even Jack Warner suffered from Zanuck's peculiar sense of humor. Just after the execution of Sacco and Vanzetti, Warner received an anonymous letter that read, "If Sacco and Vanzetti die—you die." He showed the letter to Zanuck and Al Jolson before turning it over to government agents who had received fifteen similar letters from other executives. Warner was advised to hire a bodyguard. One night, when he was working late, he walked across one of the sound stages. Wrote Warner, "The cluttered labyrinth was blacker than the inside of an eight ball, and I was feeling my way when a pistol suddenly cracked the silence. I hit the floor, with adrenaline jolting me like a hot line as three more shots split the shadows over my head. I could see the brief daggers of light they made, and the powder smell drifted down. I aged ten years, and I lay there and wondered who in hell was going to save me from these killers. Then the lights flooded the big barn, and I looked up from my undignified huddle to see Jolson and Zanuck laughing so hard they were bent over like fishhooks."

Zanuck was like an overbearing football coach; he became a natural leader in anything his group thought to undertake. Even if he was wrong, he could convince everyone that he was right. Once, Neal McCarthy, a wealthy Los Angeles lawyer, approached Zanuck's polo team at the Riviera Club and invited them to invest $5,000 each in a racetrack he and a syndicate of investors were planning to build. Zanuck convened the team in a football huddle and declared, "This guy is crazy. Who in hell will go to see racing in Hollywood? Everybody is too busy." The team turned McCarthy down. The project became the highly successful Santa Anita racetrack, and each $5,000 share would have paid Zanuck and his friends an annual 100 percent dividend for years after. By 1950, a share was worth $65,000. Years later, some of his hangers-on mourned that, had it not been for the despotic Zanuck, some of them would have reaped thousands of dollars in profits.

In fact, only Zanuck was too busy to go to the track. He was busy building his own legend. His success and his control over so many people and important decisions inflated his self-confidence to new dimensions. His stuttering magically disappeared. He began smoking the fat cigars that the public later came to view as the symbol of moguldom. He would tap them languorously when making pronouncements to subordinates, jam them in his face and suck to show concentration, and smash them into an ashtray when he lost his temper. He ceased doing things for himself. He didn't dial his phone; a secretary carried out the humble task. He didn't shave; a personal barber came to his home to do it. He didn't drive; he hired a chauffeur. He couldn't take time to visit the dentist—a personage he feared more than death and income taxes—so he had one bring his chair and all his equipment to the studio. Producer Milton Sperling recalled the first time he ever saw Zanuck. "He was carrying his polo mallet and was followed by his retinue of stooges. Suddenly he stopped, walked over to the stage wall, and peed on it, all the while talking over his shoulder to the people he was with."

In 1933 Zanuck's own privileged world was suddenly in jeopardy. The Depression finally hit Hollywood. President Roosevelt had declared a bank holiday in March, and the studios acted together to order salaries of all producers, directors, actors, and other employees in the creative end of the business cut in half while they figured out how to tighten up expenditures. The Academy of Motion Picture Arts and Sciences would decide when full pay was to be restored.

At Warner Brothers it was left to Zanuck to announce the pay cuts to employees. He was violently opposed to the cuts but reluctantly met with his aggrieved subordinates and reassured them that their full pay would be restored by April 10. As that day grew near, Harry Warner, the brother who managed studio finances, decided that he could not resume full pay until April 17. Zanuck was furious, and he and Harry had a bitter quarrel. One evening, Zanuck and his fellow Warner Brothers producer Hal Wallis dined at the Brown Derby before one of their customary all-night sessions running movies in the cutting room. After a drink and some spirited wrangling about how various features were to be edited, they spotted Harry Warner poking his head in the door. He motioned Zanuck to come outside. Several other diners looked up curiously; most people in Hollywood knew who Zanuck and Warner were and that they were involved in an ongoing dispute. Zanuck gave Wallis a "this is trouble" look, rose from his seat, and disappeared outside. Wallis and the other diners could hear shouting from the street. Zanuck reappeared looking "flushed and irritable," reported Wallis. He "sat down and ordered another drink. 'What happened?' I asked him. 'The inevitable,' he replied. 'I'm leaving Warners and I'm not coming back.' "

*   *   *

Zanuck's impulsive resignation was an act of courage. He left without asking for a settlement for his unfinished contract. Virginia was already pregnant with a second child, Susan, who was born on August 30, 1933. Zanuck's leave-taking was also an act of cunning, however. For some time he had pondered starting his own film company. He would never have control of the purse strings at Warners; too many brothers were competing with him. All of the other major studios were similarly dominated by large Jewish families full of sons, sons-in-law, grandsons, and nephews. He had to strike out on his own eventually—so why not choose a moment when his value was high and resign over a dispute in which he had championed the underdog?

Warner Brothers was in great shape when Zanuck left. He had reorganized the studio's sprawling operation into one of the most efficient in Hollywood. The average cost of a finished negative he produced was $225,000—a figure much lower than movie budgets at all other major studios. His hit production of *42nd Street*, which had kicked off a new musical cycle, had already pulled in $2.5 million. Twenty completed negatives were in New York waiting for release, and ten more were ready for cutting. People in the industry speculated that Harry Warner had simply not understood that it was Zanuck and not his brother Jack who was the vital element in the studio's success. *Time* magazine declared, "Possibly Warner merely meant to cut off his own nose to spite his face, but if so, he made a bad mistake. He cut off his head."

Zanuck did not want for job offers. Almost immediately he received a call from his poker-playing buddy, Carl Laemmle, inviting him to work at Universal on a few pictures a year. He wasn't certain that he should accept. He decided to walk over to Universal to see Laemmle, and on the way, on Hollywood Boulevard, he stopped at a cigar store. At the very same moment, Sid Grauman had also dropped in to buy cigars. When he learned where Zanuck was going, he asked him to wait five minutes. He rushed to a telephone, called Joseph Schenck, president of United Artists, and set up a breakfast appointment at Schenck's apartment the next morning. Zanuck never got to Universal.

Stodgy businessman Joseph Schenck seemed an odd match for the hyperkinetic Zanuck; but the two men seemed to be the answer to each other's needs. Schenck and his family, who were Russian immigrants, had popped up all over the film business. His brother Nicholas served as president of MGM, and Joseph had independently produced features starring Fatty Arbuckle, Buster Keaton, Constance Talmadge, and Norma Talmadge, who later became his wife. In 1924 Joseph was appointed chairman of the board of United Artists, but creative disputes, and Schenck's impending divorce from Norma Talmadge, had left the company moribund and Schenck dispirited—until Zanuck came along.

Winning Zanuck, Hollywood's most prolific and popular young producer, would put United Artists back in business and revitalize Schenck's career. The two men ate breakfast and reached an agreement after five hours. Schenck gave Zanuck a $100,000 advance on his $5,000-a-week salary. Soon after the deal was struck, Zanuck was playing polo with his friend, producer Sam Engel, who was to join him in the as yet unnamed new company. The two men collided and fell off their mounts, and the bumped, bruised, and annoyed Zanuck shouted, "For God's sake, you play like this game was played in the nineteenth century!" Inspired, Engel suggested that the new company be called Twentieth Century.

Ownership of Twentieth Century Pictures was split among Zanuck, Schenck, William Goetz, who was MGM kingpin Louis B. Mayer's son-in-law, and a couple of banks, which put up the loans. All Zanuck had to do was produce movies—a dozen a year. He got space to do his work at a UA lot and distribution through the UA marketing group. Zanuck pulled a skeleton crew out from Warners to staff his new company. Raymond Griffith, the comedian who had suggested he write a book, was now a producer; and George Arliss, one of Warners' most distinguished actors, lent the new company a touch of class. Zanuck had only a handful of other actors—including Loretta Young and Constance Bennett—but he could trade for big stars, many of whom worked for presumably friendly MGM. Zanuck's first production in 1933 was *The Bowery*, a lively comedy-melodrama of turn-of-the-century street life with Wallace Beery. In his first year, Zanuck's company spent $4.5 million on the first twelve productions and earned $3 million in receipts on the four that were already in release. That was enough to pay off the cost of the first four pictures and to defray most of the expenses of the remaining eight, which hadn't been released. Twentieth Century's backers breathed a sigh of relief and content.

He spent most of his time working. He was happily busy—acquiring scripts, rewriting, revising, casting, and supervising. He also began proclaiming. Reporters wanted to ask him searching questions: What is the future of cinema? What does it reveal about public taste? What does a producer do, anyway? Zanuck was eager to tell them. Harry Brand, the studio publicist, cranked out press releases and polished articles under Zanuck's byline. In a 1933 *New York Times* piece, Zanuck made his job sound more important than FDR's. Knowing what to do with the budget a producer is given is "a grave responsibility full of traps for the unwary." A single oversight can ruin the work of months. A producer faces "strain," "worry," "demands," and more "worries." Censors, laborers, temperamental artists, and exhibitors besieged him at every turn, and, if all that wasn't enough, there was the fickleness of the public's fancies. He made himself sound like the hero of a remake of *The Perils of Pauline*.

Reporters had fun with Zanuck. In 1934, only a year after joining forces with Schenck, Zanuck and Virginia—who was three months pregnant with the couple's third child—stopped in New York on their way to an African safari. After a full day in the executive trenches at

United Artists headquarters, Zanuck invited *New York Herald Tribune* reporter Joseph W. Alsop, Jr., to his bouquet-packed suite at the Sherry Netherland Hotel. According to Alsop, Zanuck wore "a vermilion and yellow silk dressing-gown decorated with painted polo ponies"—an astounding sight for the conservative Alsop, who caustically dubbed the producer "Hollywood's newest Napoleon." Zanuck's vision of the future of movies was much more dazzling than his dress, however. He predicted that producers would do Shakespeare and opera.

"Public taste is like an ascending spiral," he told Alsop. "The movies, in them we have the first medium that's ever got to the whole public, the mob. Now, when movies began they drew off the people from the theater who just wanted an easy sensation, who were looking for bandits, and pure heroines, and heroes and villains and all that. Well, pretty soon, people got tired of that, so they moved on to something else, and then to something else and so on, regularly. Each time the move was made it was toward a more complicated, artistic type of picture." Alsop failed to recognize the visionary in Zanuck. He saw only the silly, pompous young climber. "[Zanuck] leaned back in his chair under a frond from one of the rose baskets to let that sink in," wrote Alsop.

Some of the cruelest cuts came from writer Alva Johnson, who profiled Zanuck in *The New Yorker* in November of 1934. Johnson declared that in Hollywood, where everything operated in reverse, college men worked for high school alumni, and high school alumni worked for grammar school alumni. Zanuck was so successful that one might mistakenly conclude that he had stopped school in the sixth rather than the eighth grade. Johnson praised Zanuck as "a great journalist" who ripped his ideas right off the front pages and sold the excitement to the public. Yet Johnson couldn't resist taking a poke at Zanuck's vocabulary. He quoted Zanuck to the effect that his new company gave him more time for "betterment and correctment." At story conferences "Things may tiffle and blore and ruggle, but everyone knows exactly what Zanuck is saying," he added. He was unselfconscious about his pronunciation; he said "admirable" by tacking an "able" onto "admire." Johnson told how a writer was fired for correcting Zanuck when he described a man as a "milestone around her neck."

Zanuck's embarrassment at the publication of the *New Yorker* profile must have been eased by the birth of his third child in December 1934. It was a son, an heir, a little replica of himself. He named the boy Richard Darryl. Zanuck stage-managed Richard's birth as he had those of his two daughters.

Of course, most of the publicity he received—some of it cranked out by his own subordinates—was favorable. A typical sampling proclaimed, "What Zanuck lacks in education, he more than makes up in uncanny genius and daring initiative, a rare combination that has brought millions into the coffers of his companies and fame and fortune to him." Zanuck himself maintained an engaging modesty— for the record, anyway. In 1935 *Time* published a letter from him complaining that the magazine had mistakenly reported that he had come to New York that spring to "gloat" over his two new pictures, *Les Misérables* and *Cardinal Richelieu*. "Facts are as follows," he corrected. "Producer Zanuck came to New York before either picture had opened to quiver and tremble and hope that the public and press would allow him to gloat. Strangely, public and press were unanimous, thank Heaven."

By April 1935, when he turned up in New York to complain to Frank Nugent about the California income tax, Twentieth Century Pictures, under his leadership, had released eighteen productions. Only one—*Born to Be Bad*, with Loretta Young—was a flop. Zanuck had commanded the respect of the critics by kicking off a new cinema cycle—a batch of costume dramas with artistic pretensions. His first— *The House of Rothschild*, in which George Arliss leads his persecuted family out from usury into the wonderful world of stocks and bonds and floats the largest loan ever—had proved to be one of the biggest hits of 1934. He followed that with more historical dramas: *The Affairs of Cellini*, *Cardinal Richelieu*, and *Les Misérables*. He was well aware that he had initiated a new cycle, cynically quipping that *Les Misérables* was merely *I Am a Fugitive from a Chain Gang* in costume.

Zanuck was carrying the entire United Artists organization, and he and Schenck knew it. He was entitled to 10 percent of his movies' income, but soon after he had released his first group of movies, he read the fine print in the hurriedly drawn contract and learned—like many luckless Hollywood performers down through the generations— that his deal gave him a cut of net rather than gross. UA's stockholders, who made almost no movies at all, received their share of profits off the top. That and a bit of old-fashioned creative accounting left him with little more than his salary. Of course, $225,000 a year would have been plenty for most people, but Zanuck was a man who spent nearly every dime he ever earned. The hunting trips, the chauffeurs, the polo ponies, the club memberships, and all the other lavish trappings he felt he and his family deserved kept him right on the very edge of his income. Every year he would try to save; almost always he found himself in the red. He needed more money, and he needed equity in something that would grow. Schenck had asked the board of United Artists to vote Twentieth Century a block of UA stock, a move that would have rewarded Zanuck with a share of gross profits, but Samuel Goldwyn had opposed the idea. Schenck worried that his star producer might jump to another studio.

In April 1935 Schenck popped down to Florida to meet with Fox Film Corporation president Sidney R. Kent. Local news gatherers spotted the two men on the beach and speculated that they were planning to build a giant $10 million superstudio in Miami where movie producers could avoid the proposed California income tax that Zanuck had whined about to the *New York Times*. The superstudio story was a bluff to cover their real purpose: putting Darryl Zanuck and Twentieth together with the Fox Film Corporation. Once one of the most prominent studios in Hollywood, Fox had declined in the 1930s after its founder, William Fox, was convicted of stock market manipulation. Fox's one strength was its distribution organization and its hundreds of movie theaters. What it lacked were movies to show in them. Surely Darryl Zanuck could supply the needed new productions.

It took two months for Schenck and Kent to work out the complicated merger that would release Twentieth Century from United Artists and merge it with Fox. A Byzantine exchange of stock left Zanuck, the reason for the deal in the first place, with 183,979 shares of common stock. Zanuck's share of the common—about 30 percent was disproportionately small compared to the amount of work he was soon to be assigned. The new hyphenated company was to produce fifty-five pictures a year, twenty-nine of which would be personally supervised by Zanuck. *Fortune*, in December 1935, only a few months after the merger, proclaimed, "To Darryl Zanuck, just thirty-three last September and quivering with energy, that job appears simple enough. All he need do is read, revise, cast, film, cut, assemble, and release one picture every twelve days."

Zanuck had ample resources to deploy, for he now controlled an empire. At his disposal was one of the biggest production budgets in Hollywood, as well as Movietone City, Fox's ninety-six-acre lot in Westwood; it was jam-packed with housefronts, gardens, jungles, small-town streets, and a Manhattan vista complete with an elevated railway. In August, however, only a month after he marched onto the lot like a conquering general, one of the studio's major star assets was lost: Will Rogers, Fox's box-office reliable, died in a plane crash into a frozen Alaska river. The studio's other major human property was Shirley Temple who, newswriters were proclaiming, was, at age seven, past her prime.

The question was: Would Zanuck be boosted to new heights or buried by the giant Fox bureaucracy? He approached the challenge with the single-minded drive of the man Alsop compared him with—Napoleon. Every project planned or under way came in for a reevaluation. All scripts were read in four days and nights. The results were dramatic: willy-nilly, screenplays were tossed away, movies were canceled, and the payroll was slashed. Zanuck brought in some of his own people, writers Nunnally Johnson and Bess Meredyth, director Roy Del Ruth and producer Raymond Griffith, and signed three new players to add to Fox's skimpy adult-star roster, which so far could boast only Janet Gaynor and Warner Oland, who played Charlie Chan. Loretta Young, Warner Baxter, Victor McLaglen, and Ronald Colman were added, and Zanuck negotiated special movie deals with Wallace Beery, George Raft, and singer Lawrence Tibbett.

In August 1935, Fox shareholders officially ratified the deal and a seven-year employment contract for Zanuck at $250,000 a year. Salaries for Kent, Schenck, and Zanuck were to cost stockholders fifty cents a share. Kent, however, shouted down those who complained at the annual meeting. "We earn it. . . . When I took this company in April 1932, it had $37,000 in debt. . . . Without these three men, I wouldn't give ten cents for the stock. We pay stars $8,000 and $9,000 weekly and make money out of them. Zanuck, who directs these stars and creates stars, is worth $5,000 a week. It may be more money than bank presidents are paid, but bank presidents can't make moving pictures."

And for a brief heart-stopping moment, it appeared that Zanuck could not make them, either. Two months later, his first production—*Metropolitan*, starring Lawrence Tibbett—was ready to roll. The movie, about a baritone getting his first break, an operatic version of *42nd Street*, was a critical success when it opened at Radio City Music Hall in New York. It never drew much of the moviegoing public, however. Zanuck called it "a big bust."

His second movie—*Thanks a Million*, with Dick Powell, a musical about a singer who accidentally becomes a politician—seemed destined to be a failure. When Zanuck previewed it at a theater in Santa Monica, the audience hated it. He was sick at heart. Later that night he ran it again for himself at the studio. How could he have made such a bomb? he wondered, all alone in the bathroom. Back in the cutting room, when he began to play around with the movie, he found the problem. He cut out twelve minutes and shuffled some of the scenes around. When the movie previewed again, this time in Santa Barbara, the audience was ecstatic. The movie was a success and, more than any other, Zanuck thought, put Twentieth Century-Fox in business.

By November, *Time* magazine was already issuing plaudits for two more movies produced on his watch: *Show Them No Mercy*, a daring story about kidnappers, which *Time* described as "a drama so compact and terrifying it makes other G-men stories seem like Mother Goose," and *The Man Who Broke the Bank at Monte Carlo*, "an adventure story designed to fit Ronald Colman's elegant offhand romanticism." Zanuck had another grabber in the works—a movie called *The Country Doctor*, which starred the nearly newborn Dionne quintuplets. Once again he was on top.

With his reign secure, Zanuck reestablished his imperial court to laugh at his jokes and suffer his pranks. Aidan Roarke, the polo player, joined the studio. His major function, according to Twentieth Century-Fox screenwriter Philip Dunne, was to play polo and "to hit the ball up to Darryl so that the boss, an aggressive but only average performer on the field, could score a lot." Zanuck hired Fidel La Barba, an Argentinian flyweight, to box with him daily. Zanuck bragged that he instructed La Barba never to go easy on him, but, says

Dunne, he "most certainly pulled his punches or Zanuck wouldn't have survived to produce the movies." Otto Lang, who was Zanuck's ski coach on Sun Valley vacations, became a producer.

Every day Zanuck would lunch at the Café de Paris, Fox's elegant commissary, surrounded by his fellow executives and hangers-on. He installed himself in a vast wood-paneled office. Every paintable surface was done in a deep metallic "Zanuck green" that a company mixed for him on order. He would sit at one end behind a giant desk that stood in front of a backdrop of zebra skins and other trophies from his African safari. Hard-backed chairs lined the walls; one was stationed right in front of the desk. "You felt like you had to walk miles and miles to get to his desk," said Walter Scott, a scenic designer who occasionally paid trembling business calls on Zanuck. "It was the same kind of setup Mussolini had; it made you feel very small and powerless." Scott recalls that he was almost too nervous to make the long walk to the desk and would stand near the door showing artwork from afar.

Behind Zanuck's office was a connecting suite with a bathroom to which he retreated—often right in the middle of story conferences. The assembled producers, writers, stenographers, and directors would sit in silence as Zanuck exited, peed loudly into the toilet, and flushed. Writers speculated that, in emulation of Charlie Chaplin, Zanuck kept a dictionary in the bathroom to consult when one of them used a word that he didn't know. Another small room housed a bed where he took naps before long nightly film editing sessions. It was to this small suite that he summoned female contract players for some diversion on the casting couch. He arranged everything—even his adulteries—for his own convenience. Who, after all, was going to stop him? He was making a fortune for the studio; anything he did, short of breaking the law, was fine with his bosses and colleagues. "He wasn't criticized for it," said Milton Sperling. "Hell, they envied him." And young women, if not always eager to pander to his needs, were certainly willing. "He could make a woman wealthy overnight," declared Sperling.

In theory, a young woman could depart unnoticed by way of a back door; however, everyone at the studio knew of the afternoon trysts. Though Sperling once hyperbolically asserted that the studio practically shut down every afternoon at four for half an hour while Zanuck had his way with an ingenue, he amends that "It wasn't really every day, but it happened often enough." Martha Newman Ragland, widow of studio musician Alfred Newman, recalled that when she was a contract actress with Fox in the 1940s, "Many girls got the call—I don't know what they did about it—but, yes, they got the call." She herself never received the "call," possibly because she was already dating Newman or, she speculated, chuckling, "because I wasn't Zanuck's type." Though several of the actresses he bedded won parts and other favors, he strictly kept most important business decisions insulated from his office hideaway. He never got serious about any of the women. To him they were merely pleasurable breaks in the day—like polo, lunch, and practical jokes.

His cold, cruel jokes grew meaner than ever. One favorite was to sneak cheese into the food of a hapless subordinate who was allergic to dairy products. Zanuck would laugh heartily when the man began wheezing and breaking out in blotches. He had a special script called *Lucky Baldwin*, which he reserved for new writers. They received as their first Hollywood assignment the task of rewriting the script and vested in it all the language and literary style that they dreamed of putting on the silver screen—only to discover that Zanuck had no intention of making the script into a movie. Zanuck was often thoughtless and rude, elbowing others aside to be the first to pass through a door, rudely stalking ahead of older men, leaving them running breathlessly to catch up with him.

Yet, for all that, many writers, directors, and actors *wanted* to work for Darryl Zanuck. Writers in particular felt at home at Twentieth Century-Fox. Their work was hardly treated like the Bible; it had to survive the fire of the constant conferences in which Zanuck often reshaped a story into a form unrecognizable to its creator. As one writer remarked, "Zanuck loved my screenplay. He wants to rewrite it." Once he signed off on the script, however, it was immutable. Directors were forbidden to change it, and Zanuck rarely visited sets. Nunnally Johnson wrote that if a director made so bold as to mess around with a script, Zanuck would act "as if he had insulted everybody's mother and the American flag." Maybe so—but once the film was made, Zanuck took it to the cutting room where he and his chief editor, Barbara McLean, were free to do violence to the original story—righteous violence sometimes, but violence nonetheless.

Perhaps his subordinates' loyalty grew from Zanuck's skillful management, which proved nearly infallible until he had to manage his son Richard thirty-five years later. Zanuck seemed to know exactly what buttons to press to make people leap happily to do his bidding. Says Philip Dunne, "He undoubtedly pushed over those who were intended by nature to be pushovers, but for men and women of integrity, he showed only consideration and respect." Zanuck displayed those qualities not out of any overwhelming concern or love for those upstanding members of his staff but because doing so would help him achieve what he wanted. "[Writer] Lamar Trotti, Nunnally Johnson, and I would never be treated badly," says Dunne. They would never have stood for it, so he treated them well.

Then, too, Zanuck was loyal to the final product. No matter how disastrous a movie seemed to be, he declared it the best, the greatest, or the first. When he visited neighborhood theaters to screen a movie and gauge the audience response, he would invent an excuse if the reaction was negative. When the viewers coughed and wheezed, indicating that they were bored to tears, Zanuck would tell his staffers, "Terrible cold season. Everyone has the flu." Once when huge numbers of people got up and left in the middle of a movie, he remarked that they were night-shift workers leaving for their jobs at a nearby factory. Dunne recalls that when he released a movie that drew almost no ticket sales, Zanuck consoled him with the thought that "More people saw it than saw the goddamn ballet."

As Zanuck surveyed the scene in which he starred early in 1936, he could hardly have been less than ecstatic. He loved what he was doing, and everybody on both coasts longed to get near him, to catch some of the magic. Of his appearance at a Waldorf-Astoria cocktail party in his honor that January, a *New York Times* reporter observed with equal measures of awe and irony "The fact that Mr. Zanuck, whose court is almost as numerous as that of the Little Corporal and whose personal erg output is alleged to be something in the neighborhood of Boulder Dam's, was right there in the Basildon suite along with the rest of us seemed to perk everybody up more than the two bars and the excellent turkey and ham." Zanuck's position, he added, "was less that of a guest of honor than of the ball in some annual gridiron clash like the Army-Navy game. We had him for just a moment, but we fumbled him and saw him being borne away by superb interference to another corner of the room. For one moment, though, we spoke to Mr. Zanuck. Nobody can take that away from us."

*   *   *

Zanuck surely thought that he could go on doing what he was doing forever. Indeed, his greatest movies—*The Grapes of Wrath, How Green Was My Valley, Pinky, The Snake Pit, Gentleman's Agreement,* and *All About Eve*—were still ahead. Perhaps the public's taste was not an ascending spiral, but Darryl Zanuck's was. He was building and building, trying to rise in understanding, in knowledge, in experience, in greatness. He could not rest content with mere success. Indeed, he sometimes expressed the opinion that almost any jerk with solid financial backing could be a producer. He had to go one step beyond everybody else, or none of what he had won would matter.

If his strivings were the main event, his family was a sideshow. He rarely returned home from the studio before midnight—much too late to see his children. Nonetheless, as Virginia told a reporter, Zanuck would break all the nursery rules and tiptoe into the rooms where his children lay sleeping. One by one, he would pick up his babies, rock them in his arms, and kiss their cheeks. Certainly he must have believed then that everything he did was for them.

The next morning he would leave for the studio right on time. Sometimes he saw the kids; sometimes he didn't.

TWO
HOLLYWOOD WIFE

∎

Virginia was often to wonder why her marriage had crumbled. She was certainly as beautiful a woman as her husband could have asked for. She was understanding, forgiving, and involved in his interests. She supported Zanuck, no matter what he chose to do. She tolerated his many affairs. She bore him three attractive children. Virginia organized her family's routine to suit her husband's convenience. She was known as a loyal friend and a gracious hostess. Even when her prodigal husband returned after an absence of seventeen years, she eagerly and happily took him back without recrimination. After his death, she continued to uphold his dignity in the lengthy and embarrassing court battle over his estate. Virginia Zanuck thought herself the perfect Hollywood wife.

Unlike Edith Goetz or Irene Mayer Selznick, the social lionesses who were daughters of producer Louis B. Mayer and wives of film executives William Goetz and David Selznick, Virginia Fox had not been bred to the role. Indeed, she had never aimed to be a consort to any man. She had come to Hollywood to become an actress, but when she wed Darryl Zanuck, she seemed to collapse into a safe and comfortable dependency. Marriage to such a high-voltage man was anything but safe, of course, and she certainly knew that life with Darryl Zanuck would not proceed predictably.

Virginia Fox felt free to take risks because her own childhood had been stable and comfortable. Her parents, Frederick and Marie Oglesby Fox, were solid burghers of German descent who settled down in Wheeling, West Virginia, after their marriage in 1898. Frederick was a beer salesman and later, after West Virginia prohibited alcohol in 1914, he moved his family to St. Petersburg, Florida, where he became involved in the import-export business. Virginia was born on April 19, 1902, and her brother, Frederick, Jr., arrived two years later.

The Foxes had high hopes for their children. When Virginia was fourteen, they boarded her at the Aiken Open Air School, a private school in St. Petersburg. Aiken was not a finishing school; girls took a college prep course that included English, math, science, and Spanish. Virginia became a close friend to the principal's daughters. Together the girls played tennis, talked about clothes and boys, hid trembling in closets during violent Gulf storms, and attended the movies. Virginia was always star-struck. "She wanted to be in the movies right from the very start," said Mrs. Merrill Merrill, one of Virginia's schoolmates. "Really, there hadn't been that many good movies by that time, but she just loved the idea." Everyone agreed that Virginia had movie-star looks. She was "so pretty, just like a doll," said another friend. Virginia's mother nurtured her aspirations. Mrs. Fox always saw to it that Virginia wore the finest clothing in the most up-to-date styles. She made many of her daughter's frocks herself.

Virginia's dreams of stardom seemed outlandish, recalled Mrs. Merrill. "We didn't believe that Virginia was really meant to be an actress," she added. Almost every other girl wanted to get married and settle down. Virginia, however, was determined to strike out on her own.

Like her future husband, Virginia saw herself as a person with a destiny. Her father wanted her to go to college after she graduated from high school in 1920, but she couldn't see the point of further classroom study when Hollywood was where she really wanted to be. Her mother, who shared Virginia's dream, convinced her husband that their daughter should be allowed to test the waters in California. For Virginia's graduation, the Foxes gave her a new car, and the whole family went west to install her at the Studio Club, the Los Angeles women's residence that catered to actresses.

The Foxes envisioned their daughter becoming a film star like Mary Pickford, "America's sweetheart," or Norma Shearer, who starred in

The Flapper. Virginia's first job offer, however, was a part as a bathing beauty in Mack Sennett's movies. The Foxes disapproved. Virginia's years at boarding school—independent of her mother and father—had prepared her to oppose them, however. She took the job over their objections.

Virginia may have grown up a sheltered little girl, but she was game to try almost anything. Young actresses had to be physically strong and daring in the days of the silents when sight gags and wild chase scenes carried most comedies. Hanging upside down from an elk's head was the kind of acting movies then required. Her good looks won her film parts easily, although she also quickly attained a reputation for a boisterous sense of humor and a love for the fun of performing. Soon she was playing leading lady to Buster Keaton.

Like many women of her day, Virginia believed she should be able to do anything a man could do—wear pants in public, smoke, drink, and even discuss sex. Also like many women, she was a freethinker, but not a free lover. Although she attended movieland parties where men paid her plenty of attention, she was not the most adventurous flapper. She spent most of her evenings studying her lines, visiting her parents, who summered in California, and chatting with fellow ac-tresses. Several of them—Virginia, Colleen Moore, Ruby Keeler, Loretta Young, and Ann Harding—formed a club, which they called "Our Club," a name they thought terribly chic and exclusive. Mary Pickford served as honorary president. Their purpose was high-minded—to help new actresses get jobs. However, they usually ended up helping one another. When one member was rejected for a part, she would quickly call all the others so they could try out.

The girls met at one another's houses and sat on the floor drinking hot chocolate and eating cookies. They talked movies and gossiped for hours about who was sleeping with whom, who had recently suc-cumbed to cocaine, and how much so-and-so was earning a week. They desperately wanted to be thought outrageous, madcap, and unconventional. F. Scott Fitzgerald, the storyteller of the generation lost to alcohol and high times, was their very favorite author, and they spent time in serious discussion of the Russian Revolution, which fashion demanded they call "the great experiment." They loved the poetry of Edna St. Vincent Millay. Said Colleen Moore, the star of *Flaming Youth* and the decade's quintessential flapper, "We were always quoting, 'My candle burns at both ends; It will not last the night; But ah, my foes, and oh, my friends— It gives a lovely light!' We felt it would be the height of existence to burn a candle at both ends. Even at one end."

Virginia was cool to Zanuck when she first dined and danced with him. He seemed shy and awkward to her—certainly nothing special. But when he asked her to marry him for the umpteenth time, she consented. She would attach herself to him, thereby making his greatness partly her greatness. Being the wife of such an extraordinary man—someone exempt from the usual—would exempt her, too. She could be the stunning companion to a genius. Still, her friends must have been surprised when she decided to give up acting soon after her return from her wedding trip in January 1924. There was no hint that Zanuck required such a sacrifice. What others might see as a giving-up, however, Virginia would view as an easing-up. Marriage relieved her of the daunting problem of constantly trying to be *her*. There was no longer any question about who she was—she was Mrs. Darryl Zanuck. She would do whatever a Mrs. Darryl Zanuck should do.

*   *   *

Virginia must have wondered later whether she had made the correct choice; her first years as Zanuck's wife were not happy. There were many times when she was so discouraged that she thought of running home to her mother. Not quite so often she actually did run home to her mother. Mrs. Fox told her that she was married to a genius; she should stick it out. Virginia later recalled to a reporter that she had retorted, "Genius—heck!"

To Virginia, who had to stick it out, her husband sometimes seemed more like an ogre than a genius. When they first married, he was still working on the Witwer series, and to meet his deadlines, he would labor far into the night. If the writing didn't go well, he would throw a tantrum and vent his rage on her. When he finally did fall into bed, he couldn't sleep. He would thrash around and sometimes tumble onto the floor. She took to pinning his nightshirt to her pillow to try to keep him in bed with her, but he would either pop the pin open with his restless motion, stabbing himself or her, or both of them would wind up on the floor.

Her husband, she found to her distress, was more than just a temperamental complainer. He sometimes displayed a vicious streak, as he did on a trip the Zanucks took to Oregon to film the very first of the Rin Tin Tin movies. He loved the North Woods, and he spent many hours trying to roll logs into the river, as he had seen some of the woodsmen do. He kept winding up in the water. One night Virginia waited for him in their room. She had dressed up for a cast party scheduled for the evening. When Zanuck arrived, soaking wet and cold, he announced that he didn't want to go to the party—and he didn't want her to go either. She insisted. They were expected, and if need be, she would go alone. As she left the room, he followed her into the hall stark naked, screaming at her that she had no right to go without him. Embarrassed, humiliated, and angry, she stood her ground. With that, she left. When she returned to their room later that night, she found that he had slashed all her clothing—her underthings, dresses, hats, and gloves—to ribbons. She decided that was the end, that she couldn't take such behavior. She slept in the bathtub that night and vowed to divorce him. By morning, however, he had grown conciliatory. He apologized and told her he would never, never do anything like that again. She decided to stick it out.

Sticking it out became harder still when she learned that he was cheating on her. The first inkling she got came on a trip to Europe in 1926. In Vienna with another couple, they went to see a show featuring a group of chorines called the Hollywood Redheads. After the performance, the men escorted their wives back to the hotel and went off to gamble—or so they said. Hours later the husbands returned, each with a "redhead" on his arm. Viewing the scene from the balcony, Virginia grabbed a potted geranium and directed it at her husband's pate. Her aim was true, and he was temporarily stunned. She threw a fur coat over her nightie and rushed downstairs. As usual, he was apologetic come morning. To make up for the evening, he gave her an expensive wristwatch. Oddly, she treasured the present even though it reminded her that her husband had strayed.

After he won the job as chief of production at Warners in 1927, work became even more demanding. Even when he played—at hunting or cards—he worked as hard as he did on the job. After the long nights viewing rushes, he would take a steam bath at the Los Angeles Athletic Club. There he would discuss scripts with Jack Warner and his other buddies. His new status and higher salary made life easier for Virginia. The couple could now afford the big house Zanuck had insisted they buy, as well as a maid to do all the cooking and cleaning. Virginia was free to spend her days shopping with girlfriends and her evenings waiting for her husband to return, or viewing movies with him at the studio.

With his new power came new abuses. He could now carry on with women at work, presumably without Virginia finding out. He spent so much time at the studio that she could scarcely question his where-abouts. She didn't expect him to turn up every evening for dinner, and even when he did, he went back to the studio to work deep into the night. She was not inclined to be a doormat, but she wasn't the type to mount a full-scale investigation to find out what her husband was doing. Unfortunately, an aggrieved husband, an outraged father, or a girlfriend who thought she was being helpful would tell Virginia of Zanuck's latest exploit. Some of the stories she discounted as phony tidbits churned out by the Hollywood rumor mill. Others, she be-lieved, came from women who invented tall tales just to hurt her feelings.

Nevertheless, she couldn't wish away all of the stories. "Virginia was smarter than most people gave her credit for," said a woman friend who was married to one of Zanuck's polo-playing pals. "She knew what went on, she wasn't ignorant of what happened. But I guess she had to put up with it—that is, if she wanted to stay married." Zanuck's extramarital escapades infuriated Virginia, however, and occasionally she would react violently. Myrna Loy recalled that when Zanuck was once involved with a Warner Brothers starlet, Virginia appeared at the studio with a pistol. "She wasn't letting him fool around in those days," said Loy. When Virginia learned that her husband seemed to be smitten with Dolores Costello, who appeared in *Noah's Ark* and *Tenderloin*, she threw him out. When he finally returned to make amends, he found an empty house. She had gone to visit her relatives in St. Petersburg. He implored her forgiveness from afar with jewelry, flowers, and gifts, but she refused to be reconciled with him. Finally he journeyed to Florida and persuaded her to come back to him.

No matter what Virginia did, she couldn't keep her husband faith-ful. She fussed with her appearance, but her good looks, trim figure, and stylish clothing were not enough to prevent him from straying. Despite his extramarital wanderings, he still behaved amorously to her. Ardent lovemaking was not something she was comfortable with. She felt a bit embarrassed by physical attention, but she didn't dislike it by any means. Her coolness, though, seemed to work in her favor, for the more standoffish she acted, the more interested he seemed to be.

Virginia couldn't bring herself to blame Zanuck completely. He was surrounded every day by irresistible young actresses. Virginia convinced herself that the studio liaisons meant nothing to him. Most of them lasted no more than an afternoon or evening. Indeed, his ability to bed women with such frequency seemed to make her believe her marriage was even more valuable because he always came home to her. Perhaps she sometimes even relished his escapades. In later years she would boast to her friends, "Oh, DZ was going with what's-her-name back then," or she would ask one of her kids, "Who was Daddy seeing then?"

Virginia felt, moreover, that her husband valued her. A former actress, she knew his business, and she kept up with events at the studio. Indeed, his staffers often were stunned—and sometimes dismayed—by the store he set by her opinions. If she told him that a scene didn't work or that a script was no good, he listened. He would often proclaim to producers and writers at a script conference, "Mrs. Zanuck doesn't like that," and they would have to change it. In 1936 she virtually discovered—or perhaps uncovered—Tyrone Power, who became one of Twentieth Century-Fox's most reliable box-office attractions. Fox was chronically short of stars partly because Zanuck truly believed that good stories were more important than big names. He was looking around for a young beau for the heroine of a movie called *Girls' Dormitory*. "I wanted to get the best-looking sonofabitch in the world," he later told a reporter. Tyrone Power tested for the part. Said Zanuck, "To me, he looked awful. But Mrs. Zanuck, who watched the test with me, said, 'He's awfully good-looking if he'd only cut his hair.'" The order was given to shear Power's locks, and he got the part. The actor had only one brief scene at the end of the movie, but at the preview, two-thirds of the audience responding to questionnaires demanded to know who the young man was. Zanuck immediately rushed him into the starring role in *Lloyds of London*.

Zanuck respected his wife's refinement and gentility—two qualities he lacked. The way he talked sometimes made her blush. A script was "bullshit," he would announce. "It made me vomit." He spit on the sidewalk and sometimes even peed on the street when Virginia and their friends were looking. He could be arrogant, and he was always striking ridiculous poses. Though short and skinny, he seemed to think of himself as Ernest Hemingway. When he planted his foot on the running board of a car, he posed as though he had an elephant's head underneath his shoe.

Virginia was often startled, sometimes appalled, but occasionally thrilled by his derring-do. One night after a polo match, he came into her bedroom while she was primping for a dinner party and announced, "When you turn around, don't worry, but I got hit in the face with a ball, but don't worry. I'm a fast healer." When she did face him, she was stunned. His entire forehead was black-and-blue, his nose was squashed to a pulp, and his eyes bulged from his skull. She later learned that a ball had hit him so hard that an artery in his nose was severed. He had almost bled to death. Luckily, a doctor who doubled as a referee had saved Zanuck's life by holding his nose in place. Still, her husband insisted on joining their guests for dinner with two cotton sponges dangling from his nostrils. The next day Virginia proudly told her friends, he went to the studio as though nothing had happened.

*   *   *

At parties, polo matches, picnics, and premieres, Virginia mingled with studio executives and Warner Brothers stars—James Cagney, Lew Ayres, Joan Blondell, Mary Astor. On screen in movie after movie, Zanuck faithfully portrayed the common man during the American Depression. Virginia's real world, however, was a round of dinners, dances, new gowns, and exciting company.

Her carefree existence and high status as a Mrs. Mogul had not made her feckless, however. As the wife of the production chief at Warners and later at Fox, she took on the role of First Lady, dispensing kind remarks, gifts, favors, and hugs. Friends remember her in those years as a woman who was incredibly kind and thoughtful. One producer's wife recalled that when she was in labor with her first son, Virginia drove all the way from Santa Monica to Good Samaritan Hospital downtown to sit with the producer and his mother-in-law. "She brought me a bottle of Joy and some sandwiches for my husband and mother to eat and cards [for them] to play with." Virginia waited through the hours with them until the woman gave birth. "I was not one of her best friends, though she was very fond of my husband," she adds. "I wasn't one of her intimates; she did that kind of thing for everybody."

The Zanucks—particularly Virginia—were loyal to a fault. Michael Romanoff, who had passed himself off as a Russian prince among the social climbers of Hollywood, became one of the couple's best friends. Many in Hollywood doubted Romanoff's royal credentials, but not the Zanucks. They stood by him even after the Los Angeles newspapers exposed him as a Brooklyn-born faker. Romanoff recalled two decades later, "Everybody canceled any invitations they might have given me. Not the Zanucks. . . . [They] used to bring hot meals to me up in my hotel room—a cheap, grubby little room. And they were never patronizing. Other people, having the cupidity I lacked, scorned me. Darryl and Virginia manifested the most extraordinary maturity."

Devoted wife that she was, Virginia did everything her husband did. They went to Sun Valley on vacation, and Zanuck fell in love with skiing. For a time the couple had a home in Sun Valley, Idaho, where Zanuck would take one-month working vacations complete with stenographers, screenwriters, and typists. He took ski lessons from Otto Lang, who later became a Twentieth Century-Fox producer. "Because Darryl took up skiing, Virginia took up skiing," says a friend. "He went hunting; and she joined him. In fact, there was almost nothing he did that she *didn't* do—except play polo, of course." Zanuck recruited Edward Leggewie, a college French teacher, to help him learn French. Virginia later lamented that she hadn't joined him in his lessons.

The African safari, which Zanuck decided to undertake early in 1934, was particularly hard on Virginia. She had given birth to Susan only six months before and was already pregnant with her third child, but she was game for the adventure. According to a friend, "Her doctor advised her not to go. He thought the idea was crazy because she was in her treacherous third month, but she was determined to go. And she did."

Virginia's nerves could hardly have been anything but frazzled by the trip, but she wanted to see it through. In an article for *Esquire*, Zanuck later wrote: "I wanted to leave my wife in Capri, but she had already been inoculated against the more common types of African diseases and decided it would be a shame to waste all the serum. So, we were off, completely off, as our friends made a point of remarking." Though the trip was not quite as grueling as the voyage made by Humphrey Bogart and Katharine Hepburn while filming *The African Queen*, it did prove exhausting. The party usually rose at four in the morning to hike for hours on foot. Even the bearers had blisters and swollen feet. Zanuck took chances with his life that were truly frightening. At one point, the group was surrounded by a herd of angry elephants. A bearer grabbed the camera Zanuck was wielding and shoved a gun in his hands; it was too late to draw a bead, however, and the whole group had to flee. Wrote Zanuck, "I don't believe I ever ran so fast in my life. . . . It was a quarter mile to the edge of the forest. I think I could have made it had it been five miles." Virginia rose to the occasion valorously. On the same day that Zanuck bagged a leopard and a lion, she also shot a lion.

Fortunately, Virginia's exertions had no ill effect on her pregnancy. In December of 1934, when she gave birth to the Zanucks' third child, a healthy boy named Richard Darryl, *Time* magazine ran a formal portrait of the family. Virginia held Richard—who was dressed in a lacy christening gown—gracefully, almost as though he were a spray of flowers. Darrylin and Susan perched on their father's knees. Zanuck wore a stunned expression; he seemed almost surprised that he had become a staid paterfamilias. Later he was to tell reporters that he hadn't really wanted to become a father; he had been reluctant to be tied down. "I had a very nervous temperament," he said.

He needn't have worried too much, for he and Virginia had the money to live a free-wheeling life, unencumbered by homely routine. Zanuck had toyed with the idea of building a ranch house in Hidden Valley, where he kept his polo ponies in one of the most elegant stables in southern California. However, says Walter Scott, the Fox scenic designer and a friend of Virginia's, that plan never worked out because Zanuck had to be near his studio. In 1934, just before Richard was born, the couple rented a cottage on the "Gold Coast" of the Santa Monica beach, jammed in among the mansions of Louis B. Mayer, Mary Pickford, and other screen aristocrats. The Zanucks liked the beach so much that they bought the property and built a three-story house. Like the other film palaces on the strip, the house presented blank garage doors to the street outside. Inside the wrought-iron gate, however, was a garden reminiscent of New Orleans with beds full of brightly hued flowers. The living room faced the garden. Beyond the house lay a large swimming pool and a shimmering expanse of the Pacific. The couple's bedroom faced the sea. Zanuck had learned to accommodate his wife's taste; it was she who would be in charge of selecting the furniture. She chose from a virtual storehouse of eighteenth-century antiques the Zanucks had acquired on a trip to England. "They had bought four marble fireplaces that they just couldn't use," said Walter Scott.

Eventually the family wound up with two houses placed side by side and connected by a second-story walkway. The Zanuck adults lived in the original home while the newer residence housed the three children and their governess, Alma Diehl. The Zanucks could live their lives undisturbed by 2:00 A.M. feedings or the clutter of toys and cereal bowls.

The children were little terrors—not just Darrylin and Susan but also Richard, whom Alma perceived as perfect. They all perpetrated their share of tricks. Zanuck, fearful that some Bruno Hauptmann type might steal his beloved babies, hired a security guard to protect them. The kids delighted in stealing the man's gun and sticking it in his back. Dick shot beans at a passing car and once, with a friend, tied up Elizabeth Taylor in a closet for a joke. She apparently didn't think it was funny because, years later, when the two were negotiating a contract, he said, she yelled at him about the incident.

Their high jinks might have seemed cute to some, but there was a nasty quality to many of the pranks. They displayed a disregard for other people, a careless arrogance. Virginia's close friend Margaret Shands felt that the Zanuck kids could be very thoughtless, even later, as young adults. One day she was working in her garden next door to the Zanuck compound. Susan and some friends were on the other side of the fence, frolicking in the swimming pool. Margaret Shands heard Susan mention something about a full ashtray and, a few seconds later, witnessed ashes and cigarette butts showering her flowers. Susan had merely tossed the contents of the ashtray over the fence. Mrs. Shands wanted Susan to know that she knew where this garbage was coming from. "Why, where did all these cigarette butts fly in from?" she inquired loudly enough to be heard on the other side. Susan never apologized.

Whatever Alma conveyed to the children, however, could never have been as important as what their parents taught them by the way they lived. The kids saw two people who pretty much satisfied themselves without reference to anybody else. Virginia was involved with Zanuck, and Zanuck was involved with himself. Said Walter Scott, "He didn't run his home like he ran the studio. The children were not controlled by Virginia or Darryl, they were controlled by Alma [Diehl]. . . . There was not what you'd call a family thing." According to Mrs. Shands, Virginia was so focused on her husband's needs that she pretty much turned the care of the children over to Alma. "The Zanucks didn't really raise their kids—they let Alma do everything," added Mrs. Shands. Zanuck was an absentee workaholic father, and Virginia had a heavy social schedule. After her husband took charge of Twentieth Century-Fox in 1935, Virginia was in great demand. Filling her life were tennis games, swimming, shopping expeditions, hairdresser appointments, parties, and premieres. When her husband worked at night—almost always—she would often join him for dinner or meet him at the studio to view rushes by his side.

Zanuck wanted his children to learn how to do things, but he didn't take time to teach them himself. His French tutor, Edward Leggewie, dropped by every morning to drill the children in conversation. "They were average students," said Leggewie. "Anyway, it was difficult for them to concentrate with the beach and sea nearby. They were more interested in swimming." A formidable White Russian called Captain Naff was the children's coach in water sports. One of Zanuck's grooms taught them how to ride, and by the age of eight Darrylin had become an accomplished horsewoman. Father and children played badminton and tennis together, though a disquieting competitive furor seemed to infect everything Zanuck did with his son. Always the scenarist, Zanuck made up stories to tell his kids. The major character was Gyppie the monkey—one of the alter egos of Darryl F. Zanuck, as he was later to admit. The stories were not the stern moralizing tales with which some parents bore their kids to death—about eating broccoli or getting good grades. They were fun; Gyppie was invariably a naughty little monkey who got into scrapes but managed miraculously to triumph in the end.

Richard received memos from his father emphasizing the responsibilities of a young man with advantages. Zanuck did not see his daughters as similarly obligated. They were not going to be powers at the studio. The two little girls had everything that two little girls could possibly dream of possessing. There were closets full of ruffly dresses, pinafores, riding habits, coats, and patent leather Mary Janes. Their dad bought each child a pony, and every year when the Zanucks traveled to Europe on vacation, the ponies came along on the steamship. A frequent visitor to the Zanuck home was Shirley Temple, one of Twentieth Century-Fox's major stars. Most little girls in the 1930s would have just died to meet the dimply, good-natured moppet. Darrylin and Susan got to play with her all the time. But to them she was nothing special. After all, Shirley Temple worked for their father. In fact, almost everybody they met—from Tyrone Power to Rita Hayworth—was dependent on their dad for something.

Virginia stressed the importance of good manners to her children, particularly to Susan and Darrylin. Early on, they learned to write cordial thank-you notes, to mingle graciously, to be seen but not heard at parties and gatherings. Neither parent seemed to put a premium on good grades or intellectual accomplishment for their daughters, and both girls were rather indifferent students. As adults, they would pen gracious letters to friends and acquaintances—full of misspellings and grammatical errors.

Zanuck was determined that his daughters would mix with the crème de la crème of Los Angeles society. Zanuck was generally not a snob or a social climber himself, but where his daughters were concerned, he wanted the best. He entered first Darrylin and later Susan in the exclusive Marlborough School in Hancock Park, a preserve of capacious mansions, and the Zanucks were one of the few Hollywood families to gain admittance to the choosy Midwick Country Club. If Susan and Darrylin were among the best girls in Los Angeles, Zanuck reasoned, they would meet the best men and ultimately have the best kind of life possible. Like their mother, they would adorn the arms of important men.

*　　*　　*

In her early years of marriage, Virginia had complained bitterly about the number of hours her husband spent at the studio, but after about five years, she gave up on him. Even when her prodding brought him home, he spent all the hours after dinner reading and revising scripts. She became more understanding as his incredible investment of time in work continued to pay off. Out of the Twentieth Century-Fox movie factory rolled musicals, historical dramas, romantic comedies, Shirley Temple vehicles, and Fox Movietone newsreels. Virginia attended almost every opening. In the late 1930s there was a premiere nearly every week. Her reaction to the pictures was emotional and romantic. She would weep openly and unselfconsciously when a picture moved her. Indeed, Virginia's tears were the goal toward which many Fox writers and directors labored. Recalled Elia Kazan in his recent memoir, "The ultimate praise Darryl could pay any film was: 'Virginia cried.' "

As her husband matured as a filmmaker, Virginia and the moviegoing public found more in his late 1930s and early 1940s productions that moved them. Zanuck had turned out a number of movies that were to become classic depictions of the social themes of the Depression. One of the best, released in 1941, was *How Green Was My Valley*, the story of a Welsh family caught in a miners' strike. Philip Dunne, who wrote the final script, recalled that some studio executives in New York had found the story too controversial. "[Zanuck] wrote a defiant letter to New York saying that this was the finest script he had ever had, that some day he would find a way to make this picture, even if he had to take it to another studio—which was a dire threat indeed." A few months later, Zanuck's bosses caved in and granted him the right to produce the picture—though on a budget of only $1 million. The final product was the gripping tale of a family beset by poverty and fear and its heroic efforts to survive. The public loved the film, and it won Best Picture at the Academy Awards that year.

The Grapes of Wrath, which had appeared a year earlier, similarly set Zanuck apart from other producers who were busy with escapist themes and musicals starring leggy blondes—not that he didn't produce his share of those, too. However, the story of the Joad family, who lost their farm in the dust bowl and took to the road to eke out a living as itinerant Okie farmworkers in California, sent shivers up and down movie viewers' spines.

Anti-Okie feeling ran high, however, and the movie had its problems. Many Californians connected to agricultural interests threatened to boycott it. Zanuck received letters threatening him and his family. He became concerned about his children, worried that some offended grape grower might kidnap or murder them. Virginia was frightened when she heard of the threats, but it never occurred to her to ask her husband not to produce *The Grapes of Wrath*. It was unlikely she could have deterred him had she wanted to, but she had little desire to do so. Neither Virginia nor her husband was particularly moved by the political overtones of the movie. Both were conservatives and staunch Republicans. The saga of the Joad family was simply great human drama. Virginia felt that if her husband could face down threats, the whole family could back him up. So the Zanucks hired a guard to protect their home and kids. The three children were driven to and from school by limousine.

Still, it sometimes seemed to Virginia that everyone was after the Zanucks. As if the ire of the Okies' bosses wasn't enough, the government started to look into the personal finances of Hollywood moguls. In 1939 the Justice Department revealed that it was investigating Zanuck's tax returns and those of his partner Joseph Schenck. The government informed the Zanucks that they owed over $730,000 in back taxes for 1935 when Zanuck had received stock in the merger of Twentieth Century-Fox. Zanuck was furious; he felt he had paid enough. Practically all his income, he sometimes claimed, went to the U.S. government. He was determined to fight the assessment, and in April 1940 he and Virginia filed a protest with the Tax Appeals Board. Later the Internal Revenue Commission claimed that Zanuck had underpaid his gift taxes. In 1939 he and Virginia had transferred a total of thirty thousand shares of Fox stock to a trust for their three children. The government asserted that the stock had been undervalued by the

Zanucks. In both cases, the government won, and Zanuck had to cough up thousands of dollars.

Schenck faced even more serious problems. The government claimed that he had evaded paying over $412,000 in federal taxes by taking lavish deductions for personal expenses: $136 to fly his personal masseuse from Los Angeles to New York; $536 for his barber; $2,100 for a weekend vacation for himself and two girlfriends; and $40,000 for maintenance of his yacht. The IRC was determined to make an example of Schenck. In 1940 he was indicted for tax fraud.

Virginia and Darryl were nervous. Zanuck himself had written off thousands in personal expenses, and friendly reporters whispered to him that John Cahill, the U.S. attorney in New York, planned to indict him, too. The stress in the Zanuck household increased. Virginia believed that her husband was right to fight IRC claims on their savings. They had too little as it was, because they lived so well. But she did not want her husband to go on trial and air their personal finances to the world. In 1941, just before Schenck's trial, the Zanucks negotiated with the government and paid thousands of dollars more.

During Schenck's highly publicized trial that spring, the scandal widened to cover studio payoffs to unions to quell strikes and other labor disturbances. Several industry bigwigs—Charlie Chaplin, Irving Berlin, Chico Marx, and Will H. Hays, president of the Motion Picture Producers and Distributors of America—testified in Schenck's behalf. Zanuck and his wife were notably absent. Schenck resigned from his studio post during the trial. In April he was convicted on two counts of fraud and handed a prison sentence of three years, which was later reduced to a year. He was paroled after four months in the federal correctional institution in Danbury, Connecticut, and rejoined Fox as chief of production soon after.

*   *   *

By the time Schenck returned to Fox in 1943, however, Virginia's husband had undergone a dramatic transformation in philosophy. He had become much more serious and worried about the fate of America in the choppy waters of world politics. The catalyst for the change lay in his experience of World War II. From the time the Nazis stopped rattling sabers and invaded Poland in 1939, Zanuck was convinced that the United States would have to enter the war. Always eager to be where the action was and to take part in it himself, he longed to don his old uniform. In 1940 he was commissioned a lieutenant colonel in the reserves and began coordinating Hollywood's efforts to make training films and propaganda features.

The job was insufficient to slake his thirst for adventure, however. One day he arrived home in Santa Monica and announced to Virginia that he had won an appointment as a full colonel with the peculiar proviso that he would be allowed to return to civilian life at any time. Well acquainted with her husband's lust for danger, she was quite worried. She was partly mollified when she learned that he was to work on training films in New York City. But after only a week he won a posting to London to serve as a liaison with the British army and oversee production of training films. Zanuck thrilled to the excitement of the blitz, albeit from a luxurious suite at Claridge's. Fortunately, the censors prevented Virginia from knowing what her husband was really doing—venturing forth on a perilous nighttime air raid on German-occupied France with Lord Louis Mountbatten. Of a long letter he sent her, she received only a package of sand with the one-sentence message that it came from an enemy beach. At least, she reasoned, he had survived to report this much.

After a dull spell producing another training film in the Aleutians, Zanuck was reassigned to Washington, and Virginia breathed easily once again. She organized the entire family to join him. Alma Diehl spent days helping Virginia pack clothes in tissue paper. At the last minute, however, Zanuck called Virginia and told her excitedly that he had been dispatched to Europe for a secret mission that would involve "bullets, blood, lights, and color." She was crushed. Not only wasn't she to see her husband then, but like all women with men in the war, she was worried that her husband would be killed.

In Los Angeles, she threw herself into work for the USO. Alongside Myrna Loy and other stars, she passed out coffee, doughnuts, and good cheer to soldiers who were stationed at military bases. With several Fox celebrities, she put on a series of shows for servicemen heading overseas. Once in a while she would politely dance with an officer at one of the many army-sponsored war bond drives, but her mind was always on her husband's safety.

Much to his joy, Zanuck had none of it. His "secret mission" was to produce a movie of the Allies' North African campaign. He stayed in Africa for three months, sniffing out danger like a bloodhound. His unit crew was not always thrilled; he seemed ever anxious to be in the thick of the fighting. Subordinates respected him, though. He slept on the ground with them and never pulled rank. Some days he took on one of his World War I jobs—carrying the stretchers of the wounded.

Virginia, who read of her husband's exploits in the newspapers, greeted the news of his impending return to the United States late in 1942 with tremendous relief. Frantic to bring the realities of the war to the home front, he had wangled transport from Africa to Brazil to Washington and then to New York. Virginia met him there but saw him little more than she had when he worked as production chief at Fox. Betty Rivkin, a stenographer who had been drafted to help with the final production of the North African film, recalled that "Zanuck was so driven to produce the movie that all of us—the whole crew—stayed in the studio for six days and nights. We slept on couches or on the floor. We never went home."

The final production of *At the Front in North Africa*, which was ready for the theaters in March 1943, suffered more shelling from the critics than Zanuck had sustained in all his adventures. *Time* accused Zanuck of trying to dress up the film with "arty shots of tank treads, dawns, sunsets." By contrast, Zanuck's log of his war experience, published a month later as *The Tunis Expedition*, won praise for its no-nonsense style and solid reporting. But Zanuck was stung by the criticism of his movie. He complained in a letter to the *New York Times* that what moviegoers saw was the real thing. "We did not jazz it up or slip in a few clips from the stock library," he said in defense of the project.

Virginia was hurt for her husband. He had risked his life for his country—a second time—only to be mistreated by a bunch of critics who had done little more during the war than watch movies. She was even angrier when more barbs issued from congressmen who began complaining about "instant Hollywood colonels." Zanuck, they charged, had conducted the army's business while still on the Fox payroll. They were only partly right. Always mindful of money, Zanuck had collected his paycheck until August of 1942, when the army asked him to step down officially from his studio post and waive his salary. Still, the accusations were an affront. In April 1943 he asked to be placed on the "inactive" list. Senator Harry Truman, Zanuck's chief critic and head of a committee investigating quickie commissions, called the producer a quitter and asserted, "I don't believe in these fellows backing out."

Zanuck later appeared before Truman's committee and testified that Hollywood had made almost no money on its war department films. Truman wrote him a letter of apology. However, Zanuck stuck to his decision to quit. With his extravagant personal expenses, he couldn't live without his salary forever. Virginia was aggrieved on her husband's account. Even dinner at the White House with President Roosevelt did not completely appease her. To her, Zanuck was a greater hero than ever before. The whole episode seemed outrageous. Her husband had jeopardized his life and given up his pay merely to be smeared by Congress.

Much to Virginia's surprise, Zanuck stayed at home for days on end after his resignation from the army. He swam and exercised and read but refused to return to the studio until Joseph Schenck and Spyros Skouras, the newly appointed president of Twentieth Century-Fox, settled the mess made by William Goetz, who had been chief of production in Zanuck's absence. Goetz, Zanuck felt, had used the storehouse of film properties he had built up without adding anything new. More offensively, Goetz had redecorated his office and turned his little casting-couch annex into a file room. The Zanuck-green walls had been painted Goetz-blue. Further, Goetz had asked to form an independent production company, perhaps as a way of bowing out of the scene gracefully. He wanted Darryl Zanuck to have no say in how he produced his movies. Zanuck was violently opposed.

Within weeks, Goetz was out. He began his own company, International Productions, at Universal and eventually became production chief after the merger of the two firms. Virginia was a bit distressed by this turn of events. Goetz's wife, Edith, was one of Hollywood's "Saturday night ladies." Invitations to her elegant dinner parties were a mark of social success in Beverly Hills. The Goetzes and the Zanucks had not been close; Virginia and her husband usually circulated with actors and other celebrities while the Goetzes mixed with movie industry executives. Now Virginia had reason to fear that she and her husband would be cut forever from the A-list.

Not that the Zanucks were in such great demand by the A-list's denizens. Indeed, Zanuck himself had a reputation for such outrageous and strange behavior—much of it apocryphal—that some people were leery of any close association. H. Brad Darrach, a *Time* writer, recalled a tale about a bizarre party Zanuck threw in the early 1940s, a story that circulated around Hollywood for years: "Supposedly, he invited about six hundred people or so to a huge cocktail party. And at the party there were shit canapés—yes, they were made out of shit. And everybody ate them and said, 'My, how delicious,' and Zanuck ate one, too." It seems hard to believe that a perfect hostess like Virginia Zanuck would allow her husband to serve such fare to guests, and Darrach did not give the story much credence. He added, however, "Many people believed it. Knowing what the man was like, people found strange anecdotes completely believable. They thought Zanuck was capable of practically anything."

After Goetz's disappearance, Zanuck jubilantly took control at the studio like MacArthur establishing a beachhead on Manila. He later bragged that he entered his office, sat down at his mammoth desk, and with one sweep of his arm, cleared the surface of all Goetz's scripts. He lit up a cigar, summoned his employees, and announced that he was "through with the crap." He was going to make pictures with "real significance."

One of his first efforts at quality soon after his return in 1943 was the screen version of *The Ox-Bow Incident*, a grim and moralistic tale about a lynching, which starred Henry Fonda. During Zanuck's absence, Goetz had canceled the movie, but Zanuck revived it because it was the type of high-minded movie he believed Fox should be producing. He and his wife parted company in their opinion of the final cut, however. She looked for commercial value; he was trying to climb that ascending spiral of taste. When Virginia saw rushes, she loudly declared that the studio should be ashamed. The movie, she felt, was too depressing to make any money. This time Zanuck ignored her advice and released the movie. The critics gave it good notices, but it made only a small profit.

A film biography of President Woodrow Wilson was Zanuck's next do-gooder project in 1945. Zanuck felt that Wilson, who envisioned a world united to solve its problems in the League of Nations, had an important message to deliver the postwar audience. He threw himself into *Wilson* with characteristic intensity, and he lavished money on the movie as though Fox coined it. He had crews build elaborate reproductions of the U.S. Congress chamber and the Palace of Versailles. So proud was he of the movie that he determined to premiere it in Omaha, near his birthplace. Late in 1944 he packed his family and a batch of celebrities on a train to Nebraska, making a glory stop, complete with a parade, in Wahoo, where he was born. On the first night, the Omaha theater was packed. On the second night, almost no one showed up. Though the war was still raging, he had run up against the nation's still-strong isolationism. Like Napoleon, Zanuck left his equipage of celebs in the sticks and hightailed it back to the studio. *Wilson* flopped in New York and Los Angeles, too. Audiences found it long, boring, and preachy.

Virginia ached at her husband's humiliation, but he was not one to be easily discouraged. In 1946 and after, he continued trying to save humanity through movies, with a strong set of war dramas including *The House on 92nd Street*, *13 Rue Madeleine*, and *Call Northside 777*. But one of his biggest triumphs was a 1947 production, *Gentleman's Agreement*, based on Laura Z. Hobson's exposé of anti-Semitism in America. Though Zanuck had never displayed racial or religious prejudice in conducting his own business, he seemed an odd person to bring the best-seller to the screen, since he was virtually the only producer in Hollywood who wasn't Jewish. Indeed, Elia Kazan, who directed the movie, believed that Zanuck had "no strong feelings about the theme. . . . Darryl was interested in whatever would make a good story." Yet he refused to give up the project at the urging of Jack Warner and other Jewish producers who felt, said Kazan, that the movie might "stir things up."

When Laura Hobson timorously tiptoed into his grand office to ask him why he wanted to turn her book into a movie, he responded self-consciously, squirming a bit. She said, quoting him: " 'I have three children, Darrylin and Richard and Susan.' He was looking past me, as if he were looking at the faces of his son and daughters, then all in their teens. 'If this country ever did go fascist,' he went on, 'and they said to me, "Well, Pop, what did *you* do to stop it? You had the studios, the money, the power—what did *you* do to fight it off?" . . . I want to be able to say to them, "Well, I made *Wilson,* and then I made *Gentleman's Agreement,* I made *Pinky.*" ' " Hobson didn't take him very seriously. She recalled him adding, "Anyway . . . I felt in my bones your book would be a sensation, and I wanted to be *in* on a sensation." She tartly observed, "If I ever were to find myself a bit skeptical about all the higher motives, I never once doubted this one."

*   *   *

Unlike profits, Zanuck's progeny were almost abstractions. He sent them typewritten memos urging them to brush their teeth, study, and behave—things he had never bothered to do. His son, Richard, was to be good at athletics, get good grades, and inherit the studio. Zanuck was already asking Dick what he thought of particular movies and scripts. The girls, however, were to be girls, with fluff-filled minds, pretty dresses, and clean-cut boyfriends. Although he doted on his elder daughter, Darrylin, Zanuck was too much of a traditionalist to picture *her* following in his footsteps—or having any career at all. She and her sister Susan were to attend high school, parties, and football games, find eligible men, and marry. They would always live in style, because in 1935 he had established $1 million trust funds for each of his children. They would start receiving income from the trusts when they reached age twenty-six. When they died, the principal would go to their children.

Virginia did not take exception to Darryl's unstated plans for the girls. She put no particular premium on learning; her letters, like those of her daughters, are full of misspellings. Her daughters spent much of their time driving around town in the Cadillacs their indulgent father had bought them, buying clothes, swimming, surfing, and dating. "Both of the girls would climb up over the wall of the house to get out late at night and meet boys on the beach," said Virginia's friend, Martha Newman Ragland. "They were pretty wild."

Virginia looked the other way—or perhaps never looked at all. Her time was completely taken up with her husband. When Darrylin began to get serious about a UCLA student and lifeguard named Robert Jacks, he was welcomed into the Zanuck family circle. Tall, blond, blue-eyed, well mannered and well spoken, he appealed to the entire family. The young couple announced their engagement in 1949 and planned to marry a year later. Darrylin went off to Finch College in Manhattan that fall, leaving Virginia more time to devote to her husband. Almost before she could reorient herself, however, Darrylin called to inform her parents that she had eloped with Jacks to Covington, Kentucky. Darryl and Virginia could scarcely believe that their daughter, barely eighteen, could have married without consulting them. Virginia's dreams of giving her eldest child a large church wedding ended. "I believe that she was secretly relieved," declared Martha Ragland. "Darrylin was so wild, Virginia was glad to have her settled down." Zanuck hired Jacks to work at Fox as a producer, and the young couple settled down to life in a small home in Brentwood.

As her children became adults, Virginia could focus even more on her husband. She ran the family's routine to suit his convenience. A direct line to the studio had been installed in their bedroom, and the first thing he did every morning, after gazing out to sea for a moment, was to call his secretary and inform her to "send Sam down." With that notification, his personal barber, Sam Silver, would climb into his Pontiac and motor down Olympic Boulevard to the sea. The two men would convene in the Zanuck living room, which was decorated with century-old French wallpaper depicting George Washington's arrival in New York Harbor. Sam would retrieve from a cupboard a collapsible leather contraption that metamorphosed into a flimsy replica of a barber's chair. Zanuck would climb on to face a wall of bric-a-brac he and Virginia had assembled from their globe-trottings. One of Zanuck's favorite pieces was a miniature of a bear mating with a yowling dog. Sam would then shave his charge while he sucked on the first cigar of the day. Virginia had the cook prepare a breakfast for her husband, which he consumed while making quick work of the *Los Angeles Times*. Sometimes he would sit by the pool and read scripts, but more often, he would get in his Zanuck-green Cadillac and drive to the studio. (After the war, he had decided that doing one's own driving was more dashing than being ferried about town by a chauffeur.) Virginia wouldn't usually hear from her husband until four or four-thirty, when he would call to talk to the children. On Thursday nights, the two might dine out or attend a party.

During the winter months, Darryl, Virginia, and sometimes the children would travel to Palm Springs by airplane or car. In 1943

Zanuck had bought Joseph Schenck's estate in Palm Springs. Virginia, who loved wordplay, christened it Ric-Su-Dar, using the first syllables of the names of the three children. During the war, the estate had served as a USO inn for soldiers. The walled-off compound, which took up most of a block near the town's center, contained two structures—a two-story main house, where the family and servants stayed, and a pool house with four bedrooms and a living room, which guests came to call the "casino." Separating the two whitewashed buildings with their red tile roofs was a seventy-foot pool offering relief from the burning desert heat. Tall date palms, lemon trees, and tamarisks provided shade, and pink, white, red, and yellow flowers bloomed in the beds that bordered the manicured lawn. The Zanucks added a tennis court behind the pool house.

When Zanuck first visited the house to determine the work that was needed, he found an old croquet set. He began to play and, once he became accomplished, took up the sport with a vengeance. Every weekend, celebrities would stream to Ric-Su-Dar to relax or play croquet. The two activities were mutually exclusive, since Zanuck took the sport so seriously. The players parked cars around the perimeter of the field and trained the headlights on the croquet matches, which ran deep into the night. Later, Zanuck installed floodlights, which lent the lawn the atmosphere of Yankee Stadium.

Joseph Cotten was a frequent guest. Other regulars at the "Palm Springs Yacht Club" included Mary Lee, Douglas Fairbanks, Jr., David Niven and his wife Hjordis, Jennifer Jones and David Selznick, Mr. and Mrs. William Powell, Gregory Ratoff, Moss Hart, Spyros Skouras, Clifton Webb, Tyrone Power, and Louis Jourdan. The chief activity, of course, was croquet, and the lawn was dotted with sturdy white wickets, a scoreboard, and other equipment. "If you didn't play croquet," wrote Cotten in his autobiography, "you saw Darryl and the others only at lunch, cocktails, and dinner."

Darrylin recalled in an interview for a Palm Springs magazine years later that the games got so rowdy at times that disgruntled neighbors summoned the police because of "all the screaming and yelling. They thought somebody was being murdered. What was really happening was that Daddy was shouting that he had seen Clifton Webb or some other player move their ball and, a couple of times, in the heat of the play, Howard Hawks threw his mallet down and left in a huff. . . . They used to get very, very wild."

Virginia was the proud queen of the weekend doings. She hired a regular chef and a pastry chef to feed the guests, who sometimes numbered as many as forty. She would have breakfast served outdoors at six or seven tables. At eleven o'clock, the croquet game would begin, while the nonplaying visitors frolicked in the pool or batted balls around the tennis court. Virginia would call a halt to play about two hours later, and everybody would adjourn to the big Spanish patio where long tables had been set up. An informal lunch would usually last for two hours. "By that time," said Darrylin, "Daddy was raring to go again with the croquet and they'd go back to it." Virginia and the women would prowl the Palm Springs shops for clothing in the afternoon. At seven o'clock, the entire party would meet in the casino for cocktails. Then they would troop off to the main house for dinner—another two- or three-hour affair.

When the game ended before dark, according to Cotten, "there was dancing to the phonograph or a wild game of charades in the billiard room." Jennifer Jones, Selznick, the Powells, and Charlie Chaplin—who, ironically, "always won the booby prize," according to Cotten—vied with one another to present the best pantomime. Virginia was a canasta fiend, and she would recruit a foursome who would retire to a corner to play. Other entertainment would embellish the evening. Noel Coward or Judy Garland would sing. Richard Rodgers might play, and, Cotten said, "Sometimes when the stars lowered themselves over the desert to within touching distance, Spyros Skouras would recite Greek poetry in his native tongue."

Pocahontas (Pokie) Noonan Seeger, a friend of Susan Zanuck, recalled another Palm Springs pastime—a popular Hollywood game called Murder. At lunch each guest would receive a card. The person who got the ace of spades was the murderer. Later a servant would inform another guest that he or she was the victim. The victim had to stay put until his "body" was discovered. "Once Virginia was sunbathing nude alone on a sunroof upstairs, and she learned that she was the corpus delicti," said Mrs. Seeger. Always one to abide by rules, Virginia waited hours and hours to be found. Unfortunately no one came upon her. "She was so sunburned she looked like a boiled lobster," added Mrs. Seeger. Zanuck himself always played the role of the prosecutor. At dinner he would grill his guests until he trapped one of them into confessing. "He could be very intimidating," remembered Mrs. Seeger. "I would get apprehensive when he questioned me."

Zanuck continued his practical jokes during the weekends, and though Virginia supposedly disapproved, she howled with laughter at his antics. She didn't deplore all his jokes, she once declared, because he could take it as well as he dished it out. One favorite ploy was to hand a new guest "my personal mallet." Zanuck claimed it was so delicately balanced that it would turn a new croquet player into a virtuoso magically. Supposedly the finest wood from the Himalayas or from Lebanon gave it the proper heft and so on. Of course, after the third or fourth shot, the mallet would break into a million splinters. To the guest's horror, Zanuck would wail, "Oh, my God, that mallet is irreplaceable." Another trick was the erratic ball. It would veer aimlessly no matter how truly a player hit.

While strolling to Saturday night dinner once, Zanuck, by prior arrangement, shoved talent agent Fefe Ferry right into the swimming pool. Virginia's mouth set in a thin line. This was too much—a guest dressed in evening clothes was now sopping wet and humiliated. Though she was tricked out in a gown and diamonds, she did not pause but jumped into the pool herself—as though a dunking were a Zanuck pre-dinner tradition like cocktails and hors d'oeuvres. Louis Jourdan, to save his hostess from embarrassment, dived in also. Soon all sixteen guests were splashing around in their finery. The butler appeared and announced with aplomb, "Madam, dinner is served." Zanuck's joke on his wife had backfired. Guests noted that Virginia managed to maintain her composure no matter what. Once, several of the men began tossing around hassocks in the main house as though they were beach balls. Virginia was starting to seat her guests at dinner. One of the hassocks hit and broke a chandelier. Through the crash she could be heard calmly directing, "And you sit here, darling, and you sit next to her . . . and you . . ."

The Palm Springs pool house was designed for dalliance. Each of the rooms had two entrances—one that led to the casino and another that opened to the yard. If croquet, tennis, shopping, dining, and drinking were not enough to amuse the guests, there was always the opportunity to play musical beds, and many joined in wholeheartedly.

Virginia monitored the goings-on closely so that she could render a full report to the rest of her friends come Monday. She was the ear to a thousand confidences from female guests. Said John O'Grady, a Los Angeles detective who worked for her many years later, "She loved being in on the adventures and misadventures of Hollywood stars—she just loved that—for example, when Rita Hayworth thought she was carrying Aly Khan's baby, though she had come to Ric-Su-Dar with another man." Virginia was always ready with good advice. Added O'Grady, "Mrs. Zanuck told her to marry Aly and packed her off on a plane to Los Angeles."

Despite the competitive games, the heavy-handed practical jokes, and the heated nighttime wanderings, weekends at Ric-Su-Dar were always relaxing—unlike Beverly Hills get-togethers where people were made to dress up in showy, uncomfortable clothing and dine at tables littered with so many pieces of silverware that they didn't know which fork to pick up first. At Virginia's home, guests could wear slacks and shirts or golf skirts and T-shirts. She never fussed or hovered. People unwound gracefully and beautifully under her care. When the weekend was over, the Zanucks' driver would convey them to the airport. Back to the rat race. For Zanuck, the work week began on Sunday afternoon when his stenographer Molly Mandeville came down to Palm Springs to collect scripts, memos, and other paperwork so that it would be in the pipeline at the studio when he returned late Monday morning.

*   *   *

Zanuck continued his constant studio sexual entanglements with women throughout the late 1940s. For a time he was interested in Merle Oberon, star of *Wuthering Heights* and *A Song to Remember*. Virginia knew of the attraction and mentioned it—almost proudly—to several friends years later, and she and Oberon remained quite friendly. Virginia ungrudgingly entertained Zanuck's girlfriends at her home, acidly commenting to a friend that failing to do so would cut down the guest list considerably. Everybody at the studio knew that Zanuck often called on the busty blond pinup girl Carole Landis for his traditional afternoon sessions. Landis, who committed suicide in 1948 over a go-nowhere love affair with actor Rex Harrison, had earlier been involved sexually with Jacqueline Susann, who later wrote *Valley of the Dolls*. Some Hollywood gossips began to think that Zanuck preferred women who preferred women. Sidewalk psychologists, when they dissected his character, concluded that to ease some nagging childhood insecurity, he had to possess women who didn't really want him. The more common view was expressed by Myrna Loy: "Darryl, undersized, with prominent buckteeth, always seemed to be overcompensating to prove his potency."

Despite his continuing flings with women, Zanuck could be very, very jealous of his wife. At one movie premiere in 1949, Virginia was smoothing her gown so that she could be photographed. One of the photographers dropped to his knees to rearrange a batch of cables and wires near her feet. Zanuck misinterpreted the gesture and grabbed the hapless photographer by the collar, ready to punch him in the nose. Only Virginia's quick intervention saved them from fighting.

It's not clear how Virginia saw her husband's drive to bed woman after woman. Such goings-on seemingly ceased to trouble her, for she no longer appeared at the studio with sidearms. Nor did she threaten to leave her husband. Perhaps she came to believe that Zanuck's creativity and genius justified his betrayals. Indeed, his ability to produce movies that entertained, informed, and grabbed the public's imagination seemed greater than ever before. In 1948 he stunned the public with *The Snake Pit*, an exposé of mental hospitals. A year later came *Pinky*, a daring story for the times about an interracial romance; and then, in 1950, the Academy Award–winning *All About Eve*, the unforgettable tale of an excessively ambitious, back-stabbing young actress. That year, *Time* put Zanuck—crowned with a twirl of celluloid film—on its cover and christened him the king of the moviemakers. When Virginia attended the premieres and the testimonials honoring her husband, she could comfort herself with the thought that her tolerance was contributing to his greatness and, by indirection, her own. *Time* saw things that way. According to the magazine, she was such a wonderful person that her attachment to Zanuck itself proclaimed the man's quality.

Virginia must also have sensed that Zanuck needed her—perhaps even more than she needed him. Moss Hart, a frequent visitor to Ric-Su-Dar, observed that Zanuck had no close male friends. "He is really quite lonely, he doesn't trust anyone. . . . He must suspect most of his friends because of his position." Zanuck had comfortable relations with women who worked for him as secretaries or film editors; however, they never got close to him. And his afternoon entanglements seemed mechanical and unfeeling. According to Hart, "Virginia was his only real friend."

Virginia may have made her peace with her marriage, but her husband was restive. He began telling friends that someday soon he would like to chuck everything. Moss Hart told reporters that Zanuck had once announced to him: "I'm going to go on for about six or seven years, and then I'll pick up and go maybe to Europe, Africa, New York. One thing I won't do is sit in Santa Monica and read in the *Hollywood Reporter* about what goes on and wonder why I wasn't invited to parties. I don't accept invitations now, but I do receive them, and I don't want to know how it is not to be invited anymore." As usual, Zanuck was jumping ahead, looking into the future. He didn't like what he saw—aging, decline, neglect, and death. He didn't want to face that. Perhaps he could opt out.

By 1951, when the Zanucks made one of their annual trips to Europe, he was ready for something new. Ironically, it was Virginia whose life suddenly careened in an uncertain direction. While strolling down a boulevard one day on the French Riviera, the couple ran into Alex D'Arcy, an Egyptian-born character actor, who was passing the time at an outdoor café. With him was a striking woman with gray-green eyes, brown hair, and exotic-looking high cheekbones. Her name was Bayla, or Bella, Wegier. The foursome dined together that night, and both the Zanucks were charmed. To Virginia, Bella was particularly appealing. Despite her dazzling beauty, she had the reticent air of a poor orphan.

Indeed, life had treated Bella harshly. Born in Poland in 1927, she had emigrated to France with her family and had grown up in the Jewish district of Paris. In 1941 she was interned in several concentration camps, and her brother was deported to Germany, where he was killed by the Nazis. Her parents had fled to the unoccupied zone, and her mother kept trying to obtain her daughter's release. The papers finally came through, and Bella was freed on December 30, 1943. Only a day after her liberation, all the other inmates were shipped to Germany; she had narrowly escaped death.

By the time the Zanucks met Bella, however, she had ceased to be quite so tragic. She had won a few beauty contests and done some modeling. In 1950 she had married Alban Cavalcade, a French industrialist, and mingled with the Riviera's café society. Her husband encouraged her to participate in curious events called automobile fashion shows in which awards were given for the honor of modeling the most stylish clothing while posing in the snazziest car. Bella had picked up prizes at Cannes, Enghien, and Deauville, coincidentally the sites of Europe's most popular casinos. Acquisition of fine clothing and jewelry was now her chief hobby. Frantic gambling was her occupation. When she met the Zanucks, she was down on her luck. She had separated from her husband, and she was deep in debt. Though she owed so much to her hotel that the management had impounded her luggage and clothing, the day after her first meeting with the Zanucks Bella managed to scrounge up enough money to send Virginia flowers.

The Zanucks were not averse to playing vacation benefactors— Darryl for the usual reason. Soon after their first dinner in Cannes, he began meeting Bella on the sly, and they became lovers. With her connection secure, Bella appealed to him for money. Her financial situation was dire. She needed $2,000 to pay off her creditors immediately. After she rendered a tearful presentation of her problems, Zanuck agreed to help her. He told Virginia that the poor girl was in desperate need. Virginia endorsed her husband's plan to help. Kindness demanded that they treat Bella as they might want their daughters treated should they need money. They advanced Bella funds within a day.

Virginia could not have been completely deceived. Her husband's interest in Bella, she must have been certain, was not merely fatherly. He could hardly help feeling attracted to someone so young and beautiful. However, Virginia, too, found Bella's appeal magnetic and irresistible. She wanted to guide Bella, to assist her, and simply to be with her. They lunched together almost every day in Cannes and toured the shops. Virginia loved helping Bella choose just the right scarves and shoes, giving her advice about men friends, and accompanying her on nighttime visits to Riviera clubs. Everyone took notice of Bella when she and the Zanucks entered a room. Virginia felt proud to be with such a refined and lovely young woman.

When the time came for the Zanucks to return to Los Angeles, however, Virginia was heartbroken. She couldn't bear the thought of leaving her protégée behind. She wanted Bella to join them in California, but Bella had other ideas. With the Zanucks' cash in hand, she could pay her bills and return to the gaming tables. A year later, however, when her marriage ended and her money ran out, she wrote Virginia, saying that she might like to visit America. The Zanucks invited her to stay with them in Santa Monica. She arrived on November 20, 1952, and promptly moved into the beach-house annex. Susan and Alma Diehl were its only other occupants; Darrylin was living with her husband in Malibu, and Richard had gone off to Stanford University that fall.

Bella became Virginia's constant companion. "Every time I went over to the house to visit Susan," recalled Terry Moore, "there were Virginia and Bella playing cards." Susan steered clear of Bella—she was unable to understand her mother's infatuation—but Virginia introduced Bella to her own circle of friends, and she was invited to Beverly Hills parties as though she were a member of the family. Virginia lavished attention and gifts on her young friend. They swam together, played tennis together, and shopped ceaselessly. Virginia eagerly supplied her with everything she could possibly want. She made special visits to her jeweler to buy Bella a diamond wristwatch and a ring. Virginia was smitten. People began to talk about the strange relationship. Their explanations of Virginia's behavior ranged widely. Some thought she was just giving rein to maternal instincts, befriending Bella as she would a daughter. Others came to believe that at age fifty Virginia had discovered that she was a lesbian.

The ever loyal Virginia hardly seemed the type to betray her husband with another man, much less a woman. In the early 1950s homosexual behavior was considered either criminal or sick. Bella did seem to call forth strong feeling from Virginia, but it was unlikely that a sexual liaison would actually have occurred unless Zanuck himself either endorsed it or participated in it.

To Virginia's distress, Bella constantly threatened to leave Los Angeles. She often talked about her longing for Paris and about how boring Los Angeles was compared to Europe, with its shows, restaurants, sidewalk cafés, and gambling casinos. She also missed her family. Virginia, frantic to keep Bella in America, quickly came up with a solution. If her husband could promote the young woman as a film star, then Bella would have a career; she would have to stay. Virginia appealed to her husband, and he happily announced to Bella one day early in 1953 that the studio was going to grant her a screen test. Bella later said that she was taken aback. She wasn't sure she had any dramatic talent. Indeed, it appeared that she had been looking for a temporary meal ticket, not a passport to stardom. However, she aimed to please her mentors. Somehow she passed the test and began receiving regular paychecks as a contract actress. Virginia, who acted as Bella's unofficial personal manager, decided that the name Wegier was hardly likely to excite box-office attendance. Her protégée needed a new name. Bella was taking on a life and an importance that Virginia and her husband had created together; she rechristened her Bella Darvi—borrowing the first syllables of *Darryl* and *Virginia*.

Now Bella was visiting the studio daily, for the acting lessons she desperately needed. There Zanuck was lord and master, and he was free to resume his affair without inhibition. Bella became a regular visitor to his office-hideaway, ostensibly to discuss business. Zanuck starred her in *Hell and High Water*, an early feature in CinemaScope, which was wasted, said critic Bosley Crowther, "on a ridiculously melodramatic tale" in which Bella Darvi "does not succeed convincingly." Unwilling to admit that perhaps Bella was not the great talent he and Virginia had hoped for, Zanuck cast her in *The Egyptian*, another wide-screen extravaganza, this one starring Marlon Brando. After the actors went through their first reading, Brando quit, reportedly because of his reluctance to work with Darvi. Zanuck had to substitute Edmund Purdom at the last minute. Bella did not have the leading role, but screenwriter Philip Dunne recalled that his boss was so taken with the "mildly talented woman . . . [that he] asked me to rewrite a scene for her and then accompanied me to the set to gain her approval of the changes." Later, at lunch with Nunnally Johnson, Dunne asked how Bella could possibly exert such magical control over Zanuck. "Well, Bella made Darryl take her to bed," Dunne remembered Johnson saying. "Until then, Darryl thought it was somethin' you did on a desk."

Virginia had succeeded in bringing her protégée to the silver screen, but in a way, the project had backfired. Bella now spent her days under

Zanuck's supervision, not hers. His wardrobe masters chose Bella's clothing and makeup. His publicists wrote her biography and selected the parties she attended. Virginia had hoped that bringing Bella into her home would keep her in control of the three-way attachment. She had been the keystone of the relationship. Once Bella's new career got under way, however, she was unneeded. Her link to Bella had weakened, and Zanuck's had strengthened.

Susan, however, supplied a powerful distraction to her mother. Virginia's younger daughter had an itch for the stage. She had already sung in a few nightclubs. Her friend Terry Moore was heading up a troupe of Hollywood performers who were to entertain soldiers in Korea under the auspices of the USO, and she had invited Susan to join the group. Virginia was a bit reluctant to allow her daughter to travel to a war zone, but she finally gave in. Her days were taken up helping her daughter organize for the trip. Susan was rehearsed by comedian Tommy Noonan, whose wife, a former chorus girl named Pocahontas Crowfoot, became one of her best friends. Charles LeMaire, chief costumer for Fox, designed Susan's dresses.

When the tour ended in February 1954, Zanuck threw a party in honor of his daughter and Terry Moore. He invited more than four hundred guests. "The party was at Ciro's," said Moore. "The marquee read 'Welcome Home, Terry and Susan.' All the studio heads were invited, and because we had just come back from Korea, the party had an Oriental theme. We all wore makeup to look like Mandarins and dressed in Oriental costumes." Tyrone Powers's wife, Linda Christian, attended wearing a wraparound skirt and a thick lei to cover her breasts, and Mitzi Gaynor donned a coolie hat and a mini-sarong.

During the evening, recalled Philip Kunhardt, former managing editor of *Life* who was then a reporter in the magazine's Los Angeles bureau, "Zanuck was really in his cups. A trapeze had been left on the stage by one of the nightclub performers, and Zanuck stopped the band to announce that he was going to perform chin-ups." Much to everyone's surprise, Zanuck yanked off his jacket and shirt and dropped his suspenders. "The studio P.R. people had forbidden us from taking pictures, but Loomis Dean, a *Life* photographer, wriggled his way to the front and got the whole thing on film," said Kunhardt. Dean barely made it out of the room in one piece. "Some goons tried to beat him up," added Kunhardt. Zanuck performed four regular chin-ups successfully, but when he tried to raise and lower himself one-armed, he failed. "Dean masterfully got his pictures and got the film out of the camera and into the camera before they [the goons] got to him," said Kunhardt. The film was shipped to New York for publication in the magazine.

Had Kunhardt and Dean stayed, they would have been able to publish an even stranger picture: the sight of a very tipsy Virginia Zanuck grappling with her husband over the trapeze. Some thought she was trying to stop him, but Pokie Noonan Seeger knew that Virginia was trying to do a chin-up herself. As always, Virginia wanted to do everything that Zanuck valued. How else to impress on him that she, too, was vital and playful just like Bella Darvi, other than by copying his antics? A hush fell over the spectators as they gaped goggle-eyed at the bizarre scene.

At home later, Virginia apparently came to her senses. She turned on her husband. She announced that he had embarrassed her with his display of foolishness. To her mind, he was behaving like a fraternity brat, not a fifty-one-year-old business executive. Under his influence, she had acted as dumb as he had. He had tried to make himself the center of attention when the night was supposed to belong to Susan. Virginia stormed off to bed.

Within days of the event, Bella left the Zanucks' home and moved into the Doheny Avenue apartment previously occupied by Marilyn Monroe. Pokie Seeger said that when Susan returned from Ciro's that evening, she caught wind of Darryl's affair with Bella Darvi. She had overheard them in Bella's room right down the hall from her own. "Susan told Virginia about it, and Virginia sent Bella packing," said Seeger. Susan may have been less shocked by her father's relationship with Bella than by her mother's. She knew of his studio dalliances because one of her dearest friends, Corinne Calvet, who had appeared in *Rope of Sand* and *What Price Glory?*, had been at the receiving end of a Zanuck afternoon proposition. Pierre Savineau, Susan's second husband, said she discovered that Virginia was deeply in love with Bella. "Virginia was gay, and the Zanucks had a *ménage à trois*," he declared. "It was a family secret." When Virginia learned from her shocked daughter that Darryl had been involved with Bella on his own, "she became jealous" and sent her from the house, he said.

Pokie Seeger discounted Savineau's story. "That was just vicious Hollywood gossip," she said. And Hollywood did buzz with stories. Virginia never discussed Bella Darvi even with her closest friends. "She never talked about her problems," said Martha Newman Ragland. "I never asked her, either, but I had heard the rumors that she was involved with Bella."

For a short time, Zanuck moved out of the house, too, but he came back hat in hand, as he always had before. Virginia had reason to believe that the affair had been put to rest. True, she had lost Bella, but once again her husband had returned to her, reconfirming the importance of their relationship. Pretty girls might come and go, but he would always need her in his life. And it looked as though Bella would go for good. In August *The Egyptian* opened to unfavorable reviews. The *New York Times* declared, "Bella Darvi [who plays] the heartless gold digger, smiles and postures without magnetism or charm." Much to Virginia's disgust, Bella later starred in *The Racer*, but that role, too, was a failure. The *Times* pronounced that Darvi "contributes very little in the way of excitement or sincerity."

Susan was shocked and upset by her parents' involvement with Bella Darvi, according to Savineau. She wanted *out*—out of her family and out of their household. She felt that their behavior was sick and perverted. Two months after Bella Darvi left the Santa Monica house, Susan announced to her parents that she planned to marry André Hakim, a French Jew ten years older than she. Zanuck approved the match. He had known Hakim since World War II when the Frenchman was working for U.S. Naval Intelligence. After the war, Hakim had come to New York and eventually won a job as a Fox television producer. Like Zanuck, Hakim was tiny and full of explosive energy, and, according to Zanuck's friend Art Buchwald, "he was very much in love with Susan."

Once again Virginia was to be denied the opportunity of having her daughter wed in an extravagant movieland ceremony. Susan was so eager to become Madame Hakim and move out of her parents' orbit that she gave her mother and father only a few days' notice. With their families and a few friends, the couple went to Las Vegas to be wed at the Little Church of the West at the Last Frontier Hotel on April 18, 1954, only two months after she learned of her parents' sexual involvement with Darvi. The ceremony was brief and uneventful, recalled Pokie Seeger, "except that Susan and André held their kiss so long that Darryl said he thought that the police would come and haul them off to jail for obscene behavior." To ease her exit from the family, Susan had persuaded her father to send Hakim to work at Fox's Paris office. After the wedding, the group retreated to Palm Springs to spend Easter Sunday together. The following week, Susan and André left for Paris.

Back at the beach house—now almost completely empty—Virginia had to face the fact that her husband's affair with Bella Darvi was not over. Even when Bella, discouraged by the unfavorable notices, took off in 1955 for the playgrounds of Europe, Zanuck found obscure business that would take him to Paris. When Bella popped up in New York, he always happened to be there at the same time. He equipped Bella with an American convertible, mink coats, and jewelry and installed her in a lavishly furnished apartment on the Rue Léon-Bonnat in the swank Passy district of Paris. For some reason he couldn't get enough of the woman. He had to be with her. They were spotted kissing passionately and openly at Maxim's on New Year's Eve at the end of 1955 and nightclubbing at the White Elephant.

Still, Virginia hung on. This, too, would pass, she reasoned. Some new starlet was certain to grab his attention. His restlessness would not disappear, however. The old pleasures—sports, practical jokes, power-playing at the studio, afternoon delights—no longer satisfied Darryl Zanuck. Like everyone else in Hollywood at the time, he was busy revising his own life to make it appear unfulfilling and directionless. Psychiatry had become the rage among the celebrities and executives of the film industry, and, reported Ezra Goodman, an entertainment correspondent for *Time*, the psychoanalytic approach had encouraged show-biz folk to discover hidden misery in their lives. "Their misery goes back to some traumatic experience long ago. In the past, most everyone in Hollywood was happy and cheerful in print. Today, the reverse is true. It is fashionable to be miserable," wrote Goodman.

Zanuck retained a psychoanalyst. Goodman noted that at lunch one day with Zanuck "and his high-priced producer stooges" in Fox's executive dining room, "all of these wealthy and voluble gentlemen dummied up when Zanuck started talking and listened quietly and respectfully without once opening their mouths except to eat. The only ones at the table who said anything occasionally were I, seated at

Zanuck's right, and a man identified as his psychoanalyst, seated on his left."

Always at one with a new trend, Zanuck became fashionably miserable, too. Once he had described his childhood as happy. Suddenly it was fraught with pain, alcoholism, abuse, and loneliness. He now complained that his work, which had been so consuming and involving all his adult life, held no satisfaction. When dissected by a shrink, his marriage must have appeared a sham. Indeed, everything seemed to get on his nerves. The studio grind was just too much. He had to supervise ten to twelve major productions each year—he was tired of it all. He complained violently that he couldn't make any money; he had to pay 90 percent of his salary and dividends to the government. That was outrageous, he told reporters. And he couldn't stand the fact that actors, writers, and directors were refusing to work on salary. They had the temerity to demand portions of net or gross profits. Why, they wound up getting more money than he! "I am a creative man," he said. "I don't want to worry about these things."

The powers that be at Fox were also beginning to think that Zanuck shouldn't be bothered by such things. Spyros Skouras, the new head of the corporation, had had his troubles controlling the bumptious producer all along. Indeed, Zanuck had always thought very little of the theater owner, announcing to his flunkies that if Skouras liked a script, it was bound to be a dud. Zanuck would sometimes lock himself in the cutting room for nighttime editing sessions, and when Skouras pounded on the door, Zanuck would caution his co-workers to be quiet and pretend they weren't there. Now, however, Skouras encountered new affronts. Zanuck was hardly ever in Los Angeles. He ran the studio by cable from Paris. Fox executives met with him in London in the fall of 1955 to beg him to mind business, but he was not interested. Skouras seemed to want Zanuck out of the company.

In March of 1956 the studio publicity apparatus began making quiet noises that Zanuck was leaving. He conferred with lawyers in New York, rushed off to see Bella in Paris, and returned for a lightning visit to New York to iron out the details of his leave-taking. That month the news was announced: he was to become an independent producer for Fox and would operate his new company, DFZ Productions, from Europe. Many concluded that Skouras had dumped him. Said Martha Newman Ragland, then wife of Alfred Newman, the studio's chief composer, "We thought Darryl was fired." If so, the fact was kept secret. To all intents and purposes, Zanuck had merely resigned.

*　　*　　*

Virginia learned the news the same way the rest of Hollywood did—by reading the trade papers. She could scarcely believe what was happening. Surely her husband meant for her to accompany him to Europe? The answer, however, was no. Her husband returned for a few days in April to announce that he was leaving her, the studio, the children, the houses, and everything else. He told her that he had to find out what was "on the other side of the hill." He asked her for a divorce, but she refused. Though he told her he would probably never return to her, she would not agree to make their parting permanent. He was to remain her husband no matter what the circumstances. He did not press the issue. Just as he maintained a lifeline to the studio by working as an independent for Fox, he wanted to keep her as a tie to the home and family he was giving up. He seemed to need a way to get back if he had to someday. She wouldn't have to worry; he would take care of her. His lawyers were to draw up a separation agreement that would grant her more than half their assets.

In moments Zanuck was gone. He jumped into a studio limousine and told the driver to take him to the airport. Virginia was left to tell Darrylin and Richard what had happened. She put the best face she could on the startling news. Their father was not gone for good; he would be back. As days passed without a letter, a card, a call, or a cable from her husband, the dreadful reality of her situation became clear. Many of her Hollywood friends dropped her. Now that she was no longer the consort of the studio's king, she held little appeal for them. "Virginia was terribly, terribly lonely," said Pokie Seeger.

Instead of a living husband who left his socks on the floor and demanded chipped beef on toast, Virginia had memories, talismans, and omens to nurture her hope that he would return. She kept a picture of Zanuck on her bedside table and took it with her wherever she went. Soon after the Zanucks' breakup, Seeger's then husband, Tommy Noonan, went on a business trip. Virginia invited her daughter's friend, pregnant with her first child, to stay with her at the Santa Monica beach house. "Virginia begged me to sleep in Darryl's bed," recalled Seeger. "She said that if a woman who was going to have a baby stayed in his bed that somehow it would be a good sign to bring him back." Seeger compliantly slept in his bed, but Zanuck kept Virginia waiting for seventeen years.

*　　*　　*

In 1957, about a year after Zanuck's departure, Walter Scott escorted Virginia to a Beverly Hills party. While the two were making their separate ways through the crowd, Scott ran into Cesar Romero. The actor requested an introduction to Virginia—he had never met her. Scott brought the two together. "I'd like you to meet Virginia Zanuck," he said. Virginia responded graciously, but by the frozen set of her face, Scott knew that something was wrong. She was cool to him for the rest of the evening. When Scott drove her home, he asked whether he had done something to offend her.

"Don't you ever introduce me that way again," she replied angrily.

"What way?" Scott couldn't figure it out.

"Virginia Zanuck," she said. "I am *not* Virginia Zanuck. I am Mrs. Darryl F. Zanuck, and don't you *ever* forget it."

THREE
STUDIO BRAT

.

I t seemed a foregone conclusion that Richard Zanuck would inherit his father's position at the studio, and he did—for a time. He was often seen as a puppet, however, whose every twitch was manipulated by his father. Who was the real Richard Zanuck? Nobody knew—least of all Richard himself, who jumped around like a puppy anxiously trying to please his imposing father, as a son and as an employee of the movie industry's reigning king. His efforts went almost unnoticed by Zanuck, unless they served the elderly producer's own ambitions and convenience. When Richard began to show his father up as a has-been of fading competence, Zanuck cast him out of his studio and out of his will.

Not until 1973, when his father's career came to an end, was the real Richard Zanuck able to stand up. He went independent with his partner David Brown, and together they produced some of the most dazzling screen successes of modern-day Hollywood: *The Sting, Jaws, The Verdict,* and *Cocoon.* Then, at last, when working Hollywood referred to "Zanuck," they meant not Darryl F. but Richard D.

*   *   *

Unlike his sisters, Dickie, as his family and friends called him, was a frequent visitor to his father's workplace. He was remarkably enterprising for a rich little boy—though at his father's behest. Zanuck ordered his son to do something useful; when Richard was nine, he began selling the *Saturday Evening Post* on the Twentieth Century-Fox lot. He operated his business like a kiddie tycoon, employing four classmates from the Pacific Palisades Grammar School. The Zanuck limousine would pick them up after school and drop them on street corners where they would peddle the magazines. Dick kept the prime spot—the studio—for himself. He manned a little newsstand where he accepted a weekly delivery of eight to nine hundred issues, which he hawked from office to office. Sometimes he stood outside the Café de Paris, the studio's commissary, selling magazines. Practically everyone on the lot bought, of course, but his father did not allow Dick to accept tips, so he never made much money by movieland standards. He did get to know people at the studio, however, and became familiar with filmmaking jargon and shop talk.

The young Zanuck also picked up his father's sangfroid in dealing with stars. He could tell that his father dominated everyone with whom he mixed, from fellow tyro Jack Warner to actors Tyrone Power and Henry Fonda. At social gatherings at the beach house, the little boy saw leading men without their toupees and well-known actresses complaining about their kids and their husbands. To him, they were ordinary people.

By the time Richard Zanuck was in the sixth grade, his father was asking his opinion about scripts. Would they appeal to kids Dick's age? Sometimes Dick would join his father in the cutting room, where he was occasionally allowed to render his views on a movie. Dick would candidly announce to all present, including the movie's creators, "It stinks!" or "It's lousy!" Years later Dick squirmed with embarrassment at how thoughtlessly he had once dismissed the hard work of other people. But he had to follow his father's directive to deliver his opinion without fear or favor. Clearly Richard was a mogul in training.

Zanuck seemed to treat Dick as though he were an up-and-coming young subordinate instead of a son. In an interview for the Father's Day issue of *Los Angeles* magazine in 1982, Dick recalled that his father would issue letters to him, much like the memos he constantly shunted to his employees. They usually ran five to six pages and read like sermonettes. He would criticize a school grade, stress the importance of getting a proper night's sleep, and zealously proclaim the virtues of exercise and bodybuilding. Zanuck also warned Dick to "play it safe" with girls and avoid "infections."

More important, however, Zanuck urged on his son a philosophy of noblesse oblige. According to Dick Zanuck, "What he did was instill a certain appreciation for my position and, thanks to *his* position, a certain recognition and an inheritance of privilege and power. He instilled in me the realization that I had many advantages and that I had a certain responsibility to other people because of my position in the world." Though Zanuck himself was the son of a less-than-prominent hotel keeper, he proclaimed the importance of the Zanuck tradition—scarcely one generation long. "He would remind me of my heritage," recalled Dick. "I really had to live up to the family name."

Dick believed that the letters were confidential—between himself and his dad. He thought Zanuck typed the missives in spare moments at the studio. It wasn't until he was an adult that he learned they had been dictated to one of a fleet of stenographers who would then transcribe them along with Zanuck's studio memos. "I found out that he would tell his secretary to make some typos so that it looked like he had done the typing himself and they were more personal," said Dick. If the messages weren't personal, they were clear: "He did see me as someone in his own image. He always emphasized . . . that because I was his son I had special talents, I could 'go all the way.' "

Zanuck saw his son as an extension of himself, and apparently he had the same worries about Dick that he had about his own character and personality. He was anxious that his son appear manly, and he discouraged activities that appeared to be soft or female. When Richard was just a boy, he took piano lessons, with Virginia's encouragement. In a short while, he became quite accomplished and even performed once at the Coconut Grove. Listeners, perhaps sincere or merely toadying the mogul's son, declared that Dick was a child prodigy. However, Zanuck was not pleased. One morning when he awoke and wandered into the living room to find Dick practicing, he angrily ordered his son out on the beach to play football. Dick gave up the piano forever.

As a youngster, Dick seemed not to regard such outrageous demands as unfair. He was in awe of his abrasive, domineering father who could make other film executives quake when he barked. Once Dick remarked that he feared they would all drop to their knees if his father screamed "Crawl!" He, too, was nervous and awestruck in the man's presence. "He was a very scary person to me," he recalled. Dick's fear was laced with a heavy dose of worship. His dad was exciting, enthralling, wonderful, and commanding. Dick wanted to please this phenomenal father.

Many of his efforts to please—like the piano playing—fell flat, however. Praise was hard to come by in the Zanuck household. Even attention was a dear commodity. In the late 1940s, when Dick was in his early teens, his dad rarely put in an appearance at home because his work at the studio was so demanding. "Weeks would go by where I'd never see him, even though we lived in the same house," Dick recalled in the Father's Day interview. "I would go to school in the mornings and come back and he would still be sleeping because he had been out late the night before. On the weekends he'd leave on Friday night right from the studio and go down to the house in Palm Springs."

Virginia followed in her husband's tracks. Her whole life centered on Zanuck's activities. Everything she did traced its origin back to his needs. She shopped—to make the right appearance when she went out with him. Her frequent attendance at luncheons and charitable events—obligatory, she seemed to feel, for the wife of such an important man—kept her away from home nearly every day. And of course she, too, would abandon the kids all weekend for Palm Springs.

So it was Alma Diehl who did most of the child-raising. She was the one who formed many of Dick's values, he sometimes told people. Indeed, she was always there for him when he was a kid. It wasn't that Dick was Alma's favorite, said her niece Helen Craig. "Dick was more conscientious with his schoolwork, more particular about doing things right, and more thoughtful than the girls. Therefore, he did not need as much discipline." Alma appreciated the boy's intelligence and adventurousness, but she could be strict, too. She stressed the importance of integrity, loyalty, neatness, and order—values her little charge came to cherish throughout his life. "She was kind of a crabby lady in some ways," said Diane Jacks, a friend of Dick's. "She could lay down the law about behavior, but she was very indulgent, too."

Dick later said he felt he was spoiled. He told another interviewer that he had been "the wildest kid in the West—rough, rowdy, an all-American brat." In fact, he wasn't so much spoiled as furious.

Trying to be the perfect son, yet receiving so little recognition for his accomplishments would be likely to enrage any youngster. People remember illogical outbursts of terrible anger. They were never directed at his overwhelming father, however. That was far too dangerous for a boy to dare. His explosions were aimed at others. "My parents tried to hide me from guests because I might punch somebody in the stomach or butt him with my head," he admitted to a reporter.

Since Zanuck apparently needed to have a woman almost every day, he seemed to feel that his son should also become a skirt-chaser. Anything less in Zanuck's view was somehow not completely virile. At the outset of Dick's adolescence, Zanuck fretted privately that his only son was not sexually active; he was thirteen, and yet he displayed little interest in girls. Though such indifference is hardly unusual at that age, the older Zanuck was uncomfortable. He determined to push Dick in the right direction by stage-managing his introduction to sex.

Concerned as Zanuck was, however, he couldn't be bothered to take on the task himself. Instead, he assigned a faithful employee to the project as though it were a location scouting or a rewrite. When Dick was fourteen, Sam Silver, the studio barber, picked him up one day after school and took him to the apartment of Fox commissary manager Nick Janios. There Dick found a lush young woman. He was told merely to talk to her. One thing led to another, and Dick lost his virginity. On the way home, Dick pointed out to Sam that he would really be in deep trouble if his father ever found out about the episode. To Dick's amazement, Sam revealed that it was Zanuck who had arranged it. Unfazed by this complete violation of his privacy, Dick saw his father's rationale: "I knew that [he] was very worried, not worried, concerned about me. He never took me aside and explained anything, but he wanted me to be straightened out."

When the two saw each other, they played games—most often badminton and tennis—and Zanuck had to beat Dick. If Dick chanced to win, the game was over. Dick has told a peculiar story many, many times about wrestling matches with his father. Every Sunday night, it seems, when the Zanucks weren't in Palm Springs, they invited a group over for screenings at the beach house. Zanuck and his son sat on a couch at the back of the room. If the film began to bore Zanuck, he would wrestle Dick into a headlock until he said

"Give." This went on for years until one night when Dick was fourteen. He recalled, "I got my father in a perfect headlock, and I showed him no mercy. His face became all red, and his eyes were almost bulging. I just kept squeezing and asking him the question he had asked me all those years. He finally blurted out, 'Give.' " After that night, there was no more wrestling on the couch. "He didn't specifically say, 'Let's not do it anymore.' It just never happened again."

Zanuck had taught his son that losing equaled failure; but for Dick, winning became losing when his competitor was his father. So he turned his attentions to turf where his father couldn't compete—school. At the Harvard School, an Episcopal fortress on a terraced twenty-three-acre campus overlooking the San Fernando Valley, Dick could excel with his father's full endorsement. Dick became a big little man on campus. By the time he graduated from the military school in 1952, he had been a prefect, editor of the school paper, and the captain of cadets. He directed school theatricals and competed on the football and swim teams. His father, impressed in spite of himself, attended most of the games and meets, dragging with him his retinue of studio flunkies.

In the economy of Zanuck family love and affection, Richard was clearly one of the "haves." Although his sister Darrylin had always been Zanuck's favorite, Dick knew that as heir to the studio mantle, he stood to receive a more significant chunk of his father's scant time and attention. However, when Dick turned fifteen, there arose a new challenge to his unique position. His older sister Darrylin, who was attending college in New York, eloped with Robert Jacks, a tall, handsome blond twenty-two-year-old. Zanuck was quite taken with the young man; Bobby Jacks was athletic, self-confident, and just plain nice. Everybody liked him—Dick, too. Dick, like his father, was small, toothy, and temperamental. Zanuck immediately installed Jacks at the studio as an assistant producer and sang his son-in-law's praises to the entire family. "Dick must have been upset," remarked Diane Jacks, Dick's friend and Bobby's second wife. "Here was this tall, fantastic-looking guy—almost everything Dick was not as a teenager—and his father takes him right into the business."

Dick could not allow himself to reveal any displeasure with his father for suddenly redirecting his attention to Jacks. Dick's future clearly depended on Zanuck. Dick's anger surfaced in other ways. Just before his sixteenth birthday, Zanuck asked him whether he knew how to drive. Unlike most other fathers in America, Zanuck didn't even know whether his son had ever operated a car. Dick assured his father that, yes, he was fully competent to drive, when, in fact, he was not. The next day, his parents presented Dick with a brand-new car for his birthday. Three days later, Dick was bombing around the hairpin turns of Coldwater Canyon Drive and smacked into another car. Its passengers wound up seriously injured, and Dick's car was nearly totaled. Zanuck had to pay thousands of dollars to compensate the accident victims and to keep the incident quiet. When he learned that his son actually did not know how to drive, he exploded and gave Dick a fearsome dressing-down. Dick believed he would have to take a taxi for the rest of his natural life. However, Zanuck lost interest in his son's misdeed almost before the discussion was over and, oddly enough, began interrogating Dick about his tooth-brushing habits. A few weeks later, Dick received a second new car—a Cadillac.

Once Dick departed for Stanford in 1952, however, his father almost ceased to notice him. There had been a takeover threat at Twentieth Century-Fox, and Zanuck and his fellow executives had spent months fending it off. Several big movies that Zanuck was supervising personally were in production, including *The Snows of Kilimanjaro* and *The Robe*. Then, too, his father's protégée and mistress, Bella Darvi, had moved into the beach house, and he and Virginia were busy promoting the young woman's acting career.

At college, Dick handily achieved honor roll status, but he also found trouble. The most serious episode occurred in February of 1953 when Dick was visiting Palm Springs on a break. According to the police, Dick and two friends decided to crash a party at the home of Leon Welmas, son of the chieftainess of the Agua Caliente Indian tribe. Dick later said he had been invited. But some of the other guests objected to his presence because he'd never invited them to parties at Ric-Su-Dar. When another guest asked him to step outside, one of Dick's friends tried to intervene, but he was challenged to a fight by another boy. The four youths scuffled until one of the Indians produced a knife. Dick's Stanford friend was slashed three times, and Dick himself was roughed up by several teenagers. By the time the police appeared, Dick's new convertible coupe was vandalized—its windows broken, roof slashed, and body dented. Zanuck had to leave Ric-Su-Dar in the middle of a croquet game to get his son out of police custody. He was again angry with Dick and, this time, took away his car for three months. Eight Indian youths were arrested while Dick and his friend were treated for minor injuries and returned to Stanford.

A year later, in 1954, during spring vacation on Balboa Island, Dick was arrested when he zipped through a stop sign. Police later said they confiscated thirty-one cans of beer from his car. Balboa Island then played host to hordes of college students looking for sun, fun, and booze much as they were to do later in Fort Lauderdale, Florida, and in Palm Springs. The night before Dick was arrested, groups of college students had rioted. Police had warned that they meant to get tough, and so they arrested Dick for running a sign. The *Los Angeles Daily News* noted that this was the second time in just over a year that he had had a brush with the law.

During his college years in the early 1950s, Dick took summer jobs at Fox. He worked on the labor gang constructing sets, and occasionally in the cutting room. He also read scripts for the story department. There he met his future partner David Brown, former managing editor of *Cosmopolitan* magazine, whom Zanuck had brought out from New York in 1952 to strengthen the studio's idea bank. Dick also worked one summer writing press releases in the Fox publicity department under the supervision of Harry Brand, the studio's longtime official mouthpiece. His working stints were short-lived, however. He spent many vacations traveling by motorcycle through Europe with his friends or surfing in Hawaii. He toyed with the idea of becoming a writer; indeed, that was how his father had started out. Wherever he went, he dragged along a portable typewriter.

By the time Dick graduated from Stanford in 1956, he had dutifully prepared himself to become a mogul—only to discover that his father had renounced the throne. Dick learned, by reading the trade papers, that Zanuck was leaving the studio to become an independent producer in Paris. In a show of togetherness, his feuding parents came to Palo Alto for his graduation ceremony. Dick's immediate plans were already set. He was to fulfill his military obligation; his father had arranged for him to join the U.S. Pictorial Service, part of the U.S. Signal Corps on Long Island. After that, however, his future was uncertain. With his father's midlife crisis, Dick's position as heir to the studio had suddenly evanesced. Zanuck assured him that there would be a place for him with the new film company—DFZ Productions—but that was hardly the same as having an inside track to the top job at a major studio.

Dick was even more stunned by his father's decision to leave his wife. Zanuck was reluctant to announce the news to his son face-to-face; he worried that the conversation would be too painful—for him, not for Dick. So he fled Los Angeles and left the task to Virginia. Dick was distressed when he heard of his parents' split, but to his surprise, Virginia was calm. Her husband would be back, she declared. Their marriage was far from over.

Virginia saw the separation as a temporary fade-out in a movie destined to have a happy ending that brought Zanuck back to her. Dick was equally certain his father would never return. He had been on the studio lot frequently enough over the years to be acquainted with his dad's sexual exploits, but they had never amounted to anything significant—or so Dick thought. Surely Zanuck could have continued to satisfy his needs with other women as he always had, in his casual, fly-by-night way. His father's decision to shake off Virginia seemed a shabby way to repay her unswerving loyalty. Dick was angry, but he was also stricken with loneliness. His home had never been a particularly warm one, but now it had broken apart. His sisters were married and on their own. His father was to relocate to Paris. Even Alma Diehl had declared her intention to leave now that the Zanuck kids were grown; but Virginia pleaded with her to stay on as a companion and Alma agreed.

*   *   *

Though Dick's sympathies lay with his mother, his attachment to Zanuck had grown stronger because his autocratic father was soon his frightening boss. After his stint in the army, Dick joined his father's first independent production—*Island in the Sun* in late 1956. Fortunately, Bella Darvi no longer divided father and son for Zanuck had dropped her. In fact, he had almost *had* to give her up. Her gambling was simply too costly. In his 1957 separation agreement with Virginia, Zanuck had signed over more than half of his property to his wife. To fund his new company, he had had to borrow, and he was short of money. Bella's urgent cables desperately asking for cash to repay her mounting gambling debts put Zanuck on the spot. At one point, he was so strapped that he appealed to a fellow cardplayer, billionaire Howard Hughes, for a $50,000 loan to tide Bella over. Hughes had a courier fly a parcel of money to Zanuck in Europe, and Zanuck toted the money to France to get his former girlfriend out of hock. According to Virginia's friend, Margaret Shands, Zanuck couldn't be bothered to repay the loan. "He said Hughes would never miss the money," she said.

Dick, then a production assistant in Barbados with the crew of *Island in the Sun*, could hardly have avoided learning via gossip that his father had propositioned females on the set. Everybody wondered why Zanuck couldn't simply act his age. Actress Joan Collins, who played a young woman who learns that her grandmother is black, wrote in her autobiography that Zanuck "had grabbed me one afternoon in the corridor of the hotel, pressed me against the wall, cigar still firmly clamped between his fingers, and tried to convince me of his endurance, prowess, and endowments as one of the world's best lovers. 'You've had nothing until you've had me. . . . I've got the biggest and the best. I can go all night and all day.' " Collins said she made a hasty escape when co-star Dorothy Dandridge appeared suddenly in the hallway.

People on the set believed that Zanuck was on the prowl for a new attachment. He found it on location for his next picture, *The Sun Also Rises*, based on the Ernest Hemingway novel. He had cast Tyrone Power in the role of Jake Barnes and Ava Gardner as Lady Brett Ashley; at the last minute, a supporting female role was filled by French cabaret singer Juliette Greco. She and Zanuck were not impressed with each other when they first met. He thought she was unattractive. She had a long nose and a mop of ill-kempt dark hair; some said she didn't bathe all that often. But her eyes were colossal and her cheekbones dramatically pronounced. Greco, who fancied herself a revolutionary artiste, found the aging producer bland and no more appealing than a loaf of American white bread.

Sparks soon began to fly between the two, however. To Zanuck, Greco symbolized what was new, exciting, and untried—definitely "on the other side of the hill." Like Bella Darvi, Greco had endured a spell in a concentration camp. After the war, she had made a name for herself singing in the underground bistros of Paris. She didn't need Zanuck to succeed—a point she was fond of making to him over and over again. With her unconventional left-wing views, she could startle and challenge the mogul—tweak him for his midwestern bourgeois beliefs. When he gave her jewelry, she would temperamentally hand it back. She didn't go in for useless and expensive baubles, she would announce. Still, the temptation of Zanuck's money and power, his knowledge and command of the set, was intriguing. Soon the money, too, became important, and she accepted more and more of Zanuck's presents. Dick must have speculated that Juliette was merely another would-be actress out to curry favor with his father. By the time the crew returned to Paris, Zanuck and Juliette Greco were an item.

Dick returned to Los Angeles. At the studio, his official title was vice-president of DFZ Productions and his job called for him to be a liaison—along with his brother-in-law Bobby Jacks—between his father's company and Fox. It was their duty to work with senior executives at the studio, in an attempt to smooth over some of the mogul's more controversial activities. That was a delicate task. With Zanuck's departure, the studio had entered a new era of caution and penury, according to Fox writer and director Philip Dunne. Heading Fox were Buddy Adler, a former Columbia producer, and Spyros Skouras, whom Dunne called "Their High Timidities." Skouras and Adler were leery of turning out any movie that was even slightly offensive or marginally costly. *Island in the Sun*, Zanuck's first independent production, had a theme so controversial that the South Carolina legislature had threatened to levy $5,000 fines on any movie exhibitor who dared to show it. Zanuck countered that he would pay the fines personally if need be. "This reminds me of the burning of the books by Hitler in Germany," Zanuck told the press. Fortunately, DFZ Production's first movie was a box-office success despite the fact that it was panned by the critics.

His other independent productions did poorly, however. Zanuck had committed the fatal Hollywood error: he had come to believe his own press. He thought he was infallible, and of course he wasn't. Louis de Rochemont, producer of the distinguished *March of Time* current-events series for Fox, had diagnosed the mogul's key flaw several years earlier in an interview with *Time*. "Zanuck as a supervisor of others' productions is excellent," said de Rochemont. "He has great ability in guiding others' ability. But when he was in charge of his own stuff, he used to fall flat on his face, and no one could tell him such-and-such was a stinker or that he was all wrong. He loses his objectivity when he's going on his own."

The Sun Also Rises, Zanuck's costly second movie, was a box-office failure and was scorned by its originator Ernest Hemingway. Fox executives quailed at Zanuck's excesses since it was studio money that financed his movies. Under Zanuck's deal with Fox, he was to receive a $150,000 annual consultant's fee and almost all financing for films of his own choosing. Profits, however, were to be his. DFZ Productions—whose ownership he shared with his children—would get 50 percent of the receipts from the film after the studio recovered its costs. The losses were all Fox's. After *The Sun Also Rises*, Dick was kept busy cooling the tempers of Fox executives; he wrote memo after memo assuring them that his father's forthcoming movie would be a winner.

The movie's title was an irritating reminder to Dick of his position in the business, which Hollywood insiders typically described as "the son also rises." Many movie executives installed their less than competent offspring in important jobs, leaving them to gum up the works. Studio folk assumed that Dick, too, was probably not up to the demands of the job. Both he and Bobby Jacks had to prove that they were worthy of their titles. Said a former TV producer at Fox, "Bobby took a lot of shit and had to suffer 'the son-in-law also rises' jokes, though he didn't deserve them. He worked hard." Gradually Dick and Bobby Jacks earned the respect of their peers.

Senior executives must have been somewhat exasperated when Zanuck announced his next project—*The Deluxe Tour*, a potentially extravagant production based on a book by Frederic Wakeman. Zanuck decided to embark on his own country-hopping journey around the world, ostensibly to scout locations. He recruited a traveling party of five men, including his son and son-in-law, and borrowed from Howard Hughes a B-25 bomber retrofitted for peacetime use. The studio had to put up a percentage of the money, but for Zanuck, asserted Mary Donahue, whose husband Frank was a member of the entourage, "the whole thing was supposed to be a big tax deduction."

The jaunt provided Dick with a front-seat view of what his father's early days at the Los Angeles Athletic Club must have been like; the trip was characterized by adolescent high jinks and heavy drinking. The airplane itself was christened *Smasher*. The group laughed up-roariously when the plane buzzed beachgoers and apartment houses in Cannes but sobered up when an engine caught fire over Italy. The entire crew prepared to bail out, and finding themselves one parachute short, Dick and Bobby Jacks nobly agreed to share a parachute and tied themselves together face-to-face. Fortunately, the pilot managed to make a heroic landing at the last minute. Undeterred, Zanuck char-tered a huge commercial airplane to take the group on to Rhodes. The trip came to an end for Zanuck in Nairobi when he reopened an old ski wound on his forehead when the plane lurched and threw him against a bulkhead, and all but Zanuck returned to Los Angeles. Despite the air of levity that had surrounded the expedition, the group managed to gather 40,000 feet of film by shooting from the nose of the aircraft. Most of it proved to be useless. Zanuck never found a script that he liked, and the costs of development had mounted so pre-cipitously that a production could never be profitable. Some of the film found its way into Fox movies as stock shots, but most of it ended up in a studio vault.

Dick communicated with his father by cable from Los Angeles practically every day. The two of them devised code names for every-one they wrote about. Virginia was referred to as "Santa Monica." Spyros Skouras was "Achilles the Heel." Both father and son signed their telexes affectionately, "Love, See you later." While Zanuck was in Europe trying his hand at costly artistic productions of great mo-ment, his son was locked in the drab regime of Fox's all-business, hell-bent-for-bottom-line management team. Richard spent much of his day soothing senior executives who were upset about his father's free-spending, freewheeling ways, prodding them to grant Zanuck the money and resources they had promised him, and winning approvals. The job was exhausting and difficult. Some at the studio were con-vinced that Zanuck should be cut off cold.

Zanuck's next project—*The Roots of Heaven*, based on Romain Gary's novel about the possible extinction of elephants—turned out to be another disaster that Dick had to explain away to Fox senior executives. Gazou, the remote site that Zanuck had chosen in Cameroon, almost killed off the actors and the crew. During the day, temperatures rose to a makeup-melting 130 degrees. Expenses ran high because food, medical supplies, liquor, generators, lights, cameras, and rain-making equipment for the two campsites—one of them called Zanuckville—had to be flown in from Europe. According to Errol Flynn, eleven people, including Zanuck's son-in-law Bobby Jacks, came down with a virulent strain of African malaria. One person died from the disease. Almost everyone had dysentery, and four men developed an exotic form of gonorrhea. The critically ill—among them, Juliette Greco—were flown to Europe for treatment. Those who did not succumb to disease became mentally woozy in the heat. Even Zanuck began seeing things that weren't there. The hardiest among the crew took to drinking. Flynn attributed his own maddening health throughout the shooting to his abstinence from local water in preference to Smirnoff's.

The jinxed movie, which cost $4 million—over budget by a third—opened in November 1958 to disappointing reviews. *Time* declared that "the huge (2 hrs. 11 mins.) movie finally seems no more than a literary notion that has apparently suffered, along with CinemaScope and DeLuxe color, a severe attack of elephantiasis." Zanuck's protégée, Greco, fared no better. The *New York Times* declared that as the movie wore on, she "slips into drab decline." Executives at Fox were dismayed. *Roots of Heaven* barely earned its production costs. The veteran who had turned out so many hits seemed to be snagged in an unlucky streak. Nobody spoke out loud of canceling his deal—that would have been an unthinkable discourtesy. Some grumblers suggested that perhaps Fox ought not fork so much money over to Zanuck. Dick, however, managed to stave off cutbacks. In memos to Fox bosses, he argued for his father's projects. While Dick was laboring to keep the studio budget ax from falling on his father's neck, Zanuck himself was proposing a new two-year $30 million budget for future productions.

Dick, meanwhile, had made plans of his own. During the summer of 1957, he started dating Lili Gentle, a teenage actress under contract to Fox. Lili had come to Hollywood from Birmingham, Alabama, only a year earlier and was immediately proclaimed star material by studio casting personnel. She had already been cast in two leading roles, in *Young and Dangerous* and opposite teen idol Tommy Sands in *Sing, Boy, Sing*. She also played the ingenue role in *Will Success Spoil Rock Hunter?* The young woman had a wide smile, a low, musical voice, and a romantic nature. The couple seemed an ideal match. Though Dick was short like his father, he had striking blond good looks and an athletic build honed by years of exercise. At twenty-four, he was six years older than she and seemingly much more worldly and sophisticated. He, too, was ambitious and in love with the movies.

Dick was not averse to marriage at that time. His family had splintered, and he wanted a home of his own. His desire for a nest seemed like a repudiation of Zanuck's behavior. While his father might globe-trot with the femmes fatales of the Continent, Dick would opt for stability, tradition, order, and loyalty. Yet Lili was, in many ways, just the kind of girl Darryl Zanuck might have chosen for his son. She was pretty, young, and in a sense, not very imposing. She would look perfect at openings and parties, keep a lovely home, just as Virginia did, bear attractive children, and quietly accede to the demands of her husband's career.

Though Dick might have, consciously or not, selected a mate to meet his father's approval, Zanuck paid him little notice. He failed to appear at the couple's engagement party, which Virginia threw in November of 1957 upstairs in the czarist elegance of Romanoff's restaurant. Virginia was delighted with the match, and the evening was a very sentimental one, full of warm toasts to Dick and Lili. Zanuck didn't attend their quiet afternoon wedding at the First Methodist Church in Santa Monica two months later, either. Zanuck's excuse: he was busy scouting locations for *The Roots of Heaven* in French West Africa. Only the tiny wedding party attended the ceremony. Darrylin was maid of honor, and actor Barry Coe was best man. The only other guests were Lili's parents and Virginia. Susan was absent, understandably, in Paris and pregnant with her first child. After the ceremony, the group retired to the beach house for a small reception. Early that evening, Lili and Dick boarded an airplane for a ten-day honeymoon in Acapulco.

Few studio people took Dick seriously during the first years of his career. They assumed that he was where he was because his father put him there. One producer opines that "second and third generation people in the picture business are joke characters—more often than not." But after Dick produced his first movie—*Compulsion*, based on the novel by Meyer Levin about the Leopold and Loeb murder—the "son also rises" jokes fell flat and disappeared. Zanuck had acquired rights to the book a year before and tossed it into Dick's lap. In February 1958, only a month after their marriage, Lili and Dick traveled to New York to view the play on Broadway. His father, he told a *New York Post* columnist, "at last decided Dick was ready to strike out on his own (with a little help from pop when desired)." Being his father's son was a lucky break, he said. "I couldn't have found a better and more patient teacher—and I was a more than willing student."

After *Compulsion* was completed, Dick and Lili again turned up in New York City. Dick had grown a pencil-thin mustache to make himself look more mature. On his arm was an adoring Lili, muffled in a fur coat and an angora hat. They looked as if they had won a contest for the Most Adorable Couple of 1959. Indeed, at "21" Lili confided to Earl Wilson and his millions of readers that she was pregnant with their first child, who was due the following September.

Her husband was brimming with confidence. Wrote Wilson, "He spoke glibly of Hollywood croquet games, and of private planes and, when he mentioned a figure like 'one' or 'two,' he meant $1,000,000 or $2,000,000." Though still wet behind the ears, Dick was already proclaiming verities much as his father had done in the 1930s. He had already sectioned off an area of turf that Zanuck couldn't credibly claim—youth. "One thing Hollywood can do is present the younger generation [with] more mature subjects," Dick declared. This assertion was revolutionary stuff in the late 1950s when Fox and many other studios were shifting into full-scale production of quickie B-movies and horror flicks designed to titillate teenagers. Added Dick, "If the only pictures we make are about werewolves, the teenagers will go but they want something better." Lili glowingly endorsed her husband's views. "When they see this werewolf stuff, they laugh," she said. "They're not stupid. . . . Anyway, as Dick says, 'Don't hide things from them. Bring sex and things out into the open.' "

Compulsion, Dick reported, had previewed successfully to a bunch of bikers in Long Beach, California. "[They] looked like a real bunch of tough guys. Like a gang. I thought, 'They'll tear me apart.' But they laughed at every joke right on time—they gave me an ovation—and on their cards they said the best scene was Orson Welles's courtroom scene playing Clarence Darrow—it was the most intellectual scene. I thought it'd be dull for kids to listen to, but they loved it." The bikers weren't the only ones to find merit in the movie. Zanuck, to whom Dick had submitted the rough cut, "flipped when he saw it," according to Dick. Although the film soft-pedaled Leopold and Loeb's homosexuality, the downbeat movie was a breakthrough that earned praise from tough critics and also garnered a modest profit.

In a turn of events his father could not possibly have overlooked, Dick had become a contender. The press began to take note of Dick's plans—for a movie based on a Faulkner book and another on an original story of a writer-adventurer who travels around the world, running into "human and geographical oddities." Only a few months later, Zanuck himself trumpeted a new production: *Crack in the Mirror*, a murder mystery whose cast—except for the addition of Juliette Greco—was almost a replica of Dick's in *Compulsion*, including Bradford Dillman, Orson Welles, and director Richard Fleischer. Zanuck's movie, however, when it was released in 1960, didn't even challenge his son's success, much less match it. It failed to win over critics or audiences, and Juliette Greco didn't rate notices—even bad ones. *The Big Gamble*, Zanuck's last-ditch attempt to make Greco into a star, bombed in 1962. Richard was forced to send his father an alarming telegram.

BOARD OF DIRECTORS HERE WORRIED ABOUT FINANCES. ACHILLES THE HEEL SAYS UNWILLING TO MAKE MORE ADVANCES PENDING BETTER SHOWING MOVIES AT BOX OFFICE.

The competition between the two men was still friendly, however. Zanuck must have thought that Dick was not a very dangerous threat because he had not yet been granted carte blanche by high Fox executives. Zanuck had acquired rights to *The Chapman Report*, a fictionalized story of a Kinsey-style survey team researching sexual practices. Typically enthusiastic and undaunted by his recent failure in Africa, Zanuck declared it "the greatest material I ever read." He also gave Dick the go-ahead on *Sanctuary* by William Faulkner. Both projects were bound to trouble members of PTAs across America, but *The Chapman Report* elicited groans—most of them offscreen, from Fox executives who were reluctant to distribute the supposedly racy movie. Although Dick quickly gained code approval of the script, many were worried about it. Even Louella Parsons whined, "I wish, I wish, I wish Dick Zanuck would not make this picture. . . . I am very afraid this could well bring censorship on our heads." Dick may not have known it, but he, or somebody else, had to make *The Chapman Report*—or something like it. Movies had to start delivering what TV could not—or face extinction.

Fox decided Louella Parsons was right, however, and, just as Dick was about to start shooting, the studio stopped paying *Chapman Report* actors without informing him that the picture had been canceled. Dick was furious. This abrogation of his own authority and experience so upset Zanuck that he immediately leapt to Dick's defense. An outside threat united father and son. Zanuck regarded Fox's action as a betrayal of them both. He immediately called his friendly enemy Jack Warner, who readily agreed to underwrite and distribute the movie. Dick went to Warner Brothers to complete the picture. It was zapped by reviewers but became a solid commercial success when it was released in 1962. Dick defended the picture with ardor, writing in a newspaper piece, "the picture may be concerned with sex, but that doesn't mean it's just a sexy picture."

*   *   *

Darryl Zanuck could easily have starred in a prurient feature himself. His breach with Juliette Greco brought new embarrassment to the entire family when she published her autobiography, *Je Suis Comme Je Suis*, in 1962. The pair had always had a bumpy relationship. According to Elisabeth Gargarine, Zanuck's Paris secretary, Greco would also heap verbal abuse on him in front of his employees. Their liaison foundered on Greco's poor movie notices, and then turned to hatred. In her recounting of her affair with Zanuck, whom she twitted as "a poor little rich man," she revealed salacious details about the American mogul: that he wore brief "babydoll" pajamas and a sleep mask to bed; that he struck her during an argument on location in Africa and put out a cigar on her neck. "That cigar left a mark that no one can ever make me forget," she wrote. When she became involved with another man back in Paris, she said, Zanuck hired detectives to keep watch on her. Looking out her window one day, she saw a

Citroën packed with his private goon squad. He stood across the street waiting for her to appear. She explained to him that their affair was over. For Zanuck, it wasn't; previously, when he was completely besotted with Greco, he had indiscreetly given her two blank checks to cash for whatever sum she chose. He had his lawyer demand that she return them, but Greco's honor was offended. She decided to keep them just to make her former lover nervous.

After Greco published her memoir, Zanuck sued her for $20,000, asserting that she had made him look ridiculous. He never pursued his claim, however. In his column, Art Buchwald presented Zanuck's side of the story. The violence and detectives seemed to bother Zanuck less than Greco's anecdote about his sleepwear. "I've bought those pajamas for fifteen years at Sulka's," he maintained. "They are one of the most popular items at the store. She also said I sleep with a mask. What the hell is wrong with that?" Buchwald asked him whether there wasn't a rule about avoiding emotional involvements with women and trying to make stars out of them. "Yes, there is," came the reply. "I violated it twice. . . . When you're stuck on a girl you do a lot of stupid things. Believe me, it's the last time I'm going to do it."

That was an empty vow, however. Zanuck was unhappy without female companionship. He had left America to free himself of domestic entanglements but had found little more than disorder and disillusionment in Europe. Still, he kept up a happy front as a glamorous figure of the *beau monde,* spending evenings dining at Maxim's and Tour D'Argent and nightclubbing at Moustache. He fancied that his French was marvelous although, according to his lifelong tutor Edward Leggewie, it was only so-so. In the winter, he skied at Davos and Klosters near Saint-Moritz in Switzerland. He partied with other American expatriates—Orson Welles, William Saroyan, and Art Buchwald. Theirs was a supposedly liberated, freethinking group. Said Buchwald, "We sat in the cafés . . . at Alexander's most of the time. There was Irwin Shaw, Sam Spiegel, and Harry Kurnitz. And we sat there and talked about the world and talked about movies and everything, and the conversation was not much different than anywhere else. Except that we were very bright, we were living in Paris, and the world was great, and the food was great."

So settled had Zanuck become in his adopted city that in 1961, with Buchwald, he invested in a restaurant called China Boy, which was operated by the columnist's Chinese cook. According to Buchwald, "He put in $2,000, and Darryl at that time used to spend $2,000 on a car to Deauville or the casino at Monte Carlo. So the $2,000 was not a lot of money, except every month, he had his guy call. He wanted to know where the dividends were. He drove me absolutely crazy. He made a terrible fuss about the restaurant. I think it gave him something to do."

Zanuck had paid dearly for his "liberation." Instead of his Santa Monica beach house and his Palm Springs estate with their crowds of visitors, he lived out of suitcases at the Plaza Athenée or the Georges V. He ate virtually all his meals at restaurants. No longer did he have a giant office and gangs of flunkies to do his bidding; he worked at a table at the Relais Plaza, the hotel coffee shop. People who knew Zanuck then thought him lonely. Movie production work, which had engulfed so many of his hours, slowed to a trickle. He cast around frantically for new properties to put on the screen but found few that were usable. He began drinking heavily and sat watching television in a foreign language for days on end.

Rattling about nearly alone in the Santa Monica beach house, Virginia, according to her next-door neighbor, Margaret Shands, "kept up with him. She knew what he was doing. I don't know who her sources were, but they called her from Europe." When Virginia told her friend that Zanuck was sick, Mrs. Shands urged her to write him a note. Virginia became nervous at the prospect. "My God, Virginia, you're still in love with the man," Mrs. Shands recalled telling her. A few days later, a very excited Virginia telephoned Mrs. Shands to say that soon after she sent off her note, she had received a two-page telegram from Zanuck. "She was the happiest thing you've ever heard. That's when they made up. I had to run over to her house to read it." In the wire, Zanuck expressed strong feelings of affection for Virginia, and he had signed it, "My love, always, DZ."

Although Zanuck and his wife started communicating again, he showed no interest in returning home. He had already taken up with another young actress, a Czech-born French model named Irina Demick. Less temperamental than her two predecessors, she was happy to be the object of Zanuck's generosity. "If Darryl is not there, we are nothing," she said of herself and other Zanuck intimates. "We are satellites around the sun. If the sun is not there, we die. Before him, I never tried to make movies. If he was not there when it began, I would never be Irina Demick. I cannot be Irina Demick without Darryl Zanuck. I am a cabbage."

Zanuck determined to make a star out of her, just as he had attempted with Darvi and Greco. He gave her the part of Janine Boitard, a member of the French maquis, in his next project, *The Longest Day*. Reading the news reports of his father's continuing *liaisons amoureuses* must have made Dick writhe with irritation. He could only guess what "Santa Monica" must be thinking. He knew that Virginia had hired her own bevy of detectives to keep tabs on Zanuck, but while private indiscretions could be borne, the public scandal with Greco and the new "friendship" with Demick were fresh humiliations for Virginia. Dick disapproved of the way his father was living. "In some peculiar way . . . we had reversed roles," Dick later told *Los Angeles* magazine. "I became the father and he was the son. We had some very frank and strange discussions. They were quite unique in that I would be telling him—as he had told me years before—'For God's sake, can't you go out with the same girl twice?' . . . 'You're staying out too late and not getting enough sleep.' 'Don't make a fool of yourself in public.' Sometimes he would abide by what I said because I was living a rational life at that time. I was a married man with my own children."

By 1962, Dick was the father of two girls—Virginia Laurine, born in October 1959, and Janet Beverly, who came along about a year later. Dick doted on his daughters, and as they emerged into toddlerhood, he tried to lavish attention on them; but as his responsibilities expanded in the early 1960s, he was usually stuck at the studio—an absentee father. Lili was alone with the servants and children much of the time. Dick and Lili moved to a spacious house on Elm Drive in Beverly Hills. Like his father before him, Dick asked Walter Scott, Fox's chief set designer, to decorate his house. The fittings were strictly old Holly-wood. "Dick has always liked eighteenth-century furniture," said Scott. The house was filled with British antiques and paintings of horses.

Dick couldn't pay much attention to his young family because in 1961 he was embroiled in battles between his father, who was mount-ing a replay of World War II in *The Longest Day*, and Fox's tight-fisted executives. They had already committed millions of dollars to an extravagant remake of *Cleopatra* starring the high-salaried Elizabeth Taylor, who had also cleverly negotiated for a percentage of gross profits. Corporate directors were reluctant to sink money into Zanuck's grand undertaking. The story of the D-Day invasion of Normandy was to include dozens of actors, thousands of real soldiers, and air, sea, and land battle scenes.

At the eleventh hour, just before filming was to begin in the spring of 1961, Dick frantically called his father, who was in Europe. Zanuck had to come to New York to talk the Fox board out of canceling the movie. Zanuck flew to New York and talked to the company directors for four long hours, trying to persuade them that *The Longest Day* would be the biggest movie the studio had produced in years. In the end, they voted to let him go ahead. Back in Europe, Zanuck marshaled his tremendous energies to deploy a huge cast and massive amounts of military equipment as expertly as Gen. Dwight D. Eisenhower. Zanuck was almost as driven. Ike had made war; Zanuck was making cinema history.

Astoundingly, he completed the film in nine short months for only $8 million. He wanted to release the movie as a road show with reserved tickets and exclusive showings. Insultingly, discourteously, and outrageously, the two Zanucks thought, Fox wanted to shunt Zanuck's masterwork out to neighborhood theaters as though it were another werewolf feature.

The problems had not come as a complete surprise, however. According to director Philip Dunne, early in 1961 "the peasants revolted." Dunne and nine disaffected Fox old-timers, including writer-producer Jerry Wald *(The Sound and the Fury)* and director George Stevens *(The Diary of Anne Frank)*, decided that the company was in such dire straits that Spyros Skouras should persuade Zanuck to return to Fox. Failing that, they would accept his son Dick as production boss because he "had inherited much of his father's drive and enthusiasm," wrote Dunne in his memoir, *Take Two*. "It was a desperate measure, especially for those of us who had known Dick as a young hellion in short pants, but these were desperate times," added Dunne.

Zanuck learned that, with the burgeoning troubles on the set of *Cleopatra*, the board of directors had split into bitter factions. Spyros Skouras was unseated from his job as president and replaced temporarily by Judge Samuel Rosenman, who was unfamiliar with show business. The board was scouting a permanent appointee, but when Zanuck heard who was under consideration, he was distressed. None of the candidates had a studio background. When he pondered the matter, he realized that Fox could easily go under. The value of its stock—the mainstay of his wealth and security—had been sliding.

In Paris, Zanuck's lawyer pointed out that he could not very well complain about prospective candidates for president if he did not offer one—namely himself. With loudly proclaimed reluctance, Zanuck proposed himself as a candidate and flew to New York, where he threatened a proxy fight against management. After a four-hour corporate rumble at Fox's New York headquarters on July 25, 1962, he became president of the company.

Characteristically, Zanuck went to work on Fox's problems that very night, reading financial reports and assessing personnel. Dick, who had come to New York to stand by his father's side during the fray, was elated. Perhaps this new turn of events meant that his dad would return to Los Angeles—and possibly to his wife Virginia? That dream died quickly when Zanuck invited Dick into his suite at the Plaza and asked him who would be the best man to head production in California. Zanuck had no intention of returning to Los Angeles, he announced to Dick. He intended to stay in Europe; the very closest he would get to the studio would be its Manhattan headquarters. Dick said he would think about the question. He went back to his own room to ponder for a while. With a little trepidation, he returned to his father some time later and nominated himself. "There isn't anybody better for the job than me," he declared to his dad. "Nobody knows the studio better than I do, nobody knows the personnel better than I do, and nobody knows you better than I do." Zanuck acceded immediately. "You are absolutely right," he said.

Some members of the board were not enthusiastic about the son rising quite so quickly. "I softened up Robert Lehman, [the famous art collector and investment banker] who was completely against him," Zanuck said later. Lehman expressed reservations "about a father-son situation"—apparently worried that decision making would not be objective. Together they overrode opposition to the father-son scheme, although some executives and producers were distrustful of the young man who, in imitation of his father, once appeared at a hotel room press conference wearing a silk dressing gown and bedroom slippers.

By the end of 1962, costs were still running so high that Fox could not pay its employees or creditors; Zanuck had no choice but to shut down almost all production at the Los Angeles studio and lease some of the space to independent producers. The only project left intact was the long-running TV series "Dobie Gillis." Dick was in charge of the massive firings that followed, and he was forced to cut people he had known since he was a little boy. Director Philip Dunne, who had been laid off in an earlier cutback, recalled that the studio's joy at the return of the Zanucks quickly turned to disappointment. "This time the ax spared nobody," said he. People had "expected more of this Second Coming than to be unceremoniously chucked out into the street." All ranks of the studio hierarchy, from janitors to executives, were decimated. Ironically, the only cash available to keep Fox going came from road show rentals of *The Longest Day*. Ultimately, the picture was to vacuum up $18 million for the company and $6 million for Zanuck and his family, who were the co-owners of DFZ Productions.

After heroic efforts to contain costs and find properties, Dick triumphantly took Fox back into production in February 1963. He was particularly proud, he told reporters, to preside over the reopening of the commissary. Only a month later, Zanuck himself turned up in Los Angeles, for the first time in seven years, to announce a $50 million program for fourteen pictures in the next twelve months. On the schedule were *Take Her, She's Mine; Shock Treatment;* and *The Sound of Music*. As always, Zanuck was superoptimistic—even about his scrambled efforts to save the botched-up *Cleopatra*. He was certain that the $30 million production would break even if it took in $60 million to cover distribution and advertising. The *New York Times* was less sanguine: "More likely $74 million," guessed the reporter. Zanuck also declared that he would spend half of his time in California and half in Manhattan, where he set up semipermanent housekeeping arrangements at the St. Regis Hotel. During his busy Los Angeles visit, however, he took no time out to stop by the beach house to visit Virginia.

At the company's annual meeting at Town Hall in New York that May, mink-coated and fur-trimmed shareholders complained bitterly about Elizabeth Taylor's $1.75 million salary for her role as queen of the Nile. They also criticized Zanuck's $150,000-a-year salary, though it was much less than the $265,000 he had been earning when he left the company in 1956. "Not even President Kennedy makes that," griped a Fox shareholder from the floor. The aging mogul was hurt by these barbs but even more deeply wounded by the attack against him for hiring his twenty-eight-year-old son at $1,000 a week. "It's true that I hired Richard Zanuck who is only twenty-eight," answered Zanuck from the podium. "However, it's also true that Darryl Zanuck received the then unprecedented salary of $5,000 a week at twenty-four when he was general manager in charge of production at Warner Brothers. So we can dispose of the age element."

He might have thought that the issue would disappear, but it popped up again a year later at the annual meeting in 1964. Though Zanuck announced a quarterly dividend of fifteen cents—the first since 1961— members of the audience still had unkind words for Dick. This time, however, his father allowed his son to speak in his own defense. The younger Zanuck pointed out that the studio had completed ten pictures the previous year and had eleven movies in production. Fox had also become one of the preeminent suppliers of TV programming. Shareholders were somewhat mollified.

Any disaffection turned into adoration a year later when *The Sound of Music* became a record-breaking box-office success. The musical saga of the Von Trapp singers, starring Julie Andrews, was in limited release at only 275 U.S. theaters, but it raked in enough money to give Fox a $20 million operating profit by June 1966. When the picture went into general release, it was expected to earn even more. Early on, it earned more than *Gone with the Wind*, until then the biggest revenue-producer of all times. The saccharine family movie was held over at theaters so often that in Moorehead, Minnesota, a college group called POOIE (People's Organization of Intelligent Educatees) picketed with signs proclaiming "49 Weeks of Schmaltz Is Enough."

Much of the credit for *Sound*'s success poured right on Dick. He had assembled the cast, screenwriter Ernest Lehman, and director Robert Wise, and he personally supervised the production. Until the movie's debut, however, studio insiders were not completely sold on the younger Zanuck. He seemed not quite as brilliant and expressive as his dad. His memos were flat-footed and uninspired. In a 1964 memo to Wise, Dick wrote with corporate fussiness about agreeing to let a free-lancer take a screen credit instead of a Fox executive. "As you obviously know, Bob, I am making this decision at the expense of considerable friction and disruption within the studio organization. My decision breaks a longstanding studio policy, be it right or wrong. I am only doing this because the relationship between you and me is very important, and I do not want this issue to cloud it." By contrast, the memos of his sixty-three-year-old father packed more youthful energy. In a note to a Fox executive about movie critic Judith Crist's unfavorable review of *Sound*, Zanuck explosively remarked, "Miss Crist is an 'exhibitionist' who takes perverse and sadistic delight in wantonly attacking 'big pictures.' Until she wrote her bitter review on 'Cleopatra,' she was comparatively unknown. She has built her reputation with a knife and the evil skill of an abortionist. . . . Miss Crist uses the tactics of a concentration camp butcher. Where I would thoroughly enjoy the pleasures of inserting the toe of my ski boot in Miss Crist's derriere, I prefer to leave the job to movie-goers who in due time will take good care of her."

A Hollywood veteran, Zanuck did not shy from grabbing a little glory for himself without mentioning his son too prominently, often proclaiming *The Sound of Music* to be his own success. Whatever he might declare, however, people in the business knew that the money-making musical was Dick's doing and not his dad's. *Time* noted, "[Dick's] sometime critics grudgingly concede that the kid with the sulphurous temper has something." Dick confidently planned three more musicals to exploit *The Sound of Music*'s success: *Star!*, *Doctor Doolittle*, and *Hello, Dolly!*

Zanuck was unable or unwilling to keep to his resolution of spending half his time in California each year, for, in April of 1964, his estranged wife sued him. Virginia confided to her intimates that she was hurt because, though Zanuck had visited Los Angeles a few times since his resumption of the Fox presidency, he had never so much as called her on the telephone—even though he sometimes wrote. She had kept quiet about the $67,000 he owed her under the terms of their 1957 separation agreement—she had never liked making trouble—but for four months her husband had failed to pay half the cost of maintaining their two homes, which he was also required to do. Such defiance violated her sense of fair play. In April of 1964 she went to court demanding he pay her about $75,000.

If part of Virginia's aim was to see her husband face-to-face once more in hope of reconciliation, she was to be disappointed. Zanuck fought her claim in absentia. His lawyers denied that he owed her any money. Court papers claimed that he had pledged to pay only half of the expenses of the two homes because he was to have access to Ric-Su-Dar. He added that the $67,000 she said he owed her really was a sum on account for expenses of the house *he* should have been able to live in, but *she* had taken it over. In a cross-complaint, he asked the court to split all their jointly held property. It no longer made sense for them to own property together, since they lived so far apart, he claimed. If the court could not divide their property, then it should be sold, period, and the proceeds split between the two. Legal papers were shuffled back and forth between L.A. and New York and Europe, where Zanuck still spent much of his time, but the lawsuit, instead of drawing Zanuck to California, scared him away. He was afraid that if he turned up at the studio, Virginia's lawyer would slap him with an order to appear in court. Trial dates were set and continued and set again, but the couple never faced off in front of a judge. The lawsuit languished for years until Zanuck and his wife eventually lost interest.

Zanuck seemed completely uninterested in his wife. He and Demick had parted amicably when she married a French businessman named Philippe Wahl, leaving Zanuck free of semipermanent foreign entanglements. Instead of cleaving to one girlfriend as he had since Bella Darvi, he was sampling the wares of the Continent. His son-in-law André Hakim was to be his guide. His daughter Susan and her French husband, then living in Paris, had become habitués of the City of Lights' kinkier nightclubs. According to Pierre Savineau, Susan's second husband, the couple helpfully took Daddy on their rounds of gay clubs and floor shows starring female impersonators. Hakim, who headed up Fox's Paris operations, did everything for his father-in-law—got him tickets, ordered limousines, made restaurant reservations. He also introduced Zanuck to Parisian brothels and to young women who worked for Madame Claude, whose exclusive call-girl service catered only to the wealthiest and most powerful men in France. The madam's real name was Fernande Grudet, and she had built a career cultivating and training girls of perfect stature and physical appeal to mix in the upper echelons of French society. Zanuck's sexual tastes tended toward the unconventional. What he particularly liked, according to Savineau and Madame Claude, was watching women make love to each other. Viewing them would make him so aroused that he would choose one and have sex with her.

Not that Zanuck had to pay for female companionship. Women were eager to light his cigar and help him put on his ski boots. He sometimes dated Italian and Swedish actresses, but observers noted that Zanuck seemed indifferent. He looked lonely. Most of the time, he lived in a suite at the Georges V Hotel in Paris. In New York, he stayed at the St. Regis and in London at Claridge's. He almost never visited Fox offices, choosing instead to read scripts in his rooms and summon stenographers who would take down his thoughts for transmission to Dick or to other Fox executives. The Fox office in Paris took care of many of his personal needs. Edward Leggewie, once his French tutor but now a studio official stationed in France, kept Kleenex and bottles of Zanuck's favorite shaving lotion in his desk and sent the items over to the Georges V suite.

Though Zanuck was in charge of the company, he ran the business from afar. In many ways, he seemed to be pulling in. His only athletic activity was skiing, having long ago given up the polo and hunting of his early years as a mogul. He seemed interested in little more than movies. To shut out the glare of the sun and the strain of screenings, the producer had taken to wearing forbiddingly dark glasses. Like his eyes, his life seemed to have narrowed in its capacity to take in a great deal at once.

He seemed to want to narrow his focus on women as well. One-night and one-afternoon liaisons diminished in appeal. He couldn't be bothered with all the effort they took. He needed a woman to supply everything to him, just as the studio did. He was ripe for yet another relationship.

*　　*　　*

Genevieve Gillaizeau, a nineteen-year-old runway model, had a slightly receding chin and spoke in the heavy argot of the French suburbs. She had gone only a little bit further in school than Darryl

Zanuck himself. After their first meeting in 1965, however, which was arranged by Zanuck's son-in-law André Hakim, Zanuck began having his limousine call for Genevieve and deliver her to screenings.

About nine months later, in 1966, they became lovers. She began traveling with Zanuck and stayed in connecting hotel suites. He got her a job with Fox as a $185-a-week fashion consultant—not a taxing job by any means. Her duties required her to attend screenings with him and give her opinion on the clothing worn by the actors. The studio picked up the tab for her food and hotel bills. It wasn't long before Zanuck began talking about putting her under contract to Fox. She was bound to be a big star, he told Dick in one of their many transatlantic telephone calls.

Sitting in his cavernous suite at Twentieth Century-Fox and meditating on his daughters' bronzed baby shoes, which sat on his desk, Dick might have been completely disgusted with his father's latest foolishness; but he had personal problems of his own. His marriage to Lili Gentle was foundering on his bad temper and her headstrong ways. When they first met, Dick was often accompanied by a bodyguard to protect him when he got into fights—as he sometimes did. After nine years of marriage, however, such behavior no longer seemed as appealing to Lili as it had when she was a seventeen-year-old bride. She complained to her friends that she lived in a climate of fear. "Dick was very violent," said one. "He never hit her or anything like that, but he would get angry at the oddest things. If they stopped at a light in their car, Dick would suddenly explode because the guy in the next car looked at him too hard. Dick would get out and threaten him with a baseball bat that he kept in his car." For his part, "Dick thought Lili was too unpredictable, too temperamental," said Pierre Savineau. "Some people in the family thought she was crazy, though I didn't." Lili refuses to discuss her marriage except to note: "Dick Zanuck was always a complete pain in the ass to me."

Many women who are attracted to wealth consider such pain the price they must pay to stay married to a man of power and status. However, when Lili heard that her husband had been seen around town with a twenty-one-year-old ingenue from Maryland named Linda Harrison, she reached her limit of tolerable discomfort. Lili told friends that her husband had slept with a number of other women; she called this his Harrison Period. Linda's willowy figure and flowing dark hair made her look like the ethereal princess of a fairy tale. But, according to Mary Donahue, a family friend, Linda's personality was more down-to-earth. "She was like a sorority homecoming queen—cute, wholesome, the all-American girl." Like Lili herself, she was just the kind of young woman Dick's father would have selected for him.

Years later, Dick and Linda's union would dissolve in acidic anger, but when Dick met her he was smitten—so much so that he didn't bother to be discreet. He turned up one evening with Linda at a private club the Zanucks frequented once or twice a month even though his wife Lili was a member. That night, Virginia had invited Lili to attend, and Dick brazenly asked her to dance. "While we were dancing, I told him that I thought it was in bad taste to come to the club with Linda while we were still married," said Lili. "And, I had had a few drinks; so I belted him." Did Richard have the good grace to leave at that point? "No," said Lili. "He returned to his table and sat down. But then Virginia became so enraged that she went over there and started hitting him with her evening bag."

In 1966 Dick moved out of the family house and took an apartment with Linda at the Wilshire Westwood, one of the sleek residential towers lording it over the West L.A. landscape. Lili was stung by her husband's public betrayal. When Richard told her that he wanted a divorce, she went into an emotional spiral. "Virginia was deeply upset," said set designer Walter Scott. "She really blamed Dick." According to Margaret Shands, "Virginia called Lili on the telephone and told her to get Dick for every dime she could."

By now, Lili herself was dating someone else—Fred DeGorter, then a writer for TV and movies, but now a Los Angeles attorney. "Lili and I had a torrid romance—full of midnight meetings in parking lots and long talks about our relationship over black coffee," he has said. He was a frequent visitor to Lili's house and took her little girls to Disneyland and Knott's Berry Farm. At first, DeGorter marveled at how sophisticated and mature he, Lili, Dick, and Linda were about their parallel romances. "It was all out in the open," he said. "Dick had already moved in with Linda, and when Lili and I went out, we would run into Dick and Linda. There was no problem at all. We would say hello, and Dick and I would shake hands."

Tolerance soon turned to thuggishness, however. "Lili and I would have our problems, and when we fought, she would sometimes cry on Dick's shoulder," said DeGorter. One Friday afternoon, after he and Lili had a spat, DeGorter recalled, Dick called him at his office. DeGorter wasn't immediately available. An hour later, he returned Zanuck's call, but he was in conference. "We missed each other," he said. The next morning, Saturday, DeGorter and a friend, Floyd Sharp, decided to pay Lili a visit and drove over to her house. DeGorter heard Dick and his friends playing tennis on the court in the backyard. "Dick didn't have a court anymore, so Lili let him use hers with his buddies once a week or so," said DeGorter. Thinking to find out what it was Dick had wanted the day before, DeGorter walked around the back of the house to ask. "When Dick saw me, he went crazy. He started screaming, 'Get off my property.' Get out of here, and so on. Well, I hightailed it back to my car right away."

To DeGorter's surprise, as he was about to jump in his open sports car, Dick came rushing out the front door of the house carrying a baseball bat. "Thank God it was just a plastic bat that belonged to one of the girls," said DeGorter with a laugh. Again Dick ordered DeGorter off his property but prevented escape by trying to grab the man's car keys. He began hitting DeGorter and Sharp with the bat. "He really wouldn't have done much damage, but I had been in a motorcycle accident and I had some bandages on my head. Dick kept grabbing at my bandages, trying to get me in a headlock, and that really hurt." DeGorter managed to get the car started, and he and Sharp sped to the nearest police station to file a complaint. The city attorney declined to prosecute, so DeGorter launched a civil suit against Zanuck for battery. In court papers, Dick denied hitting DeGorter or doing him any damage. "I finally dropped my suit because I didn't want to make a big issue of it," said DeGorter. "I was still dating Lili, and I really had no lasting ill feeling against Dick." After many months of wrangling and court delays, Lili and Dick made their split formal with a divorce in 1968.

*   *   *

Anger seemed to burst out of Dick periodically. It may have stemmed partly from his work at the studio. His father could assemble a cast, director, and producer by drawing the cards of contract employees from an index file; Dick had to negotiate his way through the New Hollywood. His father wanted him to maintain the studio's power to control movies, but the business had become dominated by independent producers who insisted on shaping pictures themselves. As production chief, he would be presented with a package deal that included script, stars, producer, and director—take it or leave it. On his approval, the studio would provide the financing and the facilities. If he wound up with a failure, his job was on the line. Dick was a good deal-maker, but he often appeared anxious. He bit his nails down to the quick and worked his jaws nervously.

Despite all the provocation from the studio and his father, Dick rarely displayed temper on the job. According to a fellow producer who worked on a movie with Dick in the late 1960s, the younger Zanuck was a model of calm by contrast with his father, who did display temper at the studio. Nor did Dick rage at his father. Instead, his anger came out randomly. In letters Linda sent to the editor of the *Los Angeles Times* and to her lawyer, she claimed that her husband was violent. The letters became public because Linda had sent copies to Richard's employers at Universal Pictures, and his lawyer filed them in court as part of a request that Linda furnish him with names of others to whom she had sent the missives. In the summer of 1966, she said, Dick went on a joyride in the underground garage of the Wilshire Westwood apartments with a car on loan from a Chrysler dealer. He sideswiped two cement columns and angrily banged into two cars that blocked his exit. He was on his way to a tennis match and couldn't be delayed. He later told Linda that he was hung over from the previous night. He couldn't account for his fury, however. He admitted to her that he himself could not believe he would do such a thing.

Linda also asserted that in December 1968 Dick began hitting a man with a pool cue during a game at the Daisy Club in Beverly Hills. "A most terrible fight followed, with all the Daisy patrons watching," she said. Two bouncers separated the men and asked them to leave before the police came. She and Dick sped off with producer David Gerber and his wife Larraine Stevens. Linda shrieked at her husband, "How could you do such a thing?" and by her account, Dick started to strangle her. Gerber stopped his car at a gas station and let the two women out until he could calm Dick down. Zanuck asked Gerber to take him back to the club for his car and jacket. Okay, agreed Gerber, but he begged his friend not to make any more trouble. After retrieving his jacket, Dick jumped in his car, swerved down a narrow alleyway, and screeched around to the front of the club where he was immediately arrested for drunk driving by the police, who had just arrived, Linda said. They handcuffed Dick and stashed him in the backseat of the patrol car. He did not give up without a struggle. He kicked the driver in the head, and took a few punches of retribution in the stomach. When he arrived at the police station, he was asked to urinate in a cup for an alcohol-level test. Instead, claimed Linda, "Zanuck peed on the policeman at hand. He screamed profanity to anyone and everyone, proclaiming his rights." There is no record of any charges filed against him.

Such charges of anger and bumptiousness were balanced by Richard's reputation for making gestures of great kindness. Pokie Seeger said, "I know that Dick can get really angry when he has had too much to drink, but he was terrific to me." After her husband, comedian Tommy Noonan, died of a brain tumor in 1968, she was left with four children to raise, no money, and a desperate need for a job. She turned to her many show business contacts, but only Dick Zanuck offered any help. When she called him at the studio, "He said he'd think about it and call me back; so I figured, well, that's that." However, a few weeks later, he *did* call her back. "I think you might work at a job in the publicity department," he told her. "That's where you could fit in." He spelled out the conditions precisely. "I can get you the job, but it's up to you whether you keep it," he said. "That job made all the difference in the world to me and my children, and I will never forget it," declared Seeger. Many relatives and friends had reason to be grateful to Dick and his father, for they could count on Twentieth Century-Fox as their employer of last resort. Linda Harrison had a studio contract. Zanuck's two sons-in-law, Robert Jacks and André Hakim, continued in jobs with the company long after their divorces; many Torpins, Foxes, and other kin were also given studio jobs.

If Linda was upset by Dick's behavior during their courtship, she didn't show it when they married in a December 1969 ceremony at the Sands Hotel in Las Vegas. She had too much on her agenda. She was under contract to Fox and had already appeared in two movies—*A*

In 1924, when film star Virginia Fox married Darryl Francis Zanuck,
the two made a dashing couple—when he could remember to keep his mouth
shut to hide protruding teeth.
(Bison Archives)

Zanuck, twenty-four, behind Al Jolson (at the wheel), claimed that, as head
of production at Warner Brothers, he instructed Jolson to utter the screen's first spoken
words in *The Jazz Singer* (1927), the world's first talkie.
(Museum of Modern Art/Film Stills Archive)

Virginia was three months pregnant with her third child in 1934 when she boldly accompanied her husband on a big-game hunt in Africa.
(Kobal Collection)

Although Zanuck and Virginia waited seven years before having their first child, Darrylin, he remarked that he was unprepared for fatherhood. That may explain his stunned expression as he and Virginia pose with Darrylin, five, Susan Marie, three, and Richard Darryl, one.
(Private collection)

After the formation of Twentieth Century-Fox in 1935, the company's giant but drab-looking dream factory in West Los Angeles became Zanuck's empire.
(Bison Archives)

Above: Darrylin perched on the knee of her most favorite person with America's most favorite child actress and Twentieth Century-Fox's biggest earner, Shirley Temple.
(Museum of Modern Art/ Film Stills Archive)

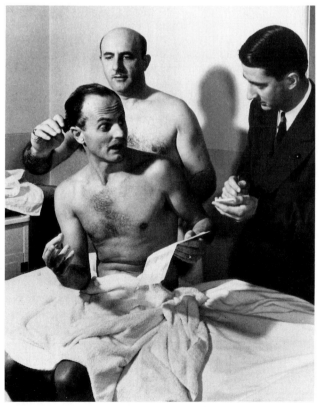

Left: As reigning king of Twentieth Century-Fox, Zanuck had a retinue that included Sam Silver, his own personal barber and masseur (*left*), and Edward Leggewie, a French tutor.
(Bob Landry/ *Life* magazine copyright 1941 Time Inc.)

Zanuck's ornate desk and vast office intimidated many, but most dreaded was the lair in the back where he auditioned actresses on his legendary casting couch.
(Bison Archives)

To Fox employees, Virginia appeared the classic president's wife—regal and remote. Yet, her reaction to the many movies she attended on her husband's arm was immediate and emotional.
(Private collection)

Top: During World War II, the entire family stood by as Virginia
prepared to christen a new ship.
(Bison Archives)

Bottom: After the war, Ric-Su-Dar, the Zanucks' Palm Springs estate
named for their children, welcomed a parade of influential visitors—Moss Hart,
Clare Booth Luce, Joseph Cotten, David Niven, and hundreds of others
who came to play croquet and enjoy Virginia's hospitality.
(Arthur Coleman Photography)

Right: Even as teenagers on a visit to their father's office, the Zanuck children had staked out their future roles: Susan (*left*) was the girl-next-door; Richard was Zanuck's admiring lieutenant; and Darrylin a glamorous princess. (Bison Archives)

Below: Susan Zanuck attended the Academy Awards presentation in 1950 with young Robert Wagner, one of her first big crushes. (Bison Archives)

Left: More influential and successful in the fifties than ever before, Zanuck constantly found himself surrounded by such Hollywood luminaries as Marilyn Monroe, Betty Grable, Lucille Ball, Walter Winchell, and songwriter Jimmy McHugh (*seated*). Yet the mogul was already proclaiming that he wanted out. (George Zeno Collection)

Below: The Zanucks made frequent trips to England and France to visit Fox operations—and vacation— in the early 1950s. (Bison Archives)

Left: Exotic-looking Bella Darvi, whose last name was formed of the first syllables of *Darryl* and *Virginia*, broke up the Zanucks' marriage, sending the entire family into a twenty-year diaspora. (Photofest)

Below: To escape her family, Susan insisted on a hurry-up wedding to Fox producer André Hakim in Las Vegas in 1954. (International Sound Photo/ Billy Rose Theatre Collection, New York Public Library at Lincoln Center)

Guide for the Married Man and *Planet of the Apes*—and was set to star in "Bracken's World," a Fox TV series. She had little time to worry that her fiancé's tantrums were anything more than adolescent outbursts. She was also kept busy moving into a new house.

Virginia, meanwhile, had decided to move to an elegant penthouse at the Wilshire Holmby, complete with a special suite for Alma Diehl, and deeded her son the beach house. For years, Virginia had kept the house exactly as it had been when her husband was in residence. "She had it redecorated periodically; however, everything had to be the same as when Darryl was there," said Walter Scott. "I had a terrible time trying to find the same fabrics and wallpaper that existed in 1940." Dick commissioned Scott to do the house again, and Linda was to make sure everything conformed to her husband's wishes—not that they were much different from his parents'. Again, Dick chose horsey wallpaper and eighteenth-century furniture.

Although he still shared his dad's taste in decor, Dick was emerging from his father's overwhelming shadow. In early 1967 the Fox board of directors had awarded him a new seven-year contract and given him the title of executive vice-president in charge of worldwide movie production. His father didn't attend the board meeting and claimed not to know the terms of the new contract, which gave Richard $300,000 in total compensation. The press happily glorified Dick, along with other young film executives, but, declared the *New York Times*, Richard was the "dean of the young'uns." Only three years ago, he was "denigrated as a puppet of his father." Now Fox was Hollywood's "hottest" studio. According to Vincent Canby, who wrote a piece on Darryl Zanuck for the *Sunday New York Times Magazine* in 1968, "Even some of Darryl Zanuck's most articulate detractors describe Richard as an effective studio chief."

Dick was clearly the heir apparent. The previous summer, the way to the top had been cleared for him when his father forced the resignation of Seymour Poe, one of the masterminds of Fox's comeback, only a week after the man had been reelected executive vice-president. According to Canby, "the critics said Zanuck was senile. . . . A more likely explanation lies in the natural antipathy that grew up between Zanuck, the instinctive, compulsive filmmaker, always impatient with corporate detail, and Poe, the shrewd, tough business mind, impatient with Hollywood-style eccentricities and a solid family man. In addition, by eliminating Poe, Zanuck consciously or unconsciously eliminated any serious competition that Richard Zanuck may have had for the presidency when his father steps down."

Canby might also have been describing the contrast between Zanuck and his son, for Dick, too, styled himself primarily as a businessman rather than an impresario. He wore conservatively cut dark suits and walked with a rigid military bearing. "Things have changed dramatically in the movie business," he told the *Newark Evening News* in October 1967. "I don't know if it's good or bad but it's more of a business now. Costs keep escalating like mad so you have to run the studio on sound business procedures. . . . Everyone is independent today. The deals are much tougher. There are few major stars and none who is an absolute guarantee at the box office."

Zanuck was uncomfortable with his son's new celebrity. By way of describing his unease, Canby told a curious tale: "Walking around the Beverly Wilshire pool one morning last fall, I met an old friend who asked what I was doing in Hollywood. Working on a story about Zanuck, I replied. 'Zanuck?' he said, looking mystified. 'I suppose he is important and he has been successful, but—well, he's still very young and not very articulate with reporters.' 'Darryl Zanuck,' I said, 'not Richard.' 'Oh,' said my friend, almost as though he had forgotten the older man. When Darryl Zanuck heard about this incident, he listened with a blank expression, then chuckled flatly. It was impossible to tell whether he was pleased." One former Fox associate Canby quoted praised Dick as an administrator and negotiator but added, "His only problem is his father. Darryl is constantly nagging him with memos, not about big things but about petty things. They waste Dick's time."

Even as the press was glorifying Richard, serious business problems were emerging at the studio. The huge movie musicals that he had hoped would capture the large audiences of *The Sound of Music* had not done well. The moviegoing public had once again changed its tastes. Instead of giant Technicolor extravaganzas with sugary themes, audiences of the era of Vietnam and social protest preferred smaller, more realistic movies. Darryl Zanuck should have sensed this, but somehow his once-perfect instinct was failing him now. *Star!* with Julie Andrews turned out to be a heavy-handed, slow-moving period piece with expensive sets and costumes. Fox was forced to take a $12 million write-down when the blockbuster fizzled. Another spectacular disaster was *Doctor Doolittle*, with Rex Harrison, which cost the studio $6 million more in write-downs.

The two Zanucks hoped that at least one movie musical—the long-running Broadway hit, *Hello, Dolly!*—would succeed. They were encouraged after a sneak preview of the movie in Scottsdale, Arizona; all six hundred viewers had given the film superlative ratings. However, the deal they had signed with David Merrick, the stage musical's producer, required Fox to withhold the movie's release until after the play had ceased to run on Broadway. In 1968, when the movie was ready to go, *Dolly* was still in its first run on stage. The movie sat in a can collecting dust and $2 million in annual interest charges. To get it out on the road, the studio engineered a complex deal that awarded David Merrick a hefty payment. Merrick admitted in a deposition that by the time he sold the play to Fox, it had lost its box-office appeal. "What persuaded me at the time was that I had Pearl Bailey in the show. I had switched to an all-black version, which had turned out to be a big hit, but Pearl Bailey's contract was running out. They didn't know that at Twentieth, and I felt that when she left, [the show] would plummet. It had, prior to that, at the tail end of the white cast. . . . So I felt it wasn't going to run until the release date anyway, and anything I could get out of it from then on would be a windfall. But they didn't know because I crossed them up."

Getting outfoxed by Merrick was only one of Zanuck's problems. Early in 1968 a Chicago columnist reported that Darryl Zanuck had suffered a stroke while he was traveling abroad. So persistent was the rumor that Zanuck decided to "show himself" in an audience with reporters at Fox headquarters in New York. Though his energetic appearance quashed most of the gossip, Dick sensed a change in his father. In court testimony given for the estate battle many years later, he said of his dad, "His condition was flawed, I would say, in 1967–68, and he showed in '68 and '69 a great improvement. And then in 1970, it became quite flawed again so that there was a roller-coaster effect. . . . He was becoming more forgetful, specifically in regard to details."

Zanuck also made business decisions that critics found bizarre. He supinely agreed to shoot both *Staircase* (which takes place in London), with Richard Burton, and *The Only Game in Town* (set in Las Vegas), with Elizabeth Taylor, in Paris to accommodate the couple's need to be together. The French location escalated the cost of both movies. Zanuck's only hope for a comeback lay in *Tora! Tora! Tora!* a $20 million Pacific basin version of *The Longest Day*. However, when that feature was eventually released in 1970, it, too, lost money. Young moviegoers were anti-war, and to them, tales of the historic battles of their elders seemed irrelevant and jingoistic.

Dick began emitting confident business noises that made him sound like the blandly reassuring coach of a losing team. The next year would be the company's biggest ever. And if the films didn't succeed financially, the studio's "nonfilm" activities would make up for losses. These nonmovie enterprises included humdrum businesses—a stake in the development of Century City, the high-rise office development in West Los Angeles, a program to explore educational equipment, large-screen TV production, and even a possible merger with another company, something his father had vehemently opposed. Dick even proposed a name change. To give the studio a new spirit, he would ask the board to call the company Twenty-first Century-Fox. "You know, I could make more money as an independent, producing two pictures a year and taking it a lot easier. But my father founded this company, we're substantial stockholders, and I want to make this company move ahead," he told a *New York Times* reporter.

Dick was given his chance to budge the studio behemoth in August 1969 when the Fox board of directors designated him president of the company. He asked for and received a $50,000-a-year raise. At age thirty-four, with a total annual salary of $350,000, he had become one of the highest-paid executives in America. That was an irritating pebble in Zanuck's shoe; his own son was now outearning him. Darryl Zanuck was to continue as chairman and chief executive officer, but he would earn only $200,000 a year—less than he had made in 1935.

The shift in power from Darryl to Richard signaled an in-house putsch. Darryl Zanuck claimed that he would still maintain "final executive responsibility," but the bylaws of the corporation had been changed to grant his son more power. The board of directors wanted to limit the elder Zanuck's say in the business—partly out of a belief that he was no longer himself. In a deposition filed in a 1971 shareholders' lawsuit against Fox, John P. Edmondson, executive vice-president of

E. P. Dutton & Co. and a Fox director, recalled, "Darryl Zanuck had been incapacitated for some time. . . . His incapacity arose out of the fact that he had broken an ankle as a result of a skiing accident in Switzerland, which did not give him the strict attendance to affairs that he would wish for."

But it was no skiing accident that had transformed the sixty-seven-year-old Zanuck. He had, in fact, suffered a stroke. John O'Grady, one of the detectives Virginia Zanuck had hired to keep track of family affairs, said, "When he went to Portugal in 1969, he had a stroke. [After that] Zanuck was not the same person. He was different then." That summer, Dick and his partner, David Brown, had approached Zanuck in New York and sold him on the idea of letting Dick run the company—to allow him to spend more time on scenarios and production. Zanuck had agreed. The two men had assured him, he later claimed, that he wouldn't be "giving up anything."

Behind the scenes, however, a coldness emerged between the father and his son. Dick felt that his father was responsible for Fox's losses; *his* job was to stem them. According to Harry McIntyre, a Fox board member, "When Darryl was the chief executive officer, he thought that Dick should clear everything with him. Dick had explained that he should have his own way and make his own decisions. This caused friction, business friction, between the two men." Edmondson testified, "The outward relationship of Darryl and his son still appeared to be cordial to the directors, but the close relationship that had existed between the two of them since Dick was in charge of the studio was the thing that had deteriorated." Zanuck would regularly countermand his son's orders. Dick would reinstate his orders, and his father would countermand them again. Said Dick later, "We played a game which was entitled 'I lose.' "

Late in 1969 *Hello, Dolly!* opened to unenthusiastic reviews and small audiences. The $24 million production was bound to be another disaster. All but done in by so many big-scale duds, Dick announced to reporters that he was going with low-budget films. He hired director Russ Meyer, whose previous movies included *Eroticon, Mondo Topless,* and *Fanny Hill.* For Fox, Meyer had already turned out *Beyond the Valley of the Dolls,* an unauthorized sequel to the original movie based on the Jacqueline Susann novel. Dick bragged that the movie cost only $2 million to make. (The company later had to fork over another $1.4 million to settle a suit filed by Susann for unauthorized exploitation of the earlier film based on her book, *Valley of the Dolls*.) Now Dick planned to let Meyer make three more films. Dick also returned to the subject on which some of his early successes were based: sex. He planned to film *Myra Breckinridge*, a book about a transsexual, and *Portnoy's Complaint*, the Philip Roth best-seller about a man's sexual obsessions.

A giant chasm was opening between father and son. Zanuck publicly endorsed Dick's plans; however, according to board member McIntyre, he quietly agitated against them. He stood foursquare against *Portnoy's Complaint*. "Dick and David Brown made a special trip to New York to persuade Darryl to permit the picture to be made, and Darryl refused to see them," recalled McIntyre. Dick was so distressed that he called McIntyre the next day and requested to have his father fire him. "I'm sorry. He doesn't have the authority to do it," replied McIntyre. "You are the president of the company." Richard took his case for the movie to the board of directors, and they turned the project down flat. Just as he had done years earlier with *The Chapman Report*, Dick got Warners to produce *Portnoy's Complaint*. The Fox board was also unhappy with Dick's other sexploitation film projects. Dick and David Brown "wanted to make pictures that it was felt were not up to Twentieth Century-Fox standards," said McIntyre. One Fox board director was so disaffected by the filming of *Myra Breckinridge* that he resigned.

While Zanuck was trying to undermine his son's projects, he produced an embarrassment of his own: *Hello–Goodbye*, starring his French protégée and companion, Genevieve Gillaizeau—or Genevieve Gilles, as she was known as an actress. She had little acting experience and could scarcely speak English; yet Zanuck was determined to make her a star. He was so besotted with his girlfriend that he bought her a cooperative apartment on East Fifty-seventh Street and spent a fortune clothing her, feeding her, adorning her with jewelry and furs, and giving her acting lessons in the vain hope of finally succeeding as a Svengali. Dick was bitterly opposed to the picture and later claimed that he begged his father not to proceed with the project; however, he never complained officially to the board of directors. Perhaps he concluded that if his father made the picture, he would be kept quiet and happy. The movie cost $5 million and barely earned $600,000 in rentals. The critics were almost as unimpressed as the audiences. Fox financial backers were distressed. Recalled McIntyre at one point, "The bank issued certain instructions to Fox . . . that we were never to permit Zanuck to make another picture with Miss Gillaizeau."

Dick conveyed the unwelcome message to his father. Zanuck was insulted. He felt that Dick's endorsement of the banks' decree not to use Genevieve in future films was a personal cut. If Dick really wanted to act like a loyal son, he would help his father find financing elsewhere. In his view, banks knew nothing about making movies. He did. He had been in the business for nearly forty-five years and had made more than six hundred movies. He was outraged that Dick was going to allow moneymen to dictate to Twentieth Century-Fox.

For Darryl Zanuck, the Genevieve insult soon became a thread in a skein of imagined conspiracies. Dick, his father was certain, was out to dump him and wreck the company. The movies he wanted to make would never go over with the public. He had gone along when Dick decided to produce *Myra Breckinridge,* but the picture had flopped when it was released in 1970 and had become a reliable source of easy gibes for critics. Now Zanuck opposed Dick's *Portnoy's Complaint* project, although it was just the kind of daring, ground-breaking movie he used to love.

The breach between father and son became more openly detectable that fall when Susan and Pierre Savineau and Dick and Linda Zanuck met with Darrylin and her family for a vacation in Acapulco. Darryl and Genevieve announced that they, too, were coming. Dick was furious when he learned from his sister that the couple had been invited. Said Darrylin, "Dickie, when he called me, was livid that Daddy was coming, and, in fact, he didn't want me to get him reservations, and I told him this is ridiculous. I haven't seen my father in a couple of years, and I wanted him to be here."

Dick did not conceal his resentment of the old man. One family friend recalled that Zanuck was holding forth to his son and some other guests about making movies in the twenties and thirties. He chided Dick for making "pornographic" films. The public didn't really want to see them—*Myra Breckinridge* had been a big flop. Dick and

David Brown, he added, were concentrating too much on stars. Stars didn't make pictures, he declared; pictures made stars. Critics didn't count, either. They made him *vomit*. They were bullshit. Dick and several others responded sarcastically, demanding that he tell them what it was like back in the old days when he was in power at the studio. Many years later in a deposition Darrylin would say that she was disturbed by her brother's behavior. Later she remarked, "During the time when they were there, it was a definite coldness on Dickie's part or a sarcasm to things that my father would say—and little needlings."

A year earlier the board of directors had retained the Stanford Research Institute, a celebrated think tank in Menlo Park, California, to study Fox's operations. The company had received the scrutiny of the think tank's M.B.A.'s, and a number of reports were issued—one or two on real estate, another on corporate cost-cutting, yet another on Fox offices. According to board member Harry McIntyre, Dick and his father parted company on the findings. If Zanuck endorsed an SRI recommendation, Dick objected to it and vice versa. The board of directors was dismayed.

Dick and Brown flew to New York to confront Zanuck. They reminded him that he had agreed to turn over the day-to-day operation of the company to them. His reply, said Dick, was that "we had put one over on him. The specifically used phrase was 'the con job of the century.' " Dick was wounded and angry. He later remarked, "During that period when he was in Europe fooling around I had many hard business decisions to make. He was acting foolishly, and there were times when I had to cover for him. He was concerned with my efforts to try to hide his lack of activity. He became a little paranoid about my help, and he interpreted that as my putting him out to pasture. That's an exact quote: 'You're trying to put me out to pasture.' "

Whoever gave orders and got them followed could not stanch the flow of red ink. In August of 1970 Fox announced a second-quarter pretax loss of $23 million. Again there would be no dividend. A cost-cutting program was put into effect; the studio would make fewer pictures until it had regained its equilibrium. However, the board was getting fed up with the Zanucks. There was so much father-son fighting that they felt Fox would never be able to get past its crisis—the worst since the dark days of *Cleopatra*. Fox was a public company; yet the Zanucks acted as if it were their own private preserve. Shareholders and board members complained that Zanuck made an expensive movie just to ingratiate himself with his girlfriend and that he had charged all her personal expenses to the studio. Genevieve decided to take herself out of the fray. In the fall of 1970 she asked Dick not to renew her contract.

Her disappearance from the ranks of Fox contract players did not mollify the Zanucks' critics. They were also becoming agitated by the perks that they read about in newspaper reports. The Zanucks, it was charged, had allowed the studio to operate a costly "club" where executives mingled. Worse yet was the "talent school" of young actresses whose job it was to mingle with the mingling executives. No evidence was ever advanced proving the existence of such scandalous doings, but the stories were accepted as truth by some shareholders. The payroll, furthermore, was packed with Zanuck family members, friends, and hangers-on. Dennis Stanfill, who became chief operating officer of Fox, was later to tell reporters that there had just been too much nepotism at the company.

Moreover, rumors had come to the attention of the board of directors and other senior executives that Darryl Zanuck and André Hakim, Susan's former husband, were involved in a so-called black-money scheme designed to siphon funds out of the company to secret Swiss accounts controlled by Hakim. According to court papers filed by Fox some time later, Hakim had commissioned several screenplays for more than $250,000. Actually, Fox contended, the scripts were either fakes or had cost much less. Fox charged that, in one case, Hakim had billed the studio $148,000 for a script that actually cost $4,500 and had deposited the difference with dummy corporations he controlled in Switzerland.

Hakim never denied that he took the money. His excuse was that he had undertaken the complicated transactions at the request of Darryl Zanuck and Fox management. "Plaintiff will show the court direct evidence which exposes Fox management, in particular Darryl F. Zanuck, as the responsible party in the alleged transactions," declared Hakim's lawyers in court papers. Harry McIntyre insisted that Dick Zanuck was not involved in any underhanded dealings. Yet Fox attorneys, trying the case against Hakim, sent official notifications to Richard in Los Angeles when they determined to depose witnesses in

Europe. He denied that he was involved in any of Hakim's question-able doings, and he was never directly named in the lawsuit.

By the fall of 1970, word that the Zanucks were on their way out had filtered down to the lower echelons of Fox employees. Pokie Seeger, who had been hired on Dick's say-so, heard the news from a New York studio executive she was dating at the time. He told her, she recalled, that the board was going to see to it that both Zanucks eventually left the company. "He warned me that I had better start looking for a new job because not only were the Zanucks going to be pushed out but all their friends . . . as well," she said.

In December the board appointed a three-man special committee to examine Fox's financial situation, its corporate restructuring, and its cost-cutting programs. The *Wall Street Journal* noted that the com-mittee was considering a proposal to oust both Dick Zanuck and David Brown. The newspaper quoted a company insider to the effect that this turn of events would require Darryl Zanuck to preside over the firing of his own son: "Fathers don't usually do this to their sons no matter what. But it's hard to see how he would have very much choice except to act on directors' recommendations." Said McIntyre, "The fact is that Dick and David never really got along with the board at all. That's why they were in line to be fired."

Dick had also come to suspect that his corporate "execution" was in the works. He placed the blame directly on his father. "I had become convinced that the breach between my father and myself had reached irreparable proportions and that it would be in the best interest of the corporation to convert my deal with the company as well as Mr. Brown's into that of an independent producing organization which would produce and distribute pictures for Twentieth Century-Fox," he recalled later in a deposition. "During this period and even before the committee was formed, I had been informed by my father . . . that we were going to be terminated." Dick was asked whether he did anything about it. He responded, "I hired a lawyer."

What was happening to Dick must have seemed like a dark and forbidding dream sequence. All his life he had worked to please his father. At Zanuck's command, he had played tennis and badminton combatively, only to find the game ending whenever he won. As a business ally, he had labored tirelessly to make his father's company succeed. He had even married women his father would have endorsed. He had said little about his father's sexual indiscretions and had allowed him to use studio money to give his father's girlfriend star status. Now Zanuck seemed to view Dick as an obstacle that had to be removed.

At her Wilshire Holmby penthouse apartment, Virginia Zanuck heard the news of her son's impending ouster, and though she still dreamed that her husband would someday return to her, she was coldly furious about Zanuck's plan to fire their only son. Such an action violated her sense of family loyalty and plain fair play. However, according to her friends, she sensed doom for her husband as well. Zanuck was sixty-eight years old—an elderly man. No matter how strongly he gripped the helm of Twentieth Century-Fox, he couldn't last forever. Dick's succession to the top corporate spot had guaranteed that the family would maintain control of the company. Now the family's position was in jeopardy.

Dick's dismissal unfolded quickly and nastily. After Christmas 1970, Zanuck presided over a special meeting of the board. The report of the special committee was read. Dick Zanuck was chastised for his lack of innovation and wastefulness, among other things. He and David Brown were invited to resign immediately. The board had adopted a resolution requesting both men to resign "without prejudice to whatever rights these individuals may have under employment contracts with the Company." Their resignations had already been prepared, and if they refused to tender them, they were told, the board would terminate their employment with the company in two days. Dick left the room to call his lawyer and read him the agreement. There didn't seem to be any point in arguing. It is common practice in Hollywood to fire first and settle contracts generously later. Much like the criminals in *Les Misérables*, the younger Zanuck and Brown ignominiously made their way out of the Manhattan building through a basement exit to avoid reporters who were eagerly awaiting the outcome of the meeting.

Later, Darryl Zanuck claimed disingenuously in a deposition, "It came as a shock. I knew that something was going to happen. I didn't know what could happen. The board would say they would take [Dick and David Brown's] power away and give the power to someone else and have them stay on—there were many alternative methods . . . but

I did not know . . . I did not suspect they were actually going through with that plan. . . . I heard them for the first time at the board meeting."

But he was not so shocked that he resigned along with his son, as many other fathers would have done. Instead, he coldly voted for the resolution to have Dick and his partner fired.

The two ousted executives flew back to Los Angeles the next day. When they arrived at the studio on the last day of 1970, they learned that they were expected to leave their offices and remove all personal property by the end of business hours. Richard's nameplate had already been taken off his door and replaced by that of another executive. Their secretaries were placed under surveillance by studio police and questioned about each item they removed. Several executives also stopped by to make sure no studio property was taken. Zanuck and Brown were required to give up the keys to their filing cabinets and offices. As if that was not humiliating enough, a locksmith appeared and changed the locks on their office doors. When Dick went out to the lot to get his car, he found a painter obliterating his name from his parking space.

Dick had once told reporters, "I'll practically do anything short of murder to achieve what I want." Now he must have felt as though he had been murdered—by his own father. "What was horrible about the whole scene was that my own father had engineered and executed my demise," Dick said later in an interview with *New York* magazine. "When I left the studio that day, I was totally destroyed. It was like a death. I lived at the beach in Santa Monica, and . . . I spent day after day walking the beach, asking myself, 'What's this all about?' I had worked so hard. I was, of course, terribly stunned and shocked that my own father was capable of doing that to me."

He did not have to worry about his future. One Fox picture—*Butch Cassidy and the Sundance Kid* with Robert Redford and Paul Newman—had already pulled in large audiences. Ironically, two other films he had assembled while at Fox, *Patton* and *M*A*S*H*, were to become money-makers for the studio. Dick didn't have to look hard for job offers. Producer Ray Stark told *Los Angeles Times* columnist Joyce Haber that he had offered the younger Zanuck a job: "I told Dick I'd love him to be in business with me. He has a better record if you look at it than anybody around. But *Tora! Tora! Tora!* and *Hello–Goodbye,* two of his old man's, must have cost him $15 million. His old man should have resigned from the board and made his son resign along with him. How can he act like that with his own son?" Virginia Zanuck added her own self-righteous jabs: "Darryl talks about *Myra Breckinridge*, not about *Hello–Goodbye*. But Darryl okayed the script for *Myra* and wanted to do a follow-up."

To Dick, the firing was like a replay of his childhood wrestling contests with his dad. If Zanuck couldn't win, he didn't want to play anymore. The old man had little to celebrate, however. His year-to-year contract was not renewed. Instead, he was to continue on "at the pleasure of the board"—an endorsement that was full of uncertainty. Within days of his son's dismissal, a batch of Zanuck supporters were purged. On January 2 Hakim was fired. Linda Harrison's contract was terminated at the end of the month. Soon Pokie Seeger was also job-hunting.

✻   ✻   ✻

When Richard Zanuck finished cleaning out his office at Fox that terrible morning after his "demise," he called his mother.

"I hope you didn't take the bust of your father," said Virginia.

"It's the only thing left in the office," replied her son.

But the younger Zanuck couldn't leave his father behind altogether. He still aimed to please. Only a few months later, Dick would be fighting to save his father.

FOUR
SA SEULE AMIE

•

enevieve Gillaizeau could never seem to remember where she met Darryl F. Zanuck, even though he was her mentor and boyfriend for eight long years and her obsession for more than twenty. In her court battle to get a share of Zanuck's estate, she testified that they were introduced in 1965 when she was a nineteen-year-old fashion model at a party at the Brasserie Lipp, a Parisian gathering place for intellectuals, crooks, politicians, and artists. At other times, Genevieve insisted she first encountered Zanuck at Maxim's—maybe in 1966. Others have disputed that story. They darkly mutter that Genevieve walked on the wild side of Parisian life, that she first met Zanuck when, as a call girl, she was dispatched to his hotel suite with another young woman.

Whatever the truth of their meeting, Zanuck fell deeply in love with Genevieve. To outsiders, the match was incongruous. She was forty-four years younger than her lover and about three inches taller. While his wizened body was dominated by dark glasses, a fat cigar, and a brushlike mustache, she was not that impressive herself. Certainly she was pretty, but hardly big-eyed and exotic like Bella Darvi or Irina Demick; and she lacked the established talent and celebrity of Juliette Greco. Superficially, the relationship seemed like a clean exchange of Zanuck's money and power for Genevieve's reasonably good looks and sexual attention.

Yet a simple trade-off could not explain why their attraction was to turn into Zanuck's longest and most serious affair. What pulled them toward each other was their common vision of the way their lives should be styled. Both the Nebraska-born filmmaker and the poor girl from the Paris suburbs yearned for sophistication, elegance, and coolness.

For years, Zanuck had been a tireless and enthusiastic eager beaver who turned out movie after movie. He had played as hard as he worked—at polo, hunting, skiing, and croquet. He had been a paterfamilias with mortgages, dental bills, and servants to take care of. Continuing that life would only remind him that he was aging. In his memoirs, director Elia Kazan noted: "Darryl's taste in glamour ran to French singer-actresses; they brought out all his cultural uncertainty. His idea of a glamorous residence was the Georges V in Paris, which was as close to a Beverly Hills hotel as a French hotel can be. He admired what he felt he lacked, international snob sophistication."

What Zanuck wanted was a style—not a life—that expressed his lack of connection to the ordinary. He didn't have a home like other people. From hotel to hotel, wherever he went, from the Plaza in New York to the Georges V in Paris or Claridge's in London, he was welcomed by hoteliers, Fox executives, servants, and drivers. As president of Twentieth Century-Fox, he would simply land on a movie, dispense his advice, and fly off somewhere else. Once he had liked to eat chipped beef on toast; now he dined every night at the very best restaurants. He was free, an American-French-Euro-sophisticate.

Genevieve fit into the fast-paced and high-toned scene as though she had been cast for it. She was not to be his wife—she was a living manifestation of his liberation from family. She was sensual and young, proving that he was exempt from the slowdown in libido that he feared his advancing age might indicate. She was a sleek bauble, a woman who could mix as easily at a diplomatic reception as at a new boîte. She belonged nowhere, so she could go anywhere.

Zanuck's new girlfriend seemed to have her own grand visions. Indeed, she had an arrogance to match Zanuck's. Only arrogance could explain her effort to lay claim to his money seven years after their liaison had ended. She, too, was somehow marvelous, special, not to be bound by routine concerns. She saw herself as one to the manner born—a woman who should have servants, designers, and hairdressers fussing over her. At age nineteen, when she first met Zanuck, she could not enjoy such a life without some financial help; she needed a Darryl Zanuck, or someone like him, to pay her way. She also had to have him because only a connection to a genius, a man who himself was detached from the petty details of living, could help her establish her own identity, her vision of herself as someone who was above and beyond it all.

In a sense, Genevieve Gillaizeau (who later adopted the stage name Gilles) started out near the bottom. Her modest beginning would have entitled her to very little. Genevieve has revealed few details about her early life. She was born on February 25, 1946, in a Parisian suburb near Argenteuil. Her mother was young, poor, unwed, and abandoned by Genevieve's father. The little girl spent the first nine years of her life in shelter homes—the French equivalent of foster homes—because her mother was too poor to take care of her.

Eventually, her mother married and gave birth to seven other children, but Genevieve never returned permanently to the family. She was sent to a strict convent school near Paris. Like most European institutions of its kind, the school was austere and cold, the emphasis on discipline, orderliness, Catholic piety, and hard work. During her vacations, Genevieve would visit her mother and her half brothers and sisters, but at school she was lonely. At the time, she felt life at the convent was very hard. Later she came to believe that somehow the school was good for her.

She left the school at age eighteen, an attractive and ambitious young woman. The nuns had praised her sharp mind, and she had thought about becoming a lawyer. However, for French girls of her background, there was no scholarship money and little chance of being admitted to a university. She and other graduates of the convent school were expected to take jobs as shop attendants or file clerks, then marry and have children. Genevieve wanted more.

Her mother urged her to live at home, but Genevieve was not about to accede. "My mother would have locked me up until I was twenty-one," she later told a reporter. In what was her first court battle, Genevieve petitioned the authorities for emancipation. She won, without too great a struggle. At age eighteen, she was on her own in Paris.

She might have had a superior mind, but people then noticed only her good looks. She had long, wavy honey-colored hair, soft blue eyes, pronounced cheekbones, a long patrician nose, and a large, pouty mouth. Only a chin that seemed slightly weak and uncertain marred her profile. Five feet seven inches tall and lean, with long, sinuous legs, she was a bit gawky, but she could wear clothes well. She felt she had a natural sense of style. With scarcely any money, she could manage to look as though she had stepped from a designer's show-room. So her choice of a job seemed obvious: she would model clothing. She was pretty enough, and besides, what else could she do? Genevieve started at the bottom—as a runway model. For many of Paris's less distinguished clothing manufacturers, she would parade garments past buyers and retailers. She earned about $50 a week, not bad for an eighteen-year-old, but still only just enough to get by on.

Genevieve has said that her affair with Zanuck began with casual dating. In interrogatories filed in court by Darrylin's lawyer Malcolm Ellis in the legal contest over the mogul's estate, Genevieve was asked whether she had worked for Madame Claude who had operated a call-girl service that catered to some of the wealthiest and most power-ful men in Europe. By 1983, Madame Claude, whose real name was Fernande Grudet, was living in Los Angeles and was subpoenaed by lawyers for Zanuck's estate to give a deposition. Madame Claude claimed to know nothing of Genevieve; but she did admit that she had operated her service in Paris for over twenty years from twenty-three different locations. She also said that Susan Zanuck's husband André Hakim had been her client and that Darryl Zanuck had also been a client in good standing for ten years. Indeed, she claimed to have introduced him to hundreds of girls. Often he had ordered up two girls who would have sex with each other. "He liked that," said Madame Claude.

Genevieve has never answered any questions put to her by the Zanuck family lawyers about working for Madame Claude. She has insisted that her first sexual encounter with Zanuck took place months after their first meeting. In Paris, the two went out together publicly. He sent his car to pick her up and bring her to screenings of Fox movies he was working on. Sometimes they went out to dinner or spent an evening at a nightclub.

According to Genevieve, she had a modeling career that was picking up speed. In 1966 Dorian Leigh, the Parisian modeling agency she worked for, sent Genevieve to New York to pose for *Glamour* magazine. She ran into Zanuck at the Paris airport when both were on their way to the United States, and he promised to call her in New York. Again, there was a round of screenings, dinners, and dates. It was during this New York stay—and not before—that she and Zanuck became lovers. Unfortunately, her visit to the United States could not be permanent because she couldn't get a green card. So, after a few months, Genevieve left for Paris. She didn't have to wait too long for Zanuck to turn up, however. He was always back and forth between Paris and New York on business. They continued to see each other. By late 1966, Genevieve had become his steady girlfriend. He called her GG.

Zanuck's associates disliked Genevieve intensely. Edward Leggewie, the mogul's longtime French tutor and then chief administrator of Zanuck's Paris operation, described the young woman's influence on the aging mogul as *"néfaste"*—which translates fairly precisely to "evil." Elisabeth Gargarine, his secretary, thought Genevieve "mean" and "hard as nails." In Madame Gargarine's view, Genevieve was something of a courtesan who was brazenly after the producer's money. Genevieve fit Zanuck's preference for what Madame Gargarine called "third-rate women." She felt that he didn't really like women—except his close employees. For him, Madame Gargarine said, women were "decoration in the background," and they were there "to go out to dinner with at ten o'clock and to sleep with." Once, when Zanuck went on holiday in the south of France, he took along a young actress and Madame Gargarine. He spent all his time dictating to Gargarine and was with the actress only for a late dinner and the night. In Gargarine's stern opinion, only third-rate women would put up with such treatment.

Even if Genevieve was third-rate, she meant to go first-class. She made nonnegotiable demands, and Zanuck eagerly met them, partly to keep her with him and partly because they made his life with her seem so special and unusual. Soon after Genevieve became Zanuck's permanent companion, she made him buy a Rolls-Royce—an uncharacteristic indulgence, even for him. She refused to beg him for every nickel and dime, and he agreed that she should have her own income. In 1966 he had Twentieth Century-Fox hire her as a "fashion consultant." Her salary was $185 a week—a generous amount considering that a clerk-typist then would have earned about half as much. She didn't have to go to an office to do her work. Her duties merely required her to attend screenings with Zanuck and render her opinion on the clothing actors wore. "We were seeing movies . . . and . . . rushes from the studio all the time, and he will ask me what do I think of the wardrobe, and this is it," testified Genevieve during the court battle over Zanuck's estate.

She began traveling with Zanuck wherever he went; curiously, they never shared the same bedroom. People wondered whether this was just tactfulness on Zanuck's part or a desire for privacy. Genevieve explained, "We just like it that way." In fact, *she* liked it that way, according to Madame Gargarine. She had demanded her own room. Zanuck acceded because it made their relationship seem so worldly and independent. In Paris the two had separate accommodations. He lived at the Georges V Hotel and she at the Plaza Athénée.

In New York, which became Zanuck's home base under the press of Twentieth Century-Fox business, the lovers kept their own accommodations. Zanuck occupied a seven-room suite at the Plaza Hotel. After Genevieve obtained her green card in 1967, he settled her in the Excelsior, then one of Manhattan's most elegant new luxury apartment buildings, less than a mile away on Second Avenue and Fifty-seventh Street. On the roof was a swimming pool beneath a glass dome that slid back to admit the sun on warm days. The bikini-clad Genevieve would spend many of her spare hours at poolside soaking up the rays of the weak New York sun. Downstairs, in front of the building often waited Zanuck's Jaguar with its DFZ-13 license plates. The car and driver were at her disposal for shopping trips and other excursions. Genevieve did not mix much with other residents of the building. Though Zanuck was forty-four years her senior, she undiplomatically announced to a reporter, "I keep pretty much to myself [because] most of the members are so old."

Apparently Genevieve's distaste for the company of the elderly never penetrated her lover's mind. Anyway, he could reason that her very attachment to him proved that he wasn't old—he was beyond aging.

Indeed, she had him believing that he was a solid member of the late sixties youth culture. Under her supervision, he would dress up in a Nehru jacket, and, at parties, the two would dance to rock music like teenagers. To anybody who asked about her close relationship with such an old man, she would declare that Zanuck was a great and loyal friend. True, he could be jealous and possessive, but she was happy with him. To Zanuck's biographer, Mel Gussow, she declared in a self-possessed manner, "He doesn't give me any trouble."

Zanuck gave her everything but trouble. He showered her with valuable gifts. The biggest was a giant diamond ring for which he had paid $150,000. He also gave her ten other rings with less costly gemstones. One was an emerald with a matching bracelet. She received earrings—one set made of gold coins from the shah of Iran—and brooches, bracelets, and watches. Then there were her furs—five minks, two foxes, a sable, an ocelot, and a fisher. The couple bought art together; Genevieve had a taste for Post-Impressionists, and she introduced her lover to their work. Zanuck paid for nearly two dozen paintings that hung on her walls at the Excelsior. In 1970, when her building went co-op, Zanuck helped Genevieve buy her apartment. He laid out a $20,000 down payment, half of the apartment's total price.

Zanuck also underwrote the cost of her wardrobe, which was sizable. "I didn't have to pay for anything," she testified in court later. Her favorite designer was Yves St. Laurent, but she also bought from Valentino and a newly popular Roman designer named Andre Laug. Genevieve owned four wigs and ten hairpieces but usually wore her hair pulled back into a knot at the nape of her neck. In 1968 she confided to a reporter that she planned to buy some Chanel creations: "I never saw her collection, but I met her at Maxim's with the Burtons," she said. "There's something sweet in her face. I like her and I think she likes me."

There were also gifts of cash. During their frequent visits to the south of France, Zanuck would try his luck at the gambling casinos. When he won, she won, too, because he gave her most of his winnings. Usually, she received a few thousand dollars; however, one day, she recalled, "When Darryl was gambling, we came out, out of the casino, the gambling place in France, and he sit on the bed, and he will share his winning, which was over $15,000. . . . He was always sharing when he win. When he lost, no." She may have received more than his winnings. "That was only part of it," asserted Pierre Savineau, Susan Zanuck's second husband, who knew Darryl and Genevieve in France. "The 'black money'—the money that came from [Susan's first husband] André Hakim—Darryl gave some of that to Genevieve, too. That's where his share went—to Genevieve." Savineau believed that Hakim charged the studio inflated amounts for screenplays and channeled some of the money back to Zanuck who, in turn, shared it with Genevieve. In a lawsuit between Twentieth Century-Fox and André Hakim, Hakim asserted that the extra money went to Zanuck to help finance one of Genevieve's movies.

In the summer of 1969, Zanuck also bought Genevieve two thousand shares of Twentieth Century-Fox stock—then worth about $50,000. It was a gift, she later claimed, to allow him to avoid taxation. She was to hold it and collect the dividends. If it increased in value, she could take the profit; the principal was to go back to Zanuck. It never did, however. He sent letters to her that seemed to forgive the debt. She could keep it all.

Savineau recalled his wife Susan remarking, on the couple's visits to France, that she had never seen her father so much in love. While the style he and Genevieve affected was sophisticated, Zanuck's Nebraska-nurtured Victorian beliefs provided a strong foundation for his attachment. He felt protective of the young girl, and he defended her to others, whatever the circumstances of their initial meeting. To him, she was not a gold digger, as some of his friends thought, but a lady. In a deposition he later gave during a shareholders' lawsuit, he described his relationship with Genevieve: "We have always been very close friends. She is a very dear friend of mine. . . . A lot of people would call her my girlfriend. I rather call her my ladyfriend. [As to an intimate relationship], I don't think that that is a question I should answer at all. I don't believe it is a question that any man should answer at all about anybody that he has respect for. You might say it about some tramp, or someone that didn't have any standing or feeling, or that he didn't have any regard for. You might say it, but he wouldn't say it for someone that is a well-bred, well-educated, lovely, charming girl."

Yet Zanuck was not so swept away by Genevieve that he entertained the idea of marriage. According to her, he said he wanted to marry her;

however, Virginia refused to give him a divorce. He also told Genevieve that he really couldn't divorce for business reasons. "He said he signed a paper where he couldn't get a divorce because of the stock," she said. Further, he was already suing Virginia to get control of Ric-Su-Dar and some of their joint property. Divorcing might jeopardize the lawsuits. However, his logic made little sense. A divorce from a wife from whom he had been separated since 1956 could hardly be damaging to the studio, though it could threaten his voting rights on some of his stock. And a divorce would lead to what he claimed he wanted in his lawsuit with Virginia: division of their jointly owned property.

At war in Zanuck were his desire for an extraordinary style of life, free from ordinary strictures, and his native Victorian principles. If he divorced Virginia, he would be a disloyal cad. If he didn't marry Genevieve, he would also be a cad. However, if he did marry her, then he would be all strung up again in another constricting, commonplace relationship. And Zanuck apparently had eyes for others than Genevieve. According to court papers in Los Angeles, a baby girl was born in late 1967 to one Paris Miller. She claimed that Zanuck was the father and named her daughter Michelle Linda Zanuck. So he elected to keep things as they were. He was a married family man who, at the same time, mixed in the jet set with a young cosmopolitan girlfriend.

Genevieve was not restive with the arrangement. If Zanuck felt he had to keep up a marriage of convenience, she understood. Many French merchants, industrialists, and politicians had similar arrangements—a formal marriage for public show and a passionate nonpublic attachment to a mistress. Besides, the life she was leading was heady and enthralling for a woman in her early twenties. The people Zanuck introduced her to were reason enough to avoid complaining. At his side, she met Frank Sinatra, Ted Kennedy, Governor Nelson Rockefeller, U.S. Ambassador to the U.N. Arthur Goldberg, Elizabeth Taylor, and Richard Burton. In 1970 the duke and duchess of Uzès threw a party for Genevieve at the St. Regis roof. With such social movers and shakers as Mrs. Vincent Astor, the William Paleys, the Rodman de Herrens, Earl Blackwell, Graham Mattison, Diana Vreeland, and Princess Egon von Fürstenberg among the guests, Genevieve was one of the least important persons in attendance. This life was a far cry from what the nuns had predicted for her back at the convent. Genevieve had always wanted more—without knowing exactly what "more" meant. Surely, this had to be it.

To Genevieve's mind, the Zanuck clan had accepted the arrangement. In 1967 Genevieve even met Virginia. Zanuck had to visit the Los Angeles studio to attend a key sales conference that brought together Fox distributors from all over the world. He wanted to go, but fretted that his wife might hit him with a court order to pay up on the old lawsuit. Eventually he called Virginia and asked what her intentions were. Much to his surprise, when he told her he was returning to Los Angeles, she was gracious and welcoming. They hadn't spoken in nearly a decade. Of course, she would love for him to return to L.A., she said. Thus emboldened, he asked her if he might use Ric-Su-Dar, and she agreed.

Virginia whirled into action. According to her friend Margaret Shands, Virginia really believed that her husband was coming home for good. She assembled a crew of servants and drove with them to Palm Springs to clean up the house and prepare it for Zanuck. They stocked the refrigerator with food and filled vases with flowers. They put new linens on the beds. The pool was cleaned and filled. Virginia waited prayerfully for Zanuck's arrival. "Then what does he do?" asked Margaret Shands rhetorically. "He comes with Genevieve."

When Zanuck and Genevieve pulled up to the gate on the appointed day, they were stunned to find Virginia waiting to greet them. Genevieve had to conclude that the two Zanucks were quite blasé. Virginia, after all, had readied a house for her husband's mistress. Virginia's face had brightened when she saw the car, but fell when she spotted Genevieve. Still, Virginia was nothing if not gracious. She welcomed Genevieve and Zanuck politely, excused herself, and left quietly with her driver.

The next day, Virginia called Mrs. Shands and recounted what had happened. Margaret was appalled. "I asked, 'What did you do?' In a small voice, Virginia replied, 'Oh, I didn't say anything. I just left.' I said, 'Listen Virginia. I told you to be nice, but I didn't tell you to be *that* nice.' " Virginia, however, had constructed her own delusion to explain her husband's close attachment to Genevieve. Added Mrs. Shands, "Virginia said, 'Oh, what does it matter? That girl is just his secretary—she doesn't mean anything to him.' " Her husband and Genevieve stayed in Palm Springs for three days and then flew back to

New York. Another five years would pass before Virginia saw Zanuck again.

Zanuck and Genevieve rarely saw Susan and Pierre Savineau, but when Dick turned up in New York on business, he would dine with his father and Genevieve. Sometimes Dick's new girlfriend Linda Harrison would join them. Every Sunday night, Genevieve and Zanuck would dine with David Brown, Dick's closest colleague and friend, and his wife, *Cosmopolitan* editor Helen Gurley Brown. All of them treated Genevieve with great civility—almost affection. In 1968 she and Zanuck had gone to visit Darrylin in Acapulco. Their reception was not just cordial—it was magnanimous. Darrylin hosted an immense and lavish party in their honor.

Still, Genevieve's life, for all its merits, had its drawbacks. Though Zanuck affected detachment, he was intensely jealous. He became nervous if she so much as met the eyes of another man—or woman, and he hired detectives to stalk her when he was not around. He retained the right to sleep with whomever he chose, however, and there were nights when he slipped off with other women.

Genevieve gradually realized that Zanuck had become an alcoholic. At one point, she said, he became addicted to Greek wine. He drank so much that he lost weight. Initially, she said she hadn't caught on because they didn't live together; he would sneak a snort from a pocket flask before a conference and then surreptitiously guzzle down more liquor after. She finally grasped the extent of the problem in 1967 when they traveled to California for a sales conference. At her bungalow at the Beverly Hills Hotel, he kept sneaking to the refrigerator where the liquor was stored. She called Zanuck's physician, Dr. Lee Siegel, who immediately gave Zanuck a dressing-down: he had to stop drinking or he would die. The producer agreed. He announced to Genevieve that he had given up the bottle, but he immediately plunged into a withdrawal so severe that he had to be helped off the plane in New York. She packed up some clothes at her apartment and joined him at his Plaza suite to nurse him through the crisis. She vigilantly kept the keys to the liquor cabinet and refused to let him out of her sight lest he order a drink from room service. Gradually he recovered and gained weight. When Siegel examined Zanuck six months later, he declared him astonishingly fit.

But while Zanuck may have given up the bottle, he was not completely fit. A year after his trip to California, he fell and broke his leg while vacationing in the south of France. Later, in 1969, he suffered a minor stroke in Portugal, according to John O'Grady, a Los Angeles private detective who worked for Virginia Zanuck. Zanuck kept the stroke a complete secret. He feared that news of his ill health might adversely affect Twentieth Century-Fox stock.

*   *   *

Several years before, Zanuck had told his friend columnist Art Buchwald that he would never again violate that old rule against using a girl he was emotionally involved with in a picture. Yet he now fell all over himself in an effort to break the rule—this time with Genevieve. More than he had been with Greco, Darvi, and Demick, he was convinced that Genevieve had the makings of a major motion picture star. She began to think so, too. In Paris she had taken an acting class, and the instructor had told her she had talent. With Zanuck's sponsorship, she could hardly fail. Indeed, she seemed already to have acquired a rather Zanuck-like insouciance. So what if she was not the world's greatest actress? If Darryl F. Zanuck wanted to turn her into a star, then he would do it—by fiat, if need be.

She and Zanuck happily set about planning her career. Both of them knew that her broken English was not equal to any great acting task. So the producer decided to start with a modest project. He cleverly designed a short feature to be called *The World of Fashion*. It would showcase Genevieve's chief asset: her ability to wear clothes. The thin excuse for the movie was to educate the public on clothing through the ages. Genevieve was to model twenty different costumes that typified high style through history. The role was a snap for Genevieve. Modeling was her game. When the movie was released in the United States in early 1969, it became a tiny smash. To save money, Zanuck had shot all the scenes in outdoor public locations, and Genevieve had worn many of her own ensembles; the movie cost only $48,000 but earned over $500,000.

At least that's what Zanuck said. André Hakim was later to claim, in his defense against the accusation of embezzlement, that Zanuck had used some of the "black money" for his production of Genevieve's short feature. According to Hakim, Zanuck directed him to have Fox purchase a phony property called *L'Echelle Blanche* because "Darryl Zanuck was producing a picture in Europe entitled *World of Fashion* starring his protégée and companion, Miss Genevieve Gilles. At the time, it was substantially exceeding budget costs, and the excessive costs were to be transferred to *L'Echelle Blanche* to make it appear that *World of Fashion* was not expensive at all." Zanuck, said Hakim, had sent a telegram to his son Richard to get his approval for payments totaling $120,000. *"L'Echelle Blanche* was a necessary picture to absorb the costs Zanuck was incurring on *World of Fashion*," claimed Hakim.

Nonetheless, Zanuck called the feature a success, and persuaded Twentieth Century-Fox to sign Genevieve to a contract. Dick reluctantly went along with his father, though he did not care for Genevieve as an actress and could only have been uncomfortable with his father's renewed efforts to play Pygmalion. Genevieve became a contract actress at a salary of $1,250 a week. Zanuck enrolled her in an intensive English course and acting school. He also hired a public relations man to get her name around town. Soon lines were devoted to her in columns written by Sheilah Graham, Douglas Watt, and Walter Scott. "Remember when it used to be B.B. for Brigitte Bardot? Now it's G.G. for Genevieve Gilles, sultry new French star," proclaimed Watt. In April 1969 Genevieve appeared in a *Life* photo spread that aped *The World of Fashion*, only this time she modeled nightclothes "that evoke the spirit of Hollywood past"—including a Kitty Foyle white-collared black nightdress, a bare-midriff pajama outfit that evoked Rita Hayworth, and a Jinx Falkenburg–style T-shirt.

By April 1969, Zanuck was preparing another movie vehicle for Genevieve. According to Zanuck, who later testified about the movie in a deposition, *Hello and Goodbye* (its name was later changed to *Hello–Goodbye*) "was brought to me by a British producer . . . Ronald Neame. And he flew over to New York and we had a long discussion and I said . . . I am very interested in Miss Genevieve Gilles getting a chance. She has made only one picture, a small picture in which she starred. . . . It was only a short film, but it was popular. I wanted to see her getting ahead. I played the role of sponsoring the film. . . . I liked the script with certain reservations. I was very impressed by the director, very impressed by the whole thing. We reconciled our differences on [the script], and he spent five days rehearsing Genevieve to find out. I said, 'It is out of my hands. It is entirely in your hands, if you think she can play the part.' At the end he said, 'Yes, definitely, I think she can play the part.' "

Ronald Neame, who had just released *The Prime of Miss Jean Brodie*, was a hot producer-director. He told a different story. "The reason Darryl brought me in was because I'd rescued a picture called *Prudence and the Pill* with Deborah Kerr and David Niven. And that particular film had one of his previous girlfriends in it." Neame had coached Zanuck's protégée, Irina Demick, through a supporting role. He added, "So [Darryl] thought I was the right fellow to handle the new one." Genevieve, in Neame's opinion, had no acting talent. "I certainly know a good actress. I directed Maggie Smith, Shirley Mac-Laine, and any number of others . . . Glenda Jackson. And so I know actresses, and this girl couldn't act. No. For sure."

Dick Zanuck, then Fox's chief of worldwide production, did not think the project would do well. It was not the script that displeased him. The movie told the tale of a Frenchwoman married to a wealthy industrialist (Curt Jurgens) yet attracted to a young mechanic (Michael Crawford)—a three-way tangle that was supposed to generate both admiration for the many designer outfits the female lead would wear and laughs for the tangled bedroom farce. If done properly, Dick thought, the movie could be a solid addition to Fox's roster of movies. Dick, however, was particularly unhappy about the casting of Gene-vieve in the starring role. Twentieth Century-Fox was a public com-pany, responsible to its shareholders. Its senior executives could not spend millions of dollars just to fulfill their girlfriends' aspirations for stardom, he argued. However, he gave way before his father's opposi-tion. When the movie project was proposed to the board as part of a production schedule in May, Dick did not utter a word of displeasure, and the board approved *Hello–Goodbye*.

Zanuck told Genevieve that his son objected to the entire venture but that he had stood up for her. He was certain that Genevieve could carry the picture. He later defended the movie and its star in his deposition in a shareholders' suit. He said he thought the movie would be a great success. "If you are interested in the career of someone," he said, "you don't put them into a story that you think will hurt them.

You only put them into something that you think will help them." He pointed out that the role was a fairly simple one. Genevieve did not have to be Sarah Bernhardt to play it, he explained. He wanted her to have the opportunity of making the picture, and he would go ahead no matter what.

And so he did. Although many Fox employees furtively laughed at Zanuck's transparent effort to bring his girlfriend to the silver screen, he took the project seriously. Indeed, he was spending serious money. He decided to shoot the film at twenty-one different locations in the south of France. One of them was André Hakim's yacht, the *Sharon Marie*, named for his and Susan's third child. Fox paid Hakim $30,000 to rent the boat for a few hours, and it never showed up in the final cut. Genevieve was allowed to keep most of the haute couture costumes she wore. A leopard coat, reportedly purchased by the studio for an estimated $40,000, was sold to her for $11,000.

An additional expense was paying out Neame's contract. After four days on the set working with Genevieve, he quit. The whole project was "misguided," he said. "I realized it would be quite impossible for me to make this film because Darryl was on the set the entire time watching the girl . . . not being the president of Twentieth Century-Fox but the boyfriend of the actress." At one point, Neame was photographing a close shot of another actor, and Zanuck sat in a chair nearby watching Genevieve feed lines to the actor so he could respond. Neame decided to print the fourth take, but Zanuck came up and whispered in the director's ear, "I think she was very, very good in the previous take." He insisted Neame use that one even though Genevieve was offscreen. Neame recalled saying, " 'Darryl, she wasn't and she's not in the picture.' That was the kind of thing that made it impossible. Darryl was absolutely besotted with this girl, but at the same time had detectives all over the place to see to it that she didn't do anything she shouldn't." Zanuck was still friendly when Neame walked off the set, but he warned, "You won't be working for Twentieth Century-Fox again." Neame answered, "Well, it's a pity, Darryl, but there it is."

The reviews of *Hello–Goodbye* were downright mean. "The sole excuse for the film appears to be that it provides a showcase for Genevieve Gilles, a former Parisian model who plays the enigmatic heroine. Chicly sheathed, dripping jewelry, and mouthing her lines in a flat monotone, she certainly cannot act," wrote the *New York Times* reviewer. The movie, which cost $4 to $5 million, took in only $600,000.

Genevieve reacted to the disaster with a Gallic shrug. Only days after the *Times* attacked her performance, she lashed out at her critics in an interview with columnist Earl Wilson. Genevieve, he wrote—caustically aping her potage-thick accent in every quote—was "acidy" about those who had blasted *Hello–Goodbye*. She and "Zanoock" would someday make a great movie, and *then* she would have a "five-letter word" for *them*. She laughed when Wilson referred to the movie as a $5 million screen test. "Yeah, my screen test cost five million dolluh, and everybody's gonna tuck about me and see my screen test," she proclaimed. Zanuck still had great confidence in her ability. "He is not enough stupid to spend millions on a girl he did not trust," she said. She grandly compared herself to Elizabeth Taylor. "Some of my scenes take only two, t'ree takes. Once Elizabeth take thirty-two takes. When she started they said she was beautiful with beautiful dress and beautiful teeth but she cannot act—the same they say about me. I get so much publicity before the picture open they expect me to be another Sarah Bernhardt. I am not Sarah Bernhardt. It is because I have star treatment on my first picture that I get bad publicity."

Characteristically, Genevieve did not conclude from her disastrous debut that acting was perhaps not her métier. As usual, she claimed that she was not responsible for anything that happened to her. First she blamed Zanuck and the publicity campaign he had orchestrated. Later her bitterness at the project's failure was targeted at Dick Zanuck and his partner David Brown. Somehow, in her mind, they—not her lover—were responsible for the flop. Years afterward, she would tell a *People* magazine reporter, "It was a bad script chosen by Dick Zanuck." Of course, Dick had had little to do with the project—except to oppose it. Now, however, Dick was telling his father that he should not make any more movies with Genevieve. It was out of the question. Banks would not finance any such projects. Shareholders would have apoplexy.

On paper, Dick had the authority to enforce his requests. A year earlier, during the filming of *Hello–Goodbye*, Zanuck had agreed to let Dick have a greater say in management of the corporation. After an

August 1969 meeting, during which Dick was elected president of Twentieth Century-Fox, Genevieve could only have become increasingly distressed that Zanuck had yielded his powers to his son. She began to see conspiracies and plots. Dick and David Brown were undercutting Zanuck. She urged her lover not to let Dick push him around—or out. She didn't have to say much. Zanuck was already convinced that he had to do something about Dick. Maybe it was time for his son to go into independent production. Indeed, Helen Gurley Brown, David's wife, said that Zanuck "thought Dick and David were plotting to wrest control of the company from him and that David, in particular, was the Svengali, as he put it. That was the beginning of the forcing out of my husband and—since he would not abandon 'Svengali'—of Dick Zanuck. It was grisly. Along with getting the sudden freeze from Darryl, whom I adored and by whom I'd previously felt so loved, his young friend Genevieve left me like the skin of a molting snake. Ugly!" So influential did Helen Brown judge Genevieve to be that she thought of appealing to her to persuade Zanuck to let the two stay on.

All Zanuck's loyalties—to David Brown, whom Zanuck had hired years before, to his son, and even to Genevieve—were washed away in the relentless surge of the producer's desire to stay on top. If Genevieve's acting career threatened his control of the company, it had to go. It seems likely that it was he who told her to withdraw from her contract. She could still continue acting. With his connections, she could get parts from other studios. She certainly had talent—it was only a matter of time before others recognized the fact. On November 5, 1970, Genevieve mailed Dick a letter from New York.

> *Dear Dick:*
> *According to my contract with Twentieth Century-Fox Productions Limited, I am to be notified by December 21, 1970 regarding my option for 1971.*
> *I would appreciate it deeply if you would not exercise my option.*
> *With my best wishes.*
> *Genevieve Gillaizeau*

Dick responded by sending his father a copy of Genevieve's letter with his own note:

Dear Dad:
  I assume you know about this. Love. See you later.
  Dick

A cable came back to Dick on November 18 from his father. Zanuck claimed—rather disingenuously and not too credibly—that he hadn't known of Genevieve's resignation until after she had sent it. He added:

> BECAUSE OF OUR PERSONAL RELATIONSHIP, SHE FELT IN THESE DIFFICULT FINANCIAL TIMES FOR THE CORPORATION THAT I MIGHT BE CRITICIZED IF HER OPTION WAS EXERCISED. HOWEVER, I KNOW SHE INTENDS TO PURSUE HER CAREER. LOVE, SEE YOU LATER. DAD.

Zanuck realized that the board might want to rid Twentieth Century-Fox of the Zanucks. Dick was young; he could start anywhere. But Fox was now everything to Zanuck. He had helped to put the company together. He had to keep his position. He saw the whole affair as a battle to maintain his hegemony over the company and his superiority over his son. If he won, he would be the stronger of the two, just as he had been when he wrestled Dick years earlier.

He set about lobbying the board of directors and readily found support. Most of the men were his contemporaries. Like him, they were entrepreneurial titans who understood his need to stay with his company. What he failed to grasp—and there seemed to be more and more things that he couldn't keep tabs on—was that winning the battle against Dick did not necessarily mean that he would really be able to retain all his power. Indeed, in the board's view, keeping the older Zanuck on was merely a ceremonial gesture—a kindness rendered to an old war-horse who had served the company well. They didn't expect that he would really run things anymore.

So when the board convened at the end of December 1970, Dick and his colleague David Brown were forced to resign. Zanuck later claimed in deposition testimony that he had abstained from voting on the report of the three-man committee that had demanded the pair's resignation. Records of the meeting showed that, in fact, he had voted to oust his son.

Dick surmised to his friends that Genevieve would probably be very happy about his dismissal, and he was right. When Zanuck reported the news to Genevieve that night, she was jubilant. What surprised her, however, was that Zanuck seemed downcast. Perhaps the ramifications of the corporate directors' work had begun to sink in. He was still CEO, but he had not been given the presidency of the company, Dick's old position. The board's executive committee was to take on the former president's responsibilities. Further, Zanuck was invited to serve *subject to the pleasure of the board*. He could be fired, just as his son had been.

The New Year's Eve "execution" of Richard Zanuck brought forth a surge of newspaper headlines. Darryl Zanuck maintained throughout that he had had nothing to do with instigating Dick's ouster. As one reporter noted, however, "Hardly anybody believes that." Many blamed Genevieve for the rift between Zanuck and his son. *Time* declared that Dick had not found enough jobs for his father's friend Genevieve Gilles. Vincent Canby, writing in the *New York Times*, also questioned why the company "saw fit to spend over $3 million on something called *Hello–Goodbye*, starring Genevieve Gilles, an actress whose chief claim to fame is her friendship with the elder Zanuck."

The cruelest gibe of all came from Walter Scott's "Personality Parade" in the *Washington Post*. In answer to a question as to whether the Zanucks fell out "because the old man would not give up his latest French babe, Genevieve Gilles," Scott responded: "Twentieth Century-Fox has come upon hard times. It lost more than $20 million last year. It owes more than $70 million to the Chase Manhattan Bank, Morgan Guaranty Trust, two other banks, and a major insurance company. . . . It is just a question of time, however, before Wall Street ousts Darryl Zanuck. The sun has set on his type of highly personal and Freudian corporate management. The banks want their money. They are not interested in the rise and fall of Darryl Zanuck's sex life."

The rest of the Zanuck family also blamed Genevieve for Dick's ouster. They all agreed that it was the Frenchwoman who had torn the family—and the company—apart. Virginia agreed, though she sided with her son. She was so angry with her husband she could scarcely contain herself. She broke her accustomed silence to tell columnist Ed Sullivan: "My son is respected by the entire industry. But the company is now run by a board of wishy-washy old men who fear Darryl and who are scared to cross him." Zanuck's betrayal of his son mirrored his betrayal of her, and her resentment of Genevieve intensified her need to take action. She announced that she would go to New York to fight for Richard.

Zanuck could not shrug off Virginia's implied threat. Under their 1957 separation agreement, Virginia still held 100,000 shares of stock in Twentieth Century-Fox. A trust set up under the 1957 separation agreement granted her husband voting rights; but he had allowed the trust to lapse. Now her lawyer was arguing that she had the right to vote the shares any way she wished. Zanuck grew more and more pettish, thinking about what she might do. Already there was a corporate takeover threat in the offing: soon after Dick was fired, MGM had made a bid to merge with Fox. Zanuck was absolutely against the idea. When David Merrick, one of the advocates of the proposed merger, asked to use Zanuck's podium at a shareholders' meeting, Zanuck declined permission. "Mr. Merrick, it will be a long time before you make it up to this dais," he announced stiffly. Now, however, his own wife might use his stock to make him suffer a takeover by another studio.

Zanuck began to try to reconsolidate his power. Soon after New Year's 1971 he wrote an open letter to Fox shareholders in the monthly newsletter, the *International Motion Picture Exhibitor*. While noting that "your company has figured prominently in the news in recent weeks," he failed to mention much, other than the fact that his son had submitted his resignation. "We have made agonizing but necessary decisions. The decks are now clear. The organization is unified around the single objective of making our company profitable again."

Genevieve confidently pronounced that Zanuck would pull another victory out of the ashes. She proclaimed to Earl Wilson (who again poked fun at her accent), "Zanooock weel save Fawx all over again, the third time—ee weel ween." Yet there was good reason for doubt. By mid-March 1971, a proxy battle was looming. Three Fox shareholders, who said they represented groups of dissidents, had joined forces to oust Zanuck and the entire board of directors.

The group claimed to control over 500,000 shares of Fox stock, out of about 8 million. They were hoping that Dick Zanuck would help their cause by persuading his mother to throw them her proxies. Dick and Virginia were said to control about 200,000 shares. (In fact, he owned only 30,000 shares outright to which his father had voting rights.) When added to the proxies gathered by the insurgents, they might swing the vote against Zanuck and his management team. The dissidents gained greater fuel for their campaign when it was announced at the end of March that Fox had lost over $50 million in its last quarter and $77 million overall in 1970.

Confusion was to beset the dissidents, however. In early April, Fox announced that Dennis Stanfill, the former controller, would be taking over as president of the company—not Darryl Zanuck, as many had expected. It was announced that the old man had given up his position as CEO. He would serve only as chairman of the board and concentrate on the production of motion pictures. Dick, already a senior vice-president at Warner Brothers, was certain that Zanuck's title attrition was a gradual stripping of power engineered by the board. They are "plucking [my father's] feathers . . . taking one toenail at a time. He developed a monster. He'll be completely out soon." Of his resignation, his father, however, would only say, "You want to know how I feel? I feel tired."

He must have felt exhausted and defeated. The press release that proclaimed that he was giving up his job as CEO "at his own request" was a face-saving lie that Zanuck insisted on inserting. Worry had been building among the directors that Fox would be lost to the insurgents if Zanuck didn't step down. The company was deep in debt and had defaulted on its bank loans. A sticking point for many wavering shareholders, according to Dennis Stanfill, was Zanuck's continued presence as chief executive officer. Already the Dreyfus Fund had voted its proxies for the dissidents, and other big shareholders were threatening to follow Dreyfus's lead. At the April board meeting, the directors had pulled a cool maneuver. Instead of firing Zanuck or asking him to resign, they simply eliminated the position of CEO. Zanuck's remaining duty as chairman of the board was to preside over corporate meetings. And it had already been decided that a lawyer—not he—would run the May shareholders' meeting in Delaware. He had been stripped even of his ceremonial duties.

Zanuck's removal from operational responsibility did not quiet the dissidents. There was no reason it should. With him or without him, the company was in default to its bankers on several loans, and the banks were clamoring for repayment. A dissident group called the Twentieth Century-Fox Stockholders Protective Committee began mailing out brochures to the studio's investors urging them to vote against management. The brochure listed several reasons for investors to vote against the management team, including giant losses, a dip in the stock price from a high of $41.75 in 1969 to $14.12 in 1971, cessation of dividend payments since 1969, loan defaults, and "disappointing returns on high-budget spectaculars." It advocated a $2 million budgetary limit on each movie. There was a short list of nine Fox movie hits—and a long list of twenty-four losers. *Hello–Goodbye* was eighth on the list at $3 million in losses. Much higher on the losers list were *Hello, Dolly!* ($13.7 million), *The Only Game in Town* ($7.7 million), *Justine* ($6.8 million), and *Staircase* ($5.4 million).

Cautiously the dissidents sidestepped the "Richard Zanuck issue"— in public, anyway. If they claimed he was responsible for Fox losses, he might vote his shares with the management team. If they claimed he was not responsible, then what was he doing while he was president of the corporation? Dick, meanwhile, said he couldn't make up his mind about what he was going to do. He, too, was receiving proxies from shareholders who had objected to his December firing. Nobody was certain how he would vote them. He seemed to be waiting for the dissidents to invite him to head their slate of candidates for the board. No public invitation was ever issued, however.

The Fox management team responded to the dissidents' attack. An ad appeared in the *New York Times* on May 5, 1971, reporting that not only had *Patton* won the Academy Award in 1970 for Best Picture but that two new productions—*The Panic in Needle Park* and *Walkabout*—had been invited to the Cannes Film Festival. Stanfill planned to limit all productions to a $2.5 million budget. No more *Tora! Tora! Tora!'s*, he announced. That was an empty gesture. The banks threatened to call in the company's loans if Fox did not stay within that limit. Ironically, the program of the insurgents and that of the management team seemed pretty much the same.

Virginia announced that she was throwing her support to the dissidents. Richard Zanuck a few days later revealed that Fox had offered him $1 million to settle his employment contract in exchange for proxies for the stock he and his mother controlled. Fox, however, claimed that it was Richard who approached the company lawyers, not the other way around. Both sides declared that they had rejected such a deal. Virginia, however, was determined to vote her husband out. "He's getting the same treatment from this group [the shareholders] that he gave my son," she said. "I want to see this whole board of directors out."

Yet, a few weeks before the annual meeting at which the battle was to be waged, Dick flew to New York to try to persuade his father to throw in his lot with the dissidents. If he didn't, warned Dick, his father would find himself completely out of a job. Zanuck remained unswerving in his loyalty to management and his distrust of his son. Like many people grown querulous with age, he was suspicious of someone he should have trusted—his son—and trusting of those who should have aroused his suspicion. His fellow directors had been telling him that the insurgents, once in control, would liquidate the company and sell its assets, and Zanuck bought that story. He couldn't abide the idea. There would be no place for him if the insurgents won, because the company itself would disappear.

On May 18, 1971, shareholders, Fox executives, and reporters converged on the Playhouse Theatre, part of the DuPont Hotel in Wilmington, Delaware. The much publicized shareholders' meeting was not very well attended, and the impassioned speeches echoed in the huge room. Questions from the floor were angry and pointed. One participant yelled out, "This meeting is a lot more interesting than a lot of Fox pictures." Richard had appeared to vote his mother's shares with the insurgents; ironically, he could not vote his own because Zanuck had retained the rights to do so himself. Although the contenders were present and ready for battle, the outcome was not clear. The tabulation of the voting proved to be too complicated to complete in one day; the results were scheduled to be announced in June at Fox's New York headquarters.

Zanuck produced a surprise, however. At the meeting, he disclosed that he would not run for his old job as chairman of the board. He had been given a new position—chairman emeritus, a title that carried little power. He gave an emotional speech: "I'll continue to be very active. I've known this business from the silent days when I started as a boy of nineteen writing scripts. I've lived with this industry. I'll never live without continuing to make a contribution."

At the meeting, a newsman asked Zanuck if the Fox management had dropped him. He replied definitively, "Under no circumstances."

In fact, they *had* dropped him. He had arrived in Wilmington the day before fully expecting to run for reelection as chairman of the board. On the afternoon of May 17, however, two board members, Harry McIntyre and William Gossett, had visited Zanuck in his hotel suite. Management had been working to firm up votes for their side. Several large blocs of stock would go their way—but only if Zanuck agreed not to run. Said McIntyre, "His resignation was the price of management continuing. So we told Zanuck, 'You may as well agree, because if we lose, you will be out anyway. The other team will toss you out.'" Zanuck quietly said he understood. He agreed to resign. He and a Fox public relations man worked out the final wording. Gossett and McIntyre rushed to inform Stanfill, who began telephoning wavering proxy holders to notify them that their nemesis was gone for good.

Zanuck dined alone that night as his fellow directors busily rounded up votes. Around eleven o'clock, Dick called him from California. In testimony months later for a private investigation by the Securities and Exchange Commission, Zanuck recalled, "[Dick] was making every effort to persuade and plead with me to vote my shares with the other side, meaning the dissidents, and that I could name my own ticket, I could do whatever I wanted . . . president of the company . . . or anything like that." His son went on to observe that "what had been done to himself and David Brown was being multiplied and done to me and that this whole scheme had been devised by Gossett and— [Dick] was quite violent on the telephone. He begged me to resist . . . this movement to demean me and take me out of a position of authority and to put me into a position where I would be embarrassed. I had brought the company back and now it was being taken away from me. That's a digest of a rather hysterical talk." Dick's central message was "Don't go for what they suggest."

There was no testimony to Dick's reaction when his father told him that he already had gone for what they suggested. Zanuck told his son that he would not vote with the insurgents and hung up the telephone. Apparently worried, however, he summoned Gossett to his room late that night. Gossett, according to Zanuck, indicated that his removal from office would be temporary—just to allow management to win the proxy contest. "His explanation," said Zanuck, "was that I was, rightly or wrongly, the chief officer of the company, and that while he himself knew that I had inherited problems from Richard Zanuck and David Brown, I couldn't go out and convince anybody I had. . . . The thing to solve the situation was to do what I had"—that is, resign.

In the middle of this discussion came another call from Dick. He asked his father to speak to Gossett directly. What ensued was a screaming match. Gossett asserted that Dick was doing his father a disservice, and eventually the two slammed down their phones. Whatever Dick had said, however, changed Gossett's approach. He threw a couple of bones Zanuck's way. The elderly mogul would be given the title of chairman emeritus of the board and a two-picture production deal—balm to Zanuck's ego.

Zanuck didn't admit that his son had helped him save face. He thought, he said, that "Richard Zanuck was calling for a double purpose, that he knew the dissidents were going to lose and that he was twisting the thing around to confuse me." The next day Zanuck voted his stock as well as that of his three children for the management team that had ousted him. Zanuck was not without anger. Henry McIntyre had traveled in the mogul's limousine to Delaware. When the meeting concluded the next day, he expected to ride back to New York with Zanuck. "He wouldn't let me in the car," said McIntyre. "I had to get a taxi to take me all the way back to Manhattan."

*   *   *

Genevieve reacted to Zanuck's ouster as though she herself had been fired. Being asked to resign is a normal, though sometimes ugly, part of business life, especially in the film industry. To her, however, the outcome had not been inevitable. She seemed to believe that it was a conspiracy directed by Virginia and Dick Zanuck. In Genevieve's view, Zanuck was extraordinary, but the Fox board had fired him as though he were an ordinary employee who had outlived his usefulness. Part of her anger stemmed from a fear and hatred of Dick Zanuck. She was certain he had plotted to get back at his father by removing him from the board. She wasn't certain how he had done it, but he was behind it all, she was sure.

Zanuck tried to tell himself that he was resigned to his retirement. However, in his heart, he was fearful. He did not know what he would do with himself. For the past half-century, he had devoted virtually every thought and action to movies. Actually, he could have parlayed his new situation into a role that meant something. This might have been an ideal time for him to step back, become an elder statesman, teach young people what he knew. But Zanuck only knew how to be a mogul. He was determined to continue making movies, and that was that. He would work out an independent-producer contract with Fox, he would turn out a major hit, and he would be back on top once again.

Genevieve was not so sanguine. Since she had met him in the mid-sixties, he had personally supervised only two pictures—the disastrous *Hello–Goodbye* and *Tora! Tora! Tora!*, which was nearly as terrible. There was no way he could turn out another *Longest Day*. His ability to charge his travel and other expenses to the company was curtailed. His employment contract with Fox would end in only two years, and after that, he was to receive only $50,000 a year as a company consultant. His prospects were lousy.

In June 1971, when the shareholders reconvened at Twentieth Century-Fox's New York headquarters to learn that management had won a clear majority, Zanuck already had plans. He had two years to go on his contract, and he was going to work them out—either as a consultant for the studio in recruiting new personnel or as an independent producer. He declared that he had a Spanish-flavor script in mind, but he *could* shoot it in Mexico. That way, he asserted—in supine harmony with the new fad for cost-cutting—he could take advantage of the Los Angeles studio, a place he hadn't visited for any length of time in years. It only remained for the company to work out a few minor contractual details. He and Fox ultimately settled on a rather sad little two-picture deal, but three months later Fox had still not approved Zanuck's contract, budget, or authority. He was raring to go, he told *Variety*, and if Fox didn't settle matters to his satisfaction, they would have to talk to his new attorneys.

In truth, he had almost nothing to do. A tiny ex-giant, he would walk his two Yorkies, Tina and Lisa, in Central Park. The Zanuck-green Jaguar with the lucky DFZ-13 plates was spotted in front of Fox's New York offices with a dent in its side. Said Genevieve, "When he lost his studio, this was the beginning of the end for him as a man. He was heartbroken, because the studio was his life, and after . . . there was no work. This is what kill him is because there was no work. There were no more telexes—after hundreds each day—no more offers, and this man was a workaholic." He suffered another loss as well. In the fall of 1971, Bella Darvi committed suicide in Monte Carlo. Only forty-four years old, she took her life by opening the gas jets on her stove. Her body was not found until a week later. All the great days and fast times were crashing to an end.

Zanuck seemed to be thinking about his own mortality. In three years he had dictated three different wills. Beginning in 1969, Genevieve had become a beneficiary. Her share of Zanuck's money was considerable—50 percent of his portfolio of tax-exempt securities, or about $500,000; the balance would be shared equally by his ten grandchildren. The rest of Zanuck's assets were to be left to Darrylin, Richard, and Susan. In September 1971, Zanuck decided to update his will to include his youngest grandchild, Craig Savineau, who was already four years old. Apparently Zanuck had forgotten about the toddler until then. In his new will, Zanuck reduced Genevieve's portion of his tax-exempts to 45 percent to give Craig a 5 percent share along with the other grandchildren. He wrote Dick out of the will completely. By way of recompense for Genevieve's "loss," Zanuck made her a "residuary legatee." In other words, she would share in the balance of the estate with Darrylin and Susan. Although his daughters were to get a greater share of the money—three-quarters—their shares would be held in trust. They would receive only the income. By contrast, Genevieve would be paid her inheritance outright—in cash.

Zanuck was not to be allowed to fade into obscurity without fuss. Already, dissident shareholders, angered by their loss in the proxy battle, had announced that they were suing Fox and Zanuck and the board of directors. The SEC had already subpoenaed records to investigate irregularities in the proxies, and in a New York court, the Stockholders Protective Committee sued the directors of Twentieth Century-Fox, Richard and Darryl Zanuck and David Merrick. The legal complaint was a roster of the shareholders' gripes. Among other things, the plaintiffs accused Darryl Zanuck of causing Fox to lay out large sums "for his personal benefit under the guise of paying for expenses of the corporation." Listed were the operation of his cars, travel, entertainment, rent, and other living expenses. Since April 1971, he had done nothing for the corporation, and all the expenses were a gift and a waste, they contended. Zanuck had also frittered away the corporation's assets by making *Hello–Goodbye* "solely to provide a starring role for the . . . friend of Zanuck"—that is, for Genevieve. Further, the complaint declared, "At great expense, the corporation in or about May 1967 brought about the resignation of Seymour Poe, its executive vice-president, in pursuance of the . . . plan of Zanuck to arrange succession of his son Richard." Richard Zanuck, plaintiffs charged, had been overpaid. The corporation had had an option to renew his 1966 contract for a salary of $165,000 a year, but had instead consistently raised his pay all the way up to $350,000 even though the pictures he produced "were notably lacking in box office appeal." All the defendants denied any wrongdoing.

That was not the only lawsuit in which Zanuck was a defendant. Richard also sued Twentieth Century-Fox and his father. Fox had not come to an agreement with him to pay out his, Brown's, or Linda Harrison's contracts, which, he said, were wrongfully terminated. Indeed, Linda had been pregnant at the time, and Fox had ungallantly fired her anyway, the complaint implied. In his complaint, Richard dropped the fact that Fox had declined to pay out his contract because of claims that the corporation said it had on him.

Zanuck's future seemed to be full of depositions and subpoenas. Indeed, he once joked to his daughter Darrylin that her brother and all his friends were suing him. And he seemed no nearer to producing a movie than he had been months earlier. Although the technicalities of his Fox contract were finally ironed out late in the fall of 1971, he was vague about his future productions except to say that they would be shot in Europe—maybe. He definitely agreed to shelve plans on a big production, *The Day Christ Died*, because the biblical epic would cost too much—about $5 million.

*   *   *

In January 1972 Zanuck visited his dentist. He told the doctor that he had felt a soreness around his molar. The dentist discovered a suspicious lesion. A biopsy revealed that it was cancer and might have spread to the lymph nodes. In early February 1972 Zanuck was admitted to Columbia Presbyterian Hospital in New York for surgery to excise the cancer from his jaw.

The operation was a lengthy and complicated one. The surgeon, Dr. Carl Feind, removed part of Zanuck's jaw, two teeth, part of his tongue, and some muscles, lymph nodes, and veins from his neck. The surgery was performed from inside Zanuck's mouth, because, said the surgeon, "he was very concerned about being disfigured." Dr. Feind managed to maintain the symmetry of Zanuck's face—"he had no deformity"—but there was a scar on his neck. Recovery was slow and painful. At first he was disoriented and uncomfortable, but he improved steadily and was released from the hospital on February 24.

So estranged had Zanuck become from his family that he did not immediately tell them that he had been ill or hospitalized. On hospital forms, he listed Genevieve as his next of kin. Dr. Feind believed that Genevieve visited Zanuck every day; in fact, she didn't even stay in New York the whole time. On January 30 she flew to Los Angeles to audition for a Paramount TV movie. Zanuck wanted her to have her chance, so she went. Zanuck acted tough and ordered her to go. No doubt he hoped she would stay but was too proud to ask. It was only after she had won a part from Paramount that she thought better of leaving Zanuck by himself. She declined the role and flew back to New York.

Only one other person took time to drop by Zanuck's sickbed: his secretary Vincenza Argentino. Nobody else knew where he was. On February 18, a maid at the Plaza Hotel found that Zanuck's suite had been burglarized. Six paintings—three of them studio fakes—had been cut from their frames. There was no evidence of forced entry, and detectives concluded that the theft was "an inside job," because the burglars seemed to know that Zanuck was not due to return and surprise them. However, the reason for his hospitalization was kept quiet. The newspapers reported that he was undergoing treatment for a broken ankle.

Back at the Plaza after his release, Zanuck couldn't eat solid food for about a month, had trouble sleeping, and complained of depression. His doctor prescribed Elavil to lift his mood. Zanuck had still not revealed that he had cancer. In May *Variety* noted, in great detail, that

Zanuck had become a daily jogger in Central Park to rehabilitate his legs. "He had been laid up for over three weeks with the swelling from ankle to the knees as a result of the second break on the same right ankle, originally from skiing but last winter as a result of a fall while getting out of the bathtub at the Plaza." He bragged that he jogged two and a half miles with his dogs Lisa and Tina, from 59th Street and Fifth Avenue up to 110th Street, where his chauffeur would pick him up. He admitted that he made several stops along the way: "What slows me down is some of the wildest wide-open lovemaking. . . . It's not to be believed. . . . The squad cars are not too interested in boy-meets-girl and/or boy-meets-boy, and I see a lot of that also. If I stop and gawk, it just doesn't faze them."

He was still announcing plans—for a movie based on an Italian novel called *The Short Cut*, a property he had purchased in 1960 about Mussolini's campaign in Ethiopia. He planned to shoot the movie in the Basque region of France. Time was running out, however. His contract with Fox would expire in May 1973. His arrangement with Fox could only be a one-picture deal—scarcely a deal at all.

Behind Zanuck's brave facade, his life was a shambles. He was in pain much of the time. During a September visit to Dr. Feind, Zanuck complained of memory loss. Said Feind, "He said he would attend board meetings, which he was supposed to run, and he would sit there and he couldn't remember what he was supposed to be bringing up, and he found it rather embarrassing unless somebody prompted him to tell him what was going on." At the time, Zanuck was not presiding over any Fox board meetings; he merely attended them in his honorary capacity. He returned to the doctor about a month later to report that his memory was worse. Recalled Dr. Feind, "He couldn't even remember any of the drugs he was taking." The physician was also concerned because Zanuck had delayed visiting the dentist for reconstruction of his missing teeth. By this time, Zanuck had also changed his cover story. Now he told people that he was nursing a fractured jaw, which was injured when he fell in the shower. His next movie would be shot in Portugal—not Mexico or France.

Genevieve was one of the few who knew of Zanuck's misery and his memory lapses. After his operation, she recalled, "he went down and down and down." There was a long spell when he refused to go out. Before, she said, it had been a premiere, a screening, or a party every night. Now she had to practically force him to leave the suite. He would dine privately with Genevieve, but he rarely went elsewhere because he was self-conscious about his face. "Like there was a hole," said Genevieve, "and he was always very conscious of the way he look." When Nelson Rockefeller invited him to a soirée, Zanuck declined in a note, according to Genevieve, "because he look like a freak. This was his expression." He hung around his Plaza suite all day long, wearing the babydoll pajamas made infamous by Juliette Greco. He watched "Hogan's Heroes" and other sitcoms and fiddled idly with the buttons on the TV set.

Genevieve's life with Zanuck had become boring, dreary, and frightening—anything but glamorous. He would take walks in the park and forget where he was. Twice he got lost and couldn't remember where he lived. He would lose his footing and trip. A few times the police had to bring him back to the Plaza. Genevieve did not know what to do. His behavior was frustrating, infuriating. She couldn't help but get angry with him. She tried to interest him in scripts and movies, but he couldn't seem to get involved. Sometimes he would tell her he had read a script, but then she would find out he hadn't. He would babble on about events that had occurred decades ago. Said Genevieve, "When he talked about playing polo, the doctor explained to me he remembers thirty years ago." He was cantankerous and paranoid. The Plaza maids couldn't get in his rooms to clean; he would refuse them entry. He wouldn't allow anybody to take a suit to the cleaners. He was constantly fretting about the dogs; he worried that they were lost or might get lost. Even when the chauffeur accompanied him on his walks with the dogs, he was anxious about where they were.

There wasn't much togetherness left between Zanuck and Genevieve. Their life had constricted too much for her. Expensive living was out. He was off the company payroll, and he had to pick up most expenses himself. He didn't think much about presents anymore. Once in a while, he gave Genevieve some cash and instructed her to buy herself something. However, the days of diamonds and sable were clearly over. Zanuck couldn't attend many parties because he was too anxious and confused. He didn't recognize some people he knew, and he was afraid that others would find out about his memory lapses. Genevieve attended some premieres on her own or with Fox executive

Christian Ferry or Prince John Radziwill. When she told Zanuck that she had found an escort for a party, he didn't seem to mind. So, after that, she didn't always bother to inform him.

She could only be desperate for relief from a life she had never sought, catering to the needs of a near-invalid. She eagerly grasped at modeling assignments—anything that took her away from him. She traveled constantly, and the trips were a welcome relief from the sad state into which Zanuck had sunk. The couple took only one trip together—to Lisbon and Paris in the fall of 1972. Edward Leggewie, Zanuck's one-time aide-de-camp in Paris, described the trip as Zanuck's pilgrimage to all the places that he loved. His health was bad then, and Leggewie thought that Zanuck's mind was starting to go. "It was a bit sad," he recalled.

During Genevieve's absences, Zanuck was marooned. She was his only friend, his last possible connection to the active working world, and she had turned away from him. She rarely called, she later said, because she was worried about the cost. Zanuck would grow frustrated at the long silences. In April 1972, during her Paris trip, he cabled her at the Plaza Athénée:

DEAR GENEVIEVE: HAVE TELEPHONED FOUR TIMES TODAY
AT EXACT HOUR YOU SUGGESTED AND HAVE BEEN UNABLE
TO REACH YOU. I STILL LIVE AT THE PLAZA HOTEL, PLAZA
9-3000, SUITE 1125. WILL AWAIT YOUR CALL.

He was so embarrassed to have to make such a pathetic plea for attention that he couldn't bear to make the cable a Darryl F. Zanuck production. He signed it, LOVE, LISA AND TINA, for his dogs.

In November of 1972, Zanuck made the first of three appearances for a deposition in the shareholders' lawsuit. He could reply to the questions fairly well if he could keep his answers general. He was fuzzy about many details, however. The transcript revealed that he couldn't give the exact address of Twentieth Century-Fox in New York and didn't remember when he had started working for the company. He wasn't sure how many shares of Fox stock he owned. At one point he said, "I think I was chairman of the board—wasn't I?" When questioned about his personal expenses, he accurately responded to his inquisitor that they were billed to the corporation but then sorted out and paid by him later; yet, except for clothing, he couldn't remember any personal expenses.

Robert Laufer, the Paul Weiss Rifkind Wharton and Garrison attorney who represented Zanuck at the deposition, did not note any troubling memory lapses or loss of control. "He was quite his own man," said Laufer, recalling with some exasperation that the mogul had annoyingly answered questions his attorney instructed him to ignore. Rather than have Zanuck reply to many details he couldn't remember, Laufer would simply stipulate the facts. "It was a very difficult and aggravating period of Mr. Zanuck's life," said the lawyer. "My role was not to tax him." Perhaps the old fox was merely being evasive to stall the examination? Responded Laufer, "He wasn't about to help Mr. Wolf," the opposition's attorney.

Only a few months later, in January 1973, Zanuck's memory was worse. Dr. Feind was certain that he was becoming senile—a condition then considered a normal part of aging by the medical profession. Feind decided to check out Zanuck's complaints about memory loss. He referred the mogul to a neurologist, Dr. Carmine T. Vicale. The specialist gave Zanuck a complete neurological examination and had him undergo a series of laboratory tests. He concluded that Zanuck was suffering an organic mental impairment of an uncertain cause. The brain had been affected by some metabolic or biochemical disorder, he concluded.

Vicale suspected that the problem might have been aggravated by arteriosclerosis or cerebral hypoxia or "unsupervised drug and alcohol intake" which would inhibit the supply of oxygen going to the brain. Additionally, Zanuck's tongue had a tendency to push forward involuntarily—another sign of mental impairment from aging. Vicale did not prescribe any treatment or new medications, because his patient was already taking Elavil and "Valium excessively." Genevieve accompanied Zanuck on a second visit to Vicale in late February. His memory was faltering, she told the doctor, and he often slept the day away. When he was awake, Zanuck seemed confused and disoriented. Vicale instructed Genevieve to find a companion to care for Zanuck. "Miss Gilles told me about his forgetfulness and his unreliability to take care of himself. And it was evident to me from discussing with him that he was not capable of looking after himself." Genevieve responded that she knew a forty-five-year-old nurse who might be right for the job.

Somehow she never got around to hiring anybody. It was difficult to find someone, and Zanuck didn't want a nurse, anyway. So, instead, she went on another trip. Zanuck was lonely. One night during Genevieve's absence, he called his secretary Vincenza Argentino at home. "He was very upset," said Argentino. "This was about one o'clock in the morning. He was very upset because he had not heard from [Genevieve] that day, and he said some things about her, and that the reason for his call was that he wanted me to change his will. . . . From what it sounded to me, yes, he wanted to change his will about her. . . . He started off with that he wanted to see his attorney in the morning because he was changing the will and that he was very upset." Zanuck began heaping insults on Genevieve. Added Argentino, "And at the time . . . he started saying things about Genevieve, you know of how he met her and where. . . . Well, he told me that he met her in a club, that she was working in a club, and that he was at the club and met her there."

When a new will was made up that February 1973, however, Genevieve was still a major beneficiary. He seemed to have no intention of changing his mind and giving more to his family. At the same time, Zanuck and Virginia settled a dispute over their joint property. The bones of contention this time were ten insurance policies whose beneficiaries were Darrylin's four children, Susan's three children, Virginia, Dick's younger daughter, Janet, and Edward Leggewie. Zanuck had taken out a $150,000 loan against the $500,000 in policies, and the companies were asking Virginia for repayment. The outcome of the dispute was not friendly. Zanuck was to repay the loan. He also agreed to Virginia's demand to supply her with a statement of money due him under employment agreements with Twentieth Century-Fox. The two further waived rights to inherit from each other. It appeared as though their long-standing separation would continue forever.

Zanuck's condition worsened. Vinnie Argentino, not Genevieve, eventually hired nurses. Only days after he signed his new will and his agreements with Virginia, Zanuck sank into "a very, very depressed and appalling state," according to Argentino. She had been away on a long weekend, and this was a routine morning visit to the Plaza after returning. She rang the doorbell to the suite, but no one answered. She took out her key to try to get in, but the door was double-locked. Worried that something had happened to her boss, she summoned one of the Plaza security guards. Zanuck, she said, "had been in bed and had been there, I would imagine, for approximately three or four days. And there was a lot of glasses around the apartment . . . and it was a mess. . . . The dogs had made on the bed, and he was right in the middle of it, and it was not very nice." Zanuck was awake but incoherent.

She immediately telephoned one of Zanuck's attorneys, Richard Paul, who instructed Argentino to contact Zanuck's doctor and to hire nurses to take care of him. Argentino continued to make daily visits to bring over the mail and help Zanuck answer it. His condition did not seem to improve. He constantly complained to Argentino about the nurses, but Argentino managed to keep him from firing them. About six weeks passed, and on March 29, one of the nurses called Argentino at the Fox office to inform her that the Plaza's house physician had examined Zanuck and recommended hospitalization. Argentino rushed over to the hotel and found Zanuck being helped into his Jaguar by his chauffeur. She got in, rode with Zanuck to the hospital, and helped with the admitting forms, which again listed Genevieve Gillaizeau as next of kin. They also noted that she was "presently not here." Paul notified Richard Zanuck that his father had been hospitalized. Argentino called Darrylin in Mexico and notified Susan in France.

Zanuck's two doctors concluded that he was suffering from a variety of maladies: acute urinary retention, fecal impaction, organic brain syndrome, and arteriosclerosis. The diagnosis of the last two ailments was based on clinical observation of his behavior. Said Dr. Feind, "He was confused, he was agitated, he was uncooperative. When questioned, he didn't know where he was. He didn't know where he lived. He was unable to care for himself. He certainly couldn't take any medications without supervision."

Within two days Zanuck's children arrived in New York. Dick flew in from L.A., Darrylin from Acapulco, and Susan—with her eldest son, André Hakim, Jr.—came from Revest-du-Bion in the south of France. Feind gave them the news. The hospital had cleared up the urinary and bowel problems. Zanuck also received blood transfusions to ease his anemia. However, the memory lapses would continue. "His mental state did not improve," Dr. Feind said. Zanuck's chart noted, "Confusion continues. Patient does appear to resent routine of hospital. . . . Patient talking about getting out and back to the hotel, watching TV, but is very confused, rambling . . . agitated." Feind pointed out to the family that Zanuck "was unable to take care of himself, and that he should be taken care of, and I didn't think the Plaza Hotel would be the place for him to go back to. I told the family that if he were around familiar surroundings and taken care of and had people waiting on him and looking into his needs, that he would get along well. This is necessary for him to get along. I did not anticipate any improvement as far as mental state is concerned."

After a few days, Genevieve turned up in New York. She was astounded, she later said, to find Zanuck in the hospital because, to her mind, there was absolutely nothing wrong with him. She would never have left, she later said, had she thought he was truly ill. Of course, she could hardly have escaped being aware of Zanuck's memory problems, since she had been advised by his doctor to hire a nurse. Genevieve accompanied Darrylin to the hospital and presented Zanuck with a sculpture of an elephant. She had bought it in Africa for him, she said. What she had been doing in Africa was a question no one asked and she didn't volunteer to answer. However, she had sent Vinnie Argentino several telegrams during her absence asking to be apprised of Zanuck's condition.

Genevieve learned from Dr. Feind that Susan, Dick, and Darrylin planned to take their father to his estate in Palm Springs. She later said in court testimony that she thought the visit was to be temporary—until Zanuck recovered his health. Later he and she would return to New York. Apparently, she never took note of the doctor's diagnosis—that her lover suffered from organic brain syndrome, that his mental capacity would not improve, and that he could never live on his own again at the Plaza Hotel or anywhere else.

Zanuck's family and his mistress were to travel to California together. On April 7, 1973, the day the producer was to be released, Darrylin said she arrived at her father's hospital room and found Genevieve dressing him and preparing to spirit him away in the Jaguar. Genevieve said she was just helping him. Dick, already back in Los Angeles, had booked the group on a direct New York–Palm

Springs flight, and somehow the entire party—Susan, Darrylin, Gene-vieve, Zanuck, Vinnie Argentino, André Hakim, Jr., and the two dogs, Lisa and Tina—got together and boarded in the first-class section.

During the tedious flight, the group became acrimonious and anxious. Darrylin and Genevieve had a spat over Zanuck's pills, and at one point the elderly mogul had tried to exit the airplane while it was still aloft. A tranquilizer lifted his spirits, and as soon as the plane landed and the doorway was open, Zanuck grabbed his dogs and bounded down the boarding steps and across the tarmac to greet his wife and son. Said Vinnie Argentino, "He walked with his wife. He took her arm. They went arm in arm. They walked away."

Genevieve had trouble accepting what seemed to have happened. Indeed, the event was difficult to comprehend. Her mentor, her companion, her lover, her provider of eight years, had suddenly, without warning, rejoined the wife he had abandoned nearly two decades earlier. Such an outcome seemed impossible. True, errant men often crawled back to their wives—but not after so lengthy a separation. How could a man desert a youthful, shapely mistress for a woman who was now seventy-one years old? Surely if Zanuck had read a script for this scene, he would have rejected it as unrealistic.

When Genevieve finally arrived at Ric-Su-Dar an hour later, Zanuck was already ensconced in the living room eating cheese and crackers and presiding over the family domain as though he had never left it. Virginia, victorious at last, happily passed around hors d'oeuvres. Genevieve tried to take control. Imperiously, she demanded to know where she and Zanuck would sleep. Dick told her to shut up, and she started screaming at him. Zanuck didn't take her side; he warned her to control herself. She angrily threw his cane at him and ran from the room crying.

Outside, by the pool, she sobbed angrily. Susan joined her and patted her on the shoulder in an attempt to comfort her. Genevieve decided to leave. But Dick barred her way to the door when she tried to reenter the house to say good-bye to Zanuck. The two scuffled, and Darrylin and Vinnie Argentino joined the fray. Soon everyone was embroiled, kicking, shoving, pulling hair, and yelling. Virginia screamed at her son from the open window: "Don't strike her! Don't strike her!" Genevieve left in a taxi, clutching her jewelry box in her arms. She never had a chance to bid farewell to Zanuck.

In the taxi she began rewriting what had happened: Zanuck had not returned of his own volition to his wife; he had been kidnapped by his son and daughters. She had not left the house voluntarily; she had been thrown off the grounds. At least, that's what she told the Palm Springs police, whom she visited right after leaving Ric-Su-Dar. She learned later from a cop who had been dispatched to the house, however, that Zanuck said he was staying with his wife. The policeman handed her a fur coat she had left behind.

Her extraordinary life with Zanuck seemed to have drawn to a close.

But Genevieve was not ready to give up on him. About two weeks later, Manhattan lawyer George Cappiello received a telephone call from Genevieve. A year or so earlier, Cappiello had helped the young woman with her application for U.S. citizenship. Now Genevieve had another request: she wanted the lawyer to accompany her to Palm Springs, because, said Cappiello, "she wanted to meet with Mr. Zanuck." He was a bit surprised that she needed the help of an attorney to get together with the aging film mogul; he knew that Genevieve had been Darryl Zanuck's longtime companion and Zanuck had been one of her immigration sponsors. Genevieve explained to Cappiello that Zanuck's family had taken him out of New York Hospital and spirited him back to the family estate in Palm Springs. Zanuck had asked her to accompany them, but soon after the party arrived, she was made to feel unwelcome. Dick Zanuck, she claimed, had practically thrown her off the grounds. Genevieve felt she had to return to find out whether Zanuck was all right.

A few days later, Cappiello flew with Genevieve to Los Angeles and then on to the desert resort. They hopped into a cab, which deposited them at Ric-Su-Dar's gate in twenty minutes' time. Said Cappiello, "I don't remember whether there was a bell or an intercom, but somehow we got the attention of the people inside because shortly thereafter, a man and an elderly woman came to the gate. The lady told us that she was Virginia Zanuck, and she must have been, because Genevieve knew her, and she knew Genevieve."

When Virginia, busy with her afternoon routine, learned that Genevieve was at the gate, she flew into a panic. After seventeen years away, her husband had finally come back to her, and she was again to be Mrs. Darryl F. Zanuck. But now Genevieve had turned up—with a lawyer—asking permission to enter the house and visit her husband. Said Rita Mahon, the maid, "Mrs. Zanuck was frightened. She was crying. And she was feeling that maybe somebody was going to come in and take Mr. Zanuck away." Virginia immediately dialed the Palm Springs police. She was determined not to let Genevieve lure her husband from her.

By the time Virginia appeared at the gate with one of the male servants to greet Genevieve, she had collected herself. Genevieve quietly asked to see Zanuck, and Virginia quietly refused. "There were no harsh words exchanged at all," said Cappiello. "However, when I looked over my shoulder, there was a cop approaching." The policeman packed Genevieve and her attorney into his squad car and took them over to the precinct house to sort matters out. Genevieve told the cops that she was very concerned about Zanuck's health. "She thought that he was not well mentally," said Cappiello. Genevieve asserted that she feared Zanuck was being kept a virtual prisoner at the estate against his wishes.

"The police were very nice—they didn't charge us with anything," said Cappiello. "And they sent out a squad car to investigate. We waited." Finally, a policeman returned. He told Genevieve and Cappiello that he had been allowed to enter the estate and see Mr. Zanuck. He found the seventy-one-year-old man sitting by the swimming pool. "The cop said to us that Mr. Zanuck appeared to be bonkers," recalled Cappiello. "He just said right out, 'This man is not playing with a full deck.' " The cop added that although he had presented himself to Zanuck as a policeman—indeed, he was wearing his uniform—the old man hadn't even bothered to ask why he was there or what was wrong. "He is living in a completely different world," the cop concluded. However, there wasn't much the police could do. Zanuck, after all, was with his family, and he didn't seem to recall who Genevieve was and couldn't say with any degree of certainty whether he wanted to leave or stay.

Cappiello and Genevieve left Palm Springs. "I went back to New York, and she went somewhere else—Los Angeles, I think, and that was the end of the matter," remembered Cappiello. However, Genevieve's fears were not eased. Zanuck was living at his own estate, attended by servants, family, and a doting wife, supplied with food, drink, and anything else he might demand—including expert medical care—but Genevieve seemed oblivious to those facts. "She felt Zanuck wasn't being well taken care of," said the lawyer. "She was concerned about his health."

Zanuck's medical condition was not her only worry, however. Added Cappiello, "She was very concerned about his—uh—his assets. She thought that his family would try to get his money."

FIVE
TWENTIETH CENTURY PRINCESSES

·

E very single morning when they were little girls, Darrylin and Susan Zanuck had breakfast served to them on trays, each garnished with a fresh rose. They ate off white china decorated with pink and gold. If they were good children and cleaned their plates, they would find inscriptions on the china that read "Good Morning, Darrylin" and "Good Morning, Susan."

Such regal luxuries were the least of the two girls' perks, however. Both young women could also command the attention of celebrities, politicians, generals, socialites, and other distinguished personalities with whom their important father circulated. Darryl Zanuck was a fount of jobs, income, and favors for many people, and they willingly stroked his daughters' feathers and presented them with gifts to show their allegiance to him. Both girls received jewelry and silver—even as children—from Errol Flynn, Clifton Webb, Tyrone Power, Betty Grable, and Merle Oberon. Darrylin used to play croquet with Shirley Temple and learned Ping-Pong from Lilli Palmer. If Zanuck was the king of Hollywood, Susan and Darrylin were its princesses.

Alas, not all the attention Darrylin and Susan received was wanted. Any public misstep could make news. When Susan had a traffic accident in 1950, the story was written up in the *Los Angeles Examiner*. Fortunately, the Zanucks had the clout to hush up details. Even though the other driver suffered broken ribs and Susan's passenger, a schoolmate, was seriously injured, there was no explanation of how she came to collide with another car.

All their lives, Susan and Darrylin could attract people because they were Zanuck's daughters. Like their parents, they were gracious and open-handed with their hospitality and money. Darrylin, in particular, displayed a strong concern for the poor, the orphaned, and the handicapped, raising funds for and donating money to charities. Yet the sisters also had inherited a strong sense of their own noblesse—to which others were obliged. To them, there was a simple rightness in their friends' willingness to do things for them. They sometimes used people carelessly; but they also became victims in their relationships with hangers-on who believed that rubbing up against the Zanuck offspring would spin gold.

On the surface, the two sisters seemed similar. They inherited their parents' small size and compact musculature. They had pretty little faces with dark brown eyes, peachlike complexions, rosy cheeks, and wide gleaming smiles—all framed by light brown hair bleached blond by the Santa Monica sun. They were attractive children, but they lacked star quality. For a 1938 photo, Darryl Zanuck posed with Shirley Temple on one knee and Darrylin on the other. While Darrylin was a good-looking little girl, she faded beside the photogenic screen moppet whose dimples almost pop off the print. The sisters shared the same temperament. Mona Skoff, one of Susan's friends, recalled, "Susan could be compliant—like a child. You would tell her to go wash her hands, and she would do it. Then, five minutes later, she would say something terrible to cut you. And she never held back when she wanted to say something nasty." John O'Grady, the private investigator who worked for Virginia, made a similar assessment of Darrylin: "She can turn on you. And she can dismiss you like you have lower status, just like that."

As a model for a child, Zanuck packed a greater wallop than ordinary dads because he was powerful outside the family, too. He seemed to rule the whole world. If he wanted something done, it got done *immediately*. To give himself a sense of who he was, Zanuck needed people to idolize him, and his daughters readily complied. Even after they grew to adults, they continued to worship him; he gave them a sense of who they were. They could fix their place in the world by their relationship to him.

Darrylin, the firstborn by two years, was her daddy's favorite. "Darrylin was Daddy's baby," said O'Grady. "Oh, when the two of them were together, that was it—she was Daddy's baby." She longed to be exactly like him—strong, authoritative, in charge. Darrylin had her father's boundless energy and seemed to want to merge with his personality by behaving like him. She could have become a film mogul herself, perhaps; but in the 1940s when she and Susan were stretching toward adulthood, girls were not deemed suitable for executive positions. Still, Darrylin was determined to make her mark, styling herself after her father yet complying with his demands. To please him, she would marry and produce grandchildren. But she would also start her own business and become an entrepreneur. And she would do it all on her own, without help from Zanuck or his friends. That was her ambition. Yet something always seemed to happen to her business projects—some snafu or loose end would tangle her up and send her scurrying back to her father or family for help.

Susan was more her mother's daughter. Like Virginia, she valued the glamour and fast living of the Hollywood community, and she loved being the daughter of the man who ruled it. Susan also idolized her father, but Virginia was her model of what a woman was supposed to be: gracious, loyal, kind, supportive, and generous. A woman's task in life was to bathe in the reflected glory of her husband, to orchestrate everything for his well-being, rarely to question his judgment, and to suffer his insults and betrayals with dignity. If her husband succeeded, then she had succeeded. All power and importance came from him. Unfortunately, few men could live up to Susan's idealized vision of her father.

Zanuck was the center of his daughters' existence. When the center went flying off to Europe to live as a high-class gypsy, the girls, too, spun off in different directions to search for what they had lost.

*   *   *

As teenagers, Darrylin and Susan were considered a bit wild. By day they attended the toney Marlborough School in Hancock Park, where they mingled with the daughters of social heavyweights. School, however, was like an extracurricular activity. The really important part of the girls' life was spent on the Santa Monica beach. Darrylin and Susan were boy-crazy, and at the beach they could easily meet young men who didn't necessarily know that their father was a famous producer.

According to Martha Newman Ragland, Virginia's friend, the Zanucks set curfews, which their daughters rarely obeyed. "The kids were kind of wild from the beginning. Alfred [Ragland's husband] would tell me how they would climb over the fence and go out on the town. And Virginia told me some stories, too. They were ordinary wild kids," she said.

"Susan drank quite a bit even when she was very young," said her friend, actress Terry Moore. By age fifteen, Susan was already sneaking into the family liquor supply or taking a thermos down to the beach, where she and her date would indulge.

Darrylin and Susan were a hit on the Santa Monica beach. Darrylin had a terrific figure and an open, friendly manner, and boys liked her. On the beach, too, Darrylin could excel. She was a strong and impressive swimmer, and she was one of the first local girls ever to master the ups and downs of the surfboard. Like her father, she enjoyed competing. Winning was important to her, and whenever there were races or meets, she was in there pushing as hard as she could. Her drive to win did not put boys off. To many of them, she was one of the gang. Susan, however, was a tad bulky from waist to knees. "She wore size twelve pants and size eight top," said Terry Moore. "She was very self-conscious about her figure." Susan was always bubbly and enthusiastic, though, and eager to participate in any adventure.

During a spring break, Darrylin brought a batch of Marlborough girls and Harvard School boys down to Palm Springs. Elsa Maxwell and Clifton Webb, both houseguests at Ric-Su-Dar, gave the girls money for an outing in the desert. Recalled Darrylin in a 1987 interview for *Palm Springs Life*, "It turned into a disaster because we Marlborough girls and the Harvard boys went out into the desert with all this food and stuff." Darrylin added, "The police were called. I got back safe. I didn't get into any trouble, but all my girlfriends from Marlborough ended up in jail and Daddy had to go get them." The fracas, said Darrylin, caused the Harvard School to change its Easter vacation schedule to avoid coinciding with Marlborough's. "That's how bad things got at our little party," concluded Darrylin. "Daddy said, 'Thanks, Elsa.' " She did not note whether her parents scolded her.

The Zanucks did not worry overmuch about propriety, either. In 1948, when they made their annual trip to Cannes, they took Susan, then fifteen, to the casino with them almost every night. French regulations barred minors from the gambling tables, but Susan was admitted at her father's special request. One night she lost her last 25,000 francs and burst into tears. Her father promptly advanced her more money. At the Eden Roc, where the Zanucks had a beach cabana, Susan shocked even the most jaded bartender by parading around in a scanty bathing suit. She would drape a brightly hued beach towel around her head to look like the Sphinx and preside at the cabana over her father's court of stars who came to pay their respects. Their homage nurtured her own arrogance. Five years later, in 1953, Zanuck arranged for Clifton Webb to escort his daughter to President Eisenhower's inaugural ball in Washington, D.C. Susan, dressed in a brand-new gown, stood poised at the head of the grand stairway to enter the room on Webb's arm—when all of a sudden she tripped, broke the heel of her shoe, and tumbled indecorously down the stairs. She picked herself up, brushed herself off, and shouted at Webb: "You nasty man. You pushed me!"

Darrylin was democratic in choosing her companions. One day, when her Cadillac ran out of gas, she made the acquaintance of a tall, blond, handsome service station attendant. His name was Robert Livingston Jacks, and he was a husky, curly-headed boy who excelled at waterskiing. Bobby Jacks was well spoken, courteous, and easygoing. At twenty-one, he had already served in the navy and was in his junior year at the University of Southern California and working at the gas station to earn spending money. He helped get Darrylin's car started, and, by way of thanks, Darrylin took him home to meet her family. Jacks was stunned to learn that she was the daughter of the film industry's most powerful executive. Virginia and Darryl liked Bobby immediately.

Darrylin and Bobby's relationship quickly turned serious. The Zanucks even invited Bobby to join them on vacation at Cap d'Antibes on the French Riviera. A few months after Darrylin's graduation from Marlborough in 1949, the Zanucks announced that their eldest child was engaged. Darrylin was to attend Finch College in New York that fall while Bobby finished his senior year at USC. The couple would wed the following summer. However, neither of them could stand to wait. In November, Jacks went to New York, picked up Darrylin at Finch, and eloped with her to Covington, Kentucky. The Zanucks were not completely unhappy about the elopement. Said Martha Newman Ragland, "I think they were relieved when she married him." "I don't think Bobby was really in love," said Diane Jacks, his second wife. "But he was in love with the ambience. I believe he was more married to Darryl Zanuck than to his daughter."

Darrylin never got back to college and neither did Bobby. His father-in-law gave him a job with Twentieth Century-Fox. The picture-perfect newlyweds set up housekeeping in the beginning of 1950 at a small house in Brentwood. They received gifts from virtually everyone in Hollywood—including demitasse teaspoons from Anne Baxter, gold and silver spoons from director Gregory Ratoff, and antique vegetable dishes from industrialist Howard Hughes. About a year later, Darrylin and Bobby bought a twelve-acre ranch up at the Serra Retreat in the Malibu hills, where they kept a number of horses. They needed more room to prepare for the birth of their first girl, Robin Lyn, who came along in February 1951. Late in 1952, Darrylin gave birth to a boy, Robert Darryl; exactly a year later, there was a second girl, Lindolyn. Just as her father named her after himself, she added "lyn" to her daughters' names. Robert was named after her husband, but his middle name was, of course, Darryl.

Unlike her mother, Darrylin insisted on running the house without the help of servants. "She entertained a lot, and she did everything herself," said her lifelong best friend Mary Donahue. "She had one woman come in to clean, but that was all. She supervised everything else, especially the care of the children." Children came first in her life. In some ways they seemed to run the household. Said Walter Scott, Virginia's friend who sometimes visited Darrylin, "You couldn't get into the room for all the crap."

Darrylin's three children didn't seem to be enough for her. In mid-1955, after lengthy bouts of paperwork, she and Bobby took in two Polish orphans, Steven and Helena. Both were older than the other kids—Steven was born in 1945, Helena in 1946. "The whole process was very expensive," recalled Diane Jacks, who became Bobby's second wife. "It was one of her [Darrylin's] little whims. It must have cost about $100,000. They went to great lengths and called on her father's help to cut the red tape." Even five kids were not enough, however. By the end of the year, Darrylin was pregnant again. In June 1956 she gave birth to her fourth child, a girl named Wendalyn.

The Jacks became members of the beach set to which Darrylin had belonged before her marriage. Mary and Frank Donahue, Norman Bishop, owner of a restaurant called Cheerio's, and his girlfriend Vee Miller would dine out or have breakfast at Bishop's place or at Frascati's or Zucchi's—all of them informal Malibu and Santa Monica beach eateries. Darrylin was generous with her friends. She took them to Palm Springs for the weekend when her parents didn't visit. "We had wonderful days," recalled Mary Donahue. "There was a maid, a cook, a pastry cook, and a butler at our disposal. They were so efficient. Once, when I was there as a houseguest, the maid even unpacked my purse. My purse!"

Few of the Jacks' friends were directly involved in movies or moviemaking. Said Mary Donahue, "Darrylin grew up thinking—and I don't know whether it was imposed on her or whether it was her own idea—she had a feeling that friends made in the picture business were not really your true friends. They were with you because of what you could do for them. It wasn't an honest situation."

Despite Darrylin's expanding roles as wife and mother, she still seemed to see herself primarily as a daughter. She was very much Daddy's girl, and his approval of her was paramount. Daddy very much approved. Jacks had become a trusted and well-liked subordinate at the studio, and Zanuck often praised the young man. For her part, Darrylin had turned out to be an energetic matron who had produced four perfect little babies for her father to dandle on his knee. Here was a new audience for his Gyppie the monkey stories, and he began recounting them to the Jacks children as soon as they would sit still. The kids identified Zanuck so closely with the monkey, that they forgot about titles like "Grandpa" or "Gramps," and simply renamed him Gyppie.

Yet Darrylin sat on the sidelines of the Zanuck family drama of the mid-1950s. At the center of her father's concern was his and Virginia's odd relationship with Bella Darvi, who had been living in the Zanucks' Santa Monica beach house since 1952. Darrylin, according to her friend Mary Donahue, was completely unaware that anything alarming was going on, despite the fact that her husband was privy to all the studio gossip. Darrylin had met Bella at her parents' home, of course, but never paid much attention to her. Though Bella was worldly enough to be considered a bit jaded, Darrylin was more mature in her own way. She was a married woman and mother to six children. She must have seen Bella as just another ingenue.

Darrylin, said Mary Donahue, didn't realize that Bella was creating a breach in her parents' relationship until 1956, when gossip columns began trumpeting the news. When Darrylin learned that her father was leaving, said Mrs. Donahue, she was stricken. "She was absolutely brokenhearted because she idolized her father—and her mother. [The scandal] was very destructive to Darrylin."

Darrylin took her father's part in the affair. To her, his faults always seemed to pale in the white light of his importance and brilliance. She acted as though the failure for the Zanucks' marriage resided with Virginia. Some deficiency in her mother's allure or understanding or love had led her father to look elsewhere. It was not simply Zanuck's venal desire to dally with a younger woman. Virginia told her friend Margaret Shands that Darrylin was angry with her—as though Virginia had been the cause of the separation rather than Bella or Darryl. After the split, recalled Mrs. Shands, Darrylin sent back all of Virginia's Christmas presents unopened. "Virginia was very, very hurt," said Mrs. Shands.

Darrylin's anger with her mother soon transformed itself into action for herself. She would not let what happened to Virginia happen to her. She determined always to be unfailingly attractive, just as her father seemed to be to the women with whom he had affairs. She fussed with makeup and clothing. She ate carefully and exercised faithfully. Though she was only in her mid-twenties and still trim after four pregnancies, she talked about having plastic surgery to improve her appearance. Bobby Jacks, according to a friend, grew exasperated with her obsession. He was constantly reassuring her that she looked beautiful. Darrylin seemed driven to show herself and her father that she could be in control sexually, just as he was. According to friends, she began flirting with other men. One of them was Patrick Dorian, an affable bartender at Cheerio's.

In August 1957, Bobby Jacks and Mary Donahue's husband Frank joined Darryl and Richard Zanuck on their quest for locations for the movie *Deluxe Tour*. Norman Bishop, who owned Cheerio's, threw a large good-bye party at "my shack on the beach." Said Bishop, "It was quite a nice party, if I do say so myself. Darrylin was very, very grateful for it. She later gave me a $600 gold cigarette lighter by way of thanks."

Darrylin had to be feeling strong and in control that August. She began receiving income from the trust fund her parents had established. Now she was free to do whatever she wanted. She was not dependent on Bobby or anybody else. In her husband's absence, Darrylin's relationship with Patrick Dorian flourished. They could see each other nearly every day. She started plans to open her own clothing shop in Santa Monica. Most startling, however, in October, she moved out of the ranch and bought a new house on the beach in the Malibu Colony.

By the time Bobby Jacks returned to Los Angeles that fall, he was presented with a stunning fait accompli: his wife was not where he expected her to be; she had left and taken the children with her.

Bobby Jacks quickly learned that Darrylin had become involved with another man; all their friends knew about it. Soon after, he had a brief affair with Mona Skoff, later Susan's friend, who was working as a waitress at Bishop's bar. "It wasn't a big thing—it was really a tiny situation," said Skoff. "I had known Bobby before, because he and Darrylin and the kids would come in for dinner. We were both having trouble in our marriages at the time. I was breaking up with my husband, and Bobby said that Darrylin was dating other men very openly. He was terribly, terribly hurt," added Skoff. In court papers, Darrylin has said that her relationship with Dorian began after she and Jacks officially separated.

In December 1957 Darrylin officially filed for divorce. She charged Jacks with cruelty, the usual contention manufactured by lawyers. No love affairs ever surfaced in the court proceedings. Many years later, Darrylin was to assert that Bobby Jacks was a drunk who occasionally beat her. In a later court dispute with her ex-husband, she declared that he once tried to strangle her and on another occasion beat her. "The first time he tried to strangle me, the second time he hit me in the face and practically broke my nose and blackened both my eyes." Most of their friends knew that Bobby had a drinking problem, but few thought it likely that beatings had ever occurred. Said Norman Bishop, "He wouldn't do it, because he didn't have the guts. He also wouldn't do it because he was a nice guy." Mary Donahue said, "I never saw Bobby hit Darrylin, and I'm sure that he wouldn't have hit her in front of others. But I believe in my heart that what Darrylin said took place did take place. She'd be foolish to say it if she couldn't back it up."

Beatings or no, the divorcing husband and wife fought bitterly about money. In December 1958, six months after their decree was granted, the court required Jacks to pay Darrylin only a dollar a year in token alimony and $25 a month in support for each of the six children.

Virginia did not approve of divorce but was surprisingly sympathetic to her daughter. She firmly believed that everything Darrylin told her about Jacks was true. She felt that for the sake of her grandchildren her daughter had no choice but to leave him and take the kids. According to Margaret Shands, Virginia had never been quite as impressed with Jacks as her husband was. However, she was thoroughly against Darrylin's attachment to Patrick Dorian, said Walter Scott. She couldn't imagine what her daughter—a graduate of the Marlborough School—was doing with such an ordinary man. Whenever Virginia talked to Darrylin on the telephone, she would ask pointed little questions about whether she was still seeing "that bartender."

Although Zanuck allowed himself a universe of latitude in his own marriage and now had linked up with singer Juliette Greco, he budged not an inch from his view that divorce for his daughter was wrong. "Darryl was definitely against the divorce simply because he was a rigid, conventional man when it came to things like that," said Mary Donahue. "He just didn't approve of divorce, even in the end, when he was not himself. He may have been against Darrylin getting a divorce from Bobby, but he did not know the truth about the things Darrylin was talking about"—namely Darrylin's claims of beatings and alcoholism. Even if he had known, he probably would have insisted she stick it out—just as her mother had. Contrary to his son-in-law's expectations, Zanuck did not fire him. Bobby Jacks was to work on and off for DFZ Productions, and later Twentieth Century-Fox, for ten years more.

Darrylin was frantic to earn more money. With a tireless energy reminiscent of her father's, Darrylin had two apparel shops going by the end of 1958—one with an overreaching French-Italian name, Pour la Contessa, on West Channel Road in Santa Monica and another simply called Darrylin's on Sunset Boulevard. The businesses were to be the new center of her life. Her romance with Patrick Dorian ceased to be as enthralling as it had been a year earlier. The two had already argued, she said in court papers, and he had left for Hawaii. Darrylin was no longer quite so interested in maintaining her image as a supermother; she hired a nanny to take care of the kids while she devoted herself to earning a living.

Eight months later, in August 1958, Darrylin left the six kids with their nanny and the shops with Mary Donahue while she took a vacation in Acapulco. By that time she desperately needed a rest because her fledgling retail empire was already collapsing around her. One of her employees was suing her for pay Darrylin allegedly owed, and she was struggling to meet the $400-a-month rent for the Sunset Boulevard store. According to Virginia's friend Walter Scott, Darrylin received loans and outright gifts from her mother to support the two boutiques.

When Darrylin visited, Acapulco was beginning to enjoy a burst of popularity with Americans. The town was growing, and the cost of living was low. Darrylin grew certain that she could earn money there, perhaps by establishing a couple of boutiques in the new hotels. Mexicans seemed incredibly easygoing and good-natured compared to the people she had to deal with in California. As it turned out, one Mexican in particular appealed to Darrylin. Julio Pineda Carranza, then twenty-seven years old, was running various recreational concessions on one of Acapulco's westernmost points of land, La Caleta Beach. Pineda was strikingly handsome. He wasn't as tall as Robert Jacks, but he was trim and muscular, with high cheekbones, a long straight nose, warm brown eyes, and an easy smile. "He ran pleasure boats for tourists, and he rented horses for people to ride—nothing much," said Father Angel Martinez, an Acapulco cleric who later became a close friend of Darrylin's. Pineda was perhaps not a mover and shaker; however, without knowing much about Darrylin or her family, he treated her respectfully and thoughtfully; and he seemed undaunted by the fact that she had six children, four of them under ten years old.

Top: Not looking anything like the humble housewife and mother of four she was in the mid-1950s, Darrylin, her first husband, Robert Jacks, Robert Wagner, and her parents attended a film premiere.
(Bison Archives)

Bottom left: Even though Zanuck had renounced his crown as head of Twentieth Century-Fox and gone independent, he was preparing his son to succeed him in the business.
(Bison Archives)

Bottom right: Zanuck tried to make a film star out of his girlfriend, French cabaret singer Juliette Greco, but most of the movies he made with her bombed.
(Kobal Collection)

Above: While his father was gallivanting around Europe in the early 1960s with his girlfriends, Richard was playing the role of Ozzie Nelson with his first wife, Lili Gentle, and the couple's daughters, Janet (*left*) and Ginny.
(Bison Archives)

Left: Under Genevieve's influence, Zanuck became natty, wearing a Nehru jacket— the Edsel of clothing— to the opening of *John and Mary* starring Dustin Hoffman and Mia Farrow in late 1969.
(Paul Schumach)

Right: In Acapulco, Darrylin became a civic leader. Few knew that her businesses were troubled.
(Mike Oliver/Acapulco News)

Below: On one of his rare visits to Darrylin in Acapulco in 1970, Darryl basked in the sun with Genevieve, who looked good even without makeup.
(Mike Oliver/Acapulco News)

On the eve of the Twentieth Century-Fox proxy battle in 1971, Zanuck was
still flaunting his power as a mogul and his reputation as a lady's man. Both he and
Genevieve were unaware that he would soon lose his job.

(UPI/Bettmann Newsphotos)

After years living apart in Mexico and France, Darrylin and Susan met in Acapulco for the marriage of Darrylin's daughter in 1972.
(Pierre Savineau)

Virginia couldn't have been happier after she won back her husband in 1973, but Zanuck's New York physicians said that he was suffering from organic brain syndrome.
(Pierre Savineau)

Richard and his second wife, Linda Harrison, celebrated daughter Ginny's birthday at a restaurant with her grandmother and sister Janet. The happy scene was soon to be ripped apart by Linda's guru, who convinced her to divorce.
(Bison Archives)

Above left: The Zanucks came to resent Richard for his success, particularly after the appearance of *Jaws* in 1975, which he coproduced with David Brown. The movie spawned nervous swimmers and millions in revenues from spinoff products like towels, cups, and posters.
(Bison Archives)

Above right: Zanuck's closest companions in retirement were his Yorkies, Lisa and Tina, whom he bequeathed in his will to Virginia. The dogs, however, had predeceased him.
(Pierre Savineau)

Left: Dino Hakim, Susan's second-born son, at his eighteenth birthday party as his grandparents looked on.
(Pierre Savineau)

Top: After Zanuck and his daughters returned to California, there were some moments of family togetherness on weekends at Ric-Su-Dar. (*Back, left to right*) Richard Zanuck, Wendalyn Pineda, Darrylin de Pineda, Virginia Zanuck, Janet Zanuck holding stepbrother Harrison, Julio Pineda, Darryl Zanuck with Lisa and Tina, Susan Savineau. (*Front, left to right*) Robin Lyn Pineda holding son Ricardo, Linda Harrison with son Dean, Ginny Zanuck, Jorge Pineda, Pierre Savineau.

(Pierre Savineau)

Bottom: Zanuck's funeral in late 1979 was the last time the family was really together. Six months later, Susan (*far right*) would be dead, and Virginia only eighteen months later. By that time, Richard and Darrylin (*center*) were feuding.

(Peter C. Borsari)

Above: Genevieve sued Zanuck's estate in 1980 for principle, she said, not money. Indeed, she owned a cooperative at Manhattan's Dakota apartments and rooms full of original art, including a bust of Zanuck.

(Harry Benson)

Above left: After she coproduced *Cocoon* in 1985, Lili Fini could take her place alongside her husband as a power in Hollywood as well as in the Santa Monica beach house he inherited from his mother.

(© Terry O'Neill/Woodfin Camp & Associates)

Above right: Darrylin, by her childhood portrait, which hangs on the wall at Ric-Su-Dar, reminisced about the good old days at the family estate for a Palm Springs magazine. Ric-Su-Dar was already up for sale.

(Arthur Coleman Photography)

The shape of a new life was beginning to emerge in Darrylin's mind. Like her father, she would escape from Los Angeles and build a new, exotic life abroad where she could do exactly what she wanted. She, too, would shake free of entanglements and find her true self. Her parents had split up. Susan had wed and was living in France, and Dick had already left the nest for marriage with Lili Gentle. Darrylin's own marriage had ended, and her boutiques were going under. If her father had wanted to escape from success, then Darrylin could also opt out.

When Darrylin returned to Los Angeles that fall, she resolved to get away to Mexico for good.

*   *   *

Susan had never had any great urge to get away. She adored being the daughter of a famous mogul and was at one with Hollywood, her father's realm. She didn't worry about receiving special treatment just because she was Darryl Zanuck's girl. She saw no reason not to take advantage of her position.

Even when Susan was a high school student, she numbered young actors and actresses among her friends. She was friendly with Robert Wagner—"actually, she had a terrific crush on him," said actress Terry Moore, who became one of Susan's best friends. She dated Keefe Brasselle, who starred in the film biography of Eddie Cantor, and hobnobbed with Moore and Corinne Calvet, the French ingenue who appeared in *Rope of Sand* and *What Price Glory?*

Unfortunately, Susan's popularity with movieland friends sometimes brought her heartache. Among others, Susan's friend Calvet became a target of Darryl Zanuck's affections. In 1949, after completing *When Willie Comes Marching Home* for Fox, the teenage French actress was summoned to Zanuck's office at five in the afternoon. She sat in a chair by his desk while he walked around making chitchat about the weather. Without warning, "He turned on his heel and stood a few feet away from me with his erect penis standing proudly out of his unzipped pants," she said. He asked her how she liked that. Too flustered to say anything, she added, "I finally managed some words. 'Please, Mr. Zanuck. I know your daughter.' " She thought that

187

comment might restrain him; however, he replied: " 'Yes, and we know she is very bright and capable of keeping secrets.' "

Susan knew many secrets about her parents, and her sympathies did not lie completely with her mother. Like her sister, she thought that somehow Virginia must have been remiss as a wife. Virginia never said anything to Susan about Zanuck's affairs; however, Susan knew that her mother had her own studio grapevine and could not be ignorant of the goings-on. Still, Susan did not understand her father or why he behaved the way he did. Sometimes she made pointed remarks to Zanuck—expressing some of the bitter feelings that Virginia herself seemed afraid to ventilate.

Susan, never much of a student, was not slated for college. She saw no need to go away when she had everything she could want right in Los Angeles. Her mother had been an actress, her dad was a producer; she decided to enter show business, too. Susan got the idea that she could sing, and while she was no Judy Garland, she could carry a tune and deliver a song with some punch, according to Terry Moore. Besides, her father could help her.

And help her he did. All the resources of the Fox movie studio were brought to bear on Susan's career aspirations. Comedian Tommy Noonan developed an act for her. Walter Scott helped with the stage set. Charles LeMaire designed Susan's costumes. "The whole thing took hundreds of thousands of dollars to put together," recalled Pokie Seeger, then Tommy Noonan's wife. She had met Susan while her husband was rehearsing with her, and the two women became lifelong friends.

Terry Moore, who met Susan when she was organizing "the act," also became a good friend. The two enjoyed glamorous days together. They would spend mornings rehearsing at the studio; then they would change into street clothes—tight-waisted, full skirted dresses, high heels, gloves, and hats—and go shopping together in Beverly Hills. Each drove a white Thunderbird. When they had spent enough money to feel as though they had accomplished something, they would stop at a restaurant and—though Susan was always watching her weight—gobble down waffles and talk about men. Then they would rush home, throw themselves into their finery, and meet once again, this time on the arms of various hunks-about-town for a party or a premiere.

Moore met all the members of the Zanuck family. She knew Darryl himself from her work at the studio. He never called her for one of his four-o'clock sessions, possibly because he knew she was seeing his friend Howard Hughes. Though Richard was ready to go to college, Moore recalled him as "an adorable little boy." She would stop by and say hello to Virginia, whose life, she felt, "was very lonely." She scarcely knew Darrylin at all. "She was married, and there was just a world of difference between being married and not being married then. You had completely different concerns."

Though Susan seemed unspoiled, she pretended to a sophistication that matched her father's. She seemed to know about a lot of things that Moore had never dreamed of. When Susan told of her sexual escapades, Moore, who was raised by a strict Mormon mother, was a little shocked, but she wasn't repelled. She was already involved with industrialist Howard Hughes, whom she would later secretly marry. Susan revealed that her first sexual experience was with André Hakim, the French film executive Zanuck had hired after they met in the war. Susan and André were riding a train together and found their way to one of the private compartments. Hakim was not her last, however. She was involved with a lot of men. For all that, Susan was still rather naive. A comedian with whom she was friendly recalled that once she had an unfounded pregnancy scare. "Why didn't you use something?" he asked. "Because the boy was Catholic," was Susan's reply.

Late in 1953, Terry Moore was asked to head up a group of entertainers who were to go to Korea to put on a show for the troops. She invited Susan to come along and do her act. Susan was ecstatic. Virginia, nervous about her daughter going into a war zone, reluctantly gave her permission. Again, Tommy Noonan worked on Susan's arrangements, and Charles LeMaire designed costumes. Moore had no such advantages. To save money, Moore's mother designed and sewed her clothing. Moore was worried that Susan's costumes would outshine her own. She and her mom decided to cook up a costume that would ensure her headline attention: they designed a one-piece ermine bathing suit with matching hat, boots, and muff.

In Korea, the rather modest ermine suit, which covered every inch of skin but Moore's legs, set off a scandal. When Moore wore it, the troops went wild. She nearly froze wearing the costume in the icy Korean winter. The military authorities were shocked, dismayed, and outraged. They insisted the costume was too revealing and announced that Moore was to be sent home. She was forbidden from continuing her performance. The next night, Susan went out on stage and announced to the soldiers that her friend had been sent packing. Then, recalled Terry, "she said, 'I'd like to dedicate the next song to my friend Terry.' She sang 'Won't You Come Home, Bill Bailey?'—which was kind of her specialty—and she sang it so sweetly, I felt like crying. And when she finished, I came running out on the stage, and we kissed. We were both crying." A few days later, the army relented. As long as Moore left the ermine suit in her trunk, she could stay with the tour.

The Zanucks prepared a huge welcome-home in February 1954 for the two girls, a party at Ciro's, which practically everyone in Hollywood attended. Susan's parents promptly got drunk and acted so peculiarly that all present were astounded. First Zanuck and then Virginia tried to chin up one-armed on a swing. "There was nothing festive or playful about the event," wrote Ezra Goodman, in *The Fifty-Year Decline and Fall of Hollywood*. "Zanuck, who had been partying for several hours, was in an odd exuberant mood. Among the edgy spectators to his extraordinary display were Zanuck's wife, Virginia . . . and Bella Darvi . . . a green-eyed French 'actress' whom Zanuck had put under contract at Fox. Zanuck, Mrs. Zanuck and Bella Darvi were an almost inseparable threesome. . . . As the illustrious Zanuck suddenly leaped to the trapeze and chinned himself with gusto, a hush fell over the crowded nightclub."

Reports of the odd incident appeared in newspapers all through the nation over the next few days. Susan was deeply embarrassed. For the previous two years, she had shared the children's annex of her parents' house with Bella Darvi. The sight of her parents publicly trying to show off to the young actress forced her to recognize that Darvi was more than a companion to her mother and more than an ingenue her father was cultivating. Her parents, she decided, were having a very strange relationship with the woman. She was later to tell her second husband, Pierre Savineau, that the three were involved sexually. She claimed to have heard and seen their encounters and was shocked and mortified. She could scarcely bring herself to acknowledge what had happened. She later told her friends that Zanuck and Bella were merely having an affair. She didn't reveal—until years later, and then only to her second husband—that the relationship was really a ménage à trois.

As Susan pursued her career desultorily and kept her distance from her parents, André Hakim began courting her seriously. Hakim was not a glamorous-looking man. His pudgy round face was topped by a thatch of black hair and punctuated with an unfashionable pencil-thin mustache. Born in Cairo in 1915 to a family of French descent, he joined his brothers Raymond, Robert, and Raphael in Paris where they operated a film distribution company. When the war broke out in 1939, Hakim came to America and picked up English by attending movies. He distributed French films to art houses and turned up in Hollywood two years later as an actors' agent. Darryl Zanuck originally met him during the war in Paris, where Hakim was involved in military intelligence. Zanuck was impressed with the man. In 1949, after Hakim had returned to Hollywood, Zanuck signed him to a long-term contract with Fox. By the time Susan grew enamored of him, he had produced two American features, *Mr. Belvedere Rings the Bell* and *The Full House*, as well as several television programs.

André was completely unlike the tall, handsome California men Susan had been dating; yet he did evoke the Continental mystery and charm of Bella Darvi and the other European women with whom Zanuck himself became involved. To Susan, André was courtly, suave, and sophisticated. He kissed women on the hand. He knew how to order wine. He had dined at the best restaurants. He spoke four languages. "I knew that Susan really loved him because he was her first," said Moore. "She went back to the man who was her first. It was sweet."

The couple's courtship was rushed into marriage by Susan, who was desperate to get away from her parents and what she thought of as their perverse affair with Bella Darvi. Susan gave her parents only a few days' notice before her April 1954 marriage to Hakim in Las Vegas, where she became Mrs. Hakim at a small ceremony attended only by her family and a few friends. According to her second husband, Pierre Savineau, Susan was anxious to get as far as she could from Virginia because she couldn't bear to be reminded of her mother's suspected lesbian affair. "She went to her father and asked him to send Hakim to Paris; so he did," said Savineau.

In Paris, Susan was often put in a strange position. When Bella Darvi arrived in town, Susan was delegated to meet the actress at the airport as part of the Fox contingent. Hakim, who was much more broad-minded about homosexuality, persuaded Susan not to take sides. Her father was living in Europe. He was André's boss and mentor. There was no point in not getting along with him. Then, too, Susan could not bring herself to judge her father harshly. He had become a citizen of the world, and as such, he had to be allowed his sexual foibles.

Susan was very serious about being a good wife. Fortunately, André did not require her to be that serious. He was earning plenty of money, and the Hakims had a large and luxurious apartment on the Right Bank in Paris and several servants to staff it. All Susan had to do was make sure that the cook and the housekeeper did their jobs. Nevertheless, she took up cooking with a vengeance and became startlingly proficient for one who as a child had her breakfast served on a tray. Still in her early twenties, Susan began looking like a slim, elegant Parisian in couturier fashions. Life in Paris for the Hakims was a whirl of parties, dinners, and nights spent dancing at *boîtes* until dawn.

The birth of André, Jr., in 1957 scarcely changed anything. Susan hired a nurse to attend him and continued with her demanding nightlife. She drank heavily almost every night. She and her husband grew bored with ordinary clubs. The couple began visiting clubs featuring transvestite entertainers and shows with a sadomasochistic flavor. Susan had always been an experimenter, eager for anything, since her comparatively tame teenage days sneaking out of the Santa Monica beach house to meet dates. Susan and André experimented with sex themselves. "They got into things involving a lot of cruelty," said Susan's friend Mona Skoff. "I gathered that Susan was on the receiving end. I also gathered that she accepted—maybe she liked it."

Hakim introduced his father-in-law to Madame Claude, the city's most prestigious madam. Darryl Zanuck's sexual horizons had widened considerably since his casting-couch days. Susan was disgusted but also intrigued by this. She resolved to be sophisticated, too—just like her father—and began seeing other men. She had a number of affairs quite openly. Hakim never complained. In 1959 she gave birth to her second boy, Raymond Edwin, who was immediately nicknamed

Dino. Unlike André, Sr. or Jr., he didn't have curly black hair. He was blond and blue-eyed. "The boy was not Hakim's," said Susan's second husband Pierre Savineau. "She told me that another man was his father."

Her marriage, however, was not shaken until 1960 when she ran away to Rome with one of Hakim's Italian business associates. Hakim pleaded with his wife to come back. She was adamant. She would not return. Hakim took the two boys, whom she had left with the nurse-maid, and went into hiding. If Susan didn't return, she would never see her kids, he declared. When Zanuck heard the threat, he pleaded with Hakim and his daughter to reconcile. The Cholly Knickerbocker gossip column reported that Hakim announced that should they di-vorce, Hakim would give Susan everything he had. "There's nothing to compare with a sporting gesture like that to make a girl think twice," declared the columnist. What made Susan think twice was something else, however. Pierre Savineau said, "Her lover left her; he abandoned her on a boat off of Italy. She was alone. She went back to Hakim."

Susan's daughter, Sharon Marie—or Sherry—was born in 1961. The girl was premature and sickly, and she didn't leave the hospital for months. Susan rarely visited. She sent her nursemaid to hold and cuddle the newborn in the nursery. She couldn't be bothered herself. She and Hakim were trying to put their lives together, but they were having trouble. They continued on their rounds of parties and night-clubs, but they were fighting. The steam had gone out of the relation-ship; they had loved each other and humiliated each other. Now there was nothing left. In 1964, Susan and her children met Virginia in San Remo for a vacation. Virginia discovered—to her shock—that Susan was covered with bruises. This was outrageous, her mother told her. She should not stand for such treatment. When André drove down a few days later to see them, Susan announced that she was finished with him. She wanted him out of her life. "All right," he said. "If that's what you really want." "That's what I want," she told him. He left without another word.

Hakim moved to Fox's office in London, but he and Susan clung to their marriage much like her father and mother. The couple separated but didn't divorce.

*   *   *

In early 1960, Darrylin threw everything she could manage into her car and drove back to Acapulco. Her kids followed a few weeks later, despite a court order forbidding them to leave L.A. without their father's permission. Darrylin claimed later that Jacks *had* signed the proper papers. Jacks always denied that he had released the children to go to Mexico.

Her path was marked by a trail of financial mishaps. Her businesses were in trouble, and when they finally folded in early 1960, she owed the bank $12,500. Her father's office sent her accountant a cold little note saying that the bank was threatening to bill Zanuck's account for the money. Left unguarded, one of her shops was burglarized at the end of 1959 with a loss of about $2,500. Her Malibu house was broken into, and a silver collection that she had started as a child was stolen. As if all that were not enough, some fifteen boxes of household goods were lost in transit to Mexico.

Darrylin seemed a chronic victim of mishaps: she lost things; she was robbed; people borrowed money and never repaid it. She often complained that her own friends cheated her. She could never prove anything, however, because she didn't keep receipts or records. She said she couldn't collect money she was owed by Dorian because her lawyer informed her that her claim was too weak to stand up in court. She invited a girlfriend to live with her and help with the kids, but soon Darrylin angrily asserted that the woman had been sponging on her hospitality. There was always a dark plot behind everything. The same friend was also given a cashier's check to hand to an L.A. bank in repayment of Darrylin's loan. It was mysteriously lost, but Darrylin had no proof the check ever existed. It seemed that off on her own, away from her father's supervision, she was helpless to manage her affairs. Perhaps she hoped that her crises would bring him to the rescue. He almost never intervened, however.

Though Bobby Jacks tried to dissuade Darrylin from marrying Julio Pineda, she wed her second husband on April 6, 1960. Over the objections of her former husband, who declared that Mexico was a hogpen, she decided that Acapulco was to be their permanent home and said she planned to renounce her U.S. citizenship, settling her family into a white stucco, tile-roofed two-story house named Casa Arco Iris (Rainbow House) on one of Acapulco's steep hills overlooking La Caleta Beach. She continued to deny her former husband the right to visit his children. In 1961, when William Houghton, Bobby Jacks's lawyer, came to Acapulco to investigate the children's welfare, he found the kids firmly under her care. They dreaded the idea of returning to their father in California. Robert, then eight, told Houghton that he didn't want to visit his father.

Oddly, Darrylin, when asked by Houghton how many children she had, ticked off only four. Indeed, few people in Acapulco seemed to know about Steven and Helena, her two adopted children. Jacks's attorney pointed out that the custody case involved *all* the children, not just the four who were living with Darrylin. Darrylin replied that she didn't know where her adopted children were, noting vaguely that her mother had told her they were enrolled in a school in Redlands, California. In fact, says Diane Jacks, Robert's second wife, "Darrylin got sick of them and threw them back at us." Steven went to military school, and Helena, she noted, returned to the United States after Steven and went to live with Jacks's brother for a time. She doesn't know where the children are now.

That fall, the Santa Monica court ruled that Darrylin could keep the kids, but she was also ordered to fly them to Los Angeles to visit her former husband. By 1965, Jacks later said, "All communication had broken down, and I didn't demand anything except to be left alone." He gave up asking to see any of the children, and he never paid anything toward their support.

By 1962, Darrylin's third full year in Acapulco, she looked like a going concern. She had opened a clothing shop at the brand-new Acapulco Hilton, selling swimsuits and resort wear. Since Mexican law forbade foreigners from owning more than 49 percent of any enterprise, she put the shop in her husband's name and said she worked for him, even though the shop was called Darrylin's.

Julio, according to several of Darrylin's Acapulco friends, did not often work in the store. Father Angel Martinez, a close friend of Darrylin's, said Julio seldom worked, period. "He came into the store once in a while, but Darrylin was busy during the week. Julio was busy on the weekends—he was hunting and fishing." Darrylin told people back in the United States that her husband ran an egg business. Few people in Acapulco ever knew about the egg business. Pierre Savineau,

Susan's second husband, declared trenchantly that Julio was disabled "by a severe allergy. He had a bad reaction to work."

Darrylin went Mexican with a vengeance. She approached Father Angel, who was pastor of a large Catholic church in Acapulco, and asked for instruction. "When I met her, she seemed like a nice, simple girl," he said. "I met her, and she asked me to give her instruction in Catholicism because she wanted to convert. She went through it all and became Catholic." Darrylin became an avid supporter of Father Angel's modest orphanage for boys. She donated personal funds and sponsored several parties and luncheons to raise money for Father Angel and a number of other local causes.

The intensity of Darrylin's commitment to children surprised Father Angel. Somehow her new husband, her own four children, the business, and the charity work were not enough to satisfy her. She was taking on children almost as her father took on girlfriends—in transient relations that were bound to end. When Father Angel met Darrylin, she had already adopted a young Mexican boy named Oscar. (Steven and Helena had completely disappeared from the picture— Father Angel had never heard of them.) Oscar's adoption never took. Darrylin told Father Angel that he wasn't fitting into the family, and she returned the boy to the orphanage. "I took him in, and he stayed with me. Then an Episcopalian couple adopted him and took him to the United States," recalled Father Angel.

Soon after Oscar departed, in 1963, she became interested in another boy, named Jorge, who lived at Father Angel's orphanage. "I was against it because she already had four children of her own, so I didn't see why," said Father Angel. "I thought that he was not right for the family. Not right. He wasn't brilliant, he wasn't very smart. He would never be *universitario*. But Darrylin wanted. I said, 'Why do you want? There are other kids.' But she loved him because he had beautiful eyes, beautiful green eyes. I told her, 'That's not a good reason,' but she had to have him. So I finally said yes."

Like Darrylin's other adoptions, this one was not permanent. When Darrylin and her family returned to the United States in the mid-1970s, Jorge stayed in Acapulco. "I see him once in a while," said Father Angel. "He has jobs from time to time, but he has never been able to get anything together for himself."

Many of Darrylin's friends were mystified by her gluttony for children. The impulse to acquire kids stemmed partly from a charitable, sensitive nature strongly affected by the many pathetic waifs who struggled for survival on Acapulco's streets. Like her father, Darrylin needed people to idolize her, and children could easily meet that need. Darrylin's friend Rita Oliver saw another hunger: "I always thought that people who were very, very lonely as children wanted to be surrounded by children when they became adults. I figured that Darrylin was somebody who had been lonesome as a little girl."

Darrylin told people that her father wrote her constantly, and according to Rita Oliver, he often called Darrylin on the telephone. "She was a real Daddy's girl," said Mrs. Oliver. "She was devoted to him." In fact, Zanuck's Paris secretary, Elisabeth Gargarine, said he almost never called, wrote only occasionally, and rarely visited. People in Acapulco believed that Darrylin's business was a big success; however, friends of Virginia's back in California were hearing a different story. Virginia often told them that her daughter was barely scraping by. Both Margaret Shands and Walter Scott asserted that Virginia was constantly bailing her daughter out with money and gifts. By the mid-1960s, she rebounded enough from her losses to expand into producing her own textiles and fashions. Eventually she was to own four outlets at various Acapulco hotels and a fifth store in Mexico City. After she began marketing her clothing to Bonwit Teller in New York in 1965, she could hook up with Zanuck, who was spending much of his time at Fox's Manhattan headquarters.

Darrylin's parents, by then, had been separated for nearly ten years, and there were no signs that he was interested in a reunion with his wife. Darrylin later noted in a court deposition that her father was dating several people. On one occasion, when he was supposedly involved with Genevieve Gillaizeau, Zanuck had dinner with his daughter and invited another ingenue to join them. He asked Darrylin not to tell Genevieve.

Darrylin's trips to New York included surgery as well as work and play. She was still obsessed with her appearance, and eagerly submitted to the ministrations of Manhattan plastic surgeons. "Her father could help her with the bills," said Pierre Savineau. "He had his profits from *The Longest Day*." Martha Newman Ragland, wife of Fox composer Alfred Newman, recalled Virginia telling her that Darrylin had had virtually every plastic surgery procedure then available. Darrylin's mother was astounded by her daughter's obsession to be physically perfect. Mrs. Ragland remembered Virginia telling her that one day, while visiting Acapulco, she noticed a girl walking by who had a perfect little fanny. When she took a second look, Virginia saw that the perfect little fanny belonged to her daughter. "Virginia realized that Darrylin had her fanny lifted, too!" said Mrs. Ragland. "She really laughed."

Darrylin's name appeared frequently in the society section of the *Acapulco News*. In the late 1960s, celebrities were constantly flying down to Acapulco to work or vacation. Indeed, by 1968, the town had become a resort retreat for the rich and famous. Merle Oberon, who had been one of Darryl Zanuck's major infatuations during the late 1940s, had married an Italian industrialist and built a grand villa near La Quebrada, the cliff where divers entertain tourists by plunging hundreds of feet into the ocean. Darrylin and Julio would often wine and dine visiting entertainers—from Ed Sullivan to Chuck Mangione. For a brief time in the late 1960s, Darrylin hosted an Acapulco radio show that filled her audience in on celebrity comings and goings.

Partly because of her Hollywood connections, Darrylin was sought after by the major American charitable group—the Foreign Friends of Acapulco, which held fund-raisers for local causes. She had the pull to induce big-name celebrities to put on shows that would bring in contributions from local donors. At first she was very close to the group, but then she mysteriously turned on them. Just as she had claimed in the past that friends had cheated her, she now felt that the Foreign Friends of Acapulco were using her. Further, the group was exclusionary. It prohibited Mexicans from membership, a policy to which she took exception. In 1968 she broke with many people in the American community and formed her very own rival charitable group: it was called DAR, which means "to give" in Spanish. The letters stood for *dar, ayudar, y recordar*—"to give, to help, and to remember." The major recipients of DAR aid were the Acapulco fire department—Darrylin bought the city its first fire engine—and Father Angel's orphanage.

Most members of Foreign Friends took the breach philosophical-ly—but "Darrylin was always melodramatic about everything," remembered her friend Emi Fors. "Every event was a big crisis." Darrylin actually came to believe that Foreign Friends were plotting against her. In 1968 she warned her accountant not to take tax deductions for money contributed to DAR, because it was not a U.S. charity and "my enemies in Foreign Friends of Acapulco hate me and might report me to the authorities."

Darrylin's preoccupation with her own melodrama was overshadowed by the real drama enveloping her father and brother over control of Twentieth Century-Fox. In 1970 Zanuck and Genevieve visited Acapulco along with Richard and Linda Harrison. Darrylin noticed, she later said in a deposition, that Dick was very curt with Zanuck and cold to Genevieve, who spent most of her time sunning her bikinied body on a lounger at the Villa Vera, a European-style hotel where she and Zanuck stayed. Father Angel found Zanuck rather ungracious and self-involved. Darrylin proudly introduced the priest to her father while he was on the dance floor at the Villa Vera. Father Angel was ready to spout the praises of his benefactress to her father, for indeed, Darrylin had helped his orphanage tremendously over the years, but Zanuck "never stopped dancing with his friend long enough to shake my hand," he recalled.

Darrylin could hardly have escaped knowing that the friction between her father and brother was serious. That fall, when she visited Los Angeles and dined with Dick, she had to have heard about the growing troubles between father and son. When the news came from Virginia at the end of the year that Zanuck had engineered Dick's firing, Darrylin was stunned. No one could have predicted such an incredible outcome. She was sympathetic to Dick; she was certain that Genevieve had somehow persuaded Zanuck to oust his son. Her father would never do such a peculiar thing on his own. Then, when Zanuck himself was booted upstairs to a meaningless position as chairman emeritus in mid-1971, Darrylin took his side. As far as she was concerned, he had been ruined by Twentieth Century-Fox and its crafty board. Much, much later, she saw her father's ouster as Dick's fault. She noted in a court deposition that her father had sent her letters asserting that "Dickie had turned on him . . . Dickie went behind his back to the different stockholders and tried to get them to go along with him and put my father out. . . . He also said that what hurt him and shocked him the worst was when André Hakim, Sr., called him, and David Brown asked him to come over to his suite . . . in the hotel, I think it was the Beverly Wilshire, and that they [Richard and Brown] wanted André to also go against Daddy."

When he went into the hospital for his cancer surgery in early 1972, Zanuck kept his daughter, and everyone else, in the dark. In July, Darrylin was set to host an important family gathering. Her twenty-one-year-old daughter Robin Lyn had become engaged to Ricardo Lomelin, the brother of a well-known Mexican bullfighter. Darrylin planned a big wedding, at which Father Angel was to officiate, followed by a reception at the Hilton. She expected everybody in the family to turn up to celebrate. Virginia arrived, accompanied by two close men friends, Thomas L. Shirley and Ed Meena. Shirley was a stockbroker at Blythe Eastman Dillon, and Meena worked for Paramount as a prop man. Meena had originally come from Mississippi and knew Virginia's friend Margaret Shands from gatherings of native Mississippians in Los Angeles. She had introduced Meena and eventually Shirley to Virginia. The two men, both of them tall and handsome, quickly became part of her social circle. They attended parties together and dined at Chasen's. Usually Meena escorted Virginia, and Shirley dated Martha Newman, whose husband Alfred had died. Shirley was always investment-minded. "He would get Virginia off in a corner of the room and try to talk her into buying something-or-other," remembered Mrs. Shands. Later Virginia was to see dark plots in Shirley's salesmanship.

Darrylin's sister Susan and her husband Pierre Savineau also flew to Acapulco for the wedding, and Dick attended with his wife Linda. The only one in the family who didn't come was Zanuck himself—the one who counted most. He was much too busy—with what, no one could be certain, since he scarcely had any work then. No one in the family knew that Zanuck's health was very poor. His absence was an embarrassment. Virginia was infuriated by her husband's neglect of his grandchild; she was also bitterly disappointed that she wouldn't be seeing him. Darrylin was disinclined to fret about his nonappearance. She could not understand her mother's obsessive desire to see Zanuck when it was obvious that he was not interested in her.

*   *   *

Virginia was very much interested in Zanuck, however. Margaret Shands recalled that she found Virginia still obsessed with Zanuck when she visited Ric-Su-Dar one summer weekend in 1972. She sometimes wondered why Virginia had not simply divorced Zanuck and remarried. Even though Virginia was nearly seventy years old, her figure was as trim as it must have been when she had been a Mack Sennett bathing beauty back in the 1920s. Her dyed auburn hair shone. Only Virginia's skin revealed her age. The sun had taken its toll, and her face was quite wrinkled.

Shands had brought Virginia a copy of *The Happy Hooker,* one of the publishing sensations of the early seventies. The book recounted Xaviera Hollander's steamy adventures as a New York call girl. Shands wanted Virginia to see the book not for any particularly prurient interest, but because it contained a passage about Zanuck. Earlier that week, a gossipy friend had telephoned Shands to find out whether Virginia had read it. "Look for the part about the American movie magnate," counseled the caller. "You'll be able to see that it's Darryl— very, very thinly disguised. His name isn't there, but you'll know that it's Darryl." Shands ran out and bought a copy and quickly found the pertinent passage.

Though the reference to Zanuck made her queasy, Mrs. Shands gave the book to Virginia, reasoning that her friend might get a charge out of it. Then, too, if Virginia was hurt by her husband's sexual exploits, it would be better if she received the news of his latest from a friend rather than from some catty Hollywood hostess. Besides, Mrs. Shands knew that Virginia hungered for any news of her husband. In the sixteen years since he had left her, she had gathered information on him and his paramours more prodigiously than a reference librarian. She had sent him birthday cards and notes. She had even sued him. Anything to keep him a part of her life.

Still, Shands grew anxious, watching her friend as she read the passage. She knew exactly what Virginia was reading because the words were burned in her memory:

> One of the rare cases of men over sixty still being strong enough to screw is an American movie magnate, and I know this because he has made love to me several times.

This famous man always specifically requests me and another of my girls to come to his suite in the Plaza Hotel, where he waits for us dressed in an expensive silk morning gown.

There is very little conversation when we arrive, and we usually have time to admire his original Dali and Picasso canvases before his imported girl friend saunters in with the air of someone just passing by, then undresses and lies on the bed.

For some strange reason the movie man never makes love to his young girl friend although he keeps her in high style and has bought her a co-op in a luxury East Side building.

The two hired girls undress as well and begin to make love to the foreign girl while he sits there, his gown falling open, of course, in a splendid Louis XV chair. And I must say for an antique himself, this movie man has got a beautiful big cock.

After the three girls on the bed have been making it for about fifteen minutes—with one girl kissing the foreigner's breasts while I give it to her with my vibrating tongue—she curls around and whispers in my ear: "All right, I'm going to fake it now." And she pretends to have an orgasm to please her movie-magnate lover. . . .

After she pretends to climax, the tycoon takes off his robe and screws one of the hired girls, usually me. And I must say he is pretty strong and fantastic for over sixty—as long as you close your eyes.

Shands recalled Virginia laughing when she finished reading. "That's DZ, all right," declared Virginia. "Everything fits. He lives at the Plaza. He has a silk dressing gown. And he has those paintings—but, of course, they're not originals. They're just a couple of fakes the studio made up for a movie. And that's his trashy little French friend Genevieve." Shands pointed out that maybe the girlfriend was somebody else. Zanuck's companion Genevieve Gilles had not been named—it could have been another woman.

"Oh, don't be ridiculous," responded Virginia firmly. "Of course it's Genevieve. She's imported. And he bought her a co-op apartment on East Fifty-seventh Street. That's her. I am certain that's Genevieve. And it's just what I thought about her all along. . . . You see, DZ doesn't really have anything to do with her. She's just a companion. He gives her money, and she pays the bills. She keeps track of his schedule. He's not really involved with her. See!" Virginia grabbed the book off her lap and pointed to the text. "He doesn't even sleep with her. She means nothing to him."

Shands was surprised that Virginia seemed somewhat invigorated by the book, even a little pleased. The fact that Zanuck hadn't actually had intercourse with the woman Virginia believed to be Genevieve gave Virginia a peculiar hope. Odd, Shands thought, because that was at best a technical distinction. Maybe Zanuck hadn't slept with her, but, if *The Happy Hooker* accurately described his activities, then he might as well have. Most wives would have been hurt and horrified, but not Virginia. She viewed the anecdote as a victory for herself. If her husband confined his sexual adventures to prostitutes, then in his heart he still really loved *her*.

He didn't seem to want to return to her, however. Several months later, in February 1973, when Zanuck signed a new will, Genevieve remained a major beneficiary. At the same time, he and Virginia finally settled a long-standing legal dispute over some insurance policies. It looked as though the two of them would continue their separate lives.

* * *

Only a month after signing the will, in March 1973, Zanuck was admitted to the hospital. Darrylin received the news by telephone at one of her boutiques in Acapulco. Vinnie Argentino called to report that Zanuck was quite ill. Said Darrylin, "She didn't go into [it at] any length because I became very hysterical about it. I was very upset. She just said, 'Your father is very, very sick, and I think he needs you.' . . . I rushed back to my house, got an overnight case, and got a ticket." Darrylin was certain her father was dying.

Still wearing her tropical clothing, Darrylin braved New York's early spring chill and went straight from the airport to the hospital where she met Dr. Carl Feind, her father's physician. The doctor told her that Zanuck hadn't eaten for three weeks. She was shocked when she went to his bedside. "He was very, very weak. He looked very thin and . . . very, very old . . . from when I had seen him last." Although Feind and his colleague, neurologist Carmine Vicale, thought Zanuck extremely disoriented, Darrylin didn't find his behavior strange in any way, she later said. He recognized her immediately and demanded, "What the hell are you doing here?" She was afraid to tell him she had come because she believed him to be seriously ill, for fear of upsetting him; so she casually announced that she was in New York on business.

Dick and Susan, accompanied by Susan's sixteen-year-old son, André Hakim, Jr., also arrived in New York. After listening to the doctors' verdict that Zanuck was suffering an organic brain syndrome—which now would be called Alzheimer's disease—and would probably never recover his memory and other mental faculties enough to care for himself, the family had to decide what to do about their father. It was clear that he could no longer stay on his own at the Plaza Hotel. He needed to recover from his physical illnesses in a therapeutic environment—perhaps a nursing home. Dick, according to Darrylin, suggested a rest spa in Switzerland, which made some sense. Zanuck, after all, loved Europe, and what else could the family do? Darrylin said she was outraged by the idea. Her father had a perfectly good home in Palm Springs. He would certainly improve faster in a warm climate. Dick was doubtful. He didn't know what Virginia would think of her husband visiting Ric-Su-Dar, and he couldn't imagine his father leaving Genevieve to return to the West and to his wife.

Richard telephoned his mother in California to get her reaction. Not too surprisingly, she ordered, "Bring my husband home." When the children told Zanuck that he should stay for a while at Ric-Su-Dar, he placidly agreed. He didn't seem to be worried about a possible clash between his estranged wife and his self-possessed mistress. Darrylin had already begun to wonder whether Zanuck's feelings for Genevieve had chilled. When the French model returned from travels unknown to visit her lover's bedside, he seemed not to want to be alone with her. Darrylin said in a deposition later, "We all arrived [at the hospital], Vinnie, myself, and Genevieve, and she said that she had been in Africa. . . . They didn't have too much to say to each other. . . . Vinnie thought maybe they wanted to talk alone, so I started to get up, and my father kept asking me to stay, and then finally I went outside for a few minutes, and afterwards Daddy asked . . . to speak to me alone. . . . He asked me why did I bring her, why did I go out [of his room], and I said, 'I thought you wanted to see her,' and he said, 'I don't want to see her!' "

Feeding Darrylin's penchant for melodrama, Zanuck darkly muttered that he hadn't eaten because he was afraid he was being poisoned. Could he be talking about Genevieve? More likely, he was irrationally accusing the staff at the Plaza because, during his eight-year liaison with Genevieve, she had never lifted a hand to cook him so much as a boiled egg. Still, Zanuck told Darrylin to get an airline reservation for Genevieve so that she could accompany him to Palm Springs.

In the battle over Zanuck's estate nearly ten years later, Darrylin claimed that Genevieve was planning to steal Zanuck away without the family's knowledge. When Darrylin arrived at the hospital on the morning of April 7, 1973, to help her father get ready for the trip, she said she found Genevieve getting him dressed for a drive in a car parked downstairs. Genevieve said she was merely preparing Zanuck for the flight. Somehow Zanuck managed to calm both women, and the party proceeded to Kennedy airport; however, the trip to California was marred by friction between them. They argued over who should give Zanuck his medication, who should sit next to him, and who should talk to him. By the time the plane landed late that afternoon, everybody was frazzled.

Everybody but Zanuck, who fairly leapt down the boarding steps from the plane and tore across the tarmac to see Virginia. He immediately took his wife's arm as though the two were strolling to a dinner party after an afternoon of croquet. When Dick whisked his reunited parents away, Darrylin was left to travel with Genevieve—the discarded mistress and daughter together in the backseat of Ed Meena's car.

Genevieve's mood did not improve when she arrived at Ric-Su-Dar. After insulting Virginia, throwing a cane at her lover, and screaming at Dick, she ran to the patio. It was Dick who stopped her from saying a final good-bye to Zanuck, but when the scuffle broke out, Genevieve and Darrylin were the two who tangled most viciously, pulling hair, kicking, and pushing. Darrylin took blows from her father's mistress and delivered a couple of strikes of her own with a determined self-righteousness. She was fighting for Daddy.

SIX
TOGETHER AGAIN

·

A
t last, the Zanuck family had been reunited. They had recaptured Darryl from Genevieve, from Europe, from his endless wanderings, and restored him to his proper place among them. Unfortunately, their trophy was in sad shape. Zanuck's weight had slid down to about ninety-eight pounds, and he wore a rope to keep his pants up, since no belt he owned was tiny enough. He was pale and weak. He didn't like to bathe or shampoo his hair and, as a result, had developed a crust on his scalp. His ears were filthy and stuffed with wax. He was also incontinent.

The morning after his father's return, Dick departed for Los Angeles. The two sisters, Tom Shirley, and Ed Meena stayed behind for a week to help out until Virginia got the house together. The labor was divided up neatly. Susan, who was used to cooking, took charge of the kitchen. Darrylin did the marketing. Alma Diehl, Shirley, and Meena helped straighten up the house, and Virginia took care of Darryl.

In the middle of the bustle sat Zanuck. He watched TV constantly and occasionally got himself wet in the pool. He stroked and petted his Yorkies. He seemed oblivious to the goings-on about him. Virginia quickly began hiring a staff for the house. She had her hands full with Zanuck. Every day his bedclothes had to be changed because "he wet and soiled his bed," said Rita Mahon, the housekeeper. He also needed help in getting dressed. Mrs. Mahon, a former beauty salon attendant, cleared up Zanuck's encrusted scalp by washing his hair and oiling the dry skin. Darrylin, however, did the most. No task deterred her. It was she, said Mrs. Mahon, who managed to clean her father's ears.

In Palm Springs, Darrylin became better acquainted with Ed Meena and Tom Shirley, who, only a decade older than she, were more her contemporaries than Virginia's. The pair visited Ric-Su-Dar nearly every weekend. The two men were both quite taken with Darrylin, and the three became good friends. Every morning, while eating toast and sipping coffee in the breakfast room, Darrylin would listen while Shirley, a stockbroker, proclaimed his investment ideas. He made it sound easy to make money in the market.

Zanuck himself was rarely in the mood to discuss money. He now had little control over his own funds. A month earlier, Virginia had persuaded him to put all of his money and stock in a "household trust" that would be managed by a bank. The income would go to pay his share of expenses. Zanuck had docilely agreed to the arrangement. Most of the time he seemed very subdued, though his behavior could be as shocking as ever. Said Meena, "On several occasions, we would be in the living room in the guest house. One end was the bar. And Mr. Zanuck would go behind the bar—and . . . he would urinate in the sink."

Even during Zanuck's first week at home, according to Ed Meena, Virginia, Darrylin, and Susan had a great many conversations "about how to get Genevieve Gilles out of the will." The discussions intensified when Darrylin returned in June 1973. They seemed to go on every single day, recalled Meena. "Got tiresome," he added. Virginia and Darrylin kept after Zanuck to change his will so that Genevieve was not his principal heir. He seemed confused about who she was. At one point, Meena remembered him responding, "Why would she be in my will? Who is that person?" The elderly mogul, who had once ordered people around like a general, was now completely suggestible. He would ask his wife, "What should I do?" Virginia would tell him to sit and watch TV, and so he did.

That summer of 1973, Paul Weiss Rifkind Wharton and Garrison, Zanuck's New York law firm, received typewritten letters from the mogul directing them to draft another will, even though Zanuck had written a new one only two months before returning to Palm Springs.

Genevieve was to be excised. All she would "inherit" was a forgiveness of any debts. A portfolio of municipal bonds would be divided among the grandchildren, and the rest of the estate would go to Darrylin and Susan. When the new will arrived in Palm Springs for Zanuck's review, however, he didn't seem interested. Virginia was annoyed, according to Meena, who was still a regular visitor.

The exclusion of Genevieve from Zanuck's will doesn't seem to have been the product of a family conspiracy so much as a simple result of the former mogul's forgetfulness. He seemed unable even to remember who in the world his ex-girlfriend was. A couple of years later, *Daily News* columnist Charles McHarry called Zanuck and asked for some kind recollections of his former female friends. Zanuck, he reported, "claimed to remember nothing of" Darvi, Greco, Demick, or Gilles. Not that he had much help in recalling. When Genevieve sent him a bouquet of red roses for his seventy-first birthday in September 1973, Virginia intercepted them and ripped them to shreds.

Like many victims in the early stages of senile dementia, Zanuck was slipping in and out. Much of the time, sufferers of the disease have trouble focusing on or remembering what happened five minutes before, then unexpectedly bear down with remarkable clarity. That October, Zanuck's two attorneys Richard Paul and Robert Laufer flew from New York to Palm Springs to meet with the retired producer. The lawsuits with Twentieth Century-Fox had finally been settled, and they wanted to explain the terms. The final outcome was somewhat humiliating for the mogul. He was required to give up his $50,000-a-year consultant's job with the company. Laufer didn't find his client lacking in mental acuity. "He understood everything we said, and he asked all the right questions." Zanuck also examined his new will, which he signed on October 31. He reminisced with the lawyers about the good old days at Twentieth Century-Fox. "It was a pleasant visit except for those two dogs," said Laufer. "They kept nipping at our ankles, which Zanuck thought was very funny."

At the beginning of 1974, Darrylin gave Thomas Shirley control over her trust fund. She felt that she had to have more money. The Middle East oil crisis had begun to cause a recession in the United States, and not as many tourists were visiting Acapulco. Shirley began trying to reshuffle her investments to produce a bigger yield. He replaced a second trustee, a lawyer, with his friend Ed Meena. That was an odd choice, since Meena, a studio prop man, could not claim to be a sophisticated financier. When Shirley began managing all of Darrylin's Stateside financial dealings, he found a mess. In September he learned that the IRS was threatening to seize Darrylin's trust fund in payment of her 1967 tax bill.

In 1975, Darrylin began to think about selling some of her jewelry. Over the years, her mother and father and their friends—including Joseph Schenck, Betty Grable, Merle Oberon, Douglas Fairbanks, Sr., Tyrone Power, and Clifton Webb—had given her many fine pieces. She took some of them to Emi Fors, who now owned several jewelry shops in Acapulco. Fors was serious about acquiring some of them to sell in her stores. However, the inclement economic climate had slowed her business, too. She decided that she couldn't afford to buy.

Fors was shocked and upset to learn only a few months later that the entire collection—worth about $250,000—had been stolen. Typically, Darrylin had no insurance. She and her husband Julio and their new grandson, Ricardo, then about eighteen months old, had been staying at the Holiday Inn in Westwood. The Pinedas had put the jewelry in a valise and stashed it in the trunk of their brown Ford LTD. Julio noted after a round of golf one afternoon when he put his clubs in the trunk that everything was where it was supposed to be. The next morning, when he was on his way with the baby to Marine Land, he found that the valise was gone. "I couldn't believe that they had left all that gorgeous jewelry in the trunk of their car," said Ms. Fors, shaking her head. Darrylin later said that friends had told her hotel safety deposit boxes were not secure; the valuables would be safer locked in the trunk of her car.

When Virginia heard of the theft, she was frantic. Although the West L.A. police were investigating and Darrylin was drafting press releases to alert newspapers and TV stations, Virginia decided to hire her own private investigator, John O'Grady. O'Grady, an athletic-looking man in his late forties with airline-pilot blue eyes and graying temples, was a retired commander of the narcotics unit of the L.A. Police Department. Virginia became very caught up in the investigation. She wrote so many little notes about clues to the detective that he began jokingly calling her "Ma Barker."

O'Grady, who was a licensed polygraph operator, decided to have hotel staffers and all of Darrylin's friends—including Tom Shirley—submit to a lie detector test. O'Grady became convinced that the valise had been taken by a hotel employee. He traced one suspect to Palm Springs, but the case was not solved and the jewelry never recovered. Several years later, according to a lawsuit Shirley filed for slander, both Darrylin and Virginia told their friends they were certain that he had stolen the collection. O'Grady thought the allegation was false; Shirley had passed his lie detector test with flying colors.

Zanuck was ill and no longer an energetic mogul father able to provide the money or support Darrylin needed. Like him, she seemed to want to collapse back into a previous existence that offered her more shelter. In 1975, the same year Darrylin lost her jewelry, Mona Skoff, Bobby Jacks's girlfriend from the Cheerio bar days, met three beautiful young girls who visited a boutique she owned in Santa Monica. They were selling some very original-looking hand-painted T-shirts. She decided to stock some, and the girls started telling her about themselves. They said that they had been living in Mexico for a number of years and that their mother's name was Darrylin. Bells went off in Skoff's head. Could these be Bobby Jacks's children?

It turned out, of course, that they were, but they hadn't seen their father in years and they wanted to meet him. Skoff had not talked to Bobby for years herself, but she knew from a friend that he was producing "The Waltons" for Lorimar, so she telephoned his office. He called her back immediately. "There are some people here who very much want to see you," she said. Within half an hour, he had driven to the store. "They were so happy when they saw each other. They were all crying," she said.

She was worried that Darrylin might be angry that she—"the other woman"—had reunited her daughters with their father. To her surprise, however, Darrylin invited Mona to join her and her former husband at a restaurant for dinner, and the meeting went very smoothly. Later, Skoff said she learned from Jacks that Darrylin had begun making noises about getting back together with him. He rebuffed her, and Darrylin was miffed with Jacks and angry with Skoff. "Darrylin thought I had something to do with it," she said.

In August 1975, Darrylin launched a lawsuit against Jacks for some $40,000 in back child support. She declared that she and her husband

Julio "have supported the children ever since we have been in Mexico, and, because of their substantial expenditures, we are continually in debt." Her bill for payments due included Steven and Helena who had not been under her direct care since she moved to Mexico. The suit seemed to have little merit. Darrylin had never pressed Jacks for payment, and the ten-year statute of limitations had already lapsed. To get the statute of limitations waived, Darrylin had to show good reason why she had not tried to collect the money from Jacks earlier. She came up with some strange excuses. Jacks, she contended, was a wife-beater. Jacks claimed in court papers that "These alleged beatings are the product of seventeen years of altered memories of a few heated arguments *which never led to any physical altercations.*" In any case, he would have had to reach very far to hit her in Mexico, since he was living in Europe at the time.

Darrylin had another even less plausible rationale. Patrick Dorian, who had long before relocated to Hawaii, was the villain. He "took some pictures of me in my Malibu home. In those pictures I was wearing a lace bra and panties approximately the size of a bikini. The next day I asked for the negatives and he destroyed certain negatives in my presence. Approximately two weeks later I had an argument with Mr. Dorian and he went to Hawaii." Subsequently, she said, when she asked Jacks to pay child support, "He stated to me if I continued to demand the money from him he was going to see my father received some very pretty pictures of me naked. . . . I would also be seeing myself on playing cards, trays, etc. . . . I never dared ask [Jacks] again and this was actually one of the reasons I decided to leave the United States." Jacks denied that he ever made such a threat. Dorian has said, "A lot of what she's said is untrue, but I don't care to say anything. Why kick a dead horse?" The Santa Monica court did not find Darrylin's case compelling and dismissed her petition in 1976.

In the midst of the battle, Darrylin added another child to her brood. Her daughter Robin Lyn's marriage had already ended, and the young woman decided to go back to school. Darrylin had eagerly taken over the care and raising of her grandchild Ricardo. Though the arrangement was initially intended to be temporary, it became per- manent after Robin remarried. Darrylin's life in Mexico meanwhile was coming loose at the seams. By late 1975, she owed money for store rent, inventory, and taxes, and a creditor had gone so far as to file a

$20,000 lien on Casa Arco Iris. Virginia came to the rescue with $80,000.

Few of Darrylin's friends in Acapulco knew about her financial troubles. In November 1975 she arranged a showing of Richard's newly released hit *Jaws* at the Acapulco Convention Center to benefit DAR charities. The weekend was to be a social as well as a charitable high mark. After the movie, there would be cocktail parties, including one at which artificial sharks would swim in a pool. Richard Zanuck, Linda Harrison, David Brown, his wife Helen Gurley Brown, Robert Shaw, Richard Dreyfuss, and Steven Spielberg were all on hand for the festivities, which were orchestrated, according to the *Acapulco News*, by "the petite and vivacious blonde who founded DAR, Darrylin Zanuck de Pineda, who went after all this like a shark." In editor Mike Oliver's weekly column, it came out that Darrylin had put her clothing shops up for sale. She had grown tired of the garment business. She thought she might start a children's shop at one of the hotels, and she intended to write a book about her dad called *Darryl Zanuck as a Father*. She declared that she had no plans to leave Acapulco.

It came as a surprise to all her friends in Acapulco when, late in 1976, Darrylin pulled up stakes and moved to a Santa Monica house that Virginia owned. Darrylin told a few of her friends that she was going home to care for her father. "I never did know exactly why she went back," said her friend Emi Fors. "She seemed to be doing all right here."

✳   ✳   ✳

In 1966, two years after her split with André Hakim, Susan Zanuck fell in love with a Frenchman named Pierre Savineau. Then thirty-three years old, he was the kind of man a woman dreams about. Tall and well built with a tanned craggy face and gray eyes, he exuded Gallic charm. "Ooooh, what a gorgeous man!" squealed Susan's friend Terry Moore, who met him on a visit to France. Savineau was a can-do type who could pilot a boat, fly a plane, fix the plumbing, and throw together a coq au vin without consulting a cookbook.

After a spell with the French army and its intelligence service, he became a yacht captain and worked for some of the wealthiest men in Europe. For a time he captained *La Favorita*, the boat owned by Egypt's King Farouk, a client of the famous Madame Claude, who some thought was Genevieve Gillaizeau's mentor. He had also worked as a consultant to Lloyds of London in investigations of nautical disasters. Savineau had achieved some notice in France. He was friendly with a number of doctors, and one night they began discussing people's tolerance for pain. The group divided into two camps: one believed that pain was inherently physical and susceptible to control only by drugs. The second faction, to which Savineau belonged, insisted that pain could be controlled by the mind. They wanted to conduct a strange experiment: operate on someone without anesthesia—though they didn't hold out much hope of finding a willing subject. "I said, 'I will do it,' " recalled Savineau, and he did. In 1966 the doctors removed his appendix without anesthesia. "I didn't feel nutheenk," he said with nonchalance. He thought the procedure lasted only nine minutes when it actually took seventeen minutes. The story made the French newspapers and TV reports, and, for a few months, Savineau was a celebrity.

If Susan thought that her father was manly, she must have been amazed by Pierre Savineau. After all, Darryl Zanuck, for all his adventures in the two world wars and his feats at hunting and polo, had always been afraid to go to the dentist.

Susan met Savineau when her sailboat fell into disrepair and she needed someone to fix it. A friend of Savineau's recommended him for the job, and he examined the boat and visited Susan at her rented villa in the south of France to give her an estimate. He moved in almost immediately. Both were swept away—she by his obvious assets. Now, years later, Savineau is hard put to remember just why he fell in love with Susan. "She was good-looking, yes, and she was only a social drinker then," was all he could muster.

By late 1966, Susan was pregnant with Pierre's child. Savineau liked life to be neat and shipshape. He insisted that Susan divorce Hakim so that they could marry. He, too, was separated but not divorced. They both cleared all the paperwork and married in early April of 1967. Savineau quickly learned that his wife's life was in disarray. "She had a thirty-gallon trash bag full of unopened mail and bills," he said. When he went through it, he found that five or six lawsuits had been filed against her by disgruntled creditors. Savineau spent four months clearing up the mess. He also discovered that a former boyfriend had borrowed money from her and taken a diamond necklace worth nearly two million francs to cover his gambling debts. "He was a kind of pimp in my opinion," proclaimed Savineau. "I made him pay back the money a few years later."

At their large wedding in Cannes, Susan wore white even though she was five months pregnant. Virginia flew in all the way from Los Angeles, but Zanuck did not attend. Susan sold her apartment in Paris and bought a villa. A few months later she gave birth to Craig. She hired a second nursemaid to help Louise de la Rivière, the children's nanny. The two older boys were sent away to school in Paris. Pierre told Susan that she should be taking care of her own children, but Susan had grown up a Zanuck. She wasn't about to give up her nightly rounds of the clubs to spend her days changing diapers.

The family stayed on in the bougainvillea-draped house in the hills above Cannes. Every day the car would take the children to the beach, and on weekends the family would sail on their boat. Although Zanuck spent most of his time in Paris, the Savineaus saw him only when he was on vacation in the south of France. "The family was not close," said Savineau. "It was 'hello–good-bye' on Christmas and birthdays—nothing more." Zanuck usually stayed at the Hôtel du Cap on Cap d'Antibes or at the Hôtel Biblos in town. Always at his side was Genevieve, his girlfriend. She was blond and tall and beautiful— much younger than Susan. But everyone got along. There were times when all of them—Zanuck, Genevieve, Savineau, Hakim, the kids, and the nannies—would take a day-long cruise on the Mediterranean on Hakim's yacht, the *Sharon Marie*. "It was a nice life," sighed Savineau, remembering the easy days and nights.

Susan remarked to Savineau that she had never seen her father so deeply in love, but Savineau was unimpressed with Genevieve. He knew by her accent where she came from. "She always kept everything a mystery. She was from the Paris suburbs. I said, 'You are from Argenteuil,' and she answered, 'Close enough.'" Savineau had a definite feeling that Genevieve didn't like men too much. She was simply after Zanuck's money, he thought. As for Zanuck, Savineau was convinced that the aging mogul preferred women who didn't prefer men. "All the women Darryl was involved with were like that," he insisted. Pierre Savineau, however, was not one to criticize. He liked to talk to Genevieve, and they sometimes reminisced about Paris, and Zanuck seemed happy. "*Ça m'est égal,*" Savineau would say with a shrug.

Virginia occasionally flew over from the United States to visit. Susan had confided to Savineau that her mother had had an affair with Bella Darvi. He believed the story. Once, in 1968, when Virginia arrived in Cannes, Susan and Savineau decided to take her around to the nightclubs. They ran into Bella Darvi. Savineau was certain that Bella knew Virginia was in town—"there had been little announcements in the newspapers," he said. "Bella wanted to show off, make Virginia mad." Bella entered the nightclub, accompanied by two men, and the three of them paraded to a prominent table. Savineau's mother-in-law, when she spotted her one-time houseguest, lost her composure completely. "She jumped out of her seat and leapt up on a table and tried to reach for Bella's throat," said Savineau. "I had to pull her off. I picked her up by her collar and the seat of her pants, she was so little, and put her back in her chair. Then the two big men, they started making trouble. I said, 'You want to make trouble? Okay, fine,' and one of them, he hit me, and I knocked him down, and then I punched the other one. I had a bruise on my face, but that was okay." In the confusion, the Savineaus and Virginia beat a retreat. Savineau attributed Virginia's outburst to distress that her affair with the actress had ended badly, though one could also conclude that Virginia was angry at the woman who had stolen her husband.

Savineau was not happy about the way life was going in Cannes. He wanted Susan to attend to the children. She seemed to pay scarcely any attention to them and they were growing up wild. Susan was drinking too much. Running around to nightclubs all the time was no way for a mother of four to act, in his opinion. He longed to move to the country, where, he felt, the children would be exposed to ordinary people and solid values. Susan at first was unenthusiastic, but Savineau was a forceful character. After a great deal of stalling and wrangling, she agreed they would look for a farm or a ranch. They picked out a place in Revest-du-Bion, a small farming community about 150 miles north of Cannes. To pay for the farm, Susan sold her villa and Savineau a pleasure craft he owned. Savineau built a barn and bought a flock of sheep. He also acquired a small plane and joined a flying club. That way, he could fly the family up to Paris or down to Nice whenever they wanted. Susan threw herself wholeheartedly into country life. The Savineaus employed two or three farmworkers to help with the ranch, and Susan took on the job of cooking for all of them.

Life in the country eventually began to pall for the normally bubbly Susan. She missed the nightlife of Paris and Cannes. Her natural optimism crumbled even more after she returned from escorting her father—along with Darrylin, Genevieve, André, Jr., and Vinnie Argentino—to Palm Springs in 1973. She later told Savineau that when she arrived at the New York hospital where her father lay ill and found him disoriented and confused, she was so upset about his condition that she could scarcely stand to be in the room for longer than fifteen minutes. After a brief visit, she would have to lie down. Only her sister could bear to stay with him for any length of time.

If Susan was anxious to have her father change his will, she never told her husband. Said Savineau, "She didn't mention it." She probably had little time to think about it, because in June 1973, shortly after her return from the United States, she was thrown headlong into a new drama reminiscent of her father's World War II spy movies. A warrant had been issued by the Swiss government for the arrest of her former husband André Hakim on charges of fraud by Twentieth Century-Fox in the so-called black money scheme. The French government had already seized his passport, and his arrest appeared imminent. Hakim called on Pierre Savineau for help.

Savineau had no doubt that Hakim was guilty of all charges. He had always lived beyond his means; he had a house in London, a flat in Paris, and a villa in Cannes. He owned a Rolls-Royce, a Jaguar, and a Porsche. Savineau, however, was convinced that Darryl Zanuck had engineered the fraud and that Hakim had been caught in his intrigues. Even though Susan pleaded with her husband not to get involved, he set off to rescue Hakim. Savineau was always ready to play the hero and had grown to like his wife's former husband. So he and André, Jr., then sixteen years old, traveled to Paris to see what they could do for the besieged French producer.

Hakim had not yet been arrested, but he was certain the police were on their way. Savineau and André, Jr., stashed him in a car and drove all night to the Italian border. Hakim managed to talk his way past immigration officials using his son's passport. From Italy Hakim flew to Los Angeles.

The Savineaus followed Hakim a few years later. Their life together in Revest-du-Bion was eroding quickly. Susan seemed bored. She drank a lot and, some days, never left her bedroom. The house was always in disorder. Meanwhile, André, Jr., and Dino infuriated Savineau. They were spoiled and arrogant, he complained. The ranch wasn't making a profit, and the family was forced to live on Susan's trust fund income. Susan seemed to want to go home to California, maybe to leave Pierre, but she couldn't come to a decision. In 1976 she learned that her older sister Darrylin had moved, with her husband and four children, to Los Angeles from Acapulco. Susan worried, too, that her sister was after Zanuck's money.

But money could not have been the only thing that drew Susan back to California. On her own, she had never managed to make a life for herself that was as clearly defined as the one she'd had in her youth, when she was Daddy's girl. In those days, her father had sat like a sun in the heavens, and she and her family had been bathed in his fame and importance. By contrast, her own life seemed squalid and empty. She seemed eager to become a part of the Zanuck legend again. She nagged at Savineau to leave France. André, Jr., was already living with his grandparents at Ric-Su-Dar in Palm Springs, and Dino was with André, Sr., in Los Angeles. Half of the family was already in California, Susan argued; they should go, too. Savineau finally agreed. Still, the two fought constantly. Their war of words often turned physical. Susan and her daughter Sherry argued, too. "Mom would shove me around," said her daughter. "One day Pierre got into it, too, and Mom fell down and broke her hip." They decided to depart for Palm Springs as soon as Susan was released from the hospital. The Savineaus—with Susan in a wheelchair—decamped suddenly, without selling the ranch or engaging a caretaker.

When the family finally arrived at the big gates of Ric-Su-Dar in

Palm Springs, Savineau immediately spotted Zanuck waiting for them in front of the glass doors. He was wearing bathing trunks and a polo shirt. He greeted them warmly but seemed vague about who everybody was.

Darryl Zanuck's condition had by this time become a matter for an all-family cover-up. Virginia did not want to believe that her strong, self-willed husband was not in command of his faculties. It was difficult enough to supervise his care, to make sure he didn't wander away or hurt himself. So strong was Virginia's denial that it left both family and friends confused. Savineau said he did not think that Zanuck was senile. Indeed, Zanuck would talk authoritatively about the good old days. Still, the former mogul would often ask the same questions over and over again, even after they had been answered. Zanuck was never allowed to leave the estate unaccompanied. Only Richard seemed able to face the sad truth. In 1976 he told a reporter who asked after Zanuck that his father was senile and living with Virginia in Palm Springs.

Friends who visited Zanuck usually did so under Virginia's watchful eye. They came away from Ric-Su-Dar with the impression that all was well. Pokie Seeger, who saw the Zanucks at a fiftieth wedding anniversary party soon after Zanuck's return, thought that the former magnate seemed "Okay—maybe just a bit subdued." Margaret Shands, during her annual visits, found that Zanuck always remembered who she was, but he had a funny walk. "He dragged his foot." She called it a "syphilitic walk" and speculated to friends that Zanuck had contracted a venereal disease that had affected his brain.

Most victims of Alzheimer's disease suffer complete loss of recent memory but can competently discuss events that occurred years earlier. When Zanuck's old friends visited, they found the one-time mogul in fine fettle. Henry McIntyre, Zanuck's former Fox colleague, visited with his wife and another Fox executive in 1976. "When I saw him, he was more himself than he had been in years," he said. "Darryl was *not* delighted to see me. Not at all. I was a party to the other side in the 1971 proxy fight, and he remembered. No problem with his memory there." Zanuck wouldn't sit with McIntyre or talk to him. He confined himself to conversation with the other executive. In March 1976, on the evening of the Academy Awards presentation, Zanuck had given an interview to television reporter Gloria Greer of KMIR-

TV in neighboring Palm Desert, California. She recalled that Virginia dropped Zanuck off at the station but didn't stay for the interview. "Of course he was able to answer questions; otherwise, I wouldn't have had him on the air," said Greer. The subject of the interview was the good old days in Hollywood. Greer added, "He was not senile by any means, but upon review of the tape at a later date I'd have to say I prompted him a bit."

*   *   *

If Susan hoped that her father would provide some kind of spiritual rescue, she must have been disappointed. Zanuck no longer carried any clout in family doings, and without him in command, the family began to collapse. Virginia was now the linchpin of the entire clan, and she confronted crisis after crisis.

The Savineaus settled down in the house Virginia had rented for them, but the empty days seemed to play on everybody's nerves. Susan continued her heavy drinking, and Savineau couldn't work because he didn't have a green card. The two older boys were constantly making trouble. They took drugs—Dino with a fervor that the entire family found scary. They were picked up for drunken driving, and they were constantly getting into accidents. The boys were never arrested because, said Savineau, once a year Virginia Zanuck gave an important officer on the Palm Springs police force a $10,000 "contribution." The "charity" was the policeman's personal bank account.

Mona Skoff, Bobby Jacks's one-time friend, met Susan soon after the Savineaus moved to Palm Springs. Darrylin's daughter Robin Lyn had driven up from Los Angeles to visit her aunt, and she called Skoff, who had remarried and moved to the desert resort herself. "My aunt would love to meet you," Robin Lyn told Skoff. Eventually, Susan and Mona Skoff became close friends. She quickly became aware of the constant crises overwhelming Susan. Soon after her arrival in Palm Springs, Susan's rental house burned to the ground. According to Sherry, Savineau was desperate for money; so he and Dino decided to set a car on fire and collect the insurance money. The fire spread to the rest of the house, and the family escaped only by chance. Savineau insisted that only Dino was behind the scheme. "Anyway, the car was registered to Virginia, and she collected the money," said Savineau.

Susan panicked; she and Sherry narrowly escaped. She knew she should do something, but her resolve always melted in a new round of drinking.

Money had become a bigger and bigger issue. The Savineaus were still living off the income from Susan's trust fund, and it was not yielding enough. Most of the money had been invested in Twentieth Century-Fox, and the company had not been healthy since the late 1960s. Virginia Zanuck and her Los Angeles business manager, the blustery Henry Bamberger, were urging Susan to allow him to sell the stock. He wanted to reorganize her portfolio and buy stocks that would throw off more income. Fox hadn't paid investors much of a dividend for years. Susan was reluctant to sell, according to her son André, Jr., but "Virginia and Bamberger were constantly after her. You have to sell them." Finally, in late 1976, she agreed. She had about 30,000 shares, and the sale earned some $300,000. A few months later, in May 1977, Virginia gave a broker permission to sell about half of Zanuck's 68,000 shares.

That same month saw the beginning of a deep distrust among the Zanucks. Only days after Zanuck's stock was sold, Fox released *Star Wars*. By that fall, Fox prices had climbed to over $40 a share. When Susan heard the news, she was hysterical. "She was up in arms and crying," said Mona Skoff. She was constantly railing at her sons and her friend that somehow her brother had done her out of the money. Added Skoff, "There was a lot of name-calling. Susan had this terrible, terrible anger about it. She would be in tears—'My brother, he cheated me.' " Susan finally decided to confront Bamberger in his office at Century City. She took along Skoff and her two boys. The scene was very unpleasant. Susan wept and accused Bamberger, who tried to reason with her. Dino got very excited and threw a punch at Bamberger. The business manager called for security and had all of them thrown out.

According to Savineau, Susan believed that her brother was behind all the stock sales. "She thought he was trying to take over the company," he said. When the effort fell through, went her theory, he simply sold the stock he had amassed, netting a huge profit from the family shares. Bamberger asserted that Dick had nothing to do with the stock sales. Indeed, that same year, when Richard filed a list of his assets in court for his divorce from Linda Harrison, he professed to owning only one share of Fox stock. Bamberger maintained that Susan's Fox stock had to be sold to produce more income for her family. "Nobody in that family—not one of them—worked or made money," he said. "Susan had to support all of them. So I had to figure out ways to generate more income. It would be nice to have the virtue of hindsight, but I didn't know that Fox would go up. I did what I thought was right."

Bamberger's account made sense. Stock analysts had not been immediately impressed with *Star Wars*. Fox stock had not done well for years; it was unclear whether the success of the movie would have a major impact on the stock. Indeed, six months passed before the stock began its surge. Yet Susan believed herself to have been swindled, and she had had some bitter discussions with her mother about the matter.

The strange conspiracy theory grew out of a deep rancor toward Richard that had begun to pervade the entire family. He had had big successes—*The Sting* with Robert Redford and Paul Newman had appeared in 1973—and earned tens of millions. He had bragged to reporters after the release of *Jaws* that his one movie made more money than everything his father had done in a lifetime of production.

His family had come to resent his good fortune—and it was his own fortune—and he knew it. He later told an interviewer, "I was the only working member of the family. My two sisters lived off the residue of the family fortune. . . . What was disturbing to my two sisters and even, strangely enough—and I'll never quite understand this—to my mother, was that I was becoming more successful than my father. There was a basic, almost unrealistic resentment when the receipts from *The Sting* and *Jaws* came in. . . . Their attitude toward me changed. It went beyond envy. A *dislike* set in."

Dick Zanuck had recovered in good form after his December 1970 ouster from Twentieth Century-Fox. Only a few months later, he and David Brown had hooked up with Warner Brothers. Unfortunately, Warners never seemed to want to do anything, and after a year, the Zanuck-Brown team departed for Universal where they rebuilt their careers in a grand way. First came *The Sting*, which won the Academy Award for best picture of 1973, the year the elder Zanuck returned home. Then, in 1974, with a virtually unknown director named Steven Spielberg, Zanuck and Brown produced a critical success, *Sugarland Express*. Along the way were a couple not-so-dashing movies—*The Girl from Petrovka* and *The Black Windmill*—but they were soon followed by *Jaws*, the blockbuster that munched up about $150 million in domestic box-office receipts. Dick's share of the profits reportedly came to $20 million.

That much money could arouse the green-eyed monster sleeping in any relative's soul. Dick's millions seemed only part of what made his family unhappy with him, however. Perhaps if he had taken on his father's role as the idolized center of their lives who gave them walk-on parts in his dramatic successes, they would have been satisfied. But he was unwilling to follow that scenario. So they criticized his conduct as a husband and father.

By 1972, Dick's second wife, Linda, had become discontented. Her marriage to Dick had had to withstand unnerving applications of stress. Only a year after they wed, Dick was fired by his father; then came his lawsuit against his dad and Twentieth Century-Fox; and, finally, he went through two job changes. Linda, meanwhile, was raising four children—the couple's two toddlers, Dean and Harrison, as well as Ginny and Janet, Dick's teenage daughters from his marriage to Lili. Since their parents' divorce, the two girls had bounced back and forth between their mother and their father, finding no easy refuge in either home. Linda had a full-time housekeeper, a nursemaid, and other servants to help, but she seemed overwhelmed anyway. To her, her husband seemed overly preoccupied with money. A bit of resentment tinged her feelings toward her husband. According to court records, she was disappointed that she had not been given the supporting role of police chief Roy Scheider's wife in *Jaws*. The part had instead gone to Lorraine Gary, wife of Sidney Sheinberg, then president of MCA/Universal, the company producing the film. Linda was hurt, she later said, that her husband had not stood up for her. Complaining about aches, pains, and burning sensations in her bones, she had confided her woes to her masseuse, who recommended that Linda see the Maha Genii Vincentii Turriziani, a Christian guru who had installed himself in an apartment on Vermont Avenue.

To all but the spiritually desperate, the scrawny sixty-five-year-old religious leader, with his long unkempt hair and wire-rimmed glasses, must have seemed unappealing. From his perch on a chair that disciples called "the mercy seat," the Maha Genii, who headed up the Risen Christ Temple Light of Translation Foundation, declared that he was a conduit for a God-given holy light that could cure diseases and ease stress. Soon Linda became one of the Maha's most ardent disciples. Most of the Zanuck clan who heard about Linda's beliefs thought that the Maha was no more genuine than a rubber chicken and twice as ridiculous. But Linda was not to be deterred. She was convinced, she told everybody, that the Maha could cause great things to happen in people's lives by sending them the Light, and she was certain that the success of *The Sting* could be laid at the Maha's mercy seat.

The early seventies were guru-time in California, and nearly everybody in Beverly Hills had a personal swami; so Linda's attachment to the Maha initially seemed more stylish than weird. One spring night in 1974, however, she came home from a foundation meeting and announced excitedly that she had broken through to a new spiritual self. She had proclaimed her belief that the Maha Genii was Jesus Christ, and in return, he had given her a new name—Augusta Summerland—in recognition of her spiritual rebirth. Thereafter, she was fanatically devoted to him. That summer, when she and Dick were in Massachusetts to film *Jaws*, she called the Maha daily. She even asked his advice on whether the children should be vaccinated.

Linda begged Dick to visit the Maha and take part in his meditations. Dick was too involved with material things, she complained, and needed more spiritual guidance. The Maha himself seemed peculiarly interested in the material things he thought were so terrible for everyone else: he urged Linda to get her husband to tithe his income to the Maha to prove his selflessness. Though Dick was deeply in love with Linda, he did not accept either suggestion.

But Linda was adamant, and their fights about the Maha grew more and more bitter. Though she clung to the Maha Genii with the loyalty of a Girl Scout, she fretted about a guilty secret that she later revealed in testimony in a court battle between herself and the guru: her involvement with the Maha had become sexual as well as spiritual, and she had slept with him. In September of 1974 she and Dick had a violent quarrel about the Maha that began at dinner in Newport Beach, where they had a second house. Her screams, she said, brought Dick's fifteen-year-old daughter Ginny running into the bedroom, begging her father to stop. Then and there, Linda said, she determined to get away for a few days; she left a week later on September 28, 1974.

A few weeks later, Linda struck back. In October 1974 she sent long letters to the editor of the *Los Angeles Times* and to her husband's superiors at Universal describing in excruciating detail Dick's violent nature as well as her marital difficulties. In Newport Beach, during their argument about the Maha, she wrote, Dick threw her on the bed, pinned her down by sitting on her, and delivered karate chops to her face. Her leave-taking, according to the letter, provoked her husband even further. Around midnight on the day she left, he and David Brown had paid a visit to the Maha Genii at his sanctuary. Dick bluntly accused the Maha of trying to break up his marriage. The guru countered that it was Linda who wanted to end the marriage.

In fact, as a jury later concluded in a court battle between Linda and the Maha, her spiritual adviser had been prodding her to divorce. Reluctant and uncertain of herself, Linda later said she could break up her marriage only if the Maha stood by her. He apparently agreed to do so—for a price: one-half of any settlement she might win from her wealthy husband. On that night in 1974 the Maha's claims to be a neutral party must have struck Dick as outrageously disingenuous because, when he heard them, said Linda in her letters, he dashed across the sanctuary to the mercy seat and began throwing punches at the Maha, who fended off the blows with his feet. Dick smashed a statue and pulled down several paintings by the Maha. The Maha managed to escape to a small back room, but Dick pursued him there, pushed him down on a couch, picked up a chair, and smashed it across his legs. Brown finally got his friend to leave, but on his way out, Dick pulled down two more religious paintings.

The ugly incident might have faded away, but Linda had gone public with her letters, which described several other violent episodes. The worst was an argument between Dick and his younger daughter, Janet, who was then fourteen. According to Linda, Dick became so enraged with Janet that he shoved her down the stairs. When Dick received the letters from his bosses at Universal, he showed them to his attorney, who sent a letter to Linda's lawyer demanding that she stop circulating "scurrilous and false" stories. All the documents were filed in court as part of their divorce suit, and the Reuters news service picked up the story and sent it out on the wire.

Dick stood to lose everything he valued—his wife, his children, and even his connection to Universal. He finally had his lawyer call Linda to say that Dick would give the Maha Genii 10 percent of his income and visit him once a week for a one-on-one session. Anything to keep the peace. One friend close to the family recalled, "Dick didn't want to divorce Linda, because he didn't want to give up half his money. So he decided to look the other way and forget about the Maha."

Little peace was to be had, however. Dick never paid the Maha, but Linda gave the greedy guru her own money. She charged gifts for the Maha on her credit cards and turned over nearly all of her allowance to him. But the Maha was still not satisfied. In the spring of 1977 he telephoned Linda and Dick and escalated his demands. He wanted 10 percent of their income *and* of their assets. The Maha argued that, by counseling Linda, he was giving Dick spiritual help, too, and should be paid like a talent agent or a personal manager. The phone call made Linda very anxious; she feared that if her husband didn't pay, he would lose his spirit, and she would be yoked in life to a materialistic person. Finally, to keep the family together, Dick made a counteroffer of a $50,000 flat fee. The Maha instructed Linda to accept.

That summer, after Dick went east to begin filming *Jaws II*, Linda moved to their Newport Beach home and filed for divorce. She consulted the Maha about every move she made, calling him several times a day. She was receiving $2,000 a month for living expenses, but gave the entire amount to the guru. When she and her husband officially parted in late 1977, Linda won a $2.5 million property settlement. By February 1978, she had given half of it to the Maha. Only a few months later, he broke with her.

Virginia was not thrilled with this turn of events, but she fretted still more over Dick's relationship to his two daughters, Ginny and Janet. Both had been drawn into the family turmoil over the Maha. Linda had taken them to see the guru, and they seemed to fall under his sway. They skipped school, and Richard worried that they were in-volved with drugs—and he was right. "The girls were living with me at the time, but their father wanted them with him," said their mother, Lili Gentle. "He never filed any court papers; it was just a nagging thing. I never refused him the right to see his kids, and I finally let them visit him for three months in the summer. They just ran amuck down there. Linda was deeply involved with the Maha Genii, and that was a tremendous contribution to their problems. The kids had stabil-ity with me, but with Linda, they ran amuck, and that led to their involvement with drugs. But, it never got so bad that they needed drug treatment or stole the silver to get them. They were very unhappy." Dick tried to clamp down on his daughters and enforce strict discipline, but they responded by running away. For a time, they lived on the Santa Monica beach, stealing garbage from dumpsters for food. Both Virginia and Darrylin felt that Dick should try to get them back or give them money—something he had plenty of—but he seemed disinclined, perhaps fearing that his funds would only go to buy drugs. Keeping his money seemed terribly important to him—maybe because it served as proof that he had bested his competitive father. His mother and sisters thought his behavior selfish. By 1978, they found more fuel for their anger. Richard was getting serious about another young woman, whose name, like his first wife's, was Lili—Lili Fini. The judgment of the family was that his new girlfriend was as self-centered as he. Darrylin remarked sarcastically, "He's finally found a woman who is his match."

*   *   *

Darrylin had more reason than anyone else in the family to begrudge her brother's wealth because she had lost most of her trust fund. Toward the end of 1977, she claimed in court papers filed in a dispute over her money, she made a horrible discovery. Her fund, at one time worth $900,000, had been whittled down to $324,000. She didn't know how she would live without her income. She told Virginia that Thomas Shirley, her investment adviser, had cheated her out of the money. Virginia believed everything her daughter was telling her. At Thanksgiving dinner that year, Virginia railed to all her guests—including Susan and Savineau—that Tom Shirley had stolen Darrylin's money. Furthermore, he had taken Darrylin's jewelry. The man was dishonest and crooked, she raged, and her daughter was going to sue.

Most of Virginia's friends believed Darrylin's story. Margaret Shands said she had always been suspicious of Shirley—and, to a lesser extent, of his friend Ed Meena. Shirley was always trying to sell *her* investments. She recalled that once, during a visit to Palm Springs, Shirley took her to see a motel he wanted to buy. "He didn't have any money; he wanted *me* to put up the money," said Shands. When she declined to invest, she added, "he made the statement that he had the richest damn friends in the world, and not one of them would part with a penny. When Shirley was in charge of Darrylin's trust fund, he bought himself a big house and drove a Mercedes-Benz," recalled Mrs. Shands.

John O'Grady, who looked into the matter for "Ma Barker," concluded that Shirley had not done anything wrong. "He only got about $30,000 in commissions over several years. I think Darrylin was pressing him to make a lot of money fast, and he made mistakes, errors of judgment."

Darrylin's financial dealings with Shirley were nothing if not mysterious. She may have been naive, but she apparently never questioned the selection of Ed Meena, the prop man, as Shirley's fellow trustee. About the same time she claimed to have discovered that Shirley had looted her trust fund, she borrowed $17,000 from him. She never repaid the loan. At least that was his contention. She waited until 1979—two years later—before she sued him. She charged him with breach of fiduciary responsibility and a host of securities violations, claiming that she was an innocent who invested with a trusted adviser who assured her he could produce growth and income. Instead, she asserted, he churned her account. Shirley promptly went to court to get back the $17,000. She responded in a countersuit that she never borrowed the money. One of Darrylin's suits against Shirley was dismissed, and the others faded from the judicial calendar because they weren't pursued. By 1980, however, Shirley claimed his credibility with customers had been ruined. He left his brokerage firm and had little remaining in savings. For her part, Darrylin survived on the income from the remainder of her trust fund and on loans from her father.

* * *

Darrylin didn't visit Palm Springs all that often, but when she did, she and Susan were cool to each other. Susan did not feel that her sister loved her—at least, not at the end. One night, her friend Mona

Skoff recalled, she went to Susan's house to visit. "My sister Darrylin hates me," Susan stated, adding, "And I hate my sister, too. She is a wicked, wicked, vicious person."

Susan never revealed the source of their animosity. "It seemed as though it must be something that went way, way back," said Skoff. Their relationship seemed to have grown into broad dislike. Darrylin thought Susan was too wayward. Susan believed Darrylin was "a snake, a conniving snake." Darrylin hated the fact that Susan had no control over her children. Susan thought that her sister held too tight a rein on hers. Darrylin was sloppy with her money; Susan was almost tight. Susan was a drunk; Darrylin was a health freak.

Meanwhile, Susan's marriage to Savineau was falling apart. Although Savineau has said that he never touched Susan, both André, Jr., and Sherry claimed that their mother and stepfather beat each other up all the time. Susan was smaller, so she got the worst of it. According to Sherry, her mother's face was often black-and-blue and swollen like a balloon. Savineau already knew his marriage was over. When Susan hit him with a cast-iron frying pan, he called the police and filed a complaint. Virginia Zanuck begged him to withdraw it, but he refused. He wanted to make sure that he, too, would have grounds for divorce. Virginia began making threats to him: if he didn't drop the complaint, something might happen to him. One day, as he got into his car after buying groceries at the local supermarket, he was approached by a former police officer. According to Savineau, the policeman warned him that if he didn't drop the complaint against Susan, he would be sorry; some people would come to the house and beat him up. Savineau grabbed the man by the collar and drew his face through the car window close to his own. He then pushed the button to close the window on the policeman's head. "I told him that if he did anything to me, I would go to the Palm Springs police and tell them about the $10,000 Virginia had paid him each year to keep everything the Zanuck kids did all hushed up," said Savineau. That night Savineau had several friends come to the house to stand guard. Nothing happened.

There seemed to be no limit to what the Zanucks would do to get rid of him, however. Savineau had been frantically trying to get a green card so that he could work and move out; it seemed stalled for months. Finally, he called up an immigration official in Los Angeles to find out what was delaying the card. The official was surprised. The green card had been mailed to Ric-Su-Dar but had come back three days later with a note from Virginia Zanuck saying that Savineau no longer lived in California and had returned to France. Savineau has also claimed that Susan and her mother tried to make him appear to be a child molester. He came home one night to find two of Sherry's schoolmates waiting for him in his bedroom in various states of undress. He said he told them to get dressed and leave, but the incident became part of Zanuck family gossip. Pokie Seeger, Susan's friend, felt that Virginia's accusations were well founded. "There was a very dark feeling in that house, very dark," she said.

It turned darker still one day in July 1978 when Savineau returned after shopping to find the family's rental house on El Chorro completely vandalized. His stepson Dino had slashed open mattresses and taken a golf club to the walls. China had been smashed, food was thrown on the floor, Susan and the children were gone, and nobody knew where they were. It was only after André, Jr., called that Savineau learned the reason for the mess. André told him that Dino believed Savineau had sexually molested his sister Sherry; Dino had torn up the house in anger. "Pierre never did anything to me," said Sherry years later. "That was a ridiculous idea. He never touched me like that. I think Pierre did have eyes for one of my friends. Maybe there was something there, but he acted like a father to me."

Though Sherry tried to remonstrate with her brothers and mother, Susan decided to stay away. Unbeknownst to Savineau, she had holed up with her kids in a suite at a Holiday Inn only a few miles from home. Savineau was terribly upset. Susan had taken their only child, ten-year-old Craig, and Savineau didn't think she could care for him properly. She was constantly drunk and never made an effort to give the child regular meals, see that his clothes were washed, or take him to school. Savineau had done all that himself. When he finally found out where Susan was, he called and told her that if he didn't see Craig, properly dressed, attending summer school each morning, he would complain to the police and to the child welfare agencies. Every morning he drove by the school to make sure that Craig was in attendance.

After a month, in August 1978, Susan filed for divorce. In an affidavit, she asserted that her husband had repeatedly beaten her and their son. "The attacks have at times been so violent as to cause severe bruising, lacerations, and broken bones." The anger, she said, arose from money problems. "About six months ago, my husband demanded that I give him . . . $2,500. When I informed him that I did not have the money, he became very agitated and threatened me with physical abuse. He also called my mother . . . and created such a threat to her that she, fearing for my safety, gave him the money he demanded." Savineau has denied making any such demand.

Life in the hotel was squalid. Susan was sometimes too drunk to go out to dinner, and the family ordered room service. "I think we spent $20,000 at that hotel," said Sherry. The suite was filled with litter and day-old meals. Gradually, the kids started going back to Savineau, who was still living at the house on El Chorro. "First Sherry, then André," said Savineau. "Then even Dino came back. They had to. They needed to eat and get their wash done." Savineau went to court and demanded custody of Craig. Susan, he declared, "is a confirmed alcoholic. . . . She regularly (many times a week) will get drunk and fail to feed the child, or send him to school." He asked for about $1,000 a month for himself and Craig.

A few months later the court decided in his favor. Craig was returned to his father, and Susan was ordered to pay support. Shortly thereafter, Savineau, who had finally received his green card, got a job on a construction project, and Susan's payment was reduced by half. He moved out of the house on El Chorro; Susan was still at the hotel, alone and depressed. Everybody had deserted her. Even her older children were gone. Sherry had moved in with a girlfriend's family, and the two boys spent most of their time in Los Angeles. One day, Virginia called her daughter at the hotel and learned, to her horror, that Susan had checked out. The desk clerk told Virginia that Susan had said she was flying to Paris. "We all knew that Susan probably went back to Revest-du-Bion," said Savineau.

Virginia was frightened by her daughter's departure. There was no telling what Susan, who was so often drunk and forlorn, might do, left on her own at the deserted ranch. Virginia begged Savineau to fly to France and retrieve his estranged wife, but he refused. He didn't think that Susan would come back with him. Virginia settled on Dino, then nineteen years old. He was the most charming of the Hakim children and Susan's favorite. If anybody could persuade her to return, it would be he.

However, months went by, and Susan remained in France. Dino called once in a while, but he seemed to be stoned. He demanded that Virginia send more money. He had wrecked a car. Later, he wrecked another. Virginia grew more and more anxious. Now she had not one but two relatives footloose in France. So she called detective John O'Grady. He flew to France and quickly located Susan at her home in Revest-du-Bion. "This was a ten-bedroom house, but it was a piece of s-h-i-t," he recalled. "It was dirty, and there were flies everywhere and pigeons all over the place, flying inside and out." Susan was alone, but she didn't want to go back to Palm Springs. Dino, said O'Grady, "was selling drugs and shit all over Europe."

When O'Grady arrived at Susan's house, he was hungry. "There was nothing in the house to eat. The *fromage* had flies all over it. Well, I finally found a steak, but there were no frying pans. So I got a pot, washed it off, and put the steak on to cook. I had fried one side, and I was about to turn it over, and along flies a pigeon and—plop— there went my steak. When I told Darrylin about that, she laughed till she was sick."

O'Grady said he virtually had to kidnap Susan, who was hooked on alcohol and prescription drugs. He somehow got her to Paris and checked her into a hotel but had to lock her in the room. For part of the night, he sat by her bed and held her hand. On the flight back to the United States, he fed her little sips of white wine. He finally got her back to Palm Springs and took her to the Eisenhower Hospital. O'Grady stopped by Ric-Su-Dar to report to Virginia. "I told her that her daughter would be dead within the year," he said. O'Grady's verdict shattered Virginia, who was not in the best of health herself. From years of heavy smoking, she had developed emphysema, and her days in the sun had led to bouts with skin cancer. She had lost weight, and her hair was thinning. The stress of caring for her husband and dealing with her family's myriad problems had taken its toll. She was often weak and tired.

But it was Darryl Zanuck himself who lay ill and dying. In October 1979 he fell ill with pneumonia and was admitted to Desert Hospital in Palm Springs. After a month, his doctor thought he had improved, but his health again deteriorated. In December, his lungs became so congested that he was put on a respirator. Virginia and Susan kept a vigil at his bedside where they were joined by Richard and Darrylin. On December 22, 1979, Darryl Zanuck died.

Virginia decided to hold her husband's memorial service in Los Angeles because he had spent so much of his life there. The family traveled in their limousine, following the flower-bedecked hearse for ninety miles on Interstate 10 through the broad desert mountains down into Beverly Hills. Two hundred people had come to United Methodist Church of Westwood for the funeral. As Zanuck himself would have noted, it wasn't a sell-out crowd. That was not surprising, since he had spent most of his recent years in New York, Paris, and Palm Springs and had outlived many of the people he worked with in his heyday.

Inside, Virginia greeted people as the family proceeded to the front pews, which were tied off with black velvet ribbons. The family's Santa Monica contingent was already in place—Dick, his new wife, Lili Fini, and his two sons. Ginny and Janet, his daughters, were sitting with Darrylin, her husband, and their kids. Susan, who stood next to Sherry, appeared faded and shrunken. Though she was two years younger than her sister Darrylin, she appeared years older.

After the congregation heard a reading from the Bible by the preacher, Orson Welles delivered the eulogy. "In our Hollywood community," boomed the mountainous actor, "we hear on sad occasions such as this various leaders referred to and hailed as giants of the motion picture industry. Of all that number, very few have truly deserved such a description. And nobody has deserved it more than Darryl Zanuck." Welles praised Zanuck for his movies—*Grapes of Wrath, Gentleman's Agreement, All About Eve, The Snake Pit, Pinky, The Longest Day.* "Darryl's commitment was always to the story. For Darryl, that is what it was to make a film, to tell a story. . . . He was tough. That was his job, but he was never cruel or vindictive. What a rare thing it is to say in this competitive game of ours, he was a man totally devoid of malice. He had a great sense of irony, a great sense of humor, even about himself . . . he was a friend. I don't mean just my friend. I think friendship was something he was very good at. That's why it's just so hard to say good-bye to him."

Darrylin wept openly while Virginia and Dick sat impassively. Susan was quiet. Perhaps the drinks she had had in the limousine helped ease the pain.

Zanuck was buried at a small cemetery in Westwood. It was Darrylin who composed the inscription—so embarrassingly lengthy it must have given the stonemason a bad case of tendonitis—on Zanuck's tombstone. Though it was a personal message from her to her father, it sounded like a résumé:

DARRYL FRANCIS ZANUCK
BORN, WAHOO, NEBRASKA, SEPTEMBER 5, 1902
PASSED ON PALM SPRINGS, CALIFORNIA, DECEMBER 22,
1979
COFOUNDER, PRESIDENT AND PRODUCER OF
TWENTIETH CENTURY-FOX STUDIO, DOCTOR OF
HUMANITIES, UNIVERSITY OF NEBRASKA, LINCOLN,
NEBRASKA.
MASON FIFTY YEARS, RECEIVING HIGHEST DEGREE.
IN HIS LIFETIME RECEIVED SUCH A HOST OF
DEGREES, DIPLOMAS AND AWARDS FROM ALL OVER
THE WORLD THAT IT IS IMPOSSIBLE TO STATE THEM
ALL.
PRIVATE WORLD WAR I OVERSEAS, 14 YEARS OLD,
WORLD WAR II COLONEL, ACTIVE DUTY OVERSEAS,
U.S. SIGNAL CORPS, ALGIERS.
LISTED BELOW ARE A FEW OF THE SERVICE RIBBONS
AND DECORATIONS HE WAS PROUDLY AUTHORIZED TO
WEAR:
VICTORY MEDAL, WORLD WAR I
MEDAL OF FRENCH LEGION OF HONOR WITH ROUGE
ROSETTE, WORLD WAR I
ASIATIC PACIFIC CAMPAIGN RIBBONS AND
EUROPEAN-AFRICA–MIDDLE EASTERN CAMPAIGN
RIBBONS.
A MAN WHO USED HIS IMAGINATIVE CREATIVE
GENIUS TO DELIVER INSPIRATION THROUGH HIS
CELEBRATED MOTION PICTURES. HE IMPARTED A
LIFETIME MESSAGE OF DECENCY, LOVE,
PATRIOTISM, JUSTICE, EQUALITY AND HOPE
THROUGHOUT THE NATION AND THE WORLD. BELOVED
HUSBAND, FATHER, GRANDFATHER AND GREAT-
GRANDFATHER. I LOVE YOU, DADDY. YOU WILL
NEVER BE FORGOTTEN.
I LOVE YOU,
DARRYLIN

*   *   *

Two months after her father's death, Susan won a divorce decree, but the property settlement had not been made final. She agonized that she had been swindled again—this time by Pierre Savineau. It had been nearly impossible to sell the ranch in France, but finally, after they had filed for divorce, there was a deal in the works. Savineau and Susan both flew to Paris to sign the papers. In their lawyer's office, however, they fought over the proceeds from the sale. Susan said she had supported the family, and she wanted it all. Savineau asserted that he had sold his boat to help purchase the farm. She finally agreed to split the proceeds. Back in California, however, she ordered her lawyer to stop Savineau from collecting the money, then changed her mind and ordered the transfer of funds to go through. She wavered back and forth. Finally her lawyer won a court injunction to stop the transfer, but Susan had changed her mind again. She informed Savineau, who diverted the money to another bank.

After Savineau had collected his share of the money, he lost interest in Susan, married a young Mexican woman, and took her and his son Craig to Oklahoma to make a new start. Susan lived alone at the vandalized house on El Chorro. Standing at the end of a cul-de-sac in one of the less dauntingly wealthy sections of town, the spacious ranch-style home gave no hint of anything other than bourgeois orderliness and comfort. Inside the tidy-looking house, however, all was chaos. Dirty dishes were piled in the sink. There was never any clean laundry. The dog chewed up rugs, furniture, and clothing. André, Jr., and Dino popped in and out, sometimes failing to show up for months. Whenever they disappeared, so did miscellaneous pieces of silver and jewelry, which they sold to buy drugs. Susan finally took what was left of her jewelry collection to Ric-Su-Dar for safekeeping. "She wanted my grandmother to hold it for her," said Sherry.

Susan's appearance had been coarsened and mutilated by years of drinking. Virginia had her driver pick Susan up once a week and take her to the beauty parlor, just to help her daughter keep her appearance up. There her blond hair was retouched and teased into order. Susan would often leave her hair uncombed, with frizzy tangles emerging, until her next appointment. Friends who saw her were shocked at how much weight she had lost. Pokie Seeger invited Susan to visit her in

Newport Beach and was stunned to find that her friend looked skeletal. "She couldn't eat anything. Food seemed to make her sick. We would go to a restaurant and order a steak, but then Susan wouldn't touch it. So we would order a lobster, and she would just pick at it. I was really scared." Her health had deteriorated along with her appearance. She suffered from blackouts and palpitations and had no energy to speak of. She sat around the house all day, rarely bothering with anything.

Her two older boys gave her little but grief. Both were heavy drug users who had an insouciant disregard for the consequences of their actions. Dino had recently stolen some blank checks from Susan and cashed them for $2,000. André, Jr., took a check from his father, cashed it, and spent the money on himself. In May 1980 he was arrested in Los Angeles for robbing a drugstore with a friend. Said Savineau later, "He finally got caught in L.A. because the Zanucks couldn't pay off the whole police force." Susan frantically hired a lawyer, who won André a suspended sentence on the condition that he enroll in a drug treatment program. He checked into a detoxification clinic at San Juan Capistrano Hospital in Laguna Beach. Almost as soon as that crisis had been dealt with, Susan faced another. In late May two men and a woman came to her house looking for Dino. They told her that her son had written them a bad check for $2,000 for drugs, and they meant to "get Dino."

Susan was so lonely that she called Pierre Savineau in Oklahoma and asked him to send Craig, then twelve, to visit her for the summer. Savineau was leery of letting the boy stay with his alcoholic ex-wife, but he agreed when she told him that Pokie Seeger's teenage daughter Susan Andrea would stay in the house and help out. As soon as school was out, Craig flew to Palm Springs. Only a few days after he and Susan Andrea were installed in the house, Dino showed up. He arrogantly offered his mother a joint, which she refused; and, when she wasn't looking, he took several checks from her purse. He called Sherry and told her that he might take a trip to Latin America.

When André, Jr., enthusiastic about his drug treatment program, talked to his mother about getting help for her alcoholism, she seemed to be interested. Signs that Susan might recover began to appear. Sherry brought her mother food every so often and stopped by the house to check on her. On June 9, Susan, Sherry, Craig, and Susan Andrea drove to a big Palm Springs drugstore for ice cream cones. The conversation was cheerful. Craig's birthday was only five days away, and Susan was planning a party for him. "She was really happy when we talked about the cake and the decorations," said Sherry. "Then my mother said to me, 'We haven't gotten along very well, but I want you to know that I will always love you.' " Sherry blinked back tears and gave her mother a hug.

Later that night, however, Susan called Sherry in a panic to report that she had coughed up blood. She had been complaining recently that she was short of breath and had pains in her chest. She had made an appointment to see a doctor at noon the next day, and Sherry volunteered to pick her up and take her. The next morning Susan Andrea and Craig dropped by Sherry's office at the Hot Dog Construction Company, where she was working for the summer. Neither of them had seen or heard from Susan that morning. They assumed she was sleeping and left the house without bothering her. Sherry tried to call her from work, but no one answered the telephone. She was alarmed and quickly drove to her mother's house.

Sherry entered with her own key. She turned down the hall to her mother's bedroom. The door was open, and she walked in. The room was a mess, as usual, with clothes strewn over the floor and furniture. Susan was sprawled on her back, half on and half off the king-size bed. Her nightgown was disheveled. She had apparently passed out the night before after drinking herself into oblivion again. It happened all the time. Sherry shook her shoulder, but the moment her fingers touched Susan's skin, she knew her mother was dead. Susan felt like ice, and a hiss of air was expelled from her mouth. Her eyes were wide open. Sherry began to cry, and then she began to scream. She couldn't believe that her forty-six-year-old mother was dead.

Sherry knelt, picked up the phone on the bedside table, and dialed the operator. She asked for an ambulance and the fire department. Then she called her grandmother and, her voice breaking, announced to Virginia that Susan was dead.

There was a long silence. Sherry waited for her grandmother to issue orders, to tell her what to do.

What came over the telephone was not Virginia's customary definitive voice but grief. She was crying brokenly. Her sorrow welled up and out and kept on coming. But the sobs that had begun in anguish seemed to take on an angry sound. Her voice turned brittle. "Murder!"

she proclaimed to her granddaughter. "Murder! Your mother was murdered. Murdered! She was killed—by those brothers of yours. Those little bastards. They did it! They killed your mother. I knew this would happen. I warned her—and now she's dead."

To Sherry, Susan's funeral three days later in Los Angeles was a sham. Most of Susan's L.A. friends hadn't seen her for decades. Virginia insisted that there be *something* held in the city so that her friends and people from the studio could attend although, ironically, Susan herself never made it to her own funeral. There was no body— just an empty casket—because the police were investigating her death. Susan had died alone, and in California any "unattended death" must be followed by a postmortem and a preliminary look by the police.

By the afternoon of the funeral, Virginia was not the only one who was suspicious about the cause of Susan's death. The coroner's office and the police were also curious. At 5:00 P.M., Lisle Ford, an investigator with the Riverside County Coroner's Office, called Detective Tom Barton, the Palm Springs policeman assigned to Susan's case. Ford told Barton that Dr. Choon Sil Koo had completed an autopsy. Because Sherry had said that her mother was suffering from chest pains, the doctor had looked for a coronary malfunction. However, he couldn't find any. Sherry had also told the coroner's investigator that her mother drank heavily, and both she and her grandmother had said they wouldn't be surprised if Susan had killed herself. There had been no evidence of suicide, however, and the coroner was waiting for the results of drug and alcohol screens. Ford added that there was a bruise the size of a quarter on the top of Susan's head and that Dr. Koo had found an injury to her brain from a blow. While the blow to her head was probably not fatal, said Ford, "the death appears to be suspicious in nature."

Barton opened a police investigation. He first visited 2320 El Chorro. "The interior of the residence was disarranged and in a filthy condition," he noted in his report. The house as a whole "was undesirable for the living conditions of the average person." Barton later described it less formally as "a shithouse."

Everybody in Palm Springs knew that Susan was Darryl Zanuck's daughter, but given the squalor of her home, Barton figured that she was short of funds. After telephoning Susan's ex-husband, André Hakim, Sr., in Los Angeles, Barton learned that she did not lack for money. Hakim, then a real-estate agent for Stan Hermann & Associates, told the detective that Susan lived on the income of a trust fund established by her father. It provided her about $3,000 a month. Her mother paid the rent on the house. Hakim supplied a possible motive for murder. He said that when Susan died, the money in the trust fund—about $1 million—would go to her four children. Hakim also told Barton about his sons' drug problems and about threats to Susan that had been made by Dino's drug connections.

Barton started checking out the whereabouts of Susan's two older boys. André, Jr., had been in the Laguna Beach hospital undergoing treatment when Susan died. He was released to attend his mother's funeral. Nobody knew where Dino was, however. His father told Barton that he thought Dino had left the country for France or Venezuela. He hadn't been seen since June 4, 1980.

Virginia and Sherry had suspicions, but the police investigation was suspended only a few days later. The county coroner's office concluded that Susan's death was not caused by foul play. Instead, the doctor had decided it was due to cardiac arrhythmia or irregular heartbeat, brought about by a "fatty liver." An enlarged liver, usually traceable to alcoholism, can make the heart malfunction. Further, the head injury Susan sustained, said the coroner, "was not enough to cause death and could have been caused when a person is an [sic] a stuporous state. She may have fallen into furniture or a corner table." The drug and alcohol tests had turned up negative; someone suffering cardiac arrhythmia could conceivably be woozy enough to stumble and fall. Detective Barton was ordered to halt the investigation. As far as the police were concerned, nobody—not Craig, not André, Jr., not Savineau, not Dino—was a suspect. Susan had died as a result of prolonged heavy drinking.

Suspicions among the Zanucks were not quelled by the coroner's report. Rumors were swirling. Sherry felt that she had to know the truth. She decided to hire a private investigator, but her grandmother intervened by putting Los Angeles detective John O'Grady on the case. He took Sherry with him to visit the coroner and meet with Dr. Koo. "He had no doubts," said Sherry. "He convinced me that Mom was not murdered. O'Grady and I both really believed that, and I was very, very relieved."

Virginia, however, was not reassured by O'Grady's report. Her distress surfaced at Susan's second funeral. Sherry and André, Jr., got the coroner to release Susan's body, and Sherry held a second service at Desert Lawn Park in nearby Calimesa. Susan had requested cremation, which distressed Virginia. She asked her granddaughter to take photos of Susan in her casket before the funeral so that she would have pictures to remember her by. "Susan looked beautiful," said her friend Mona Skoff. "Her hair was done and laid out on a pillow; she would have been proud of herself that day."

The ceremony itself was a disaster. It was held in a small chapel, and very few people attended. Virginia didn't appear until after the service began. She was trailed by her chauffeur. Her black dress hung from her emaciated frame, and her tiny feet seemed lost even in her small black shoes. Her skin was scaly and scabby from repeated bouts with skin cancer, and on her head perched a wig. The two latecomers pushed themselves into a pew behind Mona Skoff. The little sermon was momentarily disrupted by their soft "Excuse me's" and the rustling of their clothing. The organist played a hymn, and the minister rose to offer a prayer. Virginia was buzzing to the chauffeur. Her voice rose. Said Skoff, "She then started saying, 'You know, the children killed her, the children killed her.' The kids were hysterical. Sherry was crying so hard."

There was a loud "shhh!" from André Hakim's sister, but nothing stopped Virginia. The chauffeur patted her arm and whispered in her ear, but Virginia went on. "Those two were little cutthroats. This isn't the first time. Dino tried to kill her before. He threatened her. And what about those hoodlums he hangs out with?" Everyone was stricken, but Virginia defiantly continued. "They murdered her, they killed her."

André, Jr., stood, turned, and faced his grandmother. He leaned over the back of his seat and growled, "You are disgusting . . . you have no respect for your own daughter."

Even in tragedy the Zanucks were fighting.

Skoff exchanged glances with André Hakim, Sr. "I thought this just couldn't go on," she said. "Please stop this," she begged him. "You've got to do something." Hakim agreed. He went to confer with the minister. Virginia and André, Jr., were still hissing at each other like two snakes. "Let us pray," declared the minister forcefully. André, Jr., turned away to face the small altar, and Virginia sat back with her head bowed and her hands folded in her lap. "The Lord is my Shepherd, I shall not want," intoned the minister. A group of schoolchildren sang, and the organist played a recessional. Virginia and the chauffeur left before it ended. "I have a hair appointment," she announced to no one in particular.

Outside the chapel, the rest of the mourners milled about uncertainly in the sunshine. It seemed as though they should gather somewhere, but nobody knew where. The logical place was Ric-Su-Dar, but Virginia had rushed off. Mona Skoff told people to drive to the Gaiety Delicatessen in downtown Palm Springs. An hour later, a small party of mourners sat amid the bowls of pickles and jars of mustard, a quiet group eating corned beef sandwiches and cheesecake in Susan's memory. Skoff picked up the check. Sherry thanked her. Skoff responded, "I wanted to do something for Susan." She and Sherry were both crying when they parted.

Practically everybody connected to the Zanucks managed to get to one of Susan's two funerals—everybody, that is, except Susan's sister Darrylin. Her excuse was a very severe headache. "She really loved her sister. She was very upset," said her friend Mary Donahue. "She was hysterical when she got the news."

SEVEN
ALL THE LITTLE FOXES

■

I n 1980, when Genevieve Gillaizeau decided to sue the Zanuck estate to get what she believed was her rightful share of the mogul's millions, Marvin Mitchelson was her choice for a lawyer. Genevieve had always liked designer labels, and if there was such a thing as a designer lawyer, he was it. In 1980, he was still riding a tsunami of publicity after representing Michelle Triola in her palimony suit against actor Lee Marvin.

Zanuck, Genevieve told Mitchelson when they first met at her apartment on May 19, 1980, had promised to leave her nearly half his money, but a new will, already entered in probate, had cut her out. She did not appear to be a mistress in distress, however. She seemed to have plenty of money. She had accumulated a small fortune modeling for a Japanese cosmetics company and dealing in art. She owned houses in Nantucket, Malibu, and Palm Beach and an eight-room apartment in Manhattan's fabled Dakota, which also housed John Lennon and Lauren Bacall.

Still, she was ready to go to war because she felt that, on principle, she was *owed*. The lawsuit she planned to launch against Darryl Zanuck's estate seemed odd. She had not seen Zanuck since April 1973, and she had not asked him or his family for a penny since. To all appearances, she was a cast-off girlfriend, and her former lover could have rewritten his will many times since their parting without raising any eyebrows.

Proving that Zanuck's October 1973 will was invalid would be a tremendous legal challenge. In California, as in most states, there are only two grounds for a successful will contest. The first is proof that the decedent lacked "testamentary capacity," meaning that he didn't know who his natural heirs were and what property he owned. In fact, a person could be nearly demented yet still arguably meet the legal criteria for testamentary capacity. The second customary basis for a will contest is proof of undue influence—in other words, proof that someone browbeat the decedent into signing the will.

Genevieve could fill Mitchelson's ear with strange tales of Zanuck family doings, but she didn't have much direct evidence that there were grounds for either claim. She asserted that the doctors who attended Zanuck during his last days in New York had found him mentally fuzzy and dull. She couldn't argue that he didn't know his heirs, however. When Darrylin, Susan, and Richard turned up in his hospital room, Zanuck certainly knew who they were. Dick Zanuck scared Genevieve; perhaps he had pressured his father into cutting her out. Yet there was no way she could know that. She had been nowhere near Palm Springs when Zanuck signed the will. Finding witnesses to testify to undue influence would be difficult if not impossible.

Still, Mitchelson agreed to take the case. His intention was to file a "creditor's claim," arguing that Zanuck, like Lee Marvin, had made promises of lifelong support to Genevieve and intended to fulfill them via his estate. The case could only add to Mitchelson's drive to legitimize the concept of palimony. Indeed, the notion of palimony beyond the grave would certainly produce headlines. He would also challenge the will on the usual grounds of testamentary incapacity and undue influence. After the initial meeting with Genevieve, Mitchelson sent her a letter of agreement, which she quickly signed. In it, Mitchelson promised to pursue a "Marvin-type action" to win her fair share of the estate. In exchange, Genevieve was to pay the attorney one-third of any amount she won, plus a $25,000 nonrefundable retainer, which would be credited against the total fee. Mitchelson later said that he wanted a nonrefundable retainer because "It was a difficult area of law [that] I felt might be highly contested."

While Mitchelson continued to jet from city to city conducting business, he appointed his colleague Harold Rhoden to supervise drafting and filing of papers for the legal challenge. On June 19, Rhoden received a call from a man who said he represented Thomas Shirley. He had explosive news. Shirley, he said, was a Zanuck family friend who had information that the final will was a forgery. He would tell what he knew only after some money was paid to his lawyer and the private investigator who had helped him gather evidence. Rhoden arranged for a meeting in Mitchelson's office the following Saturday.

Shirley's contention was that Darrylin had told him that she forged the October 1973 will. Moreover, Virginia Zanuck had known about it and directed a person at the Bank of America to notarize the signature without seeing Zanuck sign it. Shirley said he had conducted an investigation of his own. He had hired an expert who examined the will and exemplars of Zanuck's signatures and had concluded the will was a forgery. He was inflexible on his demand for money, however. Before he would make a statement or show any of his evidence to the two lawyers, Shirley wanted $10,000 to be paid to his own lawyer and investigator.

Mitchelson and Rhoden stewed about what to do. Some handwriting experts were good, but others were not so credible. They probably would have to get their own expert to verify the results of Shirley's investigation. Moreover, he wouldn't even show his evidence until they made the payment. That, too, was troublesome. Still, Mitchelson said later, "I had the feeling that nothing would happen unless his lawyer and investigator received some sort of fee for their services." Mitchelson called Genevieve in New York that weekend and relayed Tom Shirley's story. Mitchelson cautioned her not to pay until he and Rhoden were certain of Shirley's credentials. What they did to check him out remains unclear. Nonetheless, Genevieve wrote a check to "M-3's trust account"—M-3 stood for Marvin M. Mitchelson.

The following Thursday, June 26, 1980, an employee of Leavitt's—a business that files papers for Los Angeles law firms with the cheery slogan "Leave it to Leavitt's"—drove the two hundred dusty miles east from Los Angeles to Indio, California, the county seat for Palm Springs, where Zanuck's will had been entered in probate. There he filed a creditor's claim for $15 million on behalf of Genevieve. The claim demanded $7 million to fulfill an oral promise the mogul had allegedly made to Genevieve to give her 45 percent of his estate and a share of his employee benefits and $1 million in proceeds from an insurance policy if she "devote[d] her life to him as long as he lived by being his constant companion and adviser in business and personal matters; refrain[ed] from marrying or having any personal relationship with any other man . . . and refrain[ed] from pursuing her career." The will Zanuck signed in February 1973 backed those claims. But "in October 1973, under influence of and duress from decedent's son Richard . . . and when decedent was mentally incompetent, and unknown to claimant, decedent purportedly nullified the said acts."

On the same day the claim was filed, Mitchelson and Genevieve held a press conference at the Mayfair Hotel in New York to announce the legal action. The lawsuit immediately became an item in gossip columns across the nation. That weekend, Rhoden sent Mitchelson another petition for Genevieve's signature. This one claimed that Zanuck's will had been forged. The document had to be returned to California quickly because the 120-day deadline for challenges to the estate was drawing near. Mitchelson flew back to California on July 2 and had the forgery petition filed at the Indio court the next day. He figured he had just made the deadline.

Meanwhile Genevieve's $10,000 check had cleared, and Tom Shirley agreed to make an official declaration. It was signed about a week after the petition was filed with the Indio court. In his declaration, Shirley said that in the fall of 1975, when he was driving Darrylin from Los Angeles to Palm Springs, she confided that "the October 31, 1973 'will' had sat unsigned in front of Darryl for about two weeks, and that Darryl refused to sign it [because] he knew there was more to it than he was being told." Darrylin had added that "she could no longer stand the thought of that outsider, Genevieve, getting most of her father's money while she, Darrylin, was to get so little." Shirley then told in his declaration how Darrylin said the will had been forged.

> Darrylin told me that she told her mother that she, Darrylin, had always been able to sign daddy's signature as well as he could, and that all through school, daddy, that is, Darryl, had never signed anything, and that she, Darrylin had always forged his signature. Darrylin told me that she asked her mother, "Do you suppose we could get away with doing that with the will?"

. . . her mother, Virginia, replied that she did not think that Darryl was ever going to sign the will, and that they may as well try that because something had to be done before something happened to him.

Darrylin . . . told her mother that the only problem was that the will had to be notarized. . . . Virginia's response was, "Mary Williams at the Bank of America here in Palm Springs always takes our word for it. We can get her to notarize papers that were signed here and we just take them to her at the bank and she knows the signatures. Do you suppose we could get away with doing it that way?"

Darrylin . . . told her mother in response, "We can't lose anything by trying. Let's try it."

Darrylin said that she and her mother then got out the will and that she, Darrylin, forged Darryl F. Zanuck's name to it.

Shirley said that Darrylin and her mother saw to it that the Bank of America employee did notarize the will—though the notary public herself later insisted she had done so in Zanuck's presence. The document was later returned to Zanuck's lawyers in New York.

Shirley also stated that, after Zanuck's death in late 1979, he happened to be at the Indio courthouse on other business and, out of curiosity, asked for a copy of the will. He took it to two handwriting experts to compare the signatures with Zanuck's known signature. As luck would have it, Shirley said, he had originals of three documents that he had witnessed Darryl Zanuck sign. The experts confirmed Shirley's suspicions that the will had been forged.

The forgery was not Shirley's only dramatic revelation. He also declared that he would take a lie detector test and asked to have his deposition taken under oath at the earliest possible time because, he said, "I have on several occasions witnessed the explosive, violent and deadly temper of Dick Zanuck, and I am aware of Dick's tendency toward impulsive assaults and attacks on others. I heard and saw Dick Zanuck threaten to kill Genevieve in 1973, and I know that had Dick not been restrained physically, he would have carried out his threat. I heard Dick Zanuck threaten to kill Genevieve by drowning. I know that after I give my deposition, if anything happens to me, the deposition can be used in evidence; therefore, killing me would not profit anyone who wishes to see this forgery probated."

The contents of Shirley's declaration sounded plausible enough—or inflammatory enough—to force some kind of settlement.

Mitchelson kept the presses rolling. In its July 14, 1980, issue, *People* magazine ran a story about the lawsuit, told from Genevieve's point of view. Her account of events bore only a sketchy resemblance to what had really happened. Zanuck, she said, had been kidnapped by his son Richard. Zanuck's doctors had persuaded her to bring him back to Palm Springs, and when she and Darryl had alighted from the airplane in April 1973, "a local bodyguard" stepped on one of their Yorkies "to distract her" and then two of Richard's security guards plunked Zanuck in a limousine and took him away. When she finally arrived at Ric-Su-Dar, the living room was full of people—"most of them drunk. They were having a cocktail party. Darryl was a sick, sick old man—he was supposed to be in bed." She left and never saw Zanuck again. Not only was he mentally incompetent, she charged, but "his family kept him under sedation in California for the last seven years of his life." Furthermore, Richard had induced Darryl to change his will. "Dick really hated his father," she said.

Of the family, only Richard responded to her assertions. "I don't want a duel between myself and this person who I think is a lowlife," he told *People*. "I find the charges preposterous. I would like to see the evidence. There was a period when we [Dick and his father] didn't get along, but I considered him my best friend."

That August, Virginia wrote to her friend Margaret Shands, who had offered to testify in the case. Virginia thanked her and mentioned that she had heard through the grapevine that Shirley had said Shands would never testify because he had broken up her friendship with Virginia years before. Her tone was vituperative. "How little does this S.O.B. know!" she wrote. She hadn't any contact with her old friend Ed Meena. Virginia was angry and bitter about the turn of events. She couldn't figure out why Tom Shirley had sided with Genevieve. After all, he had only met her that one time in Palm Springs. She outlined Shirley's charges of forgery and violence, but she never denied them— even to her friend. "This will be a long drawn out costly affair, but we will win!" she declared.

By summer's end, attorneys for the Bank of America, Zanuck's executor, had triumphed in the first round. They filed a demurrer with the court against Mitchelson's forgery petition. The court could not consider the petition, argued the lawyers, because it had been filed a day after the deadline had expired. Mitchelson and Rhoden were taken aback by the demurrer. They thought they had just made it, but when they counted off 120 days from March 3, they realized that the deadline was July 1, not July 2, as they had thought. This could be a legal disaster; however, the demurrer might not be a problem. The two lawyers figured that, just as in a civil action, all they had to do was file an amendment to the first June 26 petition—the one contesting the will on the usual grounds. They would simply add forgery as a basis for the suit.

Unfortunately for Genevieve, Mitchelson and Rhoden miscalculated. About eight months later, on March 11, 1981, Judge Frank Moore of the Indio trial court sustained the demurrer. The forgery claim had been filed a day late. Deadlines were deadlines, and that was that. Forgery could not be considered in any further action. Genevieve had flown out to California to hear the oral arguments in favor of the forgery petition. When she realized that Mitchelson and Rhoden had failed, she resolved to dump them as her attorneys. She visited Mitchelson's Beverly Hills office and asked to see an item in her case file. Later that day, Rhoden told Mitchelson that Genevieve had walked out of the office with every document in the file. A few days later, she fired her attorneys. The palimony-after-death issue was never pursued.

Genevieve quickly hired a Washington, D.C., attorney, Samuel Buffone, who decided to stick with the customary rationales for an estate contest. The battle would proceed without any palimony or forgery claims. Thomas Shirley seemed dissatisfied with the new approach. In the spring of 1981 he visited the FBI and told two agents about the forgery, showed them his declaration and the handwriting samples. To prove his case, he said he would undergo a polygraph examination voluntarily. He hired an independent firm to conduct the lie detector test and mailed the results to the FBI in mid-May 1981. The examiner had concluded that Shirley was telling the truth. The FBI was not impressed, however. An agent sent Shirley a letter to announce that the U.S. attorney had declined to prosecute because of "the lack of commission of a federal crime within the statute of limitations." Any prosecutor would have to wonder why Shirley hadn't reported the forgery earlier if he had known about it since 1975.

The FBI rejection must have annoyed Thomas Shirley deeply because his friends say that Shirley told people that he was furious with the Zanucks and determined to get even. He was planning to write a book about the family that would embarrass them so badly they would never hold their heads up in public again.

*   *   *

Darryl Zanuck wasn't the only member of the family whose death unleashed battles over money. His daughter Susan Zanuck Hakim Savineau had also made out a will. Most of Susan's money was tied up in her trust fund, whose value her business manager Henry Bamberger had boosted to about $1 million by the time of her death. The structure of the trust dictated that money would go directly to her four children and bypass probate. The rest of Susan's assets were minuscule. She had only about $50,000 in property and cash, and a sizable portion of that would have to go to pay taxes and debts. Of course, Susan's estate would have been much, much larger had Genevieve not sought to challenge Darryl Zanuck's will. Susan's father had left her $100,000 outright and one-third of the balance of the estate. Now her estate could not be fully settled until the litigation was settled.

Soon after Susan's death, her two executors, Richard Zanuck and Henry Bamberger, summoned André, Jr., then twenty-three; Dino, twenty-one; and Sherry, nineteen, to Bamberger's office. Each received a check for about $250,000—their share of Susan's trust fund. Pierre Savineau was sent Craig's money for safekeeping. "Richard and Bamberger gave us the money just like that," said André, Jr. "They washed their hands of us." Indeed, in August, two months after Susan's death, Richard resigned as executor.

André, Jr., was to lament bitterly that he and his brother and sister were blithely handed so much money. Richard and Bamberger should have done *something* to supervise them, he claimed later. However, at the time, he and his brother were absolutely unsupervisable. Few people who were remotely respectable wanted to have anything to do with them.

Susan had raised Hakim's boys to be Zanuck princes. Except for their small size and prominent foreheads, Susan's three elder children bore little resemblance to their grandfather. As children, the boys wore expensive clothes, had countless toys, and could do just about anything they wanted. "We were little terrors," recalled André. They were very conscious of the fact that their grandfather was a famous filmmaker. He was living in Paris off and on while they were growing up. "When I was little, I followed my grandfather around," said André. "I visited the movie sets. I spent time on yachts in the Mediterranean. I didn't know at the time, but I couldn't have been the grandson of anyone better." Susan constantly emphasized that they were Zanucks and heirs to a family empire, and, like sponges, the boys absorbed her ideas. She endowed them with a sense of destiny. Like their grandfather, they would achieve miraculous success; unlike him, however, they wouldn't have to work too hard to do so.

Susan's daughter, Sherry, had also been imbued with the magic of the family name. To her, Zanuck was a magical source of money and power, and he dazzled Sherry with his sleight of hand. Before a screening at the Cannes Film Festival one year, when she was about seven, he asked her for a dollar. She had only one, and her mother had warned her not to lose it. Sherry couldn't bear the thought of giving up her precious dollar. But he kept coaxing her, "Give it to Gyppie. Gyppie needs it . . . please . . . you wouldn't keep your dollar from your grandpa, would you?" She finally released the crumpled bill into his palm. After all, she loved him. She couldn't be so selfish. Then, "Oh, no, it was gone! My dollar! It disappeared." He was alarmed. She was scared—what would she tell her mother? "Maybe I can find it," he said. He rummaged in her hair and fingered the skin behind her ear and, surprised, pulled out a bill. Not hers, though. Abracadabra, it had turned into a crisp new fifty-dollar bill.

Susan sent the boys to boarding school over Pierre Savineau's objections. Savineau particularly opposed dispatching Dino, who suffered from a common and easily correctable birth defect called hypospadias, in which the urinary opening of the penis is in the wrong place. Savineau feared that Dino's schoolmates would taunt him about the abnormality. Dino's later desperate drive for drugs and danger, Savineau felt, was fueled by self-hatred and vulnerability that stemmed from his birth defect. But there was another reason for Dino to feel dissatisfied with himself. "I knew he was gay," said Savineau. "I don't know how I knew, maybe by the way he acted, his behavior, but I thought he would be gay. And I was right. He grew up to be gay.

That's okay, but Dino didn't want to be gay. He didn't want to be at all. But he was. He was stuck."

Neither of the boys got along well with Savineau, but André found him particularly offensive. "He was a French commando type," said Andre. Indeed, he always seemed to be issuing orders and urging the boys to work on tasks around the farm when they were home from school. A way out emerged for Andre in April 1973, when he and his mother flew to New York to see Zanuck at the hospital. One afternoon in New York, while waiting for Darrylin to stop by, Susan and André explored Zanuck's suite at the Plaza Hotel. The place was filled with valuables—jewelry, stock certificates, and paintings. In the bedroom, right out in the open, sat stacks of currency—dollars, British pounds, French francs, and Spanish pesetas. Later, while Susan and Darrylin were talking about their father in the living room, said André, Jr., he made a second visit to the bedroom and grabbed the pile of francs for himself. That fall, after he returned to the French boarding school he hated, he used the money to finance a getaway. He spent the next year bumming around the south of France, living on the money he said he took from his grandfather. Once in a while, he got a job playing the guitar. He took drugs, but mostly he drank. "I lost track of time," he said. "My nights and days were reversed." His Hakim uncles finally forced him to return to school. In the spring of 1975 he passed his high school exams "with mention." As a reward, his mother gave him a summer trip to visit his grandparents in Palm Springs.

His father and brother were already in California. André Hakim, Sr., was living in Los Angeles in a small apartment and fighting his way through his tangled lawsuit with Twentieth Century-Fox. He couldn't get work producing anymore and had taken a job selling real estate. Susan had sent the unmanageable Dino to live with her parents in Palm Springs, hoping he might help her mother with Zanuck's care. Despite his problems, Dino was incredibly likable. Effervescent, much like his mother, and voluble, he could charm anyone with a few well-directed sentences. Unfortunately, said a police officer who knew the boy through a school program, "you could tell that he came from an unstable family unit."

Virginia was not immune to Dino's charisma, and when he arrived in California, she showered him with gifts and clothes and bought him a car. Within months, however, he had been banished from Ric-Su-

Dar. Not only hadn't he been helpful, but he had smoked marijuana openly—a practice his grandmother found shocking. He had also taken Virginia's credit cards and run up thousands of dollars in bills for expensive clothes. According to private investigator John O'Grady, "He tried to turn his grandma's place into a whorehouse." Dino had actually stashed some women of ill repute in the unused second floor of Ric-Su-Dar's main house and tried to charge admission at the door. He had a penchant for violence, though he vented his anger on property rather than on people. When he was finally tossed out of Ric-Su-Dar, he smashed his car into the gate.

André, Jr., moved into Ric-Su-Dar to take his brother's place. His job was to help out with his grandfather, to take him for walks, and accompany him to restaurant lunches. Zanuck was never to be left alone, recalled André, partly because Virginia feared that Genevieve would somehow come back and take him away with her—even though by now it had been more than two years since anybody in the family had heard from her. Besides, Zanuck's behavior was not normal. He constantly asked what time it was, grew anxious about the whereabouts of his dogs, and wandered off if left alone. One time, André Hakim, Sr., came to visit, and he, his son, and Zanuck went out for lunch at the Spa Hotel. Zanuck talked to his grandson as though the boy were his father. "We didn't know if he was all there or not," said André, Jr. He eventually decided that his grandfather was just having fun with them. Virginia had managed to get him back under her influence, and Zanuck couldn't do anything about it. He was trapped, so he played little games. "He always was a practical joker," said André, Jr. "He wore a little smile on his face."

André, Jr., was also buried in gifts from his grandmother. He got along with Virginia, he said, "until I discovered who she was." He found her incredibly possessive of her husband and mysteriously evil. He felt she was somehow keeping his grandfather captive. "It would not surprise me if it turned out that she made potions," he said. André's behavior to Virginia was sadistic. Knowing that she was listening in on the intercom system, he would encourage his grandfather to devise different ways to murder her. He would have his grandfather giggling about using rattlesnakes and scorpions as weapons. Then, according to André, they would wink and elbow each other with amusement.

In late 1976, when Susan, Pierre, and Sherry arrived in Palm Springs, André could not leave Ric-Su-Dar fast enough. "That was why my grandmother disliked me," he said. Actually, she had a few other reasons, too. He rarely did anything she felt was useful. He was chronically drunk, according to people close to the family, and often took money and jewelry from his grandmother. According to Pierre Savineau, there were problems with the police that cost Virginia thousands of dollars to get hushed up. André also wrecked a car, and a few times, he allowed his grandfather to wander far from Ric-Su-Dar, an unforgivable offense in Virginia's eyes.

Neither boy seemed terribly worried about the collapse of Susan's marriage or her drinking. They *were* concerned about her money, however. When Susan believed that she had been cheated on her Twentieth Century-Fox stock by Bamberger and her brother, the two boys were furious, too. They accompanied her to Bamberger's office, and Dino tried to punch the business manager. Indeed, without money, they were nothing. They didn't know how to earn any. The slow and ordinary path of school, college, and job didn't seem to appeal to either. If their mother didn't have money coming in, they wouldn't know how to live.

By the time Darryl Zanuck died in late 1979, all of Susan's children were out of the house. Craig was living with Pierre Savineau in Oklahoma, and Sherry, who, despite all the family disruption, had graduated with honors from Palm Springs High School, was staying permanently with a girlfriend. André was bunking with his father in Los Angeles, when he bothered to check in, which was seldom. Most of the time, he and Dino stayed with friends and stopped by to see their parents only when they needed cash. Neither boy was above ripping a few checks out of one of their parent's registers and forging a signature on them. Susan's purse and house were constantly raided. There was no Pierre Savineau around to protect her against the boys. Virginia was often on the telephone to Susan warning her not to admit them to her home.

Zanuck's youthful bumptiousness had been channeled to high ambition, but his grandsons lacked the judgment to know what to do with their high spirits. In April 1980, André, Jr., got into trouble for real. On a spring day, high on alcohol and Quaaludes, he linked up with a friend who had made a habit of stealing drugs from a Brentwood pharmacy. So frequent were the robberies that the police put the store under surveillance. His friend sent André, Jr., into the store with a toy gun and a shopping list of drugs. The police caught up with them, and André was arrested. He was later released on $10,000 bail and sent to a drug treatment program.

Dino, too, had his troubles. With a strange kind of frantic eagerness, he was trying to make big deals, just as his grandfather had. They involved, not motion pictures, but drugs. He would make drug buys with checks torn from his mother's checkbook, or he would pay with his own checks. Then they would bounce, and strange characters would come looking for him. Ten days before Susan's death, around June 1, 1980, three of his "friends" turned up on her doorstep and said that if they didn't get $2,000 that Dino owed them for cocaine, they would do something terrible to him.

When Dino himself showed up a few days later, he seemed unconcerned about the threat. He was with two men, and while Susan was out of the room, he took several checks from her pocketbook. He openly used drugs in the house and tauntingly asked his mother if she would like some cocaine. Susan turned down the offer. That night, Dino spoke to Sherry on the telephone. He told her that he had met a girl in Los Angeles who invited him to go with her to South America. He was already off on his next big deal. He flew to Colombia to make a drug buy. While he was gone, his mother died. Everybody in the family speculated that he might have murdered his mother and left town. He had a perfect alibi, however. Fledgling drug dealer that he was, he had been arrested by the Bogotá police. It took a month before the family got the news from a friend who called from Florida.

All three Hakim kids by that time were heavily involved with drugs. Only a few months after their mother's death, each of them received a check for a quarter-million dollars. Ironically, only Dino, the one most bent on self-destruction, took any precautions to safeguard the money. A routine letter had gone out to all the children from Union Bank, one of the officers of Susan's trust fund, offering investment advice. Dino was the only one to visit the bank. He had an officer set up a revocable trust for his money. Under the trust agreement, the bank would supervise investments, but Dino had the right to withdraw from principal. And withdraw he did. All the Hakim children spent their money. They did as they pleased; their lives were one long party with music, drugs, alcohol, and a lot of bad moves.

Their fun was interrupted briefly in October 1980 when their father, André Hakim, Sr., suddenly died of a heart attack. He was sixty-five years old. His elder son saw a dark plot in his father's death; somehow the Zanucks had done him in, asserted André, Jr. His father had visited one of *their* family doctors, who had given an injection of amphetamines—"the last thing you should give a heart patient." André, Jr., believed that the Zanucks wanted to do away with his father because "he was *finally* going to testify against them in the Twentieth Century-Fox embezzlement case." It was as though the Zanucks could not accept that anything ordinary—like dying of a heart attack—could possibly happen to one of them.

Such a story was completely preposterous, of course. Darryl Zanuck was dead, and the embezzlement case was ten years old. Richard Zanuck and David Brown had been rehired by Twentieth Century-Fox in 1980. Scarcely anybody in Los Angeles cared about the decade-old case against Hakim. Even more ridiculous was the notion that Hakim was going to reveal that Darryl and Dick had been part of a scheme to defraud the company of money. Hakim had never resisted naming his father-in-law as a co-conspirator and his brother-in-law as one who was privy to the scam right from the very first.

Nonetheless, André, Jr., could be heard to mutter years later that the coroner's office had investigated his father's death and found it mysterious. In fact, no coroner's report was done. Sadly, André Hakim, Sr., died with scarcely a penny to his name. He owed Susan $15,000, and when Bamberger tried to collect the money for her estate, he learned that Hakim's relatives hadn't entered his will into probate. There wasn't enough money to bother. André, Jr., had tried drug treatment again that fall. When his father died, however, he was released for the funeral. "I told them I was all right," he said. "But I was lying. All I wanted to do was get high."

Without parents to rebel against, the Hakim boys turned on each other. In mid-November 1981, only a month after Hakim's death, Dino arrived at André's rented house on Dalegrove Drive off Coldwater Canyon above Beverly Hills. As usual, Dino wanted to crash for the night. He also wanted drugs. André refused to let him in. They started screaming at each other about drugs, said Sherry, who was there at the time. "There was only a little bit left, and they were fighting about who should get it," said Sherry. "They were arguing over the last spoonful." André ordered his brother to leave, and he and a friend pushed Dino out onto the front porch and locked the door. Dino was furious. He bashed his hand through the front window and unlocked the front door. When he finally got into the living room, André was facing him with a gun. "Leave or I'll shoot," he told Dino. He fired; Sherry managed to grab the barrel so that the round missed Dino and blasted into the ceiling. André ran into one of the bedrooms. Dino ran after him. A few moments later, there were two more shots, and Dino emerged from the room with a bloody lip. Sherry fled the house, called the police from a neighbor's home, then jumped into her car and drove away. "There were lots of people there, but they all ran away, too," she recalled.

The police arrived a few minutes later. They sent for an ambulance and dispatched Dino, whose face was bloodied, to the hospital. André told them that Dino had grabbed a vacuum cleaner hose and started beating him with it; so he broke a wine bottle on Dino's face. The cops noticed the big holes in the ceiling, however. They discovered a shotgun, a .25 caliber handgun, and a vial of cocaine. André was booked on charges of drug possession and released on $1,000 bail.

Cocaine and get-rich-quick schemes drained Zanuck's grandchildren's inheritance dry. Most of the money Zanuck had put in his daughter's trust fund was converted to sparkling white powder and sniffed up. Dino also snorted heroin. The fact is that after only a few months, André was down to $6,000. Life then got grim and serious. "I made it last forever," he said earnestly. Dino made some disingenuous little attempts to refashion his life. While staying at the home of Mona Skoff, his mother's friend, he took a job parking cars. He insisted that she keep his earnings for him. He would carefully count out $20 a week for expenses and save the rest. He managed to accumulate $1,000. Just when Skoff began to believe he was finally getting his life together, he would disappear. She wouldn't see him for days or weeks, and she knew he was involved with drugs again.

Dino had a belief, said Skoff, that he would die young. "He was playing chicken with himself," she concluded. He ended his game in less time than anybody had thought possible. On April 26, 1981, he was found dead on a couch at a friend's house.

The body was taken to the medical examiner's office and identified by his brother André. The autopsy report detailed the horrifying effects of Dino's addiction. One of his nostrils was dried out completely. His lungs were congested and swollen, and his brain was slightly enlarged. He had choked on his own vomit. He had overdosed on morphine and cocaine.

André has never subscribed to that obvious conclusion, however. Just as in his father's death, he saw a dark conspiracy that might involve his relatives—or somebody. He has maintained that there were two coroner's reports. The first revealed that Dino had been murdered, but the Zanucks hushed it up; the second report stated that he died of a drug overdose. There was, however, only one report and one conclusion. Perhaps André couldn't accept that his brother had died from doing exactly what he himself was doing.

Three days later, Mona Skoff drove down to Forest Lawn to stand by the Hakim children as they buried their brother. When she found the "slumber room" where the body was laid out, she was shocked. "There was not one adult. Everybody there was a child." Sherry, André, Dino's friends—all were less than twenty-five years old. Most were under twenty-one. When André saw Skoff, he fell apart. He ordered everybody out of the room except her. "He was acting crazy," she said. "He wanted Dino to have all these things. He should be buried with his headphones and his cassettes. André wept and tried to climb into the coffin with Dino. I pulled him out and calmed him down. He closed the casket."

The funeral was held the next day. Everyone in the Zanuck family came. "They were all kind to each other," said Skoff. "There was no animosity. They were united in their grief. The whole family was pulling together. There was nothing good you could say about what happened except that. They were pulling together."

Soon after Dino's death, André checked with his brother's Los Angeles banker. Maybe Dino had left some money that he could get. The trust officer informed him that Dino had nothing. He had spent every penny. Dino had set up the trust fund to protect himself from himself, but the plan hadn't worked. "I guess we didn't do a very good job," said the banker.

The Hakim family was all but demolished. "It was all very strange," said André later. "It seemed as though one year we were all sitting at the table together for Thanksgiving dinner. Then, like in a year, nobody was left." His grandfather, mother, father, and brother were all dead. Only he and Sherry were left, and they didn't get along. By July 1982, about a year and a half after Dino's death, André, Jr., was finding it tough to survive. He petitioned the Indio court for an allowance to be paid out of his mother's remaining $50,000 in assets, claiming that he couldn't work because he was an alcoholic. Sherry filed an objection to his petition. "Petitioner André Hakim is twenty-five years old and is not physically or mentally incapable of earning a living. Alcoholics Anonymous conducts meetings during the mornings, afternoons, and evenings. Therefore, André Hakim could obtain employment and attend the programs before or after . . . hours," she contended through a lawyer. The court awarded André a temporary allowance anyway, and the bad feelings between brother and sister continued.

EIGHT
THE WAR OF THE WILLS

·

There was yet another Zanuck funeral in the fall of 1982. This time it was Mrs. Darryl F. Zanuck's. The service, held in the same Methodist church as her husband's, went off smoothly enough, but little glitches revealed a family at war with itself. André, Jr., asked Mona Skoff to accompany him to the funeral. "He had no one else left," she said. "He was not close to his sister. I didn't want to go because I hadn't known Virginia very well, but André begged me." When the two arrived at the church, she waited in a side vestibule while André visited the rest room. A batch of limousines pulled up. Darrylin emerged from one of them on the arms of two men. "She was dressed all in black and wore this very white, white makeup. She was leaning on the two men—probably one was her husband. She seemed to have this weird half-smile," recalled Skoff. By that time, André had returned, and Darrylin spotted him and Skoff. "She looked at me with such hatred," said Skoff, "and I just went back against the wall. Darrylin's children embraced and held me, but then this tall man came, and he said, 'You are asked to leave the church.' André was really upset. But I would never, never start an argument. I calmed him." Perhaps, Skoff thought, Darrylin objected to the presence of the one-time "other woman." Skoff was walked past reporters and the rest of the congregation. "I have never been so embarrassed," she said. André himself was escorted to a special pew. "The church was crowded, it was packed with people," he said. "But I sat all by myself in this one pew just for me."

Darrylin held an after-funeral reception at the Beverly Hills Hotel. Dick, who had attended the service with his wife, Lili Fini, didn't even know about the gathering until Walter Scott, Virginia's friend, happened to mention it right after the funeral. "He just turned white," said Scott. "Then he added, 'Well, I can tell you there are a couple people who won't be there.' " Indeed, Dick didn't attend. A few days later, he called Scott to ask if he had sent flowers. His sister, Dick said, had removed all the note cards from people's floral tributes, and so he didn't know whom to send thank-you notes. Embarrassed, he was calling everyone he knew to find out who had actually sent flowers.

On November 1, 1982, about three weeks after her mother's death, Darrylin and O'Grady filed Virginia's last will with the Los Angeles probate court. Darrylin's financial condition was still precarious. Her $300,000 trust fund had produced a decent amount of money during the inflationary surge of the late seventies and early eighties, but interest rates had begun to fall that year and with them her income. In any case, Virginia's will seemed to indicate that there was a rush to get Darrylin some money. She had ordered that Darrylin should be paid her $1 million "in cash . . . as soon after my death as . . . is legally possible."

Richard was already aware that his mother had made a new will because Virginia had summarily fired his business manager, Henry Bamberger. When Richard finally saw the new will and how little had been left to his sons, he was upset and determined to take to the courts. Nonetheless, he did not choose to throw down his own gauntlet. Instead, his friend and business partner David Brown filed a petition to become guardian *ad litem* for Dick's boys, Dean and Harrison, and moved to have the new will declared invalid. Richard told *Parade* that Brown was not acting for him; the suit was his partner's idea—sort of. "David loves my boys. He's their godfather. I turned over all the papers to him and let him make the decision. Were they getting a fair shake? David read the various wills, and he quickly saw how, in one, the boys would get about $2 million and how, in another, written three months later, they would get $5,000 each. It seemed most unfair to him, and he decided to file suit. I know people won't believe me, but I was too emotionally involved to make a decision in the case," he said. "I let David call the shots."

Neither the lawsuit Brown filed nor Richard's public pronouncements on the will contest made any mention of Janet and Ginny, Dick's daughters by his first wife Lili Gentle. Under the old will, they, too, would have received $1 million each. Virginia had cut down their inheritances to about one-tenth of what they had been before and given the remaining nine-tenths to Darrylin. Then living together in San Bernardino, Janet and Ginny apparently never thought to sue. For her part, Janet never understood the implications of the new will. She was always very grateful to her grandmother and to Darrylin for her $100,000 trust fund.

Through his lawyer, David Brown charged in court that Virginia was not of sound mind when she wrote her will. Darrylin, according to the petition, had "exercised undue influence over her mother because [Virginia's] mental and physical conditions were such that she had no freedom of will and her confidence was subverted." Brown claimed that Darrylin had suggested the contents of the will, assisted in its preparation, and caused Virginia to sign it. The new document was "made for Darrylin Zanuck's immediate and almost exclusive benefit." He also complained in court papers that Darrylin was not capable of administering Virginia's complex estate.

Darrylin's lawyer, Malcolm Ellis, returned Brown's serve with a hard volley. Suggestions that Darrylin was not competent to serve as executor came from Bamberger and Virginia's attorney at O'Melveny & Myers, asserted Ellis. Virginia had fired both and planned to sue them. "Unfortunately . . . Virginia Zanuck died before suit was filed," he said. Ellis went on to vow that suit would probably still be filed against them—for some unstated reason. He pointed out that Virginia had taken particular care to have herself videotaped when she read the new will and signed it. Further, in an additional videotape, "she personally addresses her son Richard Zanuck and tells him why she has disinherited him." Both tapes would be shown to two special administrators whom the court had appointed to oversee the estate until it was settled.

Ellis seemed to be threatening to make the contents of the second videotape public. Indeed, the lawyer was fond of telling people that it contained embarrassing, terrible revelations about Richard. "It is not the kind of thing that any family would want to have made public," he once remarked. Reporters wondered what could be on the "secret" tape. What was it that Virginia had said about the son she had defended so ardently after his ouster from Twentieth Century-Fox years before? Those who actually knew what was on the tape were mystified. "There was nothing scandalous at all," said Matt Cooney, the lawyer who was with Virginia when she made it. "She just expressed disappointment."

Private investigator John O'Grady, who had become caught up in the Zanucks' tangle of alliances and conflicts, was unhappy with the estate battle. He had wanted Virginia to videotape the new will to avoid arguments, but everybody was fighting anyway. He had felt all along that Virginia had gotten herself into a state. She was old, she was alone, and she felt neglected. She had developed an unreasonable "thing" about Richard, and Darrylin had done nothing to cool it. "I felt bad about Virginia's will," said O'Grady. "His [Richard's] mother was swayed, she was swayed. I felt bad about it. I wasn't for it. I even sent Dick a note about it, offering to meet with him and explain how it all came about." Dick never took him up on the offer.

Dick himself was busy with yet another lawsuit—one in behalf of his former wife Linda Harrison. His third wife, Lili, had engineered a rapprochement with Linda, and the three had become quite close. Linda had lost much of her 1977 divorce settlement from Richard to the Maha Genii. Most of the money, some $1.3 million, had gone to the Maha for the development of his church—to build temples, to spread the Word, and to provide a sanctuary for his disciples to live in. Soon after she wrote her last check to him in 1979, however, he decided that he no longer wanted to see her. He moved to Santa Barbara and declared that she was unworthy to be his disciple. Linda suffered deeply at her rejection by the Maha, and she was even more distressed when she later learned that the guru had used her money to acquire expensive real estate and luxuries for himself and his wife, the Mahara Genii.

Lili Zanuck was furious on her new friend's behalf. She urged Linda to sue the Maha for the return of her money. Dick, a man who supposedly liked his privacy, inexplicably endorsed the idea even though a lawsuit would certainly publicize Linda's sexual relationship with the guru and Dick's alleged attacks on the man and his paintings.

Still, he helped Linda find a law firm to take the case. Late in December 1982, Linda launched a lawsuit against the Maha, claiming that he had tricked her out of her money by falsely implying that he planned to use the funds for the church. The Maha's lawyers responded that Linda had made the contributions of her own free will and had not been given any assurances about the use of the money. Although Richard may not have realized it then, the litigation would last for three years and put embarrassing information about him and his family in the public domain.

*   *   *

Genevieve Gillaizeau's case had continued to steam along all through 1982. Both sides were busy trying to dig up dirt on each other. Detectives had been sent to Europe to look into Genevieve's background. The strategy was to prove that Genevieve had been neither a business adviser nor a companion to Darryl Zanuck but merely a well-compensated prostitute. Little more than dribbles of information surfaced. Not to be daunted, however, Malcolm Ellis issued a set of highly inflammatory interrogatories in February 1982 demanding responses from Genevieve. Among other things, Ellis requested that Genevieve admit:

> That when you first met Darryl Zanuck, you were employed by . . . Madame Claude.
> That you were introduced to Darryl Zanuck by Chantal Winter.
> That you and Chantal Winter performed lesbian sex acts for Darryl Zanuck when you first met him.
> That you procured a friend named Danique for sex acts with Darryl Zanuck.
> During the first six months that you dated Darryl Zanuck, you also saw other customers for Madame Claude as a prostitute.
> That you acted as a procurer of men for prostitution for your younger sister while dating Darryl Zanuck.
> That in 1969 and 1970 you supported Jean Desmoyeres while at the same time you were dating Darryl Zanuck.
> That you have an arrest record in France for prostitution. That you have an arrest record in France for theft.

To no one's great surprise, Genevieve refused to respond to the touchiest questions, arguing that they were designed to annoy and embarrass her. In any case, the strategy seemed rather pointless. If Darryl Zanuck wanted to leave his estate to an alleged prostitute, that was certainly his business. Purity is not a requirement for inheriting money.

Attorneys for the Bank of America tried to establish similar information themselves. That summer of 1982, William Campbell and Jamie Broder of Paul Hastings Janofsky & Walker had managed to interview Fernande Josephine Cook—a.k.a. Madame Claude—and had unearthed the same seamy details. However, Madame Claude shied away from stating for the record what she told the lawyers in the airy surroundings of Ma Maison. They had no hard evidence of anything.

Genevieve herself was offered a bit of dirt on the Zanucks. Tom Shirley, through an intermediary, got in touch with Genevieve from Florida. He wasn't going to give anybody information, however, until he got $15,000 for his evidence. He also wanted expenses for any trip he would have to take to Los Angeles and money for a judge and an investigator who had helped him. He also demanded another $5,000 in "hideaway money." The reason: he was afraid of Richard Zanuck. His fears were based on a jumbled and distorted assortment of details from ancient history. He claimed to have been present when Richard "knifed an Indian in the Palm Springs area, and left him for dead." That story sounded like a mishmoshed retelling of Richard's misadventure during his break from Stanford nearly thirty years earlier. Shirley also said he saw Richard push Genevieve against a vehicle and threaten to kill her after Darryl Zanuck returned to Palm Springs in 1973. Shirley called later to announce that he was giving Genevieve a deadline. If she didn't hand over the funds, he would destroy the evidence.

In yet another call to Genevieve's representative, Shirley claimed to have original documents in Darrylin's hand showing her practicing her father's signature. He also said he had fingerprints showing that she had forged the signature on her father's will. He could prove, he said, that the Zanucks were lying in court. However, without the money, he would offer no evidence. Finally, a meeting was arranged at the office of a Los Angeles private investigator between Genevieve's representative and Ed Meena, Shirley's friend. Suspicious and unfriendly, they accused each other of hiding important evidence in files and bugging the investigator's office. When everybody settled into a state of uneasy trust, Shirley put in an appearance.

He agreed to turn over his evidence without getting any money. What he offered was intriguing but not conclusive—a sheet of Ric-Su-Dar stationery on which a note had been penned from Virginia to Darrylin. Dated Thursday, it read, "Dearest Darrylin—Start your practice now, before I see you Tues 18th. Love xxxxx Me—P.S. Give back to me when I see you." On the back was written "Darryl F. Zanuck" several times. There was also an envelope dated September 14, 1973—about six weeks before the new will disinheriting Genevieve was signed. The envelope had been sent from Virginia in Palm Springs to Darrylin. On the back of the envelope was "Darryl F. Zanuck, Darryl F. Zanuck."

For hours and hours, Shirley told lurid stories about the Zanucks. He had records to back up some of what he said. He was quite an impressive witness. He seemed organized, honest, sincere—and outraged by how the family conducted itself. He was furious with them—especially Darrylin. She had taken $17,000 from him, he claimed, and unfairly charged him with losing a good portion of her trust fund, he said. Shirley was writing a book about the Zanucks. Since he couldn't do a nonfiction account without getting sued, he decided to write a thinly disguised novel about the family of a famous Hollywood mogul named Zachary Irving. Everybody in town would know who the book was about.

The resulting opus rivaled any of Darryl Zanuck's earliest potboilers and contained a strong streak of pornographic detail. The hero of the piece is Billy James—presumably Bobby Jacks, Darrylin's ex-husband. According to his first-person narrative, he meets the Irvings while working as a lifeguard on the Santa Monica beach. One afternoon, he saves their little boy Zackie from drowning. The youngster claims that his older sister Vivian pushed him out to sea in a sailboat. When the boy brings James home to be thanked by his parents, they turn out to be the famed Zachary Irvings, who rule Hollywood. James meets Vivian and her younger sister Lillian. Eventually, after several torrid encounters with Vivian on the beach and in the annex of the Irving beach house, Billy marries her.

In the manuscript, family members are seen through the eyes of Billy James. The paterfamilias, who teaches the young man everything there is to know about filmmaking, has some peculiar habits. For one, he takes nightly walks, and much like a dog, urinates regularly in a particular spot outside. He and his wife hold orgies in their home; they often take part in threesomes with other women. Vivian can't have children and therefore adopts two East European teenagers. Vivian's father seduces the young girl. Vivian, distraught about growing old and frustrated by her inability to have children, becomes obsessed with her appearance. She resorts to plastic surgery and adultery to bolster her opinion of herself. She ultimately ditches Billy and moves to Mexico where she remarries and becomes a dealer and user of cocaine who, on the sly, sleeps with a Mexican priest. Lillian, the younger Irving girl, develops a love of alcohol at an early age and marries one of her father's yes-men. Zackie, the mogul's son, has "a short-man complex," is gay, and has a lurid love affair with his business partner Daniel Block. Micheline, the mogul's French mistress, is a loyal camp follower who is banished from the family by young Zackie.

A cataclysmic denouement in the last chapter, which is called "One Generation of Greatness," finds the family destroying itself for vengeance. Though Vivian is again living with Billy James, she has an affair with the family business manager who is named Hamburg. Zackie learns about it and tells Billy James. Vivian retaliates against her brother by telling his wife about his affair with Daniel Block. Zackie and his wife quarrel, and in a rage, he beats her with a tennis racket and shoots her in the head three times. Not surprisingly, she dies. Then, in despair, he threatens to cut off his "dick," but Billy James manages to wrestle away the knife. Zackie grabs the gun and turns it on himself.

In the penultimate scene, Billy James announces to Vivian that he no longer wants to remarry her. She begs him to stay the night and make love to her, but he refuses. Like Rhett Butler, Billy James brutally kisses her off—though with an up-to-date suggestion: "Why don't you get a vibrator and go fuck yourself," he says.

Those could very well have been Tom Shirley's sentiments about his former benefactress, Darrylin. Indeed, a friend who read it believed the book was "the real story of the Zanuck family." Diane Jacks, second wife of Bobby Jacks, aka Billy James, described the manuscript as "bizarre" after she read it. Jacks had confided much about the Zanucks to her, and she knew Dick quite well. Never, never had she heard such strange and peculiar stories, however. "The well-known things about Darryl Zanuck—the things that everyone knows—they're true. But the story about Darrylin trying to drown Richard . . . well, it's just bizarre," she said. Perhaps literary agents and publishers also found it questionable because it was never published.

*   *   *

By the summer of 1982, virtually all parties to the Zanuck will contest had had their depositions taken. Richard made a startling revelation during his testimony. Genevieve's lawyer Samuel Buffone asked Richard if he was "aware of any instances in which any member of your family attempted to duplicate your father's signature?" Richard answered "yes," and went on to say, "I was never present during any instances, but I was told by my sister that she had signed either the [1973] will or the [1977] codicil and she couldn't remember which one." Darrylin, Richard testified, disclosed this information after the will was placed into probate but before Genevieve had filed her challenge. Said Richard, "We both noted the great—what we thought were apparent dissimilarities in the two signatures. . . . The signature of the will and the signature on the codicil, and she told me that she had signed one of the two documents but could not remember which one it was."

Buffone asked whether Darrylin had revealed how this had happened, and Richard replied: "It seems to me that she and my mother . . . were concerned that my father, being temperamental, crabby, unpredictable, would possibly not sign whatever document they were referring to at the time, and it seemed to me that she had been, as she related, asked [by] my mother to somehow prepare to sign the document because the lawyers were all coming out, and if he didn't sign it, you know, it would be a waste of time." Darrylin's signing for her father had been a convenience, he asserted, not an attempt to thwart his desires. Richard added, "In the two conversations I had with my sister on the subject, there was no indication that any duplication of the signature would be as a result of my father objecting to the contents of the will, that it was more a matter of expediency because people were coming."

In her own deposition, Darrylin didn't respond to her brother's allegation because she hadn't had time to read the transcript of his deposition. She had examined the note from Virginia exhorting her to "practice" and the envelope with her father's signatures on it—both of which had come from Tom Shirley. Darrylin denied ever "practicing" her father's signature. The handwriting on the notes and envelopes was her father's, not hers, she asserted. There had been no writing on the envelope when it arrived. She theorized that since her mother made a habit of requesting correspondents to return the notes and letters she sent them, Darrylin had probably mailed Virginia the letter and her father had later scribbled his signature on it in an idle moment. Buffone asked her whether she could recall other specific instances in which her mother demanded return of her letters, and Darrylin could not.

Buffone also asked Darrylin what Virginia had referred to when she talked about "practice." Darrylin's reply: she was becoming a Rosicrucian and was studying for her test. The lawyer questioned Darrylin closely about Rosicrucianism. She seemed ignorant of basic facts about the organization. When asked to make the Rosicrucian sign of the cross, she declined to do so in public, since the rite was supposed to be secret.

The matter was left at that. Attorneys for the estate asked in court that there be no more pretrial discovery on the subject of forgery. After all, that charge had been stricken from the case because Mitchelson had failed to file the forgery petition in a timely manner. Bringing such irrelevant evidence to bear on the case would merely prove misleading.

The various attorneys working for the estate and the family had developed a defense strategy. Norman Oberstein, Richard Zanuck's lawyer, had come to believe that Genevieve's case could be completely derailed. Neither Marvin Mitchelson nor any of Genevieve's other lawyers had ever challenged the codicil that Zanuck had signed in 1977. This document, which itemized only a few changes, had specifically "ratified, approved, and confirmed" his October 1973 will. So, in essence, it had "republished" the original. Nobody could successfully throw out the 1973 will without taking aim at the codicil, and nobody had claimed that Zanuck was incompetent or under duress in 1977. The family certainly could get the case thrown out of court for that reason alone.

Indeed, it would seem that the lawyers could have saved their clients thousands and thousands of dollars in legal fees by filing a motion for dismissal based on this premise the moment they discovered it. Yet they never did. If the lawyers filed such a motion, Genevieve's attorney could ask the court for permission to amend her original petition and include the codicil. That would undermine the defense's strategy. The estate's lawyers determined to wait for the trial.

In his trial brief on behalf of the Bank of America, attorney William Campbell argued that Genevieve's witnesses could not testify to Zanuck's mental capacity at the time the October will was signed. The two doctors who had cared for Zanuck in New York had no direct evidence to indicate that his mental incapacity had continued for six more months. Indeed, Zanuck could have experienced "lucid periods." Richard had testified in his deposition that his father had improved dramatically after his return to Palm Springs. Two witnesses to the signing of the 1973 will—Keith Gill and William Mohlis—had both testified that Zanuck was alert and mentally competent, and so had the Zanucks' family physician Dr. George Kaplan. Zanuck's other deficits—old age, feebleness, forgetfulness, slovenliness, personal eccentricities, failure to recognize old friends and relatives, physical disability, absentmindedness, and mental confusion—Campbell asserted, were not sufficient indicators of incompetency. Nor was there any proof of undue influence, since neither Richard nor Darrylin had been present when the will was signed. Genevieve's petition was full of allegations that Zanuck was kidnapped and held prisoner at Ric-Su-Dar, but, said Campbell, "after two and one-half years of litigation and discovery, there is not one shred of evidence to support these allegations. Numerous witnesses have testified that decedent chose to move to Palm Springs and that he was free to come and go once he was there."

Trial was scheduled for Tuesday, January 4, 1983. The Zanuck family drove from their various points of origin to show solidarity in the grubby Indio, California, courthouse. Genevieve flew in from New York. She looked rather dowdy, many people thought, no longer the cool young woman who had been Darryl Zanuck's companion. She still wore her hair tied back in a simple knot, and she wore very little makeup. Her figure was no longer perfect. Some of the Zanucks felt that she had toned herself down for her court appearance.

If those present expected to see an exciting trial, a drama on the order of *The Verdict*, Richard's newest movie, which had opened only a few months before, they were to be disappointed. Much of the initial testimony—hundreds of pages—was read into the record from depositions by Genevieve's recently recruited Riverside, California, lawyer, Don C. Brown, and his associate, Sharon Waters. The deposition of Vinnie Argentino, Zanuck's secretary in New York, described her boss's memory problems and his condition when he was alone and ill in his hotel suite, lying in his bed amid droppings made by his dog.

Over the next few days, the depositions of Zanuck's two New York doctors, Carl Feind and Carmine Vicale, confirmed the dismal prognosis—that Zanuck was suffering from "organic brain syndrome" that left him confused and likely to remain that way indefinitely. Dr. Vicale, Zanuck's neurologist, added, "I would say that the brain involvement was basically senile changes of the Alzheimer's disease type." When asked by Brown if Zanuck could understand "a complex document," the doctor replied, "No, I don't think so."

The defending lawyers, over the objection of Genevieve's lawyer, read into the record a portion of Malcolm Ellis's cross examination of Vicale, which seemed to contradict the doctor's testimony and to indicate Zanuck might have been able to understand a will after all. Ellis suggested that perhaps temporary aggravating factors could have caused the appearance of Alzheimer's disease, and Vicale agreed that was possible.

Tom Shirley's friend, Ed Meena, the first living, breathing witness to be called, brought forth details of Zanuck's life in Palm Springs that surely would have embarrassed the mogul. In visits to Ric-Su-Dar after Zanuck's return, Meena said, he observed that Zanuck needed help in getting dressed and that he refused to bathe. His driver had to take him to a health spa where he would be encouraged to shower. The elderly mogul was very docile and never left the house alone, Meena added. Meena also testified that Darrylin, Susan, and Virginia had discussed getting Zanuck's will changed. They were determined, he declared, to get Genevieve written out of the will. At one point, Meena said, Virginia had urged Darrylin to "go practice your handwriting." Ellis partially impeached Meena's impartiality by accusing him and his friend Tom Shirley of befriending Virginia in order to meet her friends and take care of their finances. Meena denied that, however.

Further evidence indicating that Zanuck was senile was provided by Elizabeth Sylvia, whose husband Henry had worked as Zanuck's personal chauffeur from 1963 to 1973. In November 1970, she testified, she went to Zanuck's Plaza Hotel suite in New York to talk to him about her husband's job. She found, however, that "Mr. Zanuck was in no frame of mind when I walk in to even talk to him because dog feces was all over everything, over him, too, and he started saying, 'Vinnie, why you late?' . . . and then he picked up—he had some dog feces in the ashtray. He picked it up to light it like it was his cigar." Zanuck, she added, had often called her husband in the middle of the night. Zanuck wanted Sylvia to bring the car by even though he had nowhere to go.

Rita Mahon, the maid at Ric-Su-Dar during the first years after Zanuck had returned to Virginia, revealed that he wet his bed and soiled it. He spent much of his time just sitting, watching TV. She could not recall ever seeing him read. She was also present when Zanuck told the family's physician, Dr. George Kaplan, that he felt confused and didn't know where he was. Mrs. Mahon said that the doctor replied something like "You'll be all right."

Richard Zanuck was the next witness to be summoned to the stand. His testimony proved very intriguing; he candidly reported that his father's memory was "flawed" in 1967 and 1968, but improved the following year when he stopped his heavy drinking. From then until his death, he drank only beer or near beer. He painted a picture of a man who was nothing like the commanding executive of a major Hollywood studio. He never telephoned Richard or answered the phone—though as Richard pointed out, "He never picked up the phone for twenty years . . . that was nothing new"—never wrote a check, and visited Los Angeles only once after his return to Palm Springs. Indeed, Richard couldn't recall his father drafting a letter or any other document around the time the October 1973 will was signed. By 1974, he claimed, his father's condition had stabilized. He still suffered from memory flaws, but they were the same as they had been earlier. Said Richard, "He would ask the same question. It was mostly, as I say, detailed things that he was forgetful on. He would ask the same question twice of you. Like what time is it? Or where are we going for dinner tonight? Or when are you going back, driving home? Questions like that. Nothing of any real significance."

Genevieve didn't testify until well into the second week of the trial. She spoke softly with a heavy French accent. According to the local Palm Springs newspaper, her story started off like a Judith Krantz novel and ended like a Greek tragedy. Her high life of nightclubs, premieres, and exotic travel with Zanuck turned completely gloomy after he lost his company and fell ill. Genevieve had considerably toned down her story of the return to Palm Springs since the lawsuit was first filed two and a half years earlier. There was no more talk of kidnapping, Yorkie-stomping security goons, or arrests. "Everything went so fast," she said. "They grabbed Darryl and put him in the car and told me to get in another car."

William Campbell, one of the lawyers for the estate, took Genevieve through a painstaking recounting of all the gifts and cash she received from Zanuck. His point was that, in a sense, Zanuck had already taken care of her. Campbell also showed Genevieve an August 1969 letter in which Zanuck gave her 2,500 shares of Fox stock worth about $50,000. She was to reimburse him for the cost of the stock but keep the profit for herself. She conceded that she had since sold the stock for about $100,000 but never repaid Zanuck or his estate. She also admitted that she received a $20,000 loan from Zanuck to purchase her first apartment. She hadn't repaid that, either.

To show that Genevieve was less than completely devoted to Zanuck, Campbell also questioned her closely about where she was in March 1973 when Zanuck was alone and distraught in his Plaza Hotel suite. Genevieve had earlier claimed that she was visiting a sister in Paris. Campbell showed Genevieve telegrams that she had sent from Africa to Vinnie Argentino in New York asking to be kept posted on Zanuck's condition. One, from the Safari Club in Mombasa, was signed "Genene Radziwill." Genevieve denied that she was with Prince John Radziwill when she sent the wire. However, she conceded that in her deposition she had admitted to being engaged to Radziwill in the fall of 1973.

Ellis came up on deck next. He challenged Genevieve's assertion that Zanuck became a near-hermit during his last year in New York. She and Zanuck went to "21" nearly a dozen times that year and to Trader Vic's every Sunday evening. Ellis also implied that she was seeing various men without Zanuck's knowledge. Genevieve heatedly replied that she informed Zanuck when she had an escort. Ellis

271

intimated that she spent much of 1972 away from Zanuck because once the mogul fell ill, the stream of gifts she had come to expect dribbled to nothing. Genevieve asserted that the mogul gave her money to buy herself "a few things." Responded Ellis: "A few things but none of these major fur coats, these $40,000 fur coats, these million and a half dollar diamond rings? You didn't buy anything that expensive with the money in 1972, did you?" She replied, "Well, a lot of thing change after that. We were not traveling on Twentieth Century-Fox expense account." He suggested that her interest in Zanuck was short-lived after he returned to Palm Springs. With the exception of her visit with her lawyer George Cappiello, she never tried to see Zanuck again. She didn't call him and claimed to have written only once.

Norman Oberstein, Richard's lawyer, seemed more intent on restoring his client's stature than in impeaching Genevieve's testimony. He asked, "In the period of May 1971 through April 1973 and prior to Mr. Zanuck's return to Palm Springs, did he ever tell you in words or substance that he was sorry that he hadn't followed the advice of his son Richard? . . . In that same period of time, did Darryl Zanuck ever tell you in words or substance that he felt he would have been better off in his life had he followed the advice of his son Richard? . . . In that same period of time, did Darryl Zanuck ever tell you . . . that he didn't blame his son for being upset with . . . Twentieth Century-Fox?" Genevieve's response to each question was an emphatic no.

In subsequent testimony, Genevieve's lawyer, Don Brown, tried to repair some of the damage done to her case on cross examination. She testified that her 1972 trips were for modeling assignments and that she took those trips with Zanuck's full knowledge. Brown also introduced letters from Zanuck to Genevieve dated October 8, 1970, which seemed to forgive her debts to him—either explicitly or indirectly. In one, written just before Zanuck checked into the hospital for his jaw surgery in February 1972, he promised that she wouldn't owe him any money.

The onlookers restlessly awaited the presentation of the estate's case. But the next morning Campbell and other lawyers on the family team came into court with a motion to dismiss the case because Genevieve's first attorneys—Mitchelson and Rhoden—had never filed a challenge to the 1977 codicil Zanuck signed to change some minor provisions of his October 1973 will. The family's and bank's lawyers contended that the codicil republished the original will, and Genevieve had no evidence of Zanuck's mental incapacity when it was signed. A day later Judge Frank Moore dismissed the case. The lawsuit, which had originally looked so interesting and peculiar, had fizzled out on a technicality.

Moore's ruling should have put an end to the fight. Instead, the decision, like a hydra-headed virus, sent litigation fever up and down nerve endings, producing new legal eruptions. Within a month, Genevieve's lawyer had filed an appeal, and the Bank of America had launched a lawsuit against Genevieve to recover money for the Fox stock she had been lent. That money should be part of Zanuck's estate, argued the lawyers. Genevieve asserted that Zanuck had forgiven all her debts.

She also sued her former lawyer Marvin Mitchelson in New York for legal malpractice, recruiting Richard Ben-Veniste, one of the Watergate prosecutors, to take the case. Winning a legal malpractice judgment can be more difficult than getting a casual date to pay alimony. The plaintiff has to prove that the attorney demonstrated an egregious lack of prudence, that his mistake caused a lawsuit to go wrong, and that the bad outcome caused actual damages. Genevieve charged in court papers that Mitchelson's failure to file the forgery claim on time and to challenge the 1977 codicil to Zanuck's will constituted breach of duty. Mitchelson asserted in his response that, while he did miscalculate the deadline for the forgery petition, it was not physically possible for him to get it to Indio on time. As far as the 1977 codicil went, Mitchelson said that it was not a settled point of law in California that a codicil republished the original. He added that he had no basis for challenging the codicil because he had no evidence that Zanuck was mentally incompetent or under duress in 1977.

There were now three different battles being waged over Zanuck money. That count, of course, did not include the case that Richard Zanuck's business partner David Brown had already filed against Virginia's estate.

*   *   *

Virginia's estate was beset by minor attackers. In November 1982, two months before the Darryl Zanuck will contest went to trial, Thomas Shirley filed a claim against Darrylin and her mother's estate for $21.5 million with the Indio, California, court. He asserted he had learned late in 1977 that Darrylin and her mother conspired to forge Zanuck's will. To prevent him from revealing their misdeed, the two women then conspired to defame him by trying to pin the theft of Darrylin's jewelry on him. They repeated the accusation to an assortment of guests who gathered at the Palm Springs house for a party on November 29, 1977. Shirley didn't learn of the slander until November 26, 1981, when Pierre Savineau told him of the incident.

The dates Shirley was juggling in the legal claim didn't really gibe. In the declaration he made for Mitchelson, he stated that he first became aware of the forgery in the fall of 1975. By 1977, when he now was saying he learned of the forgery, he had already had a falling-out with the Zanucks, not just over the pilfered jewelry, but about Darrylin's trust fund as well.

Anyway, it was all old news—and hard to prove. Virginia was dead, other people who were at the party had also died or moved away, and some who were present believed Virginia's stories about Shirley; their feelings about him had already taken on a negative cast. Said Margaret Shands, "Virginia said that Tom had stolen Darrylin's trust money, and I believed her." By the spring of 1983, it was clear that Shirley's claim was going nowhere. The Indio court had the lawsuit transferred to Los Angeles where Virginia's estate was filed for probate. The judge rejected it without explanation.

In early 1983, just after the estate case had been dismissed, Shirley found another arena in which to air his views about Darryl Zanuck's signatures: show biz. F. Lee Bailey, the famed trial lawyer, had become the star of a TV series called "Lie Detector." On the show, parties to a dispute would take a lie detector test, and a professional polygraph expert would decide who was telling the truth. In fact, the on-air "test" was mostly for show. Guests underwent two off-screen polygraph tests before the taping. Shirley was one of five hundred who applied each week for one of the show's guest spots. On March 5, 1983, he was invited to tape a segment. After an opening fanfare, the announcer declared that Thomas Shirley had dramatic information to support Genevieve Gillaizeau's claim that Zanuck's will was a forgery.

Sitting on a semicircular sofa next to Bailey, Shirley recounted the conversation he had with Darrylin on the drive to Palm Springs in 1975. Shirley admitted that he wasn't exactly sure when or how Darrylin or her mother had managed to forge a will that bore the signatures of three witnesses, but added that Virginia said she was confident that a lady at the Bank of America would notarize Zanuck's signature even though he did not sign it in front of her. Bailey countered that "we contacted the lady who did the notary . . . seal, and although she was not very talkative and wound up hanging . . . up on us . . . she did say, 'Oh, now, I went to the house and everybody was there and we all saw him sign it,' and so forth. . . . That seems to be quite a bit different than the story you got from Darrylin." Shirley replied, "Well, I had actually seen the lady, um, sign documents or, notarize documents, which had been sent from the house by me, actually."

Shirley was ushered into an isolation room, hooked up to the polygraph equipment, and asked whether Darrylin had told him about the forgery. In the background was the amplified sound of a heart—presumably Shirley's—pumping away. Bailey showed viewers two of Darryl Zanuck's signatures—one from a trust agreement Shirley saw Zanuck sign and another from the disputed will.

Shirley passed his test. Bailey revealed that a report done by a handwriting expert (the one Shirley had used originally) located ten different discrepancies between the two signatures. Baily declared, "There's no question that . . . it's not a story you made up."

When Bailey's producer informed Darrylin and Malcolm Ellis of Shirley's accusation, Ellis shot back a letter in which he asserted that "There were five witnesses to the will, two of them attorneys . . . [and] they witnessed Darryl Zanuck sign the will." Ellis also revealed that the estate's lawyers had retained their own handwriting expert, John Harris, who had verified Zanuck's signature. Ellis turned down the producers' request that Darrylin appear on the show because, he wrote, "My client is very high strung and has a serious lung and breathing problem and would not be a good subject for the polygraph." Ellis did offer the names and addresses of those who had witnessed the will so they could verify that Shirley's accusation was untrue. Ellis wound up his epistle with a lawyerly threat to sue if the program was aired.

The producers of "Lie Detector" quickly invited Keith Gill, a witness to the will, to appear on the show and submit to a polygraph examination. Gill identified himself as a lawyer who had been asked by Zanuck's attorney, Richard Paul, to review Zanuck's will for California procedure and then to come to Ric-Su-Dar to watch Zanuck execute it. Zanuck, said Gill in court papers, "was very alert. He stood erect, he'd walk with a purpose, he had a firm handshake. Uh, I would say very alert and he seemed very much in control of his mind and his person." When Gill reappeared after a brief session in the isolation booth where he was hooked up to the polygraph equipment, he received heartening news from F. Lee Bailey, who declared: "I would say without question the will of Darryl Zanuck was valid."

Despite his client's vindication, Ellis asked Bailey not to air either show. Bailey promised only a voice-over "clarification" at the end of the first show, which would withdraw any inference that Darrylin had said she forged her father's will. "In fact," declared the disembodied voice, "based on Keith Gill's later appearance on 'Lie Detector' when Mr. Gill was polygraphed as to his witnessing the signing of Darryl Zanuck's will, one thing seems to be true, that Darrylin Zanuck did not forge Darryl Zanuck's will." The second show, with Keith Gill, aired the following Tuesday.

Ellis filed a lawsuit against Bailey, the producers, the distributors, the broadcaster, and Thomas Shirley for $60 million claiming slander, "false light," invasion of privacy, intentional infliction of emotional distress, and negligence. The whole insulting fracas, according to the complaint, had caused Darrylin to "employ physicians to examine and treat plaintiff, and incurred additional medical expenses." All the defendants but Thomas Shirley denied the allegations and contended that statements were privileged as opinion under the First and Fourteenth amendments of the U.S. Constitution and under California law as well.

It is unclear how deeply Darrylin had suffered from the TV show. Its ratings were not impressive, and a few months later the series was canceled. According to court papers, she did consult a therapist. She made three more appointments but showed up only twice. The therapist, who charged $95 for each visit, labeled Darrylin's emotional distress "adult adjustment syndrome."

Thomas Shirley, meanwhile, was apparently having some difficulty sustaining an adult adjustment to a lawsuit against him for $60 million. He decided that this time he would really disappear from the scene. He gave the keys to his powder-blue Mercedes to his friend Ed Meena. If anybody came looking for Shirley, Meena was to say he was dead.

*   *   *

Virginia's estate still had not cleared probate, and in the spring of 1983 there was little hope that the case would wind down promptly. Both sides seemed to be digging in for a long struggle, and the original dispute had been complicated by extraneous issues. For one, André Hakim, Jr., who had dropped out of sight for a while, turned up in a small Oregon town where he had gone with a friend to write a book about the Zanuck saga. From the woodland glade where he was holed up, André filed a creditor's claim against the estate. He asserted that Virginia owed his mother's estate a jewelry collection that was worth at least $250,000. The jewelry Susan had taken to her mother for safekeeping had disappeared after Virginia's death, he said. The collection had included a canary diamond flower clip set in gold and platinum, containing 56 round diamonds; a lily-of-the-valley pin containing 34 Oriental pearls, 63 baguette diamonds, and 215 round diamonds; and a platinum and diamond necklace containing 834 small round diamonds, five large round diamonds, and 43 baguette diamonds. No doubt, it would have been hard to misplace jewelry like that.

The issue was never to receive any real attention from the court because André, Jr., like Marvin Mitchelson, filed his claim too late to meet the four-month deadline. A few months later, the judge simply rejected it.

What did happen to the jewelry? The Zanucks accused one another of having swiped or stolen it. André, Jr., and his sister, Sherry, believed that Darrylin took it when she emptied Ric-Su-Dar. Richard also seemed to think that Darrylin knew where the jewelry was. That spring, David Brown's attorney requested that Darrylin provide an inventory of Ric-Su-Dar and notes on jewelry given by Virginia to

Darrylin or Susan. Darrylin asserted that Susan never gave their mother any jewelry but secretly sold it to meet bills. If so, the proceeds from that sale should have turned up in her estate, but that was worth less than $50,000. Henry Bamberger, who had acted as Susan's executor, asserted in court papers that André, Jr., and Sherry had access to Susan's house and that much of Susan's property disappeared after her death.

By June, Judge Ronald Swearingen had scheduled a mandatory settlement conference to get the two sides of the Virginia Zanuck estate war together. That action prompted attorneys to work out a solution. On July 20, 1983, they petitioned the court for approval of a settlement. Most of the terms were kept private, but Darrylin agreed to set aside $1.5 million to be given to the Virginia Zanuck Charitable Foundation. The videocassette Virginia had made accusing her son of neglecting her was to be destroyed. If either party to the lawsuit revealed the contents, he or she would have to pay $1 million to the other party. Malcolm Ellis and David Brown's lawyers ultimately cut the tapes into pieces with scissors. Although the tape revealed nothing earthshaking about Dick, except his fall from his mother's graces, he thought it important enough to suppress.

Virginia's heirs paid heavily for the haste and hatred with which the elderly woman had drawn up her last will. Under the old will, a clever batch of trusts had avoided almost all federal taxation. The new one, however, had been written without much regard for tax consequences. The $12 million estate was diminished by $3.5 million in taxes paid to the federal government and another $737,000 to the state of California.

Darrylin and John O'Grady were to be the executors, and they set about paying bequests. Darrylin received the $1 million her mother had left her, O'Grady got $10,000, and Richard Zanuck's daughters, Janet and Ginny, received their trust fund income. Sherry was due to inherit $15,000, and a check was mailed to her in October. She called later to complain that she never received the check; so a new one was issued. A few days later, a Palm Springs bank placed a call to Ellis. Sherry was in his office trying to cash the first check. The second check was stopped. Sherry has said that the whole thing was just a mix-up. Virginia took care of servants as well as family. She had left Alma

Diehl $25,000 in cash and an annuity that would guarantee her $700 in monthly income. After the bequests were paid, the lawyers and special administrators weighed in with hefty bills—$200,000 for the special administrators and their attorneys and $80,000 for Matt Cooney, the lawyer who drew up Virginia's last will. Ellis challenged the lawyers' fees, claiming that his firm had done over half the work. After multitudinous filings and petitions and other legal maneuvers, the lawyers were paid far less than what they demanded. Darrylin received the residue of the estate—upwards of $4 million.

She no longer had to worry about money.

*   *   *

The end of the strife over Virginia's estate did not terminate hostilities between Darrylin and Richard. They did not fight in an intimate, familiar way, however, screaming and yelling at each other face-to-face, cursing the gods and vowing never to speak. They did battle coolly—through the courts. Like soldiers who have failed to hear of a war's end, they kept going on and on against all reason. Their father's estate now provided the battlefield.

First, they fought over the $1 million or so in deferred compensation and insurance benefits Darryl Zanuck was supposed to receive from Twentieth Century-Fox. One of the agreements Zanuck and Virginia had signed during their long separation included a provision granting her half of all his Fox benefits. According to Malcolm Ellis's thinking, half of that money should go into Darryl's estate and the other half to Virginia's estate. Virginia's portion would then go to Darrylin. Genevieve's attorneys wanted the money to go to Zanuck's estate, of course. Richard seemed disinclined to allow Darrylin to receive more money than she had already inherited. His lawyer argued that the funds should go to Zanuck's estate. Again, briefs and motions piled up in case files in Los Angeles and Indio. Finally, in 1984, an agreement was worked out to allow half of the money to flow to Virginia's estate.

The money seemed much less important to the two Zanuck children than Zanuck's personal property and Hollywood memorabilia. The Bank of America had grown very testy about property that it maintained was missing from Ric-Su-Dar. Some of the items that had been left with Virginia did turn up, but the bank kept after Darrylin about the rest of it. However, the bank didn't know what efforts, if any, Darrylin had made to find the missing items. One court petition noted that "Richard alleges that certain of the decedent's [Zanuck's] jewelry has been seen worn by members of Darrylin's family, and he has alleged through counsel, that Darrylin and her family are in possession of the decedent's jewelry and the other missing personal property." André Hakim, Jr., also insisted that Darrylin had taken most of the property. That year he ran into Roberto, Darrylin's son, who had bragged that he had their grandfather's special director's chair.

Darrylin seemed most anxious to become curator of the artifacts of her father's faded and all-but-forgotten Hollywood glory. She filed a petition asking for her father's Oscars and several other awards and miscellaneous pieces of personal property. All those things had been given to Virginia by her husband; therefore, Darrylin argued, she should get them. Richard filed an objection. Some of the items she wanted were still missing, he claimed. He demanded that the bank allow Darrylin less of her inheritance to compensate for the missing property. Darrylin petitioned the court in 1984 that some of her father's awards and Oscars be released so that they could be displayed at a Summer Olympics exhibition in Los Angeles. Richard sternly countered with another petition; his father had left the items to the American Film Institute, and that was the only place they should be displayed. Richard won that round. The court also issued an order that the Bank of America would hold all of Zanuck's personal property until it could be distributed to beneficiaries. "The Bank will pursue its claim for damages against Darrylin . . . for the missing personal property . . . provided that if any of said missing property is found, it shall be delivered by Darrylin to the bank forthwith."

Brother and sister tangled in the courts over nearly every issue, and their skirmishing escalated into a new lawsuit. In 1984, Sybil Brand, a friend of Darrylin's and a doyenne of southern California charitable giving, sued the Virginia Zanuck Charitable Foundation. According to the settlement worked out for Virginia's estate a year earlier, Darrylin and Richard were each to pick two trustees. Darrylin didn't like Dick's choices, and so the fight wore on until Richard's lawyer invoked the original settlement agreement, which called for the California attorney general to mediate the dispute. John Van de Kamp, one of Richard's friends, became state attorney general in 1983. He decided in Richard's favor.

By the time 1985 rolled around, Darrylin seemed to have grown rather bitter. Genevieve was number one on her enemies list. She blamed her father's former companion for depriving her children of their rightful inheritance. Wendalyn and Lindolyn were still living with her, and Roberto was trying to launch a snorkeling business in Cancun, Mexico, but lacked money for the venture. Robin Lyn had remarried an American, and she, too, wanted to start a business. Darrylin's kids needed the inheritance from their grandfather's estate. Not that they were deprived. "Darrylin gives them everything—maybe too much," remarked a close friend of the Pineda family. It had become Darrylin's job, as she saw it, to defend their rights. If she didn't have to wage this battle, she would be happy to move somewhere else—maybe back to Acapulco or perhaps to Lake Tahoe.

If Genevieve headed Darrylin's enemies list, Richard was a strong second. Brother and sister had fought so many times about so many issues that the breach between them had become irreparable. Movie columnist Army Archerd had referred to the pair as a "don't invite-em." The green-eyed monster seemed to play a role in Darrylin's thinking. While she was leading a quiet life in Santa Monica, interrupted only by litigation, Richard and his wife Lili, now a co-producer for Zanuck/Brown, were enjoying public plaudits for *Cocoon*, one of the film hits of the summer of 1985. Zanuck/Brown had acquired the property when they were working at Fox in the early 1980s; but Lili intimated in interviews that she alone had found it and persuaded her husband and his partner to produce it. The one-time managerial assistant—a commoner who wed a prince—had undergone a dazzling transformation. Now she was a reigning queen of Hollywood. Reporters rushed to give praise and publicity to the beautiful new mogulette, and her photograph, by Scavullo or Avedon, appeared in *Vanity Fair* and *Vogue*. At openings, she turned up in designer gowns bedecked with lace and beads.

Darrylin had mentally rewritten family history to accommodate the new resentments. She now had it that Dick had "lost" the family Twentieth Century-Fox. The Zanucks had received a mere pittance from the company compared to the amounts directors got when

Denver oil magnate Marvin Davis bought Fox in 1981 for $700 million and then resold part of it to Australian press lord Rupert Murdoch in 1985 for more than $500 million. To hear Darrylin tell it, Richard had betrayed his father, not the other way around. Darrylin altered most of the family photos. "I had a lot of pictures," she told a reporter in 1985. "But Richard was ruining them, so I taped out his face."

*   *   *

In New York, Genevieve was growing more and more frustrated. The only remnant of her life with Darryl Zanuck was litigation, which she pursued relentlessly. The legal bills had been tremendous. Genevieve had spent more than $200,000 to pursue what she considered a matter of principle. Yet, except for the trial in California, little courtroom drama had touched her life. Lawyers simply filed motions, cross motions, and demurrers. They fought one another with pieces of paper that were tucked away in the dusty basements of public buildings.

Worse yet, the courts always seemed to postpone everything. When they didn't postpone, they decided against Genevieve. In August 1984 a court in Manhattan granted a summary motion for judgment against Genevieve on behalf of the Bank of America. According to the court, she owed Zanuck's estate for the Fox stock he had lent her— $50,900—plus interest. Genevieve immediately appealed the decision. Late in 1984 a California appeals court upheld Judge Frank Moore's decision in the estate case. Genevieve's attorneys had failed to attack the 1977 codicil to Zanuck's 1973 will; therefore it was a nonsuit. Adding insult to injury, the appeals court had assessed a fine against her latest attorney, Gerald Goldfarb, for a "frivolous" appeal. He in turn appealed the decision to the state supreme court.

Genevieve's case against Marvin Mitchelson for legal malpractice had ground along for nearly two years. In court papers, the Beverly Hills lawyer had changed his mind about the validity of Genevieve's original challenge to Zanuck's estate. "Plaintiff and her counsel are well aware that she never would have succeeded in setting aside either Zanuck's October will or his 1977 codicil," he declared in an affidavit. She never had any evidence that Zanuck lacked testamentary capacity or that he was under anyone's influence or subject to duress. Mitchelson dismissed Tom Shirley's claim that Darrylin forged her father's will as "inadmissible hearsay. . . . his proffered handwriting analyses were quite suspect." He made Genevieve's case sound so stupid one wondered why he had ever agreed to represent her. He insisted that he had taken the case as a cohabitant claim, partly because she couldn't succeed in a will contest. He added, "Of course, as an advocate representing plaintiff, I acted on her belief that Zanuck was either forced to disinherit her or lacked the mental capacity to know what he was doing. However, I do not believe that . . . I should be bound by any statements that as an advocate I made on behalf of my former client."

Despite Mitchelson's arguments, the court decided for Genevieve in early 1985. Mitchelson *had* failed to exercise reasonable care when he missed the filing deadline by one day. "Missing the statute of limitations is a classic example of negligence which any layperson can understand," held the court. Mitchelson should have taken an overnight flight to Los Angeles or sent the forgery petition by Express Mail. Overlooking the codicil had been another big mistake. "In failing to challenge the 1977 codicil," the court declared, Mitchelson "failed to conform to the conduct of a competent attorney who had any experience in probate matters or who had performed minimal research in the area."

Those words may have been balm to Genevieve's feelings of victimization, but they didn't translate to any money. Her lawyer, Richard Ben-Veniste, had argued that Genevieve should receive damages because she had paid a $25,000 retainer and received nothing in consideration. To that contention, though $25,000 might seem like a high price to pay for a little paperwork, the court reasoned that Mitchelson had filed the complaint, the petition, the forgery petition, and so on. To win any damages, Genevieve would have to show that she would have won the estate battle if Mitchelson had not messed up. She had not yet done that, of course. The court decided that it could not find Mitchelson liable for legal malpractice until the California Supreme Court decided on her appeal.

No resolution of that case seemed near, and the impoverished Hakim grandchildren chafed to get their inheritances. Sherry Hakim, the little girl who had attended the Cannes Film Festival with her grandfather, was forced to take a job flipping burgers at a fast-food joint. Then she injured her shoulder and couldn't work. She applied for workmen's compensation, but only one of the two doctors who examined her declared her sufficiently disabled to collect a check. Frustrated and angry at court delays, Sherry sent Judge Frank Moore a handwritten note on March 20, 1985:

> Judge Moore:
> I do hope my inquiries to you are not annoying, but I seem to have no one else to turn to. I also want [you] to know how much I appreciate your time. A court date was set for Feb. 14, then Continued to Mar. 4—Then again continued to Apr. 1. I pray to the Lord, my grandfather (Darrell [sic] Zanuck) and to my mom that what was left may be put to the use they intended. The long delay in settlement has cost me dearly—Medically, Educationally, financially, physically, and Emotionally. Right now I am unable to work because I was hurt on the job . . . which has me begging for money from anyone who will help me just to put some food in my stomache [sic]. So hopefully April 1 will help me as my mom would want.
> Thank you again for your time, interest, and patience in listening to my confession.
> Sincerely
> Sharon M. Hakim

Just as everything was looking completely inconclusive, however, things began to break Genevieve's way. On July 1, 1985, the U.S. District Court of Appeals in Manhattan, which had heard arguments between Genevieve and the Bank of America over the controversial Fox stock, decided in her favor—more or less. Zanuck's letters to Genevieve, which seemed to forgive her debt, were ambiguous, held the three-judge panel. The case was sent back to the lower court to determine Zanuck's true intent in drafting the letters.

Only a few days later, there was more cheering at Genevieve's Dakota cooperative. California's highest court came down with a decision that was favorable to Genevieve on the estate battle. True, because she had no evidence, the court dismissed her claim that Zanuck was under duress when he signed his will. And, as for pleading forgery, Genevieve's claim *had* been filed too late and that was that. However, the court agreed with her lawyer's contention that an attack against the 1973 will embodied an attack against the 1977 codicil. The lower court should have allowed her to amend her original petition to include the codicil, because the amendment relied on the same general set of facts as the original pleadings. The court also sternly chided the defendants for their strategy of waiting until the trial to raise the issue of the codicil. Most important, perhaps, the court concluded that "there was substantial evidence that decedent lacked testamentary capacity as a result of progressive senile dementia at the time of the execution of the will. Moreover, there was abundant testimony that decedent's mental condition was progressive and could only worsen over the course of time. . . . The mental condition which vitiated decedent's testamentary capacity at the time of the 1973 will would also have existed at the time of the 1977 codicil and would have similarly affected decedent's testamentary capacity at that time." Finally, there was no evidence to support lawyer William Campbell's argument that Zanuck had experienced "lucid intervals." The case was sent back to the trial court to resolve the issue of Zanuck's testamentary capacity.

Genevieve's victories were Pyrrhic, however. None of them had given her complete vindication. Worse yet, none of them had won her a dime. All required further litigation. She had learned that lawsuits were black holes for money. Her reserves seemed to be dwindling. She could no longer book modeling assignments; income was not rolling in as it had before. In 1984 she became a licensed real-estate agent in New York and took a job with Sotheby's exclusive International Real Estate Corporation, a division of the auction house that handles homes worth more than $1 million. Even though she had her own collection of expensive real estate, Genevieve had failed to pay her final $25,000 legal bill to Don Brown, who had argued her original estate case in California. Her former appeals attorney, Gerald Goldfarb, didn't receive the final $7,500 payment she owed him, and he sued her in the Los Angeles municipal court. "I don't know why she didn't pay me," he said. "I was the only lawyer who actually won something for her." The federal government had filed a $165,000 lien against her in Manhattan for back taxes.

In early 1986 she made a peculiar decision. She called Yeshiva University in the Bronx and made an offer to its incredulous officers. She wanted to donate her interest in the Darryl Zanuck estate case to the institution. Yeshiva University seemed an unlikely candidate for Genevieve's generosity, but the gesture made a strange kind of emotional good sense. Through the testimony that had been presented at the 1983 trial, Genevieve had come to believe that her former lover had indeed suffered from Alzheimer's disease. Yeshiva University operates the Albert Einstein Hospital and College of Medicine, which conducts one of the most aggressive Alzheimer's research programs in the nation. Any money that Genevieve won in a retrial of the original case would go to the university for research into Alzheimer's disease. Yeshiva accepted her offer and took on the case.

Genevieve's deed was motivated not only by altruism but by a strong desire to get out from under the Zanuck legacy. Recalled Gerald Goldfarb, "She said that she wanted to get on with her life." He turned the legal papers over to Glenn Hardie, a young California lawyer who was to act for Yeshiva. A quick settlement seemed likely. Yeshiva was not interested in fighting on issues of principle. It merely wanted to obtain the biggest possible donation for Alzheimer's research without incurring too many legal bills. Hardie declared that he was ready to fight if need be, however. "Every lawyer would like to settle quickly," he said. "But we are prepared to go to trial if we have to do that."

*   *   *

Some of the Zanucks welcomed Genevieve's change in tactics. André Hakim, Jr., who had returned from Oregon to Palm Springs, was surviving on welfare payments. He and his sister were nearly destitute. They needed money desperately, and they wanted the case to be settled, no matter what. "Give Alzheimer's the money," he said. "Let them have something. It's a good cause. My grandfather would not disapprove. We just want this stupid thing to end." Not everybody was so eager to see everything end, however. Settlement offers were made and rejected. Private investigator John O'Grady declared in December 1986, "They will never settle with Genevieve. They don't want to give her a penny."

In November 1986, Darrylin sued her father's former companion in the Indio court for malicious prosecution. She contended that several of Genevieve's original claims about the will had been proven ground-

286

less—particularly her contention that Darrylin had exerted undue influence over her father and that she had forged Zanuck's signature. The appeals court had dismissed those two allegations. Genevieve had "acted maliciously in making the aforementioned allegations . . . out of a desire to vex, annoy, and wrong the plaintiff and to cause harm and injury to the plaintiff's reputation and to cause plaintiff mental anguish." She asked for a total of $10 million plus the costs of the lawsuit. The suit got nowhere fast. The estate contest was still undecided. The appeals court had sent it back for a retrial, and a settlement was pending.

The estate contest should have been resolved quickly, but it kept dragging on. The parties with lawyers—Richard, Darrylin, the Bank of America, and Yeshiva University—had no real reason to rush. They didn't have to worry about where their next dollar was coming from. André Hakim was, as usual, flat broke. He had borrowed $10,000 from his mother's friend Mona Skoff, she said, for "medical expenses." In the spring of 1987 he signed a note against his inheritance to repay her. Sherry had signed notes totaling more than $20,000 against her inheritances.

In February of 1987, Judge Frank Moore, who had been laboring on the Zanuck estate battle for more than six years, cleared a major roadblock to settlement. He approved a final agreement between Twentieth Century-Fox, the Bank of America, and Virginia's estate that officially split Zanuck's death benefit and deferred compensation between the two estates. There was no longer any argument about the fate of that money.

But nobody had reckoned with Genevieve's obsession. Perhaps it was something she couldn't understand herself. She filed an objection to the agreement on the Fox benefits. Her argument was succinct. If Zanuck lacked testamentary capacity when he signed his last will, then he also lacked it when he signed his employment agreements designating his wife beneficiary. She asked that the court delay a decision on the matter until the underlying will contest was decided. Judge Moore denied her standing in the matter, and she immediately appealed.

Outrage swept the Zanuck camp. An appeal could cost the estate another year of paper-shuffling and waiting. The heirs received letters from the Bank of America in April warning that the estate might be bankrupted by taxes, only a portion of which had been paid. In August 1987, Sherry and André heard from their own attorneys that the estate might grant $100,000 to Yeshiva University for Alzheimer's research. They would also each receive $100,000. "It's ridiculous," declared a drunk and disheveled André Hakim outside his sister's rented Cathedral City house on a suffocating evening a few weeks later. "The lawyers are stealing everything—they have taken it all." In fact, neither his nor his sister's lawyer had been paid anything at that time.

André had written to "60 Minutes" hoping to interest one of the investigative reporters in disclosing the epic unfairness he had suffered. He was doing this as a public service, he claimed. He wasn't the only one this had happened to, he added. He had talked to other grandchildren of famous Hollywood figures. Some of them had been mired in similar battles and left to survive on practically nothing. True, they could get jobs, he conceded, but the money had been intended for them. He said that he would refuse to sign any settlement agreement, and he asked his lawyer to sue all the other lawyers involved in the case. But his lawyer declined to help him out. He called a second attorney to take on his cause, but the second attorney called the first attorney and ultimately declined. "They are all against me," he announced, as he staggered into a friend's car and rode off into the night.

That same month, Darrylin finally won a legal victory of her own. Her case against "Lie Detector," F. Lee Bailey's TV series, had hit the mandatory settlement conference stage of litigation. The show's attorney, Tim Reuben, had tried to get the judge to throw the case out of court, but the judge had decided that there were questions of fact and law. Was the retraction, asserting that Darrylin was innocent of forgery, sufficient? Reuben had tried to persuade Tom Shirley to testify, but he couldn't be reached except through Ed Meena—and Meena declared that Shirley wasn't about to come forward. To try the case, Reuben didn't need Shirley, but it would have been better to have him on hand. The producers of the defunct show decided that they would prefer to pay a small settlement rather than take their chances with a jury. They paid Darrylin $75,000. She now had some money to mend her damaged reputation.

In January 1988, when the Zanuck estate contest seemed likely to last forever, it suddenly ended. The lawyers had finally hammered out a settlement. Yeshiva University would receive a paltry $50,000. The rest of Zanuck's money would be distributed pretty much as he had dictated in his October 1973 will. Except for the employee benefits case, all the parties agreed to make no further claims on one another for anything; Genevieve would not have to worry about paying the estate for her Fox stock. The battle, which had begun with a fanfare of press releases and exaggerated claims in *People* magazine, ended suddenly and quietly.

On January 29, 1988, Judge Moore was to approve the settlement. Only three people—none of them Zanucks—turned up in his Indio courtroom to observe the resolution of the tortured case. One was a reporter for the Palm Springs newspaper, and two were curiosity-seekers. Sherry Hakim set out to attend but lost her way in the courthouse and arrived too late to witness the end. Judge Moore beckoned to the observers to join him in his chambers where the agreement was to be made final. He then made a conference call to lawyers representing Yeshiva University and the estate. The conversation was little more than a series of "un-hunhs" and "umm-hmmms." When the phone call ended, Judge Moore announced that he approved the settlement. It was over.

Almost.

Six weeks later, Darrylin filed another suit against Genevieve for malicious prosecution. Last time, she had asked for $10 million. Now she wasn't naming any figures.

EPILOGUE
A FAMILY DIVIDED

.

By the time the will contest ended in early 1988, the Zanucks could scarcely be called a family. There are no Thanksgiving Day dinners together, no Christmas celebrations, no birthdays or anniversaries where the whole family is united. Almost all of them are on their own. Most are now far, far away from the Hollywood glory that once bathed their lives in the glow of klieg lights.

           *   *   *

Darrylin, who now lives in Palos Verdes, put the three homes her mother left her on the market—including the famous Ric-Su-Dar. The estate has been hard to sell because it sits in an older neighborhood far from the new and fashionable Palm Springs enclaves where the likes of former President Gerald Ford, Zsa Zsa Gabor, and Frank Sinatra make their homes.

Darryl Zanuck's elder daughter asserts that she is a private person and a housewife, but she has sought to become the official and very public curator of her father's memory. That may be the only way she can maintain her tie to Zanuck's greatness; none of her four children has any apparent interest in the movie business. One daughter plans to start a boutique, another is a travel agent, and a third is in sales. Her son is launching a scuba rental venture in Mexico. Her adopted son Steven was a career army officer, and Helena married in Hawaii some time ago. Darrylin's plans emerged in a May 1, 1985, *Variety* story by Colonel Barney Oldfield, which announced, "Darrylin Zanuck Pineda is outraged and she's about to do $690,000 worth of something about it!" The outrage stemmed from Darrylin's belief that biographers who had published accounts of her father's life had "considerably shortchanged him."

What they had missed, Darrylin insisted, was her father's belief in charity and loyalty—and his ability to surmount obstacles. Though the last is hardly in doubt, Zanuck's loyalty to his wife and children seemed largely imagined. Nonetheless, she was determined to create a monument of some kind to his achievements. She had been asked, she said, to contribute Zanuck's memorabilia to various Hollywood collections, but she refused. In such a display, he would be merely one of the famous rather than, as she saw him, the only one of a kind. Then she thought of restoring his birthplace, the Le Grande Hotel in Wahoo, Nebraska, as a shrine to his memory, but found it too dilapidated to repair. Finally she settled on a generous $690,000 donation from the Virginia Zanuck Charitable Foundation to the University of Nebraska for scholarships. Several qualified students each year until the year 2000 will receive $5,000 grants. Darrylin traveled to Nebraska to award the grants personally. The irony did not elude reporter Oldfield. "The scholarships will sustain people in the very environment [Zanuck] went to great lengths to avoid," he wrote.

But that was not all she planned. With Oldfield's help, Darrylin attempted a memoir of her father. Zanuck himself had provided the title for the book, she said: *Never Wear Black for Me.* At the end of 1986, she sent a proposal to her agent. The prospective book set off an all-family binge of paranoia, said Diane Jacks, who became Robert's second wife after his divorce from Darrylin. When Diane happened to see Richard while visiting California, he asked her to testify on his behalf if he sued his sister for libel. All kinds of Zanuck-style conspiracies and dark crimes were supposedly going to surface in Darrylin's book—that Richard had pulled out his father's intravenous tube when he lay dying in Desert Hospital, and that Virginia had had an affair with Alma Diehl. Neither tale was true, and Oldfield has said

291

that he had planned to include no such stories in Darrylin's book. Yet distrust among members of the family ran so deep that many strange ideas became credible. By the fall of 1987, Darrylin had abandoned the project—at least temporarily.

Robert Jacks was particularly worried about what Darrylin would say about him. His relationship with her seemed amicable enough in early 1987 when she was hospitalized for meningitis. He called to wish her well. But in August he telephoned his former girlfriend Mona Skoff, to whom he hadn't spoken in years. They talked for a long time, and he complained that Darrylin was going to publish stories about his supposed wife-beating. "I never beat her. I'm not a wife-beater," he insisted. "How can she say that about me?" He asked to see Skoff, but she was off to Catalina where she owned a boutique. He said he would meet her there, but she put him off. She was involved with another man, and a meeting with Jacks would have been awkward and uncomfortable. She offered to get together with him when she returned to Palm Springs in October.

The meeting never took place, however. Only a few days later, Robert Jacks shot himself. He was suffering from a recurrence of cancer—this time a brain tumor—and he faced a depressing future of painful treatments, disability, and death. Diane Jacks, who had divorced him years earlier, returned to help settle his affairs. Darrylin, she recalled, didn't make it to the funeral.

*   *   *

By 1987, Pierre Savineau, his wife Yolanda, and their five-year-old son Pierrique, were marooned in a trailer on the plains outside of a small dead-looking town called Seminole, Oklahoma. The couple arrived with Susan's son Craig in 1979 at the height of the Southwest oil boom. Only six months after they set up housekeeping, Susan died, and Craig's $250,000 bequest was handed over to Savineau for safekeeping.

The money was invested in business after business—land, a construction company, a French restaurant. All of them failed when oil prices tumbled, and with the bankruptcies, Craig's inheritance vanished. Savineau felt he was using the money to build for the family's future. Craig, according to Savineau, came to believe that his father had stolen it. He no longer lives with Pierre and Yolanda. "He disappeared," said Savineau. "He ran away with a woman, and I don't know where they are." Savineau wants to leave Oklahoma, but there's no buyer for his land and no money to make the move. "We're stuck here," observed the former yacht captain who begged Susan Zanuck to leave the nightlife of Cannes.

*   *   *

Genevieve Gillaizeau has left New York. She sold her Dakota cooperative and retreated to her Palm Beach house. "I expect that she will go back to France," said a friend. "That's what she has always said she wanted to do."

Still, she battles with the Zanuck estate over money. The settlement granted Yeshiva University $50,000 for Alzheimer's disease research; now, however, Genevieve claims that Zanuck's $1 million in deferred compensation and death benefits from Twentieth Century-Fox should not be part of that settlement. She is fighting for her share—40 percent. Her chances of winning are slim, but her need to stay tied to the Zanuck legend—if only by irritating his family—remains as obsessive as ever.

Excluding the amount still at issue, Zanuck's estate is worth about $3.1 million. About $500,000 should go for taxes, and an as yet undetermined amount will be used to pay legal fees. Zanuck's $1 million portfolio of municipal bonds is now worth only $585,000, and the eleven grandchildren will share it. Darrylin's and Susan's heirs will receive bequests of $100,000 each and Richard $50,000. The balance of the money will be split among Richard, Darrylin, and Susan's children—about $600,000 each. The Zanuck estate battle has been one of the longest in California history, but it is far from the most financially significant.

*   *   *

Sherry and André Hakim longed for nothing more than the day when their grandfather's estate would be settled. Six months after

Judge Moore approved the settlement, they still had not received their money. André lived for a time down the block from his sister in Cathedral City, a pit of fast-food joints and slum housing between posh Palm Springs and Palm Desert. His wood-frame rented house evoked images of Third World hovels, and his only possessions were a tape deck, a director's chair, posters, and some girlie pictures. Later he moved to an equally humble apartment and eventually to a trailer owned by his mother's friend Mona Skoff.

His plans have always been grand—to be a moviemaker like his grandfather. He has a script. He has a musical group. He has a book idea. On his business card he calls himself "André Hakim Zanuck, Producer and Director." He came close to breaking into the movie business with one film project to be created for the Los Angeles Filmex exposition in 1987. He fantasized that his uncle Richard would be present to see his movie. "Maybe then my family would say, 'He didn't turn out so bad after all,' " he added. A day later, he learned that his financial backer had backed out. His ideas sound like the ones Zanuck himself tried to promote at age nineteen, but André is thirty-one and frantic to get something going. The only thing he needs is money. Mona Skoff doesn't want him to have money—not directly, anyway. "I will try to see that maybe there will be a trust to supply housing and food—no money for drugs," she said.

Sherry, who has suffered from pneumonia and hepatitis in 1987, almost never had any cash. Living in a very humble rented cottage, also in Cathedral City, she relied on handouts from friends and occasional jobs to get by. When she got her money, she said—perhaps as much as $280,000—she would go back to France, "just for a vacation." After her grandfather's estate was settled in January 1988, she began a letter-writing and phone-calling campaign to pester various bank officers in charge of the estate to get her an advance on her inheritance, but more time passed and nothing came.

Her letter-writing campaign faltered when she fell ill again in August 1988. "I was so weak I couldn't move. I shook so much that the house trembled," she said. No one came to visit, and she didn't have a telephone. Finally, André dropped by and insisted she go to Riverside Hospital. She was suffering from an infection of the valves of the heart and might have to undergo open heart surgery. Her brother and friends occasionally stopped by to see her, and she wanted to ask her uncle

Richard for help, but was afraid to telephone him personally. The money was still uppermost in her mind. "I haven't told anybody at the hospital about it because it will all go for doctors," she said. When she got out of the hospital, she vowed, "I will have a different lifestyle."

＊　　＊　　＊

Only Richard has managed to continue the family business and keep the Zanuck name alive in Hollywood. Though Richard can earn more money from one box-office success than Zanuck took in over a whole career, he can never be quite as magnificent a mogul as his father; in the New Hollywood where agents and actors—not producers—call most of the shots, true moguldom no longer exists. Still, he continues to maintain every possible connection to his father. When he visits France each year, says Edward Leggewie, Zanuck's one-time aide-de-camp, he looks up all his father's old friends. He stays at the hotels his father patronized, and dines in the same restaurants.

His wife, Lili, has worked like a powerhouse to keep Dick's family together; she backed Linda Harrison in her lawsuit against the Maha Genii for the return of her money. Linda won a $1 million settlement from a sympathetic jury, but by that time, the Maha had disappeared and, with him, all his assets. Richard has also kept up with his former governess Alma Diehl, now ninety-eight. Unless he is out of town, Richard devotedly makes a three-hour round-trip drive to visit her retirement home in Placentia, California, once a week.

Richard's daughters are clearly families apart. Ginny, the elder, lives in Colorado with her husband and two of her children. Her eldest child lives elsewhere and has no contact with the Zanucks. Janet lives in Los Angeles with her son and daughter. Both young women are dependent on their father for money, and both, according to a close family friend, are constantly threatened with a cutoff: "They live in fear of their father's temper." When *Cocoon* opened, Richard and Lili, Linda Harrison, and the two Zanuck boys attended the premiere, but neither Janet nor Ginny showed up.

One of Lili Fini Zanuck's principal concerns—aside from her husband—is her new status as a major producer. Her schedule is packed: reading scripts, working on deals, making connections between writers, agents, directors, and actors. She began generating more column inches of publicity than either her husband or his partner David Brown. In March 1988, the two men announced an end to their thirty-year collaboration. Everybody in the industry was shocked. "I was stunned when I heard, just staggered," said a friend. "But if two men have been partners, wonderfully equal partners for years, then one of the partners makes a marriage and the wife moves into that business relationship, problems are inevitable. Of course, all David will say is that 'it was time and I'm at the age, blah, blah. And there are a few things I want to do on my own.' " Indeed, in short order, Brown signed a three-movie deal with Tri-Star Pictures. Richard and Lili will take the helm of the business.

Richard Zanuck's teenage sons are too young to be anything but question marks. Perhaps they will emerge one day to become the kingpins of some twenty-first-century show-biz domain. Richard was once asked whether he wanted his sons to follow the family business tradition. "Sure, if they want to," he said. "As a matter of fact, they'll probably knock me off."

NOTES

.

PROLOGUE: HOMECOMING

Darryl Zanuck's April 1973 homecoming: Depositions of Vincenza Argentino, Dr. Carmine Vicale, Dr. Carl Feind, and Richard Zanuck and testimony of Genevieve Gillaizeau, Richard Zanuck, and Edward Meena for *Genevieve Gillaizeau vs. Bank of America National Trust and Savings Association*, Superior Court of the State of California for the County of Riverside, Indio 6635; depositions of Genevieve Gillaizeau for *Genevieve Gillaizeau vs. Marvin Mitchelson, A Professional Corporation; Marvin Mitchelson, and Harold Rhoden*, U.S. District Court, Southern District of New York, 83 Civ 4367; Virginia Zanuck, letter to Margaret Shands, August 4, 1980; André Hakim, Jr., interview with author.

CHAPTER ONE: THE PRODUCER

Zanuck's trip to New York: Frank S. Nugent, "Meet Mr. Darryl Zanuck," *New York Times*, April 21, 1935.

Praise for Zanuck as a producer: Alva Johnson, "The Wahoo Boy," *The New Yorker*, November 10, 1934; *Variety*, August 3, 1935. Zanuck's lavish standard of living: Walter Scott, interviews with author. Zanuck styling himself as a genius: Ezra Goodman, *The Fifty-Year Decline and Fall of Hollywood* (New York: Simon & Schuster, 1961), p. 168.

Daughter's flower in Zanuck's wallet: Col. Barney Oldfield, "Wahoo, Neb. Memorial Funded by Daughter of Darryl Zanuck," *Variety*, May 1, 1985.

Zanuck as a Nebraska rube: "Dime to Million Saga of Movies' Man of the Hour," *New York Post*, May 31, 1935; "Zanuck, Biggest Man in Films, Was Once 'Rube' from Nebraska," *Variety*, August 3, 1935.

Zanuck's childhood: Mel Gussow, *Don't Say Yes until I Finish Talking: A Biography of Darryl F. Zanuck* (Garden City, N.Y.: Doubleday, 1971), Chapters 5–14; Alva Johnson, "The Wahoo Boy," *The New Yorker*, November 10, November 17, 1934; Leonard Mosley, *Zanuck: The Rise and Fall of Hollywood's Last Tycoon* (Boston: Little, Brown, 1984); "One-Man Studio," *Time*, June 12, 1950; Norman Zierold, *The Moguls* (New York: Coward, McCann, 1969); Stephen Farber and Marc Green, "DFZ and the Dauphin," *Hollywood Dynasties* (New York: Delilah, 1984); Colonel Barney Oldfield, "Wahoo, Neb. Memorial Funded by Daughter of Darryl Zanuck," *Variety*, May 1, 1985.

Zanuck's train trip: Darryl Zanuck, "Los Angeles to Oakdale, Observations of Darryl Zanuck, age 11, on his trip from Los Angeles, Calif.," *Oakdale Sentinel*, July 17, 1914.

Recollections of Zanuck as a boy: Eugene Budde, "A Penny a Head at Torpin's Loft," *The History of Antelope County, Nebraska 1868–1985* (Dallas: Curtis Media, 1986), pp. 784–86.

Zanuck in World War I: Gussow; Mosley; *Time*, June 12, 1950; "Darryl Zanuck Writes," Deming, N.M., *Oakdale Sentinel*, September 21, 1917;

"Oakdale Boy Sees Real Fighting," letter from Darryl Zanuck, 136 Amb.
Co., 109 Sanitary Train, A.E.F., Le Mans, France, November 28, 1918,
Oakdale Sentinel, December 17, 1918; "Oakdale's Roll of Honor," *Oakdale Sentinel*, August 24, 1917.

Moviemaking and screenwriting in the 1920s: David Shipman, "Hollywood
in the Twenties: The Studios," *The Story of Cinema* (New York: St.
Martin's, 1982), pp. 145–86.

Zanuck's early jobs: Gussow; Mosley; Zierold; *Time*, June 12, 1950. Jewish
movie moguls: Neal Gabler, *An Empire of Their Own: How the Jews
Invented Hollywood* (New York: Crown, 1988). Los Angeles Athletic Club;
Zanuck's attitude toward its alleged anti-Semitic admissions policies: Betty
Lou Young and Thomas R. Young, *Our First Century: The Los Angeles
Athletic Club 1880–1980* (Los Angeles: LAAC Press, 1979); *Time*, June 12,
1950. Practical jokes at the club: *Time*, June 12, 1950.

The publication of *Habit*: Gussow; Mosley; *Time*, June 12, 1950. Virginia's
birth date: Virginia Fox, enrollment card, Wheeling, West Virginia, Public Schools, January 31, 1908. Virginia's birth date as written by her
mother is April 19, 1902. The Zanucks' meeting, courtship, and wedding:
Gussow; Mosley; *Time*, June 12, 1950.

Zanuck and Rin Tin Tin: Hal Wallis and Charles Higham, *Starmaker: The
Autobiography of Hal Wallis* (New York: Macmillan, 1982), pp. 11–12;
Jack L. Warner, with Dean Jennings, *My First Hundred Years in Hollywood* (New York: Random House, 1964). Zanuck at Warner Brothers:
Wallis; Warner; *Time*, June 12, 1950. The Zanucks' marriage: Gussow;
Mosley. Zanuck's jokes at Warner Brothers: *Time*, June 12, 1950.

Zanuck's prolific screenwriting: *Time*, June 12, 1950. Critics' views of his
early movies: *Time*, June 12, 1950; " 'Advice to the Lovelorn,' " *Time*,
December 25, 1933; "Up from Jew Street," *Time*, March 26, 1934; "Looking for Trouble," *Time*, April 23, 1934; "The New Pictures," *Time*,
May 29, 1935. Also see Gussow; Mosley.

Zanuck's rise to power at Warner Brothers; his role in the use of sound: See
Wallis; Warner; *Time*, June 12, 1950. Sadly, Henry Torpin, long Zanuck's
mentor, was never to know of his grandson's elevation to production chief.
He had died in Van Nuys, California, at the home of his son, C. H.
Torpin, only a few months earlier. Opinions of *Noah's Ark*: *Time*, June 12,
1950. Zanuck's contribution to *Little Caesar*: Warner. *Public Enemy*;
origin of the grapefruit-smashing scene: Patrick McGilligan, *Cagney: The
Actor as Auteur* (San Diego: A. S. Barnes, 1982), pp. 30–32.

Zanuck's conduct in the office; listening to his employees: Philip Dunne,
Take Two: A Life in Movies and Politics (New York: McGraw-Hill, 1980);
Philip Dunne, "Darryl from A to Z," *American Film*, July–August 1984,
pp. 45–51.

Zanuck's love affairs: Mosley; James Kotsilibas-Davis and Myrna Loy, *Myrna
Loy: Being and Becoming* (New York: Knopf, 1987); Elia Kazan, *A Life*
(New York: Knopf, 1988).

Virginia's attitude toward Zanuck's misconduct: Mosley; *Time*, June 12,
1950. His supervision of the birth of his children: *Time*, June 12, 1950.

Zanuck's coterie of yes-men: Philip Dunne and Milton Sperling, interviews with author; Philip Dunne, *Take Two*; Philip Dunne, "Darryl from A to Z"; Ezra Goodman, *The Fifty-Year Decline and Fall of Hollywood* (New York: Simon & Schuster, 1961).

Duck hunting, polo, poker, and practical jokes: Gussow; Mosley; Warner; *Time*, June 12, 1950; "Darryl F. Zanuck Thrown by Horse," *New York American*, September 22, 1935.

Legend-building efforts: Stephen Farber and Marc Green, "DFZ and the Dauphin," *Hollywood Dynasties* (New York: Delilah, 1984), pp. 90–118.

Zanuck's dispute with the Warners: Wallis. Move to Twentieth Century Pictures: "Zanuck Suddenly Quits as Manager of Warners," *New York Daily News*, April 14, 1933; "Twentieth Century-Fox," *Fortune*, December 1935.

Proclamations about moviemaking: Darryl F. Zanuck, "Producer Has No Sinecure, Insists Zanuck," *New York Times*, January 12, 1935; Joseph W. Alsop, Jr., "Screen Moving toward Opera, Zanuck Holds," *New York Herald Tribune*, May 8, 1934. Zanuck's lack of education: Alva Johnson, "The Wahoo Boy," *The New Yorker*, November 10, November 17, 1934. Letter to *Time* attesting to his modesty: Darryl Zanuck, *Time*, May 20, 1934.

Shift to Twentieth Century-Fox: "Schenck to Fox," *Time*, June 10, 1935; "Zanuck and Schenck," *Time*, July 19, 1935; "Amicable Settlement," *Time*, July 29, 1935; "Twentieth Century-Fox," *Fortune*, December 1935; "Zanuck Gets Sheehan Job," *New York Journal American*, August 8, 1935. Protest by shareholders about salaries: *Time*, September 2, 1935. Experience with *Thanks a Million*: *Time*, June 12, 1950. *Time* plaudits: "Zanuck's Start," *Time*, November 25, 1935; " 'Country Doctor,' " *Time*, December 16, 1935.

The new imperial court: Philip Dunne, *Take Two*; Philip Dunne, "Darryl from A to Z," *American Film*, July–August 1984, pp. 45–51; Zanuck's office: Walter Scott, Dunne, and Sperling, interviews with author; Joseph Schrank, "Facing Zanuck," *American Heritage*, December 1983. Studio trysts: Milton Sperling and Martha Ragland, interviews with author.

Zanuck as an employer: Philip Dunne, *Take Two*; Philip Dunne, "Darryl from A to Z," *American Film*, July–August, 1984, pp. 45–51; *Time*, June 12, 1950; Elia Kazan, *A Life* (New York: Knopf, 1988).

Zanuck at Waldorf-Astoria: *New York Times*, January 9, 1936.

CHAPTER TWO: HOLLYWOOD WIFE

Virginia Fox Zanuck's youth: Mrs. Merrill Merrill and Mrs. George Beatty, interviews with author; Virginia Zanuck, enrollment card, Wheeling, West Virginia, Public Schools, January 31, 1908; Bette Smith, "Private School Was Result of Widow's Efforts to Keep Family Together," *St. Petersburg Times*, August 1, 1983; *Wheeling City Directory*, 1904, 1907, 1912; "Wheeling's First 250 Years," *Upper Ohio Valley Historical Review*; Edward C. Wolf, "The Wheeling Saengerfest of 1906," *Upper Ohio Val-*

ley Historical Review; Dr. William M. Seaman, "The Germans of Wheeling," *Upper Ohio Valley Historical Review*; 1880 Indiana Federal Population Census, Rush County, Indiana; Thirteenth Census of the United States, Ohio County, West Virginia, 1910. Virginia's flaming youth; Our Club: Colleen Moore, *Silent Star* (Garden City, N.Y.: Doubleday, 1968), pp. 111–12.

Early troubles in Virginia's marriage: Mel Gussow, *Don't Say Yes until I Finish Talking: A Biography of Darryl F. Zanuck* (Garden City, N.Y.: Doubleday, 1971); Leonard Mosley, *Zanuck: The Rise and Fall of Hollywood's Last Tycoon* (Boston: Little, Brown, 1984); James Kotsilibas-Davis and Myrna Loy, *Myrna Loy: Being and Becoming* (New York: Knopf, 1987); unnamed friend, interview with author. Virginia's attitude toward lovemaking: Margaret Shands, interview with author. Her feelings about his constant cheating: Margaret Shands and other family friends who declined to be named, interviews with author.

Virginia's discovery of Tyrone Power: "One-Man Studio," *Time*, June 12, 1950. Zanuck's polo misadventure: "One-Man Studio," *Time*, June 12, 1950.

Virginia's good deeds: Margaret Shands, John O'Grady, Walter Scott, Pokie Seeger, and others, interviews with author; "One-Man Studio," *Time*, June 12, 1950.

Virginia's involvement in her husband's hobbies: Edward Leggewie, and others, interviews with author. The Zanucks' safari: Darryl F. Zanuck, "Pity the Poor Hunter," *Esquire*, April 1936.

Zanuck's reluctance to become a father: "One-Man Studio," *Time*, June 12, 1950. The Zanucks' Santa Monica beach house: Nancy Guild, "Pacific Productions—The Beachfront Residence of Richard and Lili Zanuck," *Architectural Digest*, April 1986. Childhood of Darrylin, Susan, and Richard Zanuck: Gussow; Mosley; "Sons of the Fathers," *Los Angeles*, June 1982; Margaret Shands, Martha Ragland, Walter Scott, Edward Leggewie, and Helen Craig, interviews with author.

Virginia's emotional reaction to the movies: Gussow; Kazan.

Zanuck's late 1930s productions: *How Green Was My Valley; Grapes of Wrath*: Milton Sperling, Philip Dunne, interviews with author; Gussow; Mosley. Threats: Milton Sperling, interview with author; "William Henderson; Darryl F. Zanuck, Victim," Federal Bureau of Investigation File No. 9-451, March 1, 1939; "Frank L. Faulkner; Dorothy Lamour, James Cagney, Darryl Zanuck, Casey Wilson, Samuel Goldwyn, Louis B. Mayer, Victims," Federal Bureau of Investigation File No. 9-886, April 29, 1946. Tax problems: October 1944, Brief for Respondent, filed October, 1944 for *Darryl F. Zanuck, Petitioner, v. Commissioner of Internal Revenue, respondent, and Virginia F. Zanuck, petitioner, v. Commissioner of Internal Revenue, respondent*, U.S. Circuit Court of Appeals for the Ninth Circuit; docket nos. 108608, 108609, 2 T.C.M. (cch) 963; Memorandum Findings of Fact and Opinion, filed October 23, 1943, for *Virginia Fox Zanuck v. Commissioner, Darryl F. Zanuck v. Commissioner*, U.S. Circuit Court of Appeals for the Ninth District, docket nos. 108608, 108609, 2

T.C.M. (cch) 963; Order of U.S. Circuit Court of Appeals for the Ninth District, filed May 28, 1945, *Darryl F. Zanuck, Petitioner, v. Commissioner of Internal Revenue, Respondent, and Virginia Fox Zanuck v. Commissioner of Internal Revenue, Respondent,* U.S. Circuit Court of Appeals for the Ninth District, docket nos. 108608, 108609, 2 T.C.M. (cch) 963; "U.S. Investigating Taxes of Schenck and Zanuck," *New York Herald Tribune,* July 30, 1930; "Zanuck Fights $730,575 Tax," *New York Herald Tribune,* April 2, 1940.

Schenck's problems: "Schenck Convicted in Tax Fraud Case," *New York Times,* April 17, 1941; "Bioff Contends Million Went to Joseph Schenck," *New York Herald Tribune,* October 28, 1941; "Schenck Guilty," *Life,* April 29, 1941; and "Schenck Loses Appeal in U.S. Tax Conviction," *New York Herald Tribune,* January 22, 1942; in "Washington Dope," a correspondent's memo filed for *Time* on September 4, 1940 reporting that New York District Attorney John Cahill said that a grand jury investigating Schenck would probably indict Zanuck.

Zanuck in World War II: Gussow; Mosley; Gualt McGowan, "Darryl Zanuck Shoots Pictures in Thick of North Africa Campaign," *Milwaukee Journal,* December 12, 1942; Darryl F. Zanuck, *Tunis Expedition* (New York: Random House, 1943). Virginia's activities: "Virginia Fox Zanuck," obituary, *Los Angeles Times,* October 16, 1982. Zanuck's response to unfavorable review of *At the Front:* Darryl F. Zanuck, "Letter to the Editor," *New York Times Book Review,* April 25, 1943. Zanuck's problems with Congress: "Truman Committee Smears Zanuck but Says He's Too Valuable for Army to Lose: No Chance to Defend Given," *Variety,* April 7, 1943. Zanuck's troubles with William Goetz: "One-Man Studio," *Time,* June 12, 1950.

Shit canapés: H. Brad Darrach, interview with author.

The Zanucks' approach to *The Ox-Bow Incident:* David Shipman, *The Story of Cinema* (New York: St. Martin's, 1982), p. 615. The *Wilson* project: Shipman, p. 619; see also Gussow; Mosley; "One-Man Studio," *Time,* June 12, 1950.

Gentleman's Agreement: Elia Kazan, *A Life* (New York: Knopf, 1988); Laura Z. Hobson, *Laura Z. A Life: Years of Fulfillment* (New York: Donald I. Fine, 1986).

Daughters' teen years: Margaret Shands, Walter Scott, Martha Ragland, and Terry Moore, interviews with author.

The Zanucks' daily routine: "One-Man Studio," *Time,* June 12, 1950.

Recollections of Ric-Su-Dar: Herb Pasik, "Ric-Su-Dar Revisited," *Palm Springs Life,* July 1987; Joseph Cotten, *Vanity Will Get You Somewhere* (San Francisco: Mercury House, 1987); Elia Kazan, *A Life* (New York: Knopf, 1988); Walter Scott, Mary Donahue, Pokie Seeger, Margaret Shands, and Anna Catherine Reed, interviews with author.

Zanuck's involvement with Merle Oberon: John O'Grady, Walter Scott, and Margaret Shands, interviews with author. Attachment to Carole Landis: Milton Sperling, interviews with author. Landis's involvement with Jacqueline Susann: Barbara Seaman, *Lovely Me: The Life of Jacqueline*

Susann (New York: Morrow, 1987). Loy's view of Zanuck's conquests: James Kotsilibas-Davis and Myrna Loy, *Myrna Loy: Being and Becoming*. (New York: Knopf, 1987).

Zanuck's anointment as the king of cinema: "One-Man Studio," *Time*, June 12, 1950. Zanuck's restiveness: Moss Hart, Unquoted interview with *Time* magazine for "One-Man Studio," *Time*, June 12, 1950.

Bella Darvi: Gussow; Mosley; Margaret Shands, Walter Scott, Diane Jacks, Pierre Savineau, and Philip Dunne, interviews with author; Hedda Hopper, "Hollywood," *New York Daily News*, Feb. 7, 1953; Emily Belser, "Exotic Internee Stunned by Luck," *New York Daily News*, July 11, 1953; Earl Wilson, "Gal Who Went to Dinner Became a Hollywood Star," *New York Post*, January 28, 1954; Sidney Skolsky, "Hollywood Is My Beat," *New York Times*, April 25, 1954; Mike Connolly, "From Hunger and Violence Comes—Bella Darvi," *New York Mirror*, May 2, 1954; Louella Parsons, *New York Journal American*, August 15, 1954. Brando's reluctance to work with Darvi: Philip Dunne, interview with author.

Party at Ciro's: Phil Kunhardt, Pokie Seeger, and Terry Moore, interviews with author. Discussion at home afterward: Pierre Savineau and Pokie Seeger, interviews with author.

Bella Darvi's notices: Bosley Crowther, " 'Hell and High Water,' " *New York Times*, February 22, 1954; Bosley Crowther, " 'The Egyptian,' " *New York Times*, August 25, 1954; Bosley Crowther, " 'The Racers,' " *New York Times*, February 5, 1955.

Susan's wedding: "Susan Zanuck Weds Hakim," *Los Angeles Examiner*, April 18, 1954; Pierre Savineau and Pokie Seeger, interviews with author.

Zanuck's continuing affair with Darvi: Sydney Mirkin, "Abdication of a King: What Made Zanuck Go—The Story behind His Decision," *New York Daily News*, April 23, 1956; Sydney Mirkin, "Abdication of a King: What Made Zanuck Go—Will Not Marry Him, Says Bella," *New York Daily News*, April 24, 1956.

Zanuck's psychoanalysis: Ezra Goodman, *The Fifty-Year Decline and Fall of Hollywood* (New York: Simon & Schuster, 1961). Zanuck's complaints about Hollywood: Thomas M. Pryor, "Zanuck May Quit Active Fox Role," *New York Times*, February 6, 1956; "Zanuck Leaves 20th Century to Save on Taxes," *New York Post*, February 6, 1956; Louella O. Parsons, "Zanuck Is Planning to Go Independent," *New York Journal*, February 6, 1956; Thomas M. Pryor, "Hollywood Levies: Zanuck, Other Producers, Try to Ease Tax Burden via Ownership of Films," *New York Times*, February 12, 1956; "Long Lunch Hour," *Time*, February 13, 1956; Philip Dunne, *Take Two: A Life in Movies and Politics* (New York: McGraw-Hill, 1980).

Zanuck's difficulties with Spyros Skouras: Philip Dunne, "Darryl from A to Z," *American Film*, July–August 1984, pp. 45–51; Philip Dunne, *Take Two*.

Zanuck's final scene with his wife: Margaret Shands, interview with author. Virginia's talismans: Pokie Seeger, interview with author. Desire to remain Mrs. Darryl F. Zanuck: Walter Scott, interview with author.

CHAPTER THREE: STUDIO BRAT

Richard Zanuck's childhood: Certified abstract of birth for Richard Zanuck, California Department of Health Services, December 13, 1934; Stephen Farber and Marc Green, "DFZ and the Dauphin," *Hollywood Dynasties* (New York: Delilah, 1984); Mel Gussow, *Don't Say Yes until I Finish Talking: A Biography of Darryl F. Zanuck* (Garden City, N.Y.: Doubleday, 1971); Anthony Haden-Guest, "The Rise, Fall and Rise of Zanuck-Brown," *New York*, December 1, 1975; Leonard Mosley, *Zanuck: The Rise and Fall of Hollywood's Last Tycoon* (Boston: Little, Brown, 1984); "Sons of the Fathers," *Los Angeles*, June 1982; "Dick and Lili Zanuck Pledge to Mix Matrimony and Moviemaking from Here to Eternity," *People*, August 26, 1985.

Recollections of Alma Diehl: Helen Craig (her niece), Diane Jacks, Margaret Shands, and other friends of the Zanuck family who requested that their names not be used, interviews with author. Alma Diehl is now in a California nursing home. Richard's car accident and the knifing: Gussow; Mosley; "Zanuck's Son Beaten Up in Palm Springs," *Los Angeles Examiner*, February 24, 1953; "Balboa Island Police Arrest Young Zanuck," *Los Angeles Daily News*, March 24, 1954. Zanuck's leave-taking: Margaret Shands and Pokie Seeger, interviews with author.

Zanuck's 1956 financial arrangement with Twentieth Century-Fox: Proxy statement issued in 1964, seven years after he left the company and described in *Wall Street Journal*, April 28, 1964. According to this agreement, he was to receive a salary of $150,000 to run DFZ Productions. Fox would finance all movies made by DFZ Productions and split the profits evenly with Zanuck's company after it had recovered expenses. Zanuck's breakup with Bella Darvi: *New York Inquirer*, August 27, 1956.

Zanuck's financial arrangements with his wife: Property settlement dated November 1, 1957. Although they divided all their cash and securities, they kept both the Santa Monica mansion and Ric-Su-Dar as joint tenants. *Virginia Fox Zanuck v. Darryl F. Zanuck*, Complaint for Money on a Contract and an Account Stated, Superior Court of the State of California for the County of Los Angeles, no. 836725, filed April 13, 1964.

Zanuck's proposition to Joan Collins: Joan Collins, *Past Imperfect* (New York: Simon & Schuster, 1984), pp. 102–103.

Juliette Greco's liaison with Zanuck: Ernest Lubin, "French Girl Who Makes Art out of Popular Song," *New York Times*, June 8, 1952; "A Ghostly Wild One," *Life*, April 29, 1957; Harry V. Coren, "Little Girl Gives Her Audience a Big Hand," *New York Mirror Magazine*, June 16, 1957; Bernard Valery, "Paris," *New York Sunday News*, December 1, 1957; Art Buchwald, "She Likes Darryl, Not Zanuck," *New York Herald-Tribune*, November 20, 1958. In this story, Greco asserted, "I buy my own coats, I pay my own hotel bills, and I have always worked for myself. People have humiliated me because I am his [Zanuck's] friend." "Suzy Cables from London," *New York Daily News*, August 15, 1958; "A Double Role for Juliette," *Life*, May 25, 1960. Zanuck popped into Greco's apartment during a *Person to Person* interview with the cabaret singer. He declared, when asked about their relationship, "Juliette is not my protégée; she's the protégée of Paris and of France." Greco asserted that she said no to marriage with Zanuck. "You can't marry a married man," she observed sagely. "Juliette Says Face Is Her Misfortune," *New York Journal American,* July 30, 1960; Joe Hyams, "Juliette Greco's Idea of a Man," *New York Herald Tribune,* October 11, 1960.

Island in the Sun: Stephen Watts, "Hove to on 'Island in the Sun,' " *New York Times,* January 20, 1957; "Film Attack Scored," *New York Times,* May 11, 1957; "Zanuck Film Scored in London," *New York Times,* July 27, 1957; "New Pictures: 'Island in the Sun,' " *Time,* June 24, 1957, and Bosley Crowther, "Barbados is 'Star' of 'Island in the Sun,' " *New York Times,* June 13, 1957. Louis de Rochemont interview: "One-Man Studio," *Time,* June 12, 1950. *The Sun Also Rises:* "Hemingway's Lost Souls," *Life,* September 16, 1957; Art Buchwald, "Hemingway Again in the Fight News," *New York Herald Tribune,* November 24, 1957; *Time,* December 2, 1957; "The New Pictures: 'The Sun Also Rises,' " *Time,* September 2, 1957, and Howard Thompson, "Hemingway Classic," *New York Times,* August 24, 1957.

Deluxe Tour location-scouting trip: Gussow, pp. 197–201. Richard Zanuck's efforts as liaison: Philip Dunne, interviews with author.

Difficulties of shooting *Roots of Heaven:* Stories about this film abound; Zanuck's grandson André Hakim, Jr., observed that "Somebody should make a movie of the making of *Roots of Heaven.*" Errol Flynn, *My Wicked, Wicked Ways* (New York: Berkley, 1959); David Shipman, *The Story of Cinema* (New York: St. Martin's, 1982), p. 870; Paul Beckley, "Movies: The Long Step from Novel to Screen," *New York Herald Tribune,* April 21, 1958; Bernard Valery, "The Zanuck Story," *New York Daily News,* July 6, 1958; Art Buchwald, "Cruise on the Seine," *New York Herald Tribune,* July 10, 1958; Irene Thirer, "Zanuck Reports on 'Roots' Hazards," *New York Post,* September 9, 1958; Don Ross, "Zanuck's Big Film Subject: Do Not Kill the Elephants," *New York Herald Tribune,* October 12, 1958; review by Bosley Crowther, "Screen: 'Roots of Heaven,' " *New York Times,* October 16, 1958; "New Picture: 'Roots of Heaven,' " *Time,* November 3, 1958.

Richard Zanuck's engagement and marriage to Lili Gentle: Pokie Seeger and Lili Gentle, interviews with author. Lili is now remarried and living in the Midwest; "Zanuck's Son Weds Actress," *New York Times,* January 10, 1958; *New York Times,* January 18, 1958. Plans for *Compulsion:* Sam Zolotow, "Zanuck Acquires Levin Stage Play," *New York Times,* November 30, 1956; Shipman, pp. 900–01; Thomas H. Pryor, "Three Authoritative 'Reporters' Add Background to Production Picture," *New York Times,* October 30, 1958; *New York Journal American,* October 15, 1959. Richard's success with *Compulsion: New York Post,* February 3, 1959; Earl Wilson, *New York Post,* March 10, 1959.

Richard's plans: A. H. Weiler, "Richard Zanuck Plans Two Big-Scale Movies . . ." *New York Times,* March 15, 1959; Murray Schumach, "Combination of Two Faulkner Works Outlined by Makers of 'Sanctuary,' " *New York Times*, April 4, 1960. Zanuck's plan to copy his son: "Of Local Origin," *New York Times*, September 9, 1958; Richard Nason, "Zanuck to Make 10 Films for Fox," *New York Times*, August 5, 1959. Reviews of *Crack in the Mirror*: Howard Thompson, " 'Crack in the Mirror,' Courtroom Drama," *New York Times*, May 20, 1960; Justin Gilbert, " 'Crack in the Mirror,' Trick Film," *New York Mirror*, May 20, 1960. Telegram from Richard: Mosley, p. 315.

Chapman Report problems: Gussow, pp. 237–38; Mosley, p. 339; Farber and Green, p. 101; Shipman, p. 865; Joe Finnigan, "Scenes Shot 2 Ways to Please Censors," *New York World Telegram*, August 6, 1960; Kate Cameron, "U.S. Court Sides with Film Censors," *New York Sunday News*, February 19, 1961; *New York Times*, July 7, 1961; Thomas McDonald, "The Zanucks Chart 'Chapman Report' along Solidly Commercial Lines," *New York Times*, October 15, 1961; Bob Thomas, "A Zanuck Bolts to Warners Studio," *Los Angeles Herald*, August 8, 1961; Louella O. Parsons, "Hollywood Highlights," *New York Journal American*, February 23, 1961; A. H. Weiler, "Fox' Zanuck Doing Film at Warners," *New York Times*, July 7, 1961; Joe Hyams, "A Secret Film: All Over S-x," *New York Times*, November 6, 1961; Richard D. Zanuck, "Explains 'Chapman Report,' " *New York Journal American*, June 3, 1962.

Zanuck's breakup with Greco: Suzy, *New York Post*, May 24, 1961; Spencer Hardy, "Juliette's Romeo?" *New York Mirror*, September 10, 1961; Suzy, "Whatever Else Juliette Is, She Sure Ain't Agin' Publicity," *New York Mirror*, December 19, 1961; Alfred T. Hendricks, "Juliette Drags Zanuck down Memory Lane," *New York Post*, June 6, 1962; "Zanuck Sues over Memoirs," *New York Times*, June 6, 1962; "Producer Read Her Memoirs and Saw Red," *New York Mirror*, June 6, 1962; Art Buchwald, "Zanuck versus Greco," *New York Herald Tribune*, July 8, 1962; "Double Trouble: Darryl vs. Desdemona," *Show*, February 1963. Greco's memoir was serialized in the British newspaper, the *People*, from April 15, 1962, to April 22, 1962. About six years later, Greco recanted her autobiography, claiming that the series was written by someone else who put in details that never occurred. She and Zanuck became good friends after her marriage to another man; Gussow, p. 78; Eckert Goodman, "Zanuck Masters Film Empire, but Not All His Gals," *New York Daily News*, May 8, 1963.

Zanuck's life in Paris: Edward Leggewie and Art Buchwald, interviews with author and Don Johnston; Abel Green, "Zanuck Can't See California Return; A Paris, Not Hollywood Boulevardier," *Variety*, June 13, 1961.

Virginia's rapprochement with her husband: Margaret Shands, interview with author. Irina Demick: Gussow, pp. 221–22, 254, 277; Suzy, "Darryl Sure Knows How to Treat the Gals—Ask Irene!" *New York Mirror*, August 8, 1961; "Irina Demich [sic] Story Not Unlike Cinderella's," *New York Mirror*, September 6, 1961. *The Longest Day*: Gussow, pp. 216–35; Mosley, pp. 326–38, 339–43, 345–47; Shipman, pp. 900, 939, 1005, 1125, 1156; Eugene Archer, "Zanuck Sets Film on D-Day Invasion," *New York Times*,

December 3, 1960; Bob Salmaggi, "Zanuck Is Set to Go for Broke," *New York Herald Tribune*, December 11, 1960; Eugene Archer, "The Longest Day," *New York Times*, January 18, 1961; "Zanuck Busy with Logistics," *New York Herald Tribune*, April 9, 1961; "Zanuck Signs Top Writers," *New York Mirror*, April 19, 1961; "Zanuck Filming 'Longest Day,' " *New York Mirror*, May 13, 1961; Milton Bracker, " 'D-Day,' Zanuck's Way," *New York Times*, May 21, 1961; "The Locationers," *Time*, July 14, 1961; "Dwight D. Zanuck," *Time*, September 3, 1961; Edward Kosner, "GI 'Extras' Draw Congress Fire," *New York Post*, September 14, 1961; Martin Gansberg, "Normandy Recaptured by Camera," *New York Times*, September 17, 1961; Fred Hift, " 'The Longest Day' Dramatizing History," *Christian Science Monitor*, October 3, 1961; Ted Lewis, "Capital Circus," *New York Daily News*, October 11, 1961; "700 U.S. Soldiers to Figure in Film," *New York Times*, October 17, 1961; "Defense Department Cuts Troops for Movie," *New York Times*, October 21, 1961; "Army Aid to Film Cut," *New York Times*, October 24, 1961; Wanda Hale, "French Café Seat at D-Day Reenactment," *New York Daily News*, November 12, 1961; Louis Sobol, "Recalling a Memorable Day," *New York Journal American*, December 7, 1961; "Seeks Probe of GIs' Use in Zanuck Film," *New York Daily News*, December 30, 1961; William Peper, "Zanuck Working on D-Day Film," *New York World Telegraph*, February 15, 1962.

Zanuck's reappearance as president of Twentieth Century-Fox; Richard's rise there: Dunne, *Take Two*, pp. 100–102. Richard's proposition that he be production chief: "Dick and Lili Zanuck Pledge to Mix Matrimony and Moviemaking from Here to Eternity," *People*, August 25, 1985. Overcoming opposition to Richard's appointment: Darryl Zanuck, November 28, 1972, deposition in *Arthur Gordon, Hazel Berger, Albert Kaufman and Rebecca G. Berkowitz, Plaintiffs, against Donald A. Henderson, Francis S. Levien, William C. Michel, Seymour Poe, Spyros P. Skouras, James A. Van Fleet, David Brown, John P. Edmondson, Frederick Ehrman, William R. Hearst, Jr., William T. Gossett, William C. Keefe, Harry J. McIntyre, Paul Miller, Dennis C. Stanfill, Kevin C. McCann, Jerome A. Straka, Darryl F. Zanuck, Richard D. Zanuck, David Merrick and Twentieth Century-Fox Film Corp., Defendants*, A Shareholders Derivative Action, Supreme Court of the State of New York, Index No. 21388/72.

The dressing gown incident: Vincent Canby, "The Last Tycoon," *New York Times Sunday Magazine*, March 17, 1968. Zanuck's new regime at Fox: "Two Brokerage Concerns Acquire 22% Stake in 20th Century-Fox," *New York Times*, March 9, 1961; Louella Parsons, "Hollywood Highlights," *New York Journal American*, May 22, 1961; Murray Schumach, "Fox Makes Plans to Cut Its Deficit," *New York Times*, June 8, 1961; Joseph Cassidy and Sidney Kline, "20th Century-Fox Names Darryl Zanuck the Big Boss," *New York Daily News*, July 26, 1962; Abel Green, "Zanuck: The Man & His Credo," *Variety*, August 1, 1962; Murray Schumach, "Studio Goes to Zanuck's Son," *New York Times*, October 8, 1962; "Darryl Zanuck & Son Named Head of Fox Film Studios," *Wall Street Journal*, October 10, 1962; Frederick Christian, "Darryl Zanuck: The 20th Century

Fox," *New York Journal American*, December 9, 1962; Murray Schumach, "Fox Studio Back in Production," *New York Times*, February 14, 1963; Murray Schumach, "$50 Million Plan Described by Fox," *New York Times*, March 5, 1963; Eckert Goodman, "Zanuck: 20th Century Fox," *New York Daily News*, May 7, 1963; "Elizabeth Taylor Gets Top Film Pay," *New York Times*, May 22, 1963; "Fox Film Had Quarterly Profit, Gross Fell; Holders Talk of Cleopatra, Women Bicker," *Wall Street Journal*, May 23, 1963; Clare M. Reckert, "Fox Film Turns Loss into Profit," *New York Times*, August 23, 1963; Peter Bart, "Meeting of Fox Film Marked by Oration of Stockholders," *New York Times*, May 20, 1964; Peter Bart, "Hollywood Watching Economics as Well as the Esthetic Things," *New York Times*, July 6, 1964; Art Seidenbaum, "How to Succeed at 30," *New York Journal American*, January 31, 1965; Mel Gussow, "The Twentieth Century Fox Rides Again," *New York Herald Tribune*, February 27, 1966; Peter Bart, "Executive Suite: Accent on Youth," *New York Times*, November 20, 1966.

Profits from *The Longest Day:* "Zanuck's Personal Mopup, $5,806,595 In Two Years on 20th's 'Longest Day,' " *Variety*, April 28, 1965. Success of *The Sound of Music:* Joan Bartnel, "Biggest Money-Making Movie of All Time—How Come?" *New York Times Sunday Magazine*, November 20, 1964. Memo from Richard Zanuck to Robert Wise: March 19, 1964; Memo from Darryl Zanuck referring to Judith Crist: March 3, 1965. Dick's continuing success: "Three to Get Ready," *Time*, April 12, 1968.

Virginia Zanuck's ill feeling toward her husband: *Virginia Fox Zanuck v. Darryl F. Zanuck*, Complaint for Money on a Contract and an Account Stated, Superior Court of the State of California for the County of Los Angeles, no. 836725, filed April 13, 1964.

Zanuck's amorous activities in Paris: Pierre Savineau, interview with author; Fernande Josephine Cook, August 25, 1982, deposition for *Genevieve Gillaizeau v. Bank of America National Trust and Savings Association*, Probate Court of Riverside County, Indio 6635. Zanuck's loneliness: Edward Leggewie, interview with author.

Genevieve's background: Gussow, pp. 272–76; Martha Smilgis, "In Darryl Zanuck's Last Drama, A Forgotten French Lover Sues for $15 Million," *People*, July 14, 1980; Genevieve Gillaizeau, June 1, 1984, deposition for Affidavit in Opposition to Motion for Partial Summary Judgment, *Genevieve Gillaizeau v. Marvin Mitchelson*, A Professional Corporation; Marvin M. Mitchelson and Harold Rhoden, U.S. District Court, Southern District of New York, 83 Civ 4367.

Richard Zanuck's marital difficulties: Walter Scott, Pokie Seeger, Lili Gentle, Fred DeGorter, Margaret Shands, Pierre Savineau, and others who declined to be identified, interviews with author; also, *Lili C. Zanuck v. Richard D. Zanuck in Complaint for Divorce*, Superior Court of the State of California for the County of Los Angeles, filed February 9, 1967, No. D703260. In Declaration of Frank B. Belcher (Richard's attorney) in the divorce action, Linda Harrison is described as occupying "a position as a co-respondent although not named as such." She was deposed on April 13, 1967.

Fred DeGorter's relationship with Lili Gentle: Fred DeGorter, interview with the author. His "assault" by Richard Zanuck: Papers filed in *Fred DeGorter, Floyd Sharp, Plaintiffs, vs. Richard D. Zanuck*, Does I through X, Inclusive, Defendants in Complaint for Damages (Personal Injuries, Assault & Battery and Assault), for the Superior Court of the State of California for the County of Los Angeles, No. 919799. The suit was filed on October 17, 1967, with DeGorter asking for $250,000 in damages. Oddly, in his complaint, DeGorter states that Richard hit him with a baseball bat, but fails to mention that it was plastic.

Richard Zanuck's deal-making: John Gregory Dunne, *The Studio* (New York: Farrar, Straus & Giroux, 1968).

Incidents at garage and Daisy Club: Linda Harrison, October 20, 1974, letter to her lawyer Ervin M. Roeder, filed as part of *In re the Marriage of Petitioner Linda H. Zanuck and Respondent: Richard D. Zanuck* for the Superior Court of the State of California for the County of Los Angeles, No. WED 25920. Richard Zanuck, through his attorney, made a general denial of the letter's claims.

Richard's marriage to Linda Harrison: *Time*, November 7, 1969; *New York Post*, November 28, 1969; Twentieth Century-Fox press release, December 7, 1969; "How to Make It," *Washington Post*, December 25, 1969.

Richard's elevation to executive vice-president and further career moves at Fox: Richard Zanuck, February 15, 1973, deposition for *Gordon et al. v. Henderson et al.* for the Supreme Court of the State of New York, County of New York, Index No. 21338/1972; Bruce Bahrenburg, "New Zanuck Touch," *Newark Evening News*, October 6, 1967.

New business problems at the studio: Leonard Sloane, "For Film Makers, 2 Roads to Profit," *New York Times*, June 15, 1969; Scott Schmedel, "Fox 2nd Period Loss, Omits Dividend," *Wall Street Journal*, August 29, 1969; "Fox, Harvey, United," *New York Times*, August 29, 1969; *Fortune*, October, 1969; Mel Gussow, "Excitement Fills Premiere of 'Dolly,' " *New York Times*, December 18, 1969; "Trouble Trouble Trouble for 'Tora! Tora! Tora!' " *Life*, February 2, 1970; "Fox Film Board Votes Program to Cut Costs by $11 Million a Year," *Wall Street Journal*, August 4, 1970.

Merrick deposition: David Merrick, March 14, 1972, deposition for *Gordon et al. v. Henderson et al.* for the Supreme Court of the State of New York, County of New York, Index No. 21338/1972.

Zanuck's ill health: Stuart Byron, "Shows Self as Reply to Gossip," *Variety*, January 31, 1968; Richard Zanuck, testimony in *Genevieve Gillaizeau v. Bank of America National Trust and Savings Association*, Probate Court of Riverside County, Indio 6635; John P. Edmondson, March 28, 1973, deposition for *Gordon et al. v. Henderson et al.* for the Supreme Court of the State of New York, County of New York, Index No. 21338/1972; John O'Grady, interview with author.

Conflict between father and son: Harry McIntyre, February 21, 1973, deposition for *Gordon et al. v. Henderson et al.* for the Supreme Court of the State of New York, County of New York, Index No. 21338/1972; Richard Zanuck and Darryl Zanuck, aforementioned depositions in the same case.

NOTES

Richard's plans to make sexploitation films and his father's public endorsement: Bob Thomas, "Sex Episodes in 'Portnoy's Complaint' Fail to Faze Film-Maker Darryl Zanuck," *New York Post*, April 6, 1969; A. H. Weiler, "Meyer to Make 3 More Films for Fox," *New York Times*, February 17, 1970.

Hello–Goodbye: Henry McIntyre, deposition in *Gordon v. Henderson*. Banks' refusals to finance further pictures with Gilles: Henry McIntyre, deposition for *Gillaizeau v. Bank of America*, Indio 6635.

Changes in Zanuck's will: The Last Will and Testament of Darryl F. Zanuck, August 1970. Breach between father and son in Acapulco: Darrylin Zanuck de Pineda, June 9, 1982, deposition for *Gillaizeau v. Bank of America*, Indio 6635; family friend who declined to be named, interview with author.

SRI reports: Henry McIntyre, deposition for *Gordon et al. v. Henderson et al.* for the Supreme Court of the State of New York, County of New York, Index No. 21338/1972. Richard Zanuck often spoke as though there was one giant report on the company's future; in fact, there were several focusing on different aspects of Fox operations. Brown's and Richard Zanuck's confrontation with Zanuck in New York: Richard Zanuck, deposition in *Gordon v. Henderson*. Richard's resentment of his father's foolishness: "Sons of the Fathers," *Los Angeles*, June 1982. Stanfill's allegations of nepotism: Robert E. Dallos, "Reality Enters Fox Dream Factory," *Los Angeles Times*, November 14, 1971. Hakim's alleged fraudulent dealings: Court papers for *André Hakim v. Twentieth Century-Fox Film Corporation*, Superior Court for the State of California for the County of Los Angeles, No. C 646.

Appointment of three-man committee: Stephen Grover, "Fox Film President Richard Zanuck Said to Be Facing the Ax," *Wall Street Journal*, December 18, 1970; Leonard Sloane, "Board Meets Here Today, New President May Be Named," *New York Times*, December 29, 1971. Richard Zanuck's conclusion that he would be fired: Richard Zanuck, deposition for *Gordon v. Henderson*.

The board meeting: Richard Zanuck and Darryl Zanuck, depositions for *Gordon v. Henderson*; Anthony Haden-Guest, "The Rise, Fall and Rise of Zanuck-Brown," *New York*, December 1, 1975; Leonard Sloane, "For Film Makers." Richard Zanuck's and David Brown's humiliations upon return to Fox: Zanuck and Brown, lawsuit filed November 21, 1971, against Twentieth Century-Fox for breach of contract, Superior Court of the State of California for the County of Los Angeles, No. C 15361. Richard saying he would "do anything short of murder": Richard Zanuck as quoted in "Three to Get Ready," *Time*, April 12, 1968. Richard's career options with Ray Stark; Virginia's comment; abandonment of Zanuck's bust: Joyce Haber, *Los Angeles Times*, January 1, 1971.

CHAPTER FOUR: *SA SEULE AMIE*

Genevieve's first meeting with Zanuck: Genevieve Gillaizeau, deposition and testimony for *Estate of Darryl F. Zanuck, Genevieve Gillaizeau v. Bank of*

America, Superior Court of the State of California for the County of Riverside, Indio 6635; June 1 and June 8, 1984, depositions for *Genevieve Gillaizeau v. Marvin M. Mitchelson*, U.S. District Court, Southern District of New York, 83 Civ. 4367 (JFK). International snob sophistication: Elia Kazan, *A Life* (New York: Knopf, 1988), p. 252. Genevieve's childhood: Martha Smilgis, "In Darryl Zanuck's Last Drama, A Forgotten French Lover Sues for $15 Million," *People*, July 14, 1980.

Genevieve's meeting with Zanuck: First Amended Request for Admissions and Interrogatories, filed by Malcolm Ellis, attorney for Darrylin Zanuck de Pineda (February 26, 1982); Petitioner's Response to First Amended Request for Admissions and Interrogatories, filed by Samuel Buffone, attorney for Genevieve Gillaizeau (March 26, 1982) for *Gillaizeau v. Bank of America*, Indio 6635; Madame Claude in her August 25, 1982, deposition for *Gillaizeau v. Bank of America*, Indio 6635; Gillaizeau, depositions and testimony for *Gillaizeau v. Bank of America*, Indio 6635; Gillaizeau, deposition for *Gillaizeau v. Mitchelson*, 83 Civ. 4367 (JFK). Residency at the Excelsior: Robert McG. Thomas, "The Amenities of a Country Club Right in the Heart of Manhattan," *New York Times*, July 9, 1972.

Zanuck as sixties go-go type: Mel Gussow, *Don't Say Yes until I Finish Talking* (Garden City, N.Y.: Doubleday, 1971), p. 273; "Startime Kids," *New York Daily News*, December 15, 1969.

Genevieve's gifts from Zanuck: Gillaizeau, deposition and testimony for *Gillaizeau v. Bank of America*, Indio 6635; Gillaizeau, deposition for *Gillaizeau v. Mitchelson*, 83 Civ. 4367 (JFK). Genevieve's wardrobe: "Putting It All Together," *Christian Science Monitor*, February 16, 1971; Eugenia Sheppard, "Genevieve's World of Fashion," *New York Post*, November 14, 1968.

Cash gifts: Genevieve Gillaizeau, testimony for *Gillaizeau v. Bank of America*, Indio 6635. Hakim's beliefs about use of missing Fox funds: "Counter-Defendant's Memorandum in Opposition to Counter-Claimant's Motion for Partial Summary Judgment; Declaration of Max Fine, filed May 22, 1973, for *André Hakim v. Twentieth Century Fox Film Corporation*, Superior Court of the State of California for the County of Los Angeles, No. C 646.

Zanuck's gallant regard for Genevieve: Darryl Zanuck, November 28, 1972, deposition in *Arthur Gordon, Hazel Berger, Albert Kaufman and Rebecca Berkowitz v. Donald A. Henderson, Francis S. Levien, William C. Michel, Seymour Poe, Spyros Skouras, James A. Van Fleet, David Brown, John P. Edmondson, Frederick L. Ehrman, William R. Hearst, Jr., William T. Gossett, Paul Miller, Dennis C. Stanfill, Kevin C. McCann, Jerome A. Straka, Darryl F. Zanuck, Richard D. Zanuck, David Merrick and Twentieth Century-Fox Film Corp.*, Supreme Court of the State of New York, County of New York, Index No. 21338/72.

Genevieve's views on Zanuck's lack of desire to marry her: Gillaizeau, testimony in *Gillaizeau v. Bank of America*, Indio 6635. Zanuck's alleged fathering of a baby: *Petition for Guardianship of Michelle Linda Zanuck*, Probate Court of the State of California in and for the County of Los Angeles, filed August 23, 1983, Index No. P681428.

Genevieve's society doings: Suzy, "Smashing," *Daily News*, June 12, 1970. Zanuck's visit to Ric-Su-Dar with Genevieve: Margaret Shands, interview with author. Dinners with David and Helen Brown and Richard Zanuck: Helen Gurley Brown, *Having It All* (New York: Linden Press, 1982). Darrylin's Acapulco party: Father Angel Martinez, Acapulco, Mexico, interview with author.

Zanuck's continuing interest in other women: Darrylin Zanuck de Pineda, deposition for *Gillaizeau v. Bank of America*, Indio 6635; friends of Genevieve who declined to be named, interviews with author; Xaviera Hollander with Robin Moore and Yvonne Dunleavy, *The Happy Hooker* (New York: Dell, 1972), pp. 203–04. Zanuck's alcoholism: Gussow, pp. 274–75.

The alleged fraud: "Counter-Defendant's Memorandum in Opposition to Counter-Claimant's Motion for Partial Summary Judgment; Declaration of Max Fine, filed May 22, 1973, for *André Hakim v. Twentieth Century Fox Film Corporation*, No. C 646. The scam, said Claude Fielding, attorney to Hakim in Europe, worked like this: "The circumstances necessitating this cable and the purchase of 'L'Échelle Blanche' [a movie] were related as follows: Darryl Zanuck was producing a picture in Europe entitled 'World of Fashion' starring his protogee [*sic*] Genevieve Giles [*sic*]. At the time it was substantially exceeding budget costs, and the excessive costs were to be transferred to 'L'Échelle Blanche' to make it appear that 'World of Fashion' was not expensive at all. This meant that 'L'Échelle Blanche' had to be purchased in order to absorb some of the costs of 'World of Fashion.' It was then decided by Zanuck to substantially reduce the proposed budget on 'L'Échelle Blanche' and to have the script rewritten, or supposedly rewritten. It was Mr. Fielding's knowledge that this was the reason for engaging Miss Skarman and Miss Selling [in fact, two fashion models] under the title of script writers. In order to obtain the approval of his son, Richard Zanuck, for 'L'Échelle Blanche,' Darryl Zanuck had [a cable] drafted, disclosing to Richard that Miss Skarman and Miss Selling would be hired at a cost of $80,000, and there would be a payment of $20,000 to a dummy French director, Paul Feyder." Fox claimed that the two fashion models qua writers received only $100 each for signing a bogus contract with the company, and that Paul Feyder received only $6,000.

Hello–Goodbye and Zanuck's aims for Genevieve: Zanuck, deposition for *Gordon v. Henderson*, Index No. 21338/72; Ronald Neame, interview with Lisa Towle.

Review of *Hello–Goodbye*: Howard Thompson, *New York Times*, July 13, 1970. Genevieve's views on her movie's failure: Earl Wilson, "Getting the Word from Genevieve," *New York Post*, July 25, 1970; Martha Smilgis, "In Darryl Zanuck's Last Drama, A Forgotten French Lover Sues for $15 Million," *People*, July 14, 1980.

Letters from Genevieve and Dick regarding her contract: "Gossett-to-Motley Exchange Details Record of Zanucks and Fox Switch," *Variety*, March 3, 1971.

Zanuck insisting he abstained from voting on his son's ouster: Zanuck, deposition and testimony for *Gordon v. Henderson*, Index No. 21338/72.

One of the Fox attorneys present at the taking of Zanuck's deposition, however, indicated that he had voted to ask his son to resign. Board's intention to relieve Zanuck of operational responsibilities: Zanuck, August 2, 1971, testimony and the October 1, 1971, testimony of Dennis Stanfill, "private conference" before the Securities and Exchange Commission *In the Matter of Twentieth Century-Fox Film Corporation*, File No. HO 530.
Stories critical of Zanuck and Genevieve: "M*A*S*H*E*D," *Time*, January 11, 1971; "No Place to Park," *Variety*, January 13, 1971; Joyce Haber, "Zanuck Fires Zanuck! Is That Any Way for a Father to Act?" *Los Angeles Times*, January 1, 1971; "Walter Scott's Personality Parade," *Washington Post*, January 31, 1971.
Virginia's views about her husband's ouster of her son: Ed Sullivan, "Happy New Year," *New York Daily News*, January 1, 1971. Controversy over Virginia's voting rights for Fox stock: Zanuck, deposition for the SEC, *In the Matter of Twentieth Century-Fox Film Corporation*, File No. HO 530.
Doings of the dissident shareholders: "Dissidents Attack Big Losses at Fox," *New York Times*, April 26, 1971; Advertisement for Twentieth Century-Fox Stockholders Protective Committee, *New York Times*, April 30, 1971; "Insurgents Set Proxy War on Zanuck Film; Zanuck Is Target of Broker and Lawyer," *Wall Street Journal*, March 10, 1971; "Attorney Joins Insurgents in Bid to Control Fox Film," *Wall Street Journal*, April 1, 1971.
Zanuck's face-saving lie about his resignation as CEO; board's unease with his continuing stewardship: Dennis Stanfill, deposition before the SEC, *In the Matter of Twentieth Century-Fox Film Corporation*, File No. HO 530; Leroy F. Aorans, "The Last Tycoon Answered That He Felt Tired," *Washington Post*, April 14, 1971; Mel Gussow, "The Zanuck Mystery," *New York Times*, April 18, 1971; William D. Smith, "Zanuck Resigns as Fox Film Chief," *New York Times*, April 6, 1971. Richard's view of his father's stepping down: Gene Handsaker, "Talks of Fox Dismissal," *Newark Evening News*, May 2, 1971.
Controversy about Richard Zanuck's public intentions: A. D. Murphy, "Dick Zanuck a One-Man Minefield for Either Side in Any Fox Battle: Delicate Issues: Dupe or Showman," *Variety*, April 21, 1971; "Foe Sees 'Team' in DFZ, Stanfill: Discreet Re Dick," *Variety*, May 4, 1971; Stephen Grover, "Max Factor and Richard Zanuck Will Back Insurgent Slate in Fox Film Proxy Fight," *Wall Street Journal*, May 13, 1971; "Dick Zanuck Clarifies His Fox Shares," *Variety*, May 12, 1971. Virginia's vote: "Mrs. Virginia Zanuck Says She Will Support Fox Film Insurgents," *Wall Street Journal*, May 4, 1971.
The $1 million dollar offer to Richard: "Fox Trades Charges with Ex-President," *New York Times*, May 14, 1971. Richard's attempt to persuade his father to join the dissidents: Zanuck, deposition for the SEC, *In the Matter of Twentieth Century-Fox Film Corporation*, File No. HO 530. May shareholders' meeting in Delaware: *In the Matter of Twentieth Century-Fox Film Corporation*, File No. HO 530; Leonard Sloane, "Fox Battle Ends with Results Undisclosed," *New York Times*, May 19, 1971; "Darryl Stars in 'Z,' a Foxy Feature," *New York Daily News*, May 19, 1971;

Leonard Sloane, "Fox Management Is Seen Victor in Control Battle," *New York Times*, May 27, 1971.

Pre-meeting maneuvering with Zanuck: Henry McIntyre, interview with author; Zanuck and Stanfill, depositions before the SEC, *In the Matter of Twentieth Century-Fox Film Corporation*, File No. HO 530.

Zanuck's post-resignation plans: "The Twentieth Century Fox," *Women's Wear Daily*, September 13, 1971; Abel Green, "Zanuck 'Working Off' Rest of His 2-Yr. Contract; Will Produce 2–3 Pictures; 1st One Now More Likely in Mexico," *Variety*, June 2, 1971; Abel Green, "Zanuck Impatient to Start," *Variety*, September 22, 1971; "DFZ 'Irons Out' 20th-Fox Hassle; Set to Produce 2," *Variety*, November 10, 1971; Abel Green, "DFZ Shelves 'Day Christ Died' As Indie for 20th; Agrees with Mgmt. $5-Mil Biblical Not Propitious Now," *Variety*, December 22, 1971; Abel Green, "DFZ on Park Jog, Forgoes Coast," *Variety*, May 17, 1972. Zanuck's wills: *Bank of America National Trust and Savings Association, as Executor of the Estate of Darryl F. Zanuck, Deceased, Plaintiff-Appellee v. Genevieve Gillaizeau, Defendant-Appellant*, No. 771, Docket 84-7832, U.S. Court of Appeals, Second Circuit, Decision: July 1, 1985.

Genevieve's description of Zanuck's feelings: Gillaizeau, testimony for *Gillaizeau v. Bank of America*, Indio 6635; Earl Wilson, "She's Loyal to Zanoock . . ." *New York Post*, February 12, 1971.

Darrylin's claim that Zanuck joked about lawsuits: Darrylin de Pineda, deposition for *Gillaizeau v. Bank of America*, Indio 6635.

Zanuck's diagnosis of and treatment for cancer: Dr. Carl Feind, testimony in *Gillaizeau v. Bank of America*, Indio 6635. Genevieve's trip during his illness: Gillaizeau, testimony for *Gillaizeau v. Bank of America*, Indio 6635. Zanuck's "broken ankle": Abel Green, "DFZ on Park Jog, Forgoes Coast," *Variety*, May 17, 1972. Zanuck's lonely life in hotel suite: Genevieve Gillaizeau and Vincenza Argentino, testimony in *Gillaizeau v. Bank of America*, Indio 6635.

Genevieve's travels: Lawyer Malcolm Ellis, cross-examination in *Gillaizeau v. Bank of America*, Indio 6635, January 1982. Cable from Zanuck's dogs: Exhibit I in *Gillaizeau v. Bank of America*, Indio 6635.

Zanuck's memory loss: Dr. Carmine Vicale, deposition and testimony for *Gillaizeau v. Bank of America*, Indio 6635. Zanuck's call to Argentino: Vincenza Argentino, deposition for *Gillaizeau v. Bank of America*, Indio 6635.

Virginia's second legal battle with Zanuck: Agreement between Virginia Zanuck and Darryl F. Zanuck, February 22, 1973.

Zanuck's hospitalization: Vincenza Argentino, Genevieve Gillaizeau, Dr. Carl Feind, Dr. Carmine Vicale, and Darrylin Zanuck, depositions for *Gillaizeau v. Bank of America*, Indio 6635. Theft of paintings: "Thieves May Have Been Faked Out by Zanuck Art," *New York Post*, February 18, 1972; "Careful Casing Evident in Zanuck's Plaza Heist, Celeb Dossiers Now SOP," *Variety*, February 23, 1972.

Accounts of Zanuck's homecoming: Depositions of Vincenza Argentino, Genevieve Gillaizeau, Darrylin Zanuck, and testimony of Edward Meena and Richard Zanuck in *Gillaizeau v. Bank of America,* Indio 6635; Virginia Zanuck, letter to Margaret Shands, August 4, 1980; André Hakim, Jr., interview with author.

Genevieve's return to Palm Springs with her lawyer: Rita Mahon, testimony for *Gillaizeau v. Bank of America,* Indio 6635; author's interview with George Cappiello.

CHAPTER FIVE: TWENTIETH CENTURY PRINCESSES

Darrylin and Susan Zanuck's adolescence: Mary Donahue, Terry Moore, Martha Newman Ragland, Margaret Shands, and John O'Grady, interviews with author. Susan's accident: "Susan Zanuck in Car Crash," *Los Angeles Examiner,* October 5, 1950. Darrylin Zanuck's Palm Springs party: Herb Pasik, "Ric-Su-Dar Revisited: The Darryl Zanuck Estate in Its Heyday," *Palm Springs Life,* July 1987. Susan's conduct in the south of France: *Time,* September 25, 1948. Susan at inaugural ball: Leonard Lyons, "The Lyons Den," *New York Post,* October 15, 1966.

Darrylin's courtship and marriage: Mary Donahue, Diane Jacks, and Walter Scott, interviews with author; "Darrylin Zanuck Engaged," *New York Herald Tribune,* August 23, 1949; "Miss Darrylin Zanuck a Bride," *New York Times,* November 13, 1949; *Time,* November 21, 1949. Darrylin's wedding presents: Darrylin, January 8, 1961, letter to her accountant.

The Jacks' ranch; birth of their children: Complaint for Divorce, *Darrylin Jacks vs. Robert L. Jacks, Bank of America National Trust and Savings Association, a California corporation, Robert Jacks Productions Inc., a California corporation, Leonard Goldstein Inc., a California corporation, The Estate of Leonard Goldstein through its executor Robert Goldstein, Crown Productions Inc., Crown Productions, a copartnership consisting of G. Plasty Corporation, a California corporation, Robert Goldstein Productions, a California corporation, Robert Jacks Productions Inc., a California corporation, Bandito Productions Inc., a copartnership consisting of Dorothy Mitchum dba Dorothy and Robert Mitchum, Productions Inc., a corporation, and Robert Jacks Productions Inc., a California corporation, and Robert Mitchum dba Dorothy and Robert Mitchum, Productions Inc., a corporation, Goldstein-Jacks Productions, a copartnership consisting of Robert Jacks Productions Inc., a California corporation, Robert Goldstein Productions Inc., a California corporation, and Leonard Goldstein Inc., a California corporation, Robert Goldstein Productions, a California corporation, Dick Carruth dba Producers Film and Equipment Rental Company, Samuel Silver, Black and White Corporation One to Ten, a corporation, White and Black Partnership One to Ten, a partnership, John Does One to Ten and Jane Does One to Ten,* in the Superior Court of the State of California in and for the County of Los Angeles, No. SMD 16696, filed December 24, 1957. The numerous defendants included banks and other businesses where Robert Jacks had accounts. Defendant Samuel Silver, who, Darrylin claimed owed her and her husband $4,500, was her father's loyal barber. The couple's two adoptions: Diane Jacks, interview with author.

Gyppie: Sharon Hakim, Zanuck's granddaughter noted that all the grandchildren came to call Zanuck Gyppie, after the bumptious monkey who starred in his bedtime stories.

Darrylin's attitude toward her father's affair with Bella Darvi: Mary Donahue, in an interview with the author, asserted that Darrylin didn't like to take sides; Margaret Shands, also in an interview, claimed that Virginia felt her daughter disapproved of her mother rather than her father. Darrylin's anxiety about her looks: Author's interviews with several Zanuck friends who declined to be named. Darrylin's move from her ranch home: Complaint for Divorce, *Jacks vs. Jacks*, in the Superior Court of the State of California in and for the County of Los Angeles, No. SMD 16696, filed December 24, 1957, and the property settlement agreement in the same case, filed June 10, 1958.

Darrylin's divorce: "Zanuck's Daughter Sues," *New York Times*, December 25, 1957; "Asks $5,890 Alimony," *New York News*, February 23, 1958; also, Complaint for Divorce and other documents filed as part of *Jacks vs. Jacks*, in the Superior Court of the State of California in and for the County of Los Angeles, No. SMD 16696, December 24, 1957. Alleged beatings: Declaration of Petitioner in Support of: A. Issuance of Writ of Execution B Modification of Child Support C. Attorney's Fees and Costs, filed August 6, 1975, and Petitioner's Response to Respondent's First Set of Interrogatories, filed March 16, 1976, *In Re the Marriage of Petitioner: Darrylin Jacks, and Respondent: Robert Jacks*, Superior Court of the State of California for the County of Los Angeles, No. SMD 16696.

Darrylin's boutiques: Mary Donahue and Walter Scott, interviews with author. End of romance with Dorian: Petitioner's Response to Respondent's First Set of Interrogatories, filed March 16, 1976, *In Re the Marriage of Petitioner: Darrylin Jacks, and Respondent: Robert Jacks*, Superior Court of the State of California for the County of Los Angeles, No. SMD 16696. Darrylin suggested that Dorian departed for Hawaii soon after she and Jacks began wrangling about support payments for the children. In one of his papers in the 1957 divorce suit, Jacks complained that Darrylin had taken the children to Hawaii and planned to move there. Court papers in the divorce suit also mentioned her hiring a nanny.

Troubles at the stores: Notice to Darrylin's Inc. from Francis S. Montgomery II of Montgomery Management Company, December 15, 1959; and Complaint for Breach of Contract and Fraud, *Doris Edwards v. Darrylin Zanuck Jacks and Two Does*, Superior Court of the State of California for the County of Los Angeles, filed July 1958, No. 738869.

Darrylin's meeting with Julio Pineda: Rita Oliver, Mary Donahue, and Father Angel Martinez, interviews with author.

Corinne Calvet's encounter with Zanuck: Corinne Calvet, *Has Corinne Been a Good Girl?* (New York: St. Martin's, 1983), pp. 195–97.

Susan Zanuck's show business career: Author's interviews with Pokie Noonan Seeger, Martha Ragland, Terry Moore, and others who declined to be named. The trip to Korea: "Terry Toting Ermine Shorts on Korea Tour," *New York Post*, December 18, 1953; "Bikini-ed Terry Gets Caught in Army

Draft," *New York Daily News*, December 25, 1953; "Terry Keeps 'Em On, Stays in Korea," *New York Post*, December 27, 1953; "Terry Moore Staying On," *New York Herald Tribune*, December 27, 1953; "Catholic Woman Criticizes U.S.O.," *New York Herald Tribune*, January 28, 1954; and "Terry Ill, Blame Famed Korea Bathing Suit," *New York Post*, March 11, 1954.

Party at Ciro's: Terry Moore and Pokie Seeger, interviews with author; "Hollywood Party in the Grand Manner," *Life*, February 8, 1954; Ezra Goodman, *The Fifty-Year Decline and Fall of Hollywood* (New York: Simon & Schuster, 1961), pp. 406–08.

André Hakim's background: Press release issued by Harry Brand, head of publicity for Twentieth Century-Fox, 1952. Hakim's marriage to Susan: Pokie Seeger, interview with author; "Susan Zanuck Weds Hakim," *Los Angeles Examiner*, April 18, 1954.

Susan's marriage: Pokie Seeger, Pierre Savineau, Terry Moore, and Mona Skoff, interviews with author. Hakim's acquaintance with Madame Claude: Fernande Josephine Cook, August 25, 1982, deposition in *Genevieve Gillaizeau v. Bank of America National Trust and Savings Association*, Superior Court of the State of California for the County of Riverside, Indio 6635. Hakim's offer to resolve his difficulties with Susan: Cholly Knickerbocker, "Suzy Zanuck and Husband to Reconcile," *New York Journal American*, February 3, 1960. Susan's separation from Hakim: André Hakim, Jr., and Pierre Savineau, interviews with author.

Darrylin's leave-taking from Los Angeles: Petitioner's Response to Respondent's First Set of Interrogatories filed March 16, 1976, *In Re the Marriage of Petitioner: Darrylin Jacks, and Respondent: Robert Jacks*, Superior Court of the State of California for the County of Los Angeles, No. SMD 16696; Darrylin asserted that she spoke to Jacks at the end of 1960 and left for Mexico by car. The children followed two weeks later with their nurse. "I had a document signed by Robert Jacks giving me permission to take the children to Mexico (this was turned over to the authorities when the children left the country). Without this paper they couldn't leave the country." Jacks filed a show cause order on June 28, 1960, to modify the custody order because of Darrylin's alleged violation of the original custody order, which occurred when she took the children to Mexico without his permission.

Note to Darrylin from Zanuck's accountant: Referred to in an October 5, 1960, letter to Darrylin from her California accountant. "A letter from your father's representative in Paris was received today indicating that they had forwarded to you the note and transmittal letter. Please forward it immediately because the bank just today called and said they would have to charge the $12,500 plus interest to your father's account because the examiners were at the bank for their regular audit and inasmuch as this note was outstanding since June they had no other alternatives." Darrylin's business losses: Itemized in proof of loss statement submitted to insurance company for theft of one cultured pearl cross, a 14-carat gold neck chain, a gold locket, and a gold identification bracelet in Acapulco on August 8, 1959; letter to "Laura" from Darrylin asking that her accountant file insurance claims for silver stolen from her Malibu house, jewelry stolen "in the states a long time ago," and a recent loss in Mexico of a heavy gold charm bracelet and a ring; 1960 Federal Individual Income Tax Return for Darrylin Z. Pineda, mentioning that the inventory at her store Pour La Contessa on 150 West Channel Road in Santa Monica "was removed from the store by unknown sources leaving nothing to salvage on closing the store in January of 1960." The 1960 tax return amplified on other losses as well: "On leaving California for Mexico, 15 boxes of clothing and personal effects were shipped by train and lost in transit somewhere in Mexico, put tracers on both departures and destination but to no avail. Taxpayer lived in Malibu, Calif. before departing to Mexico in 1960. Her furnished home in Malibu was locked until storage could be arranged. In June or July of 1960, taxpayer instructed that furniture be removed and on inspection it was first noticed that her collection of sterling silver was missing. The silver collection was quite extensive and elaborate and represented a collection commenced in the taxpayer's early childhood. Taxpayer, in order to import sweaters from Italy, personally signed the Bond for Darrylin's Inc. that went broke in 1959 and she was forced to pay the Bond."

Darrylin's assertions that friends borrowed money they didn't repay: Deduction schedule for 1960 taxes, listing bad debts from two friends and a relative; October 5, 1959, letter to Darrylin from her accountant, mentioning a note due from Pat Dorian that would probably be uncollectible; note to Darrylin's accountant, written in 1962 or 1963, in which she mentions a friend—"she was an employee of mine—she borrowed that money on good faith & with no intent to pay it back. It's over a year now. I here [sic] she's here but has no intention of paying me—also all of her hospital bills, medicine, I paid when she was sick. . . . My mother called her once about the money & she said she couldn't pay it back. This should definitely be a loss." In the same note, Darrylin claimed, "It was Pat Dorian who broke into shop—another thing—I bought $3,000 worth of cashiers checks in Jan. 1961 Just before I left to cover my bills I owed in U.S. (charges etc.!) they were to be mailed by Pat Dorian who also had the numbers of the checks. When I didn't return he threatened me with tearing them up. . . . I tried to get Bank to look up numbers but they never did—I even think I had you call them—Pacific Palisades Bank—I sent a check for $1,000 to my mother in 1961 to cover some of the bills—the others she finally paid for me."

Darrylin settling down in Mexico: Juan Pano de la Barrera, September 27, 1961, deposition in Acapulco, Gro., Mexico, for *Jacks vs. Jacks*, in the Superior Court of the State of California in and for the County of Los Angeles, No. SMD 16696; Ernesto Teddy Stauffer, September 27, 1961, deposition for the same case; Syria Gomez Ocampo, September 27, 1961, deposition for the same case. Robert Jacks's opposition to her remarriage: Darrylin Zanuck de Pineda, September 27, 1961, deposition. Whereabouts of Steven and Helena: Diane Jacks, interview with author.

Jacks's nonpayment of support: Robert Jacks, September 5, 1975, declaration *In Re the Marriage of Petitioner: Darrylin Jacks, and Respondent: Robert*

Jacks, Superior Court of the State of California for the County of Los Angeles, No. SMD 16696: "I have fully complied, to the best of my ability, with all Court orders in this matter and am not in default thereunder. I have made all support payments except for the periods of time within ten years of the judgment wherein Petitioner was in contempt of Court and/or denying Respondent reasonable visitation rights to his children."

Darrylin's and Julio's activities in the 1960s: Emi Fors, Father Angel Martinez, Rita Oliver, and Pierre Savineau, interviews with author. Darrylin's claim that her husband ran an egg business: Darrylin de Pineda, 1964 listing of accounts for the year 1963 for her California accountant: "You can put I borrowed on Malibu property a $9,000 loan for personal loan to my husband's chicken farm"; Angela Taylor, "Daughter of Movie Man Prefers Fashion to Film," *New York Times*, January 28, 1965; Anne Anable, "Mexican Accent," *New York Journal American*, June 20, 1965; various issues of the *Acapulco News*.

Zanuck dating women other than Genevieve: June 9, 1982, deposition of Darrylin Zanuck de Pineda for *Genevieve Gillaizeau v. Bank of America National Trust and Savings Association*, Superior Court of the State of California for the County of Riverside, Indio 6635.

Darrylin marketing her resort wear in New York: June 1967 request for an extension on the filing date of her taxes—"taxpayer had a loss activity in the East in 1966. The amounts are being confirmed"—indicating that this venture may have been unsuccessful.

Darrylin's plastic surgery: Margaret Shands, Pierre Savineau, Martha Ragland, and others who declined to be named, interviews with author.

Breach with Foreign Friends of Acapulco: Emi Fors, Father Angel Martinez, and Rita Oliver, interviews with author; note from Darrylin to her accountant on the back of a 1969 ledger sheet: "About 'DAR,' we are not listed with the Internal Revenue because we operate in a foreign country so it would be very unwise to use DAR this year because the other charity group here 'Foreign Friends of Acapulco' hate me & who knows if they might have turned DAR's name in—I know there [sic] name was looked into since they operate illegally. We don't but legally you can't take a tax deduction on any charity outside the U.S."

Darrylin's view of rift between Zanuck and Richard and their ouster from Fox: Darrylin Zanuck de Pineda, June 9, 1982, deposition for *Genevieve Gillaizeau v. Bank of America National Trust and Savings Association*, Superior Court of the State of California for the County of Riverside, Indio 6635.

Robin Lyn's wedding: Father Angel Martinez, interview with author.

Virginia's friendship with Ed Meena and Thomas Shirley: Margaret Shands and Martha Ragland, interviews with author.

Virginia's continuing obsession with her estranged husband: Margaret Shands, interview with author: Virginia was convinced that a passage in *The Happy Hooker* (pp. 203–04) described Zanuck's relationship with Genevieve Gillaizeau.

Darrylin's visit to her father at the hospital and their return to Palm Springs: Darrylin Zanuck de Pineda, June 9, 1982, deposition for *Genevieve Gil-*

laizeau v. Bank of America National Trust and Savings Association, Superior Court of the State of California for the County of Riverside, Indio 6635.

Reunion in Palm Springs: Various depositions and in testimony for *Estate of Darryl F. Zanuck, Genevieve Gillaizeau v. Bank of America*, Superior Court of the State of California for the County of Riverside, Indio 6635; Genevieve Gillaizeau, June 1 and June 8, 1984, depositions for *Genevieve Gillaizeau v. Marvin M. Mitchelson*, U.S. District Court, Southern District of New York, 83 Civ. 4367 (JFK); Virginia Zanuck, letter to Margaret Shands, August 4, 1980; André Hakim, Jr., interview with author.

CHAPTER SIX: TOGETHER AGAIN

Zanuck's physical condition: Vincenza Argentino, Ed Meena, and Rita Mahon, depositions and testimony for *Gillaizeau v. Bank of America*, Superior Court of the State of California for the County of Riverside, Indio 6635.

Establishment of Zanuck's household trust: Trust Agreement between Darryl F. Zanuck and Bank of America National Trust and Savings Association, Los Angeles, California, May 21, 1973. By the time Zanuck's assets were put in a household trust, he had only 63,540 shares of Twentieth Century-Fox stock.

Zanuck's lack of interest in his finances and his will: Ed Meena, testimony for *Gillaizeau v. Bank of America*, Superior Court of the State of California for the County of Riverside, Indio 6635.

Background behind the redrafting of Zanuck's will, summer of 1973: Robert Laufer of Paul Weiss Rifkind and Garrison in New York, interview with author.

Control of Darrylin's trust fund, 1974: Cross-Complaint for Damages, filed October 20, 1980, in *Darrylin Zanuck de Pineda vs. Thomas Shirley and Does 1 through 10, inclusive*, Superior Court of the State of California for the County of Riverside, Indio 28006; by the end of 1973, Darrylin should have been short of funds, because her trusts, according to submissions to the IRS, yielded only $864 in income in 1971 and $821 in 1972. Problems with Darrylin's 1967 taxes: September 14, 1974, Final Notice before Seizure from the IRS to Darrylin Pineda. The IRS asserted she owed $3,308 including interest and penalties; in a note to "Tom," Darrylin asserted she had already paid up; one deduction, a $5,000 payment to a New York doctor, was disallowed by the IRS, said Darrylin, because she had paid cash and he had given her no receipt.

Darrylin's plans to sell her jewelry: Emi Fors, interview with author. Darrylin's account of the theft: Reward notice drafted on July 9, 1975. Report of the robbery: *Variety*, July 16, 1975. John O'Grady's investigation and suspicions: O'Grady, interview with author. Susan Zanuck Savineau's view of the matter: Sherry Hakim, interview with author.

Darrylin's attempted rapprochement with her former husband: Mona Skoff, Diane Jacks, and other Zanuck family friends who declined to be named, interviews with author.

Darrylin's renewal of legal hostilities with Robert Jacks; allegations of beatings; picture-taking incident: Declaration of Petitioner in Support of: A. Issuance of Writ of Execution B Modification of Child Support C. Attorney's Fees and Costs, filed August 6, 1975, and Petitioner's Response to Respondent's First Set of Interrogatories, filed March 16, 1976, *In Re the Marriage of Petitioner: Darrylin Jacks, and Respondent: Robert Jacks*, Superior Court of the State of California for the County of Los Angeles, No. SMD 16696. Jacks's denials: Hearing Brief, filed in the same case on April 13, 1976. Darrylin, he claimed, could easily have tried to collect child support, since he continued to work for her brother and father long after his divorce and regularly corresponded with the children and with Virginia and Richard; the court's decision was rendered on April 12, 1976.

Darrylin's sheltering of her grandson: Mary Donahue, Rita Oliver, and several other Zanuck friends who declined to be named, interviews with author. Virginia's financial rescue: Charles Meeker of O'Melveny & Myers in Los Angeles, letter to Licenciado Alejandro Fernandes, Ramirez de la Corte y Ritch, Amberes 5, Mexico, D.F., August 12, 1975.

Susan's life in the south of France: Pierre Savineau, André Hakim, Jr., and Sherry Hakim, interviews with author.

Hakim's difficulties from the black money scheme: Warrant of Arrest issued by the District Attorney's Office, Zurich, Switzerland, June 29, 1973. Hakim's escape from Europe: Pierre Savineau and André Hakim, Jr., interviews with author.

The Savineaus' marital and financial difficulties: Pierre Savineau, André Hakim, Jr., and Sherry Hakim, interviews with author.

Virginia's reluctance to accept her husband's senility: Richard Zanuck quoted in Anthony Haden-Guest, "The Rise, Fall and Rise of Zanuck-Brown," *New York*, December 1, 1975, "I keep him [Zanuck] up to date with what's going on in the industry, but he seems to have tuned out." Also, André Hakim, Jr., Pokie Seeger, Pierre Savineau, Sherry Hakim, Gloria Greer, Indio, California, Court Clerk Wenona Winsett, and Harry McIntyre, interviews with author; Harry J. McIntyre, May 25, 1982, deposition for *Gillaizeau v. Bank of America*, Superior Court of the State of California for the County of Riverside, Indio 6635. In a December 8, 1975, unpublished interview, Richard told a reporter that his father was physically well but senile with no memory of recent events.

The Savineaus' continuing troubles in California: Pierre Savineau, André Hakim, Jr., Mona Skoff, and Sherry Hakim, interviews with author. Sale of Susan's Twentieth Century-Fox stock: Mona Skoff, Henry Bamberger, and André Hakim, Jr., interviews with author. Fox stock performance: Earl C. Gottschalk, Jr., "Fox Is Counting on Rescue by 2 New Films, But Most Analysts Still Expect 'Down Year,' " *Wall Street Journal*, July 12, 1976; "Star Wars: The Year's Best Movie," *Time*, May 30, 1977; " 'Star Wars': Fox Investor Boon?" *New York Times*, June 3, 1977; Earl C. Gottschalk, Jr., " 'Star Wars' Fuels Takeoff in Fox Film Stock but Some Advise Awaiting Its Broad Release," *Wall Street Journal*, June 14, 1977; "Fox Film Sights Profit of 75 Cents a Share for the Second Quarter," *Wall Street*

Journal, July 12, 1977; " 'Star Wars' Has Big Gross," *Wall Street Journal*, August 17, 1977.

Ironically, at the same time Susan Zanuck was wondering about the sale of her Fox stock, a bid to take over the company materialized from a Nashville businessman, Claude Cockrell. Although he made mysterious claims to be connected to big-money backers in the East and West, he held less than one hundred shares. Some alleged that he was fronting a takeover of Fox by Richard Zanuck. Zanuck denied that, and the SEC later concluded that Cockrell was a fake. Nonetheless, Cockrell set off a flurry of trading and ultimately caused trading in Fox stock to be suspended by the SEC just before the release of *Star Wars*: "Control of Fox Film Is Sought by Group in Nashville through Purchase of Stock," *Wall Street Journal*, May 11, 1977; "Cockrell Associates in Bid for Fox Film Still Prove Elusive," *Wall Street Journal*, May 13, 1977; "Businessman's Activity in Shares of Fox Film Investigated by SEC," *Wall Street Journal*, May 16, 1977; "Cockrell Drops Move to Control Fox Film," *New York Times*, May 23, 1977; "Claude Cockrell Drops His Effort to Acquire Control of Fox Film," *Wall Street Journal*, May 23, 1977; Judith Miller, "S.E.C. Penalizes Cockrell for Fox Film Statements," *New York Times*, November 3, 1977; "Tennessee Man's Claimed Plan to Acquire Fox Film Was Fabrication, SEC Suit Says," *Wall Street Journal*, November 8, 1977. Also very mysteriously, about the same time Cockrell set off heavy trading in Fox stock, half of the Fox stock in Zanuck's household trust was sold. Richard's ownership of only one Fox share appeared in property listings filed in 1977 for his divorce from Linda Harrison.

Richard's assertion that *Jaws* earned more money than his father's entire body of work: Richard Zanuck quoted in Anthony Haden-Guest, "The Rise, Fall and Rise of Zanuck-Brown," *New York*, December 1, 1975; "Son of Darryl F., He Made His Own Name with Hollywood's Most Toothsome Grosser Ever," *People*, December 29, 1975. Family's dislike and resentment of him: Richard Zanuck quoted in Stephen Farber and Marc Green, "DFZ and the Dauphin," *Hollywood Dynasties* (New York: Delilah, 1984), p. 112. Richard's share of *Jaws* profits: "Son of Darryl F., He Made His Own Name with Hollywood's Most Toothsome Grosser Ever," *People*, December 29, 1975.

Linda Zanuck's discontent with her marriage; her relationship with the Maha Genii Turriziani: Numerous documents filed as part of *Linda Harrison vs. Maha Genii Turriziani, an individual, The Risen Christ Temple Light of Translation Foundation, a corporation, and Does 1 through 10, inclusive*, Superior Court of the State of California for the County of Los Angeles, No WEC 077722. Linda's original complaint for "breach of fiduciary duty; undue influence; constructive trust; restitution after rescission; and money had and received" was filed on December 17, 1982. She admitted to having had a sexual liaison with the guru in her first deposition, pp. 58–59. Linda's violent argument with Richard; his alleged vandalism at the Temple of Light; other incidents of alleged violence: Linda Harrison Zanuck, letter to the editor of the *Los Angeles Times*, October 12, 1974; letter to her lawyer, October 20, 1974, filed as part of her 1974 divorce action against Richard Zanuck.

The troubles of Richard's daughters, Ginny and Janet: André Hakim, Jr., Sherry Hakim, Lili Gentle, and friends who declined to be named, interviews with author; also, Darrylin's lawyer, Malcolm Ellis, interview with author, April 1985, for "War of the Wills," *Money*, July 1985.

Darrylin's remark that Lili Fini was "a match" for Richard: Darrylin de Pineda, interview with author, April 1985.

Darrylin's charge that Shirley churned her trust fund: Cross-Complaint for Damages, filed October 20, 1980, in *Darrylin Zanuck de Pineda vs. Thomas Shirley and Does 1 through 10, inclusive*, Superior Court of the State of California for the County of Riverside, Indio 28006. The claim that Virginia asserted Shirley and Meena stole Darrylin's money and jewelry: Shirley's suit for slander, *Thomas L. Shirley vs. Darrylin Zanuck Pineda, and the Estate of Virginia Fox Zanuck, Deceased, and Does 1 through 25, inclusive*, filed November 18, 1982, Superior Court of the State of California for the County of Riverside, Indio 36745. Shirley's defense: Suit to recover the $17,000 Darrylin allegedly borrowed in Complaint for 1. Money Had and Received; 2. Intentional Misrepresentation; 3. Fraud and Deceit in *Thomas Shirley vs. Darrylin Zanuck also known as Darrylin Zanuck Pineda, Does 1 through 20, Inclusive*, filed April 5, 1979, Superior Court of the State of California for the County of Riverside, Indio 28006. Darrylin's loans from her father: Attachment No. II of Inventory and Appraisement of Decedent's Assets in the *Estate of Darryl F. Zanuck* filed for *Gillaizeau v. Bank of America*, Indio 6635. The statement shows that Darrylin borrowed $68,000 from her father between December 1978 and June 1979.

Animosity between Susan and Darrylin: André Hakim, Jr., Sherry Hakim, and Mona Skoff, interviews with author.

Savineau's troubles with Susan and her children: Pierre Savineau, André Hakim, Jr., Sherry Hakim, Pokie Seeger, and Mona Skoff, interviews with author. Final days of the Savineaus' marriage: Court papers filed in Dissolution of Savineau, Superior Court of the State of California for the County of Riverside, No. D 6337, August 4, 1978.

Zanuck's funeral: "Zanuck Rites Observed," *Los Angeles Times*, December 28, 1979; "Welles About Zanuck: 'Most Of All a Friend,' " *Variety*, December 28, 1979.

Susan's battle with Savineau for control over the profits of the ranch: Susan's lawyer, Burton Marks, March 5, 1981, letter to executor Henry Bamberger's lawyer at O'Melveny & Myers, Exhibit D, Resignation of Executor; First and Final Account and Report of Executor; Petitioner for Executor's Commissions for Extraordinary Services, for Fees for Special Counsel, and for Instructions, filed July 26, 1982, in *Estate of Susan M. Savineau also known as Susan Marie Savineau, and Susan M. Zanuck Savineau*, Superior Court of California, County of Riverside, Indio 6874.

Susan's ill health: Sherry Hakim, Pokie Seeger, André Hakim, Jr., and Mona Skoff, interviews with author. Dino's and André's difficulties with, respectively, drugs and the police: Palm Springs Police Department incident report and follow-up (file no. D.R. 80-162-012). The report also recounted Susan's final days with her son Craig Savineau and Susan Andrea Noonan.

Investigation of Susan's death: Palm Springs Police Department incident report and follow-up (file no. D.R. 80-162-012); Coroner's Investigation Report, Riverside County, California, File No. 45028; Bio Laboratories Medical Group, Inc., Autopsy Protocol RC 80-619, issued July 1, 1980; Sergeant Thomas Barton, interview with author. Susan's second funeral: André Hakim, Jr., Mona Skoff, and Sherry Hakim, interviews with author.

CHAPTER SEVEN: ALL THE LITTLE FOXES

Marvin Mitchelson's career: Victor Junger, "It's Round Two of the Marvin Affair, and the Stakes Are $1.5 Million for Michelle," *People*, January 22, 1979; Pamela G. Hollie, "Divorce Mitchelson Style," *New York Times*, January 6, 1980; Patricia Morrisoe, "The Prince of Palimony," *New York* magazine, January 10, 1983.

Genevieve Gillaizeau's real estate: Property ownership records in New York City and Palm Beach, Florida; California and Massachusetts properties described by a former employee who declined to be identified and by Genevieve in a May 1985 interview with Leslie Laurence for *Money* magazine.

Marvin Mitchelson's acceptance of the case and his original strategy: Affidavit in Opposition to Motion for Partial Summary Judgment filed July 18, 1984, in *Genevieve Gillaizeau against Marvin M. Mitchelson, A Professional Corporation and Marvin M. Mitchelson*, U.S. District Court, Southern District of New York, No. 83 Civ. 4367 (JFK); letter of agreement between Genevieve Gilles and Marvin Mitchelson, signed by both, dated May 20, 1980.

Thomas Shirley's assertion to Mitchelson and Rhoden that Darrylin de Pineda forged her father's signature: Depositions and other exhibits presented as part of Affidavit in Opposition to Motion for Partial Summary Judgment, filed July 18, 1984, in *Genevieve Gillaizeau against Marvin M. Mitchelson, A Professional Corporation and Marvin M. Mitchelson*, U.S. District Court, Southern District of New York, No. 83 Civ. 4367 (JFK).

Genevieve's claim against Darryl Zanuck's estate: Creditor's Claim, filed June 26, 1980, for *Estate of Darryl F. Zanuck, Genevieve Gillaizeau vs. Bank of America National Trust and Savings Association, as Executor et al.*, Superior Court of California, County of Riverside, No. Indio 6635.

Court filing of an additional assertion that Zanuck's will was forged: Plaintiff's Statement of Undisputed Material Facts in Support of Plaintiff's Motion for Partial Summary Judgment with Respect to Defendant's Liability for Attorney Malpractice, filed June 29, 1984, for *Genevieve Gillaizeau against Marvin M. Mitchelson, A Professional Corporation and Marvin M. Mitchelson*, U.S. District Court, Southern District of New York, No. 83 Civ. 4367 (JFK).

Shirley's declaration: Declaration of Thomas Shirley, July 7, 1980, for *Estate of Darryl F. Zanuck, Genevieve Gillaizeau vs. Bank of America National Trust and Savings Association, as Executor et al.*, Superior Court of California, County of Riverside, No. Indio 6635.

The bank clerk who Shirley said had notarized Zanuck's allegedly forged will could not be located by the author; however, she seemed to have issued a denial through F. Lee Bailey on his television show, "Lie Detector," on which Shirley appeared. The exchange went, in part, as follows: SHIRLEY: She [Darrylin] had forged her father's will to his signature, uh, signature to his will. BAILEY: Did she say how she'd accomplished that? SHIRLEY: Um, with her, cooperating with her mother. BAILEY: Well, we have a copy of the document. I believe it is witnessed by three different people and then notarized by a Notary Public. . . . SHIRLEY: Hmm, right. BAILEY: . . . for the State of California. How did she manage to bring that off without his signing in their presence, as the law requires? SHIRLEY: She didn't give me the full details of it but she said that she, um, that they had a number of documents which had been notarized by the lady at the Bank of America and that, uh, her mother had told her that, um, she felt confident that they'd be able to get the lady at the Bank of America to take their word for it and, uh, to notarize his signature, even though it was not signed in front of her. BAILEY: Now, we contacted the lady who did the notary . . . SHIRLEY: Right. BAILEY: . . . seal and, although she was not very talkative and wound up hanging . . . SHIRLEY: Yes . . . yeah. BAILEY: . . . up on us . . . SHIRLEY: Yeah. BAILEY: . . . she did say, "Oh, no, I went to the house and everybody was there and we all saw him sign it" and so forth. SHIRLEY: Right. (Transcript of Shirley "Lie Detector" Segment, March 16, 1983, Exhibit A (3) Notice of Motion and Motion for Summary Adjudication of Issues, Memorandum of Points and Authorities in Support Thereof, filed January 13, 1984, for *Darrylin Zanuck de Pineda vs. F. Lee Bailey, Thomas Shirley, Lee Shamberg, Ferrine Corporation, Inc., Columbia Pictures Television, Inc., Coca-Cola Company, Inc., Metromedia, Inc., Ralph Andrews, individually, Ralph Andrews Productions, Inc., and Does 1 through 200, Inclusive,* Superior Court for the State of California for the County of Los Angeles, Case No. WEC 079582.)

Genevieve's leave-taking from Zanuck: Martha Smilgis, "In Darryl Zanuck's Last Drama, A Forgotten French Lover Sues for $15 Million," *People*, July 14, 1980.

Virginia Zanuck's reaction to the lawsuit: Virginia Zanuck, letter to Margaret Shands, August 4, 1980.

Mitchelson's and Rhoden's unsuccessful legal strategy; Genevieve's termination of their services: Depositions and other exhibits presented as part of Affidavit in Opposition to Motion for Partial Summary Judgment, filed on July 18, 1984, for *Genevieve Gillaizeau against Marvin M. Mitchelson, A Professional Corporation and Marvin M. Mitchelson,* U.S. District Court, Southern District of New York, No. 83 Civ. 4367 (JFK).

Shirley's effort to bring forgery allegation to attention of FBI: Thomas Shirley, copy of letter to Federal Bureau of Investigation agent Ralph Girardi, April 28, 1981; Merit Protective Service of California, copy of letter to Ted Gunderson & Associates, Security Consulting and Investigations, April 30, 1981; Thomas Shirley, copy of letter to Robin C. Brown of the Federal Bureau of Investigation, May 19, 1981; Edgar N. Best and Ralph Girardi, agents, Federal Bureau of Investigation, copy of letter to Thomas Shirley, May 22, 1981.

Assets of Susan Zanuck Savineau: Resignation of Executor; First and Final Account and Report of Executor; Petition for Executor's Comissions [sic] for Extraordinary Services, for Fees for Special Counsel, and for Instructions, filed July 26, 1982, for *Estate of Susan M. Savineau, also known as Susan Marie Savineau, and Susan M. Zanuck Savineau,* Superior Court of California, County of Riverside, No. Indio 6874.

Distribution of money from Susan's trust fund to her children: André Hakim, Jr., interview with author.

Upbringing of the Hakim children: André Hakim, Jr., Pierre Savineau, and Sherry Hakim, interviews with author.

Appropriation of Zanuck's francs by André, Jr.: André Hakim, Jr., interview with author.

Dino Hakim's activities in California: André Hakim, Jr., Sherry Hakim, Mona Skoff, Sergeant Tom Barton, and John O'Grady, interviews with author.

Relationship between André Hakim, Jr., and his grandparents: André Hakim, Jr., Pierre Savineau, and Mona Skoff, interviews with author.

Hakim boys' theft of checks and other belongings: Sherry Hakim, interview with author; and police investigation of Susan's death, Palm Spring's incident report and follow-up (file no. D.R. 80-162-012).

Brentwood drugstore robbery: Testimony of André Hakim, Jr., in Complaint Felony, filed April 7, 1980, for *The People of California vs. André Armand Hakim,* in the Municipal Court of Los Angeles Judicial District, County of Los Angeles, State of California, No. A080354; and Reporter's Transcript of Preliminary Examination, July 10, 1980, in *The People of the State of California vs. Lance Richard Bregel,* Municipal Court of Los Angeles Judicial District, County of Los Angeles, State of California, Division No. 90, No. A080246.

Dino's attempted drug deals: Palm Springs Police Department incident report and follow-up (file no. D.R. 80-162-012), recounting the investigation into Susan Zanuck's death.

Hakim children's heavy involvement with drugs: André Hakim, Jr., Pierre Savineau, Sherry Hakim, Mona Skoff, and John O'Grady, interviews with author.

André's suspicions about his father's death: André Hakim, Jr., interview with author. Poverty of André Hakim, Sr.: Janet L. Wright of O'Melveny & Myers, letter to Hakim's sister, filed as Exhibit C as part of Resignation of Executor; First and Final Account and Report of Executor; Petition for Executor's Comissions [sic] for Extraordinary Services, for Fees for Special Counsel, and for Instructions, July 26, 1982, for *Estate of Susan M. Savineau, also known as Susan Marie Savineau, and Susan M. Zanuck Savineau,* Superior Court of California, County of Riverside, No. Indio 6874.

Dispute between André, Jr., and Dino Hakim: Sherry Hakim, interview with author; police report of the incident, filed November 16, 1980, No. 80-788090.

Dino's efforts to reform: Mona Skoff, interview with author. Circumstances of Dino Hakim's death: Case Report and Autopsy of the Chief Medical Examiner of the County of Los Angeles, No. 81-5423, completed September 3, 1981. André's suspicions about Dino's death: André Hakim, Jr., interview with author. Dino's funeral: Mona Skoff, interview with author. André's efforts to learn whether his brother had left any money: André Hakim, Jr., and Sherry Hakim, interviews with author.

André's effort to win an allowance from his mother's estate: Sherry's objection: Petition for Family Allowance, July 2, 1982; Objections to Petition for Family Allowance of André Hakim, filed August 23, 1982, as part of *Estate of Susan M. Savineau, also known as Susan Marie Savineau, and Susan M. Zanuck Savineau*, Superior Court of California, County of Riverside, No. Indio 6874.

CHAPTER EIGHT: THE WAR OF THE WILLS

André Hakim, Jr., at Virginia Zanuck's funeral: Mona Skoff and André Hakim, Jr., interviews with author. Darrylin de Pineda's "slight" of her brother: Walter Scott, interview with author.

Virginia's desire to see Darrylin receive her money quickly: Last Will and Testament of Virginia Fox Zanuck, April 3, 1982; Petition to Probate Will, *In the Matter of the Estate of Virginia Fox Zanuck*, Superior Court for the State of California, County of Los Angeles, filed November 1, 1982, No. P 676784.

David Brown's challenge to Virginia's will on behalf of Richard Zanuck's sons; Malcolm Ellis's rebuttals: Contest and Grounds of Opposition to Probate of Purported Will, filed November 19, 1982; Petition for Probate of Lost or Destroyed Will, for Appointment of Executor, Issuance of Letters Testamentary, and Authorization to Administer Under Independent Administration of Estates Act, filed November 24, 1982; Ex Parte Petition for Appointment of David Brown as Guardian Ad Litem for Harrison Zanuck and Dean Zanuck and Order Thereon, filed November 19, 1982; Petition to Appoint Named Executors, Etc., filed December 16, 1982; Declaration of Matt D. Cooney, December 12, 1982, for *In the Matter of the Estate of Virginia Fox Zanuck*, Superior Court for the State of California, County of Los Angeles, No. P 676784. Also, Lloyd Shearer, "The Zanuck Inheritance Fight," *Parade*, 1983.

What Janet and Ginny might have received had their grandmother's April 3, 1982, will been ruled invalid: Last Will and Testament of Virginia Fox Zanuck, December 21, 1981.

Ellis's contention that Virginia's videotape for Richard contained scandalous secrets: Malcolm Ellis, interview with author. What was really on the tape: Matt D. Cooney, interview with author. Possible explanation for Virginia's rift with her son: John O'Grady, interview with author.

Linda Harrison's divorce settlement and its fate: Depositions and other material filed as part of *Linda Harrison vs. Maha Genii Turriziani, an individual, The Risen Christ Temple Light of Translation Foundation, a corporation, and Does 1 through 10, inclusive*, Superior Court of the State of California for the County of Los Angeles, No. WEC 077722.

Malcolm Ellis's efforts to get Genevieve to admit to sordid details about her past: First Amended Request for Admissions and Interrogatories, February 26, 1982, in *Estate of Darryl F. Zanuck: Genevieve Gillaizeau vs. Bank of America, National Trust and Savings Association, as Executor, etc., et al.*, Superior Court of the State of California for the County of Riverside, Case No. 6635. Genevieve's responses: Petitioner's Response to First Amended Request for Admissions and Interrogatories, filed March 26, 1982, as part of Indio 6635.

Interview of Madame Claude by William Campbell and Jamie Brodie: Deposition of Fernande Josephine Cook, August 25, 1982, for *Genevieve Gillaizeau v. Bank of America National Trust and Savings Association*, Superior Court of the State of California for the County of Riverside, Case No. Indio 6635.

Thomas Shirley's efforts to give evidence to Genevieve: Documents and interviews provided to author by a person who declined to be named.

Thomas Shirley's unpublished book: Thomas Shirley, *Hollywood Family*, Registered WGAW, Number 211790. Diane Jacks's assessment of its accuracy: Diane Jacks, interview with author.

Richard Zanuck's assertion that Darrylin signed either Zanuck's will or its 1977 codicil: Richard Zanuck, May 5, 1982, deposition for *Genevieve Gillaizeau v. Bank of America National Trust and Savings Association*, Superior Court of the State of California for the County of Riverside, Case No. Indio 6635.

Darrylin's explanation of her mother's instruction to practice: Darrylin Zanuck de Pineda, June 9, 1982, deposition for *Genevieve Gillaizeau v. Bank of America National Trust and Savings Association*, Superior Court of the State of California for the County of Riverside, Case No. Indio 6635.

Family's lawyers' codicil defense strategy: Malcolm Ellis, interview with author.

Family's case as presented by Bank of America attorneys: William Campbell, attorney for respondent, Bank of America National Trust and Savings, December 27, 1982, preliminary statement for *Genevieve Gillaizeau v. Bank of America National Trust and Savings Association*, Superior Court of the State of California for the County of Riverside, Case No. Indio 6635.

Account of trial of Genevieve's challenge to Darryl Zanuck's will: Testimony given and read in January 1983 during *Genevieve Gillaizeau v. Bank of America National Trust and Savings Association*, Superior Court of the State of California for the County of Riverside, Case No. Indio 6635; Dana Kennedy, "Film Giant's Former Lover Testifies," *Desert Sun*, January 13, 1983; Mike Katoaka, "Challenges Plague Wills of Zanuck, Wife," *Desert Sun*, January 16, 1983; and Caleb Trainer, "Judge Dismisses Zanuck Will Suit," *Desert Sun*, January 21, 1983.

Genevieve's appeal: Opinion, June 18, 1985, *Estate of Darryl F. Zanuck, Deceased. Genevieve Gillaizeau v. Bank of America, etc., et al.*, Court of Appeal, Fourth District, Division Two, State of California, No. E000453. The case filed by Bank of America against Genevieve: Opinion and Order, August 29, 1984, *Bank of America National Trust and Savings Associa-*

tion, as Executor of the Estate of Darryl F. Zanuck, Deceased, v. Genevieve Gillaizeau, U.S. District Court, Southern District New York, 83 Civ. 6175 (GLG). Genevieve's complaint against Marvin Mitchelson: Affidavit in Opposition to Motion for Partial Summary Judgment, filed on July 18, 1984, for *Genevieve Gillaizeau against Marvin M. Mitchelson, A Professional Corporation and Marvin M. Mitchelson,* U.S. District Court, Southern District of New York, No. 83 Civ. 4367 (JFK). Mitchelson's defense: Defendant's Statement of Disputed Material Facts with Respect to the Issue of Liability for Attorney Malpractice in Opposition to Plaintiff's Motion for Partial Summary Judgment Thereon, filed July 18, 1984; [Defendant's] Affidavit in Opposition to Motion for Partial Summary Judgment, filed July 18, 1984; [Defendant's] Notice of Motion, filed June 6, 1984, all from *Genevieve Gillaizeau against Marvin M. Mitchelson, A Professional Corporation and Marvin M. Mitchelson,* U.S. District Court, Southern District of New York, No. 83 Civ. 4367 (JFK).

Shirley's complaint for slander: Complaint for Damages for Slander Per Se; The Intentional Infliction of Mental and Emotional Distress; Invasion of Privacy, filed November 18, 1982, for *Thomas L. Shirley vs. Darrylin Zanuck Pineda, and the Estate of Virginia Fox Zanuck, Deceased, and Does 1 through 20, inclusive,* Superior Court of the State of California in and for the County of Riverside, Case No. Indio 36745.

Shirley's appearance on "Lie Detector" TV show: Transcript of Thomas Shirley "Lie Detector" Segment, March 16, 1983, Exhibit A (3) Notice of Motion and Motion for Summary Adjudication of Issues, Memorandum of Points and Authorities in Support Thereof, filed January 13, 1984, for *Darrylin Zanuck de Pineda vs. F. Lee Bailey, Thomas Shirley, Lee Shamberg, Ferrine Corporation, Inc., Columbia Pictures Television, Inc., Coca-Cola Company, Inc., Metromedia, Inc., Ralph Andrews, individually, Ralph Andrews Productions, Inc., and Does 1 through 200, Inclusive,* Superior Court for the State of California for the County of Los Angeles, Case No. WEC 079582. Ellis's warning to Bailey not to air the show: Malcolm Ellis, letter to "Lie Detector" show, March 11, 1983, filed as part of Complaint for Damages; Slander Per Se; False Light; Privacy; Intentional Infliction of Emotional Distress; Negligence, filed March 29, 1983, for *Darrylin Zanuck de Pineda vs. F. Lee Bailey et al.,* Superior Court of the State of California for the County of Los Angeles, No. WEC 079582. Keith Gill's appearance on second segment: Filed for *Darrylin Zanuck de Pineda vs. F. Lee Bailey, et al.,* Superior Court of the State of California for the County of Los Angeles, No. WEC 079582; Darrylin's bills from her psychotherapist—dated April 22, 1983; April 25, 1983; May 5, 1983; and June 27, 1983—were also included in case files.

Thomas Shirley's leave-taking: Author's interviews with friends who declined to be identified. The author was told, when she began searching for Shirley, that he had died in a car accident in Missouri. When state highway patrol records of roadside deaths for the previous five years failed to reveal Shirley's death, she was told he had died in Florida. A search of Florida records had the same result. Ultimately, the author learned from

American Bar Association membership records that, in 1987, Shirley was alive, well, and living in the Los Angeles metropolitan area.

Susan Zanuck's missing jewelry: André Hakim, Creditor's Claim, April 5, 1983, *In the Matter of the Estate of Virginia Fox Zanuck*, Superior Court of the State of California for the County of Los Angeles, No. P 67684; André Hakim, Jr., and Sherry Hakim, interviews with author. David Brown's assertion that Darrylin might have information about the jewelry: [Contestant's] Request for Production of Documents, filed March 3, 1983, *In the Matter of the Estate of Virginia Fox Zanuck. David Brown, as Guardian ad litem for Harrison Zanuck and Dean Zanuck, vs. Darrylin Zanuck, Richard Zanuck, Janet Zanuck Davidson, Virginia L. Zanuck, Sherry Zanuck Hakim aka Sharon M. Hakim, Andre Zanuck Savineau, aka André A. Hakim, Craig Zanuck Savineau, Don Johnson, John E. O'Grady, Mary and Ray Tousignant, Mrs. Arthur (Ruth) Mitchell, Alma Diehl, Larry Williams, Salwyn Shufro and Edward G. Shufro*, Superior Court of the State of California for the County of Los Angeles, No. P 67684. Bamberger's hint that André, Jr., and Sherry Hakim had taken it: Petition for Executor's Comissions [sic] for Extraordinary Services, for Fees for Special Counsel, and for Instructions, filed July 26, 1982, for *Estate of Susan M. Savineau, also known as Susan Marie Savineau, and Susan M. Zanuck Savineau*, Superior Court of California, County of Riverside, No. Indio 6874.

Terms of the settlement of Virginia's estate: Settlement Agreement, July 19, 1983, *In the Matter of the Estate of Virginia Fox Zanuck. David Brown, etc., vs. Darrylin Zanuck, etc.*, Superior Court of the State of California for the County of Los Angeles, No. P 67684. Tax bill for estate: Accounting of Estate, August 3, 1983, *In the Matter of the Estate of Virginia Fox Zanuck*, Superior Court of the State of California for the County of Los Angeles, No. P 67684.

Sherry Hakim's double check-cashing: Darrylin Zanuck de Pineda, interview with author, April 1985, in preparation for "The War of the Wills," *Money*, July 1985. Sherry Hakim's denial: Sherry Hakim, interview with author. Ellis's challenge of legal fees: Petitions filed on October 15, 1983, November 15, 1983, and November 23, 1983, *In the Matter of the Estate of Virginia Fox Zanuck*, Superior Court of the State of California for the County of Los Angeles, No. P 67684.

Legal battles over Zanuck's employee benefits and trophies: Petition to Determine Interests in Personal Property, filed October 22, 1984, in *Estate of Darryl F. Zanuck also known as Darryl Zanuck and as D. F. Zanuck*, Superior Court of the State of California for the County of Riverside, No. Indio 6635. Fight over trustees of Virginia's charitable foundation: *Sybil Brand v. Virginia Zanuck Charitable Foundation*, Superior Court of the State of California for the County of Los Angeles, filed July 19, 1984, No. WEC 88464.

Darrylin's feelings about the estate battle and her brother: Darrylin de Pineda, interview with the author in preparation for "The War of the Wills," *Money*, July 1985; Darrylin also noted during the interview that she felt her brother had "lost" Twentieth Century-Fox, and she claimed to have taped out his face in family photos.

Genevieve's initial legal losses: Opinion, June 18, 1985, *Estate of Darryl F. Zanuck, Deceased. Genevieve Gillaizeau v. Bank of America, etc., et al.*, Court of Appeal, Fourth District, Division Two, State of California, No. E000453; and Opinion and Order, August 29, 1984, *Bank of America National Trust and Savings Association, as Executor of the Estate of Darryl F. Zanuck, Deceased, v. Genevieve Gillaizeau*, U.S. District Court, Southern District New York, 83 Civ. 6175 (GLG).

Mitchelson's assessment of Genevieve's original case against Zanuck's estate: Defendant's Statement of Disputed Material Facts with Respect to the Issue of Liability for Attorney Malpractice in Opposition to Plaintiff's Motion for Partial Summary Judgment Thereon, filed July 18, 1984; [Defendant's] Affidavit in Opposition to Motion for Partial Summary Judgment, filed July 18, 1984; and [Defendant's] Notice of Motion, filed June 6, 1984; all from *Genevieve Gillaizeau against Marvin M. Mitchelson, A Professional Corporation and Marvin M. Mitchelson*, U.S. District Court, Southern District of New York, No. 83 Civ. 4367 (JFK). The court's decision: Opinion and Order, dated January 23, 1984, in *Genevieve Gillaizeau against Marvin M. Mitchelson, A Professional Corporation and Marvin M. Mitchelson*, U.S. District Court, Southern District of New York, No. 83 Civ. 4367 (JFK).

Sherry Hakim's financial straits: Sherry Hakim, interview with author.

Genevieve's legal victories: Opinion, June 18, 1985, *Estate of Darryl F. Zanuck, Deceased. Genevieve Gillaizeau v. Bank of America, etc., et al.*, Court of Appeal, Fourth District, Division Two, State of California, No. E000453; Opinion and Order, August 29, 1984, *Bank of America National Trust and Savings Association, as Executor of the Estate of Darryl F. Zanuck, Deceased, v. Genevieve Gillaizeau*, U.S. District Court, Southern District New York, 83 Civ. 6175 (GLG). Genevieve's failure to pay Don C. Brown: Request for Withdrawal, filed December 7, 1984, by Brown's co-counsel, Sharon Waters, *In the Matter of the Estate of Virginia Fox Zanuck*, Superior Court for the State of California, County of Los Angeles, No. P 676784. Genevieve's failure to pay Gerald Goldfarb: Gerald Goldfarb, interview with author. Genevieve's tax problem: Notice of Tax Lien, Genevieve Gillaizeau, assessed September 17, 1984, for tax period ending on December 31, 1982, No. 110-42-0443. Genevieve's rationale for turning her standing in the estate case over to Yeshiva University: Gerald Goldfarb, interview with author.

Darrylin's lawsuit against Genevieve: "Zanuck's Daughter Sues Gilles Seeking $10-Mil," *Variety*, October 19, 1986; Complaint for Damages (Malicious Prosecution), filed October 21, 1986, for *Darrylin Zanuck de Pineda vs. Genevieve Gillaizeau*, Superior Court of the State of California for the County of Riverside, Case No. 48365.

Sherry's and André's notes signed against their inheritances: *Estate of Darryl F. Zanuck, Genevieve Gillaizeau vs. Bank of America National Trust and Savings Association, as Executor et al.*, Superior Court of California, County of Riverside, No. Indio 6635.

Genevieve's objection to Zanuck's employee benefits flowing to Virginia's estate: George Young, Genevieve's Los Angeles attorney, interview with author; also Genevieve's March 25, 1987, appeal of Judge Moore's January 26, 1987, and February 9, 1987, minute orders approving the Twentieth Century-Fox settlement agreement, filed in *Estate of Darryl F. Zanuck, Genevieve Gillaizeau vs. Bank of America National Trust and Savings Association, as Executor et al.*, Superior Court of California, County of Riverside, No. Indio 6635.

Darrylin's victory against F. Lee Bailey: Settlement, August 7, 1987, *Darrylin Zanuck de Pineda vs. F. Lee Bailey, et al.*, Superior Court of the State of California for the County of Los Angeles, No. WEC 079582.

Judge Moore's approval of Zanuck's estate contest: Nate Salute and Bess Salute, Palm Springs observers, interview with author.

Success of Lili Fini and Richard Zanuck: "Lili Fini Zanuck," *Interview*, June 1985; "Lili and Richard Zanuck," *Washington Post*, June 30, 1985; "Hollywood Takes Wing as *Cocoon* Takes off in the Theaters," *People*, July 8, 1985; Susan Reed and Jeff Yarbrough, "Dick and Lili Zanuck Pledge to Mix Matrimony and Moviemaking from Here to Eternity," *People*, August 26, 1985; Stephen M. Silverman, " 'Cocoon' Team on 'Target,' " *New York Post*, September 5, 1985; Nicole Yorkin, "Lili Fini Zanuck Out of the Cocoon (Super at 30! The New Achievers: Success & Glamour)," *Harper's Bazaar*, October 1985.

Epilogue: A Family Divided

Darrylin's recent activities: Colonel Barney Oldfield, "Wahoo, Neb. Memorial Funded by Daughter of Darryl Zanuck," *Variety*, May 1, 1985; Mary Donahue, interview with author.

Robert Jacks: Diane Jacks and Mona Skoff, interviews with author.

Pierre and Craig Savineau: Pierre Savineau and Sherry Hakim, interviews with author.

Genevieve Gillaizeau: George Young, her Los Angeles lawyer, and a friend who declined to be identified, interviews with author. Distribution of funds for the estate: George Stephens, attorney for Wells Fargo Bank, which now owns Bank of America, interview with Lisa Towle.

Sherry and André Hakim: Mona Skoff, André Hakim, and Sherry Hakim, interviews with author.

Richard Zanuck and his family: Edward Leggewie, Walter Scott, friends of Janet Davidson, jury members who sat on the Maha Genii case, and others who declined to be identified, interviews with author. End of partnership with David Brown: "David Brown to Quit Zanuck/Brown: Plans to Form Own Firm," *Wall Street Journal*, March 25, 1988. Potential fights with his boys: Anthony Haden-Guest, "The Rise, Fall and Rise of Zanuck-Brown," *New York*, December 1, 1975.

BIBLIOGRAPHY

■

Arce, Hector. *The Secret Life of Tyrone Power*. New York: Morrow, 1979.

Brown, Helen Gurley. *Having It All*. New York: Linden Press, 1982.

Budde, Eugene. "A Penny a Head at Torpin's Loft," in *The History of Antelope County, Nebraska 1868–1985*. Ed., Ruth Wagner. Dallas: Curtis Media, 1986.

Calvet, Corinne. *Has Corinne Been a Good Girl?* New York: St. Martin's, 1983.

Cohen, Donna, and Carl Eisdorfer. *The Loss of Self: A Family Resource for the Care of Alzheimer's Disease and Related Disorders*. New York: NAL Penguin, 1986.

Collins, Joan. *Past Imperfect*. New York: Simon & Schuster, 1984.

Cotten, Joseph. *Vanity Will Get You Somewhere*. San Francisco: Mercury House, 1987.

Dunne, John Gregory. *The Studio*. New York: Farrar, Straus & Giroux, 1968.

Dunne, Philip. *Take Two: A Life in Movies and Politics*. New York: McGraw-Hill, 1980.

Farber, Stephen, and Marc Green. "DFZ and the Dauphin," in *Hollywood Dynasties*, New York: Delilah, 1984.

Finler, Joel W. *The Hollywood Story*. New York: Crown, 1988.

Flynn, Errol. *My Wicked, Wicked Ways*. New York: Berkeley, 1959.

Friedrich, Otto. *City of Nets: A Portrait of Hollywood in the 1940s*. New York: Harper & Row, 1986.

Goodman, Ezra. *The Fifty-Year Decline and Fall of Hollywood*. New York: Simon & Schuster, 1961.

Graham, Sheilah. *Confessions of a Hollywood Columnist*. New York: Morrow, 1969.

Gussow, Mel. *Don't Say Yes until I Finish Talking: A Biography of Darryl F. Zanuck*. Garden City, N.Y.: Doubleday, 1971.

Haden-Guest, Anthony. "The Rise, Fall and Rise of Zanuck-Brown," *New York*, December 1, 1975.

Halliwell, Leslie. *Halliwell's Filmgoer's Companion*, 8th ed. New York: Scribner's, 1985.

Henig, Robin Marantz. *The Myth of Senility*. Glenview, Ill.: Scott, Foresman and American Association of Retired Persons, 1988.

Hobson, Laura Z. *Laura Z. A Life: Years of Fulfillment*. New York: Donald I. Fine, 1986.

Hollander, Xaviera, with Robin Moore and Yvonne Dunleavy. *The Happy Hooker*. New York: Dell, 1972.

Hopper, Hedda, and James Brough. *The Whole Truth and Nothing But*. Garden City, N.Y.: Doubleday, 1962.

Johnson, Alva. "The Wahoo Boy," *New Yorker*, November 10 and 17, 1934.

Katz, Ephraim. *The Film Encyclopedia*. New York: Perigee Books, 1979.

Kazan, Elia. *A Life*. New York: Knopf, 1988.

Kotsilibas-Davis, James, and Myrna Loy. *Myrna Loy: Being and Becoming*. New York: Knopf, 1987.

McGilligan, Patrick. *Cagney: The Actor as Auteur*. San Diego: A. S. Barnes, 1982.

Moore, Colleen. *Silent Star*. Garden City, N.Y.: Doubleday, 1968.

Mosley, Leonard. *Zanuck: The Rise and Fall of Hollywood's Last Tycoon*. Boston: Little, Brown, 1984.

"One-Man Studio," *Time*, June 12, 1950.

Powell, Lenore S., and Katie Courtice. *Alzheimer's Disease: A Guide for Families*. Reading, Mass.: Addison-Wesley, 1983.

Seaman, Barbara. *Lovely Me: The Life of Jacqueline Susann*. New York: Morrow, 1987.

Selznick, Irene Mayer. *A Private View*. New York: Knopf, 1983.

Shipman, David. *The Story of Cinema*. New York: St. Martin's, 1982.

Solber, Carl. *Conquest of the Skies: A History of Commercial Aviation in America*. Boston: Little, Brown, 1979.

"Sons of the Fathers," *Los Angeles*, June 1982.

Wallis, Hal, and Charles Higham. *Starmaker: The Autobiography of Hal Wallis*. New York: Macmillan, 1982.

Warner, Jack L., with Dean Jennings. *My First Hundred Years in Hollywood*. New York: Random House, 1964.

Young, Betty Lou. *Our First Century: The Los Angeles Athletic Club 1880–1980*. Los Angeles: LAAC Press, 1979.

Zanuck, Darryl. "Darryl Zanuck Writes," *Oakdale Sentinel*, September 21, 1917.

———. "Oakdale Boy Sees Real Fighting," *Oakdale Sentinel*, December 27, 1918.

———. "Oakdale's Roll of Honor," *Oakdale Sentinel*, August 24, 1917.

Zierold, Norman. *The Moguls*. New York: Coward, McCann, 1969.

ACKNOWLEDGMENTS

∎

In writing a book about a family, you realize how much you count on a whole batch of families—not just your relatives, but wider circles of people who help you get started and see you through to the end of a venture such as this. I was fortunate to have the support and comfort of a number of families, without whom I could never have undertaken—much less completed—this book.

First and most helpful in getting me started was my entire family of Time Inc. colleagues, who were always ready with advice and friendship. Particularly helpful were: Marshall Loeb, former managing editor of *Money* and now managing editor of *Fortune*, who proposed the story on the Zanuck estate battle; Landon Jones, *Money's* current managing editor, who agreed to publish the rather unlikely story in the magazine; Joseph Poindexter, editor of "The War of the Wills," the story on which this book is based; Leslie Laurence, the very thorough reporter who helped me cover all the bases; and Nicholas Jollymore, the lawyer who vetted the story with painstaking care. Special thanks must go to assistant managing editor Richard Burgheim, who gave me a berth at *Picture Week* (while it lasted), and to Frank Lalli, executive editor of *Money*, who devised a Byzantine agreement that allowed me to work at the magazine and on this book.

Another family—though far-flung on two coasts and two continents—worked on the book itself. I am most grateful to Lisa Towle, my tireless and sympathetic East Coast anchor, who can be trusted to unearth the most sensitive material without ruffling feathers; Don Johnston in Paris, who was able to find and interview friends and colleagues of Darryl Zanuck's in a language I studied but never mastered; Laura Meyers and Mary Wormley in Los Angeles, who were always willing to find missing documents and devise new reporting angles; in New York, Caroline Baer and Darlen Obertance, who helped me organize, understand, and nail down the information I had gathered. From three of *Money*'s photo editors, Miriam Hsia, Deborah Pierce, and Leslie Yoo, I learned everything I needed to know about photo research: to get Sarah Rozen, an energetic photo researcher for *People*, who managed to find the photographs that illustrate this book. Finally, without the help of *Money* senior editor Kevin McKean, who understands the ins and outs of XyWrite software like nobody's business, much of this book would have been lost in some computer oblivion.

The vast family of people who keep track of public documents—court cases, driver's licenses, property records, birth and death records, police investigations, and all the other raw material that makes up our history must also be thanked. Particularly helpful were: Elizabeth Gresh of the St. Petersburg, Florida, Public Library; Jim Hanson of the Wisconsin State Historical Society; Lois Johnson of the Antelope County, Nebraska, Historical Society; Glenda Lipscombe, Freedom of Information Act officer of the Securities and Exchange Commission; Nina Quiros, Acapulco correspondent of the *Mexico City News*; Diane Sharp of the Geneology Library of the Indiana State Historical Society; Steven Tilley of the Department of Documents Conservation of the National Archives in Washington, D. C.; Audra Wayne of the Wheeling, West Virginia Public Library; Wenona Winsett, Clerk of the Indio, California Probate Court; and the staff of the Performing Arts Library of the New York Public Library at Lincoln Center.

The family of people who made me get it all done were remarkable for their patience and perseverance. Chief of the "how-do-you-know-can-you-find-out-and-when will it be done?" group is my agent Barbara Lowenstein, who had faith in this project from the start and who provided unerring editorial guidance. David Groff and Gail Kinn, my two cliché-killing editors at Crown, were kind, patient, understanding, and calm—true rocks of Gibraltar during my most stressful moments.

Others among the Crown family have earned my undying gratitude: Peter Davis, Fred Goss, Kay Riley, Ken Sansone, and J. Wilson Henley.

A very, very loyal family of friends generously ladled hefty amounts of reassurance on my anxieties: Lani Luciano, who always insisted that the book would so be published; Patricia Dreyfus, who offered criticism and advice on the manuscript; Susan Macovsky, who listened patiently to endless whining and complaining; Phyllis Baumann, who has figuratively held my hand through every personal and professional maxi- and mini-crisis since college; Dennis Shulman, who offered psychological insights about my subjects; and John Stickney and Julie Connelly, who had kind words at every turn.

Finally, of course, thanks must go to my own real family—both extended and nuclear. My cousins Nate and Bess Salute of Palm Springs provided me with hospitality and occasional reporting help during my visits to California. A number of relatives over the years have enabled me to muster a self-confidence I did not always feel: Robert, Doris, and Bill Harris; my uncle and aunt Robert and Dorothy Rubin; and my grandmother, Bess Glazer. Although she died in 1985, before I began this project, I felt her with me whenever I wore her diamond earrings. My parents, Harold and Rivel Moses, and my sister Frankee, have always made me feel that I could accomplish everything I set out to do, and this project was no different. My mother's advice to "make a list" stood me in good stead.

The real pillars of my existence through all the work and worry and wonder were the members of my immediate family. Important constituents of that family are Nesha Sattaur and Zenaida Gerardo, two incredibly loyal people who help operate our household. My greatest joys and rewards are my two children—my toddler, Ezra, whose antics provide diversion; and my teenage son, Max, who contributed sharp psychological insights and who donated many of his free hours to keeping an eye on Ezra. Real support came from my husband, Norman, who did most of the work necessary over the past few years to keep our family—an organism as fragile as any—together and running smoothly.

INDEX

•

Academy of Motion Picture Arts and Sciences, 38
Acapulco, Mexico, 186
Adler, Buddy, 100
adult adjustment syndrome, 276
Affairs of Cellini, The, 43
African Queen, The, 60
African safari, 59–60
All About Eve, 78
Alsop, Joseph W., Jr., 42
Alzheimer's disease, 218, 269, 286, 293
American Film Institute, 280
Andrews, Julie, 114, 124
anti-Semitism, 21, 71
Arbuckle, Roscoe "Fatty," 21, 40
Archerd, Army, 281
Argentino, Vincenza:
  at Darryl Zanuck's sickbed, 2, 3, 164, 169–170, 171, 203, 204
  deposition of, 269
  in Palm Springs, 4, 6, 172
Arliss, George, 41, 43
army training films, 67–69
Astor, Mary, 58
Astor, Mrs. Vincent, 144
At the Front in North Africa, 68
Ayres, Lew, 58

Bacall, Lauren, 241
Bailey, F. Lee, 274–276, 288
Bailey, Pearl, 125
Balboa Island, 97
Bamberger, Henry, 220–221, 248, 252, 254, 259, 260, 278
Bank of America, 268, 273, 279–280, 282, 284, 288–289
Bardot, Brigitte, 148
Barrie, J. M., 22
Barton, Tom, 237–238
Baxter, Anne, 181
Baxter, Warner, 45
Beer and Blood (Bright), 33
Beery, Wallace, 41, 45
Bennett, Constance, 41
Ben-Veniste, Richard, 273, 283
Berlin, Irving, 66
Better 'Ole, The, 28, 30
Beyond the Valley of the Dolls, 127–128
Big Gamble, The, 106
Bishop, Norman, 182, 184, 185
black money scheme, 131–132, 143, 147–148, 216–217
Blacksmith, The, 24
Blackwell, Earl, 144
Black Windmill, The, 222
Blanke, Henry, 29

Blondell, Joan, 58
Bogart, Humphrey, 60
Boitard, Janine, 110
bootleggers, 32
Born to Be Bad, 43
Bowery, The, 41
"Bracken's World," 123
Brand, Harry, 41, 97
Brand, Sybil, 280
Brando, Marlon, 82
Brasselle, Keefe, 187
Brasserie Lipp, 136
Broder, Jamie, 263
Brown, David:
  career of, 2, 90, 97, 127, 128, 151, 152, 221–222, 254, 296
  contested estate and, 259–260, 273, 277, 278
  dismissal of, 133–134, 152, 153, 159, 160, 163
  guru visited by, 224
  social life of, 146, 212
  studio politics and, 128, 130, 132, 200
Brown, Don C., 269, 272, 285
Brown, Helen Gurley, 146, 152, 212
Buchwald, Art, 85, 108–109, 147
Buffone, Samuel, 247, 266–267
Burnett, W. R., 32
Burton, Richard, 126, 142, 144
Butch Cassidy and the Sundance Kid, 134

Caesar, Arthur, 31–32
Café de Paris, 47
Cagney, James, 12, 32, 58
Cahill, John, 66
California, income tax in, 12–13, 43, 44
Calvet, Corinne, 9, 84, 187–188
Campbell, William, 263, 268, 271, 272–273, 285
Canby, Vincent, 123–124, 154
Cantor, Eddie, 187
Capone, Al, 32
Cappiello, George, 173, 174–175, 272
Cardinal Richelieu, 11–12, 43
Cavalcade, Alban, 80
Century City, 126
Chanel, Gabrielle (Coco), 142
Chaplin, Charlie, 21, 23, 25, 26, 47, 66, 75
Chapman Report, The, 106–107, 128
China Boy, 108–109
Christian, Linda, 83
CinemaScope, 82, 103
Clarke, Mae, 12, 32
Claude, Madame (Fernande Grudet), 116–117, 139, 213, 262, 263

Cleopatra, 111, 113, 115, 130
Cocoon, 90, 281, 295
Coe, Barry, 104
Cohn, Harry, 37
Collins, Joan, 99
Colman, Ronald, 45, 46
Compulsion, 105–106
Cook, Fernande Josephine, *see* Claude, Madame
Cooney, Matt, 261, 279
Cops, 24
Costello, Dolores, 56
Cotten, Joseph, 2, 74, 75
Country Doctor, The, 46
Coward, Noel, 75
Crack in the Mirror, 106
Craig, Helen, 93
Crawford, Michael, 149
Crist, Judith, 115
croquet, 74–75
Crowther, Bosley, 82
Curtiz, Michael, 29, 33, 34, 35, 36–37

Dakota, 241
Dandridge, Dorothy, 99
DAR, 198–199, 212
D'Arcy, Alex, 79
Darrach, H. Brad, 70
Darrow, Clarence, 106
Darrylin's, 186
Darryl Poster Service, 19–20
Darvi (Wegier), Bella:
  appearance of, 79, 136
  background of, 79–80, 99
  Darryl Zanuck and, 80, 84–85, 86, 87, 98–99, 116
  death of, 162
  film career of, 82–83, 96, 110, 147
  Virginia Zanuck and, 79–85, 96, 182, 190–191, 215
  Zanuck children and, 81, 84, 182–183, 190–191
Davis, Marvin, 282
Day Christ Died, The, 163
Dean, Loomis, 83–84
DeGorter, Fred, 119–120
de Herren, Rodman, 144
de la Rivière, Louise, 214
Del Ruth, Roy, 29, 45
Deluxe Tour, The, 101, 184
Demick, Irina, 109–110, 116, 136, 147, 149
Depression, 13, 38, 64
de Rochemont, Louis, 100–101
Desmoyeres, Jean, 262
DFZ Productions:
  establishment of, 87, 98
  films of, 99, 100, 101, 102–103
  management of, 100
  ownership of, 101, 113
  Twentieth Century-Fox and, 100, 101, 103, 110–111

Diehl, Alma:
  as companion, 3, 81, 98, 123
  as governess, 61, 62, 67, 93
  retirement of, 295
  at Ric-Su-Dar, 206, 207
  Virginia Zanuck's bequest to, 278–279
Dillman, Bradford, 106
Dionne quintuplets, 46
"Dobie Gillis," 113
Doctor Doolittle, 115, 125
Donahue, Frank, 101, 182, 183–184
Donahue, Mary:
  on Darrylin Pineda, 181, 182, 185
  on Darvi, 183
  on *Deluxe Tour*, 101
  on L. Harrison, 119
  shops overseen by, 186
  on Susan Savineau's death, 240
Doorway to Hell, 32
Dorian, Patrick, 183, 184, 185, 186, 194, 211
Dorian Leigh, 140
Dreyfus Fund, 156
Dreyfuss, Richard, 212
duck hunting, 34–35
Dunne, Philip:
  on Darryl Zanuck's coterie, 34, 46–47, 49
  on Darvi, 82
  scripts by, 64
  on Twentieth Century-Fox, 100, 111, 113

Echelle Blanche, L', 148
Edmondson, John P., 126–127
Egyptian, The, 82, 85
Albert Einstein Hospital and College of Medicine, 286
Eisenhower, Dwight D., 111, 180
Ellis, Malcolm, 139, 260–261, 262, 269, 271–272, 275–279
Engel, Ruth, 56, 59–60
Engel, Sam, 36, 40
Esquire, 60
Excelsior, 141

Fairbanks, Douglas, Jr., 74
Fairbanks, Douglas, Sr., 209
Farouk I, King of Egypt, 213
Faulkner, William, 106
Ferry, Christian, 167
Feind, Carl, 164, 165, 168, 170–171, 203, 269
Ferry, Fefe, 76
Fifty-Year Decline and Fall of Hollywood, The (Goodman), 190
film industry:
  evolution of, 42
  power structure in, 20–21
  repetition in, 28
  screenwriting and, 19, 22–23
  social movements and, 13, 38, 64, 124
  sound introduced in, 31
  teenage audience and, 105

Fini, Lili, *see* Zanuck, Lili Fini
Fitzgerald, F. Scott, 53
Flaming Youth, 53
Flapper, The, 53
Fleischer, Richard, 106
Flynn, Errol, 103, 176
Fonda, Henry, 70, 91
Footloose Widows, 30
Ford, Lisle, 237
Foreign Friends of Acapulco, 198
Fors, Emi, 199, 209, 212
42nd Street, 39, 46
Foster, A. F., 20, 23, 32
Fox, Frederick, 52–53
Fox, Frederick, Jr., 52
Fox, Marie Oglesby, 52–53
Fox, William, 21, 44
Fox Film Corporation, 44–45
Full House, The, 191
Fürstenberg, Princess Egon von, 144

gambling, 142–143
gangster movies, 12, 32–33
Gardner, Ava, 99
Gargarine, Elisabeth, 107, 140, 141, 197
Garland, Judy, 2, 75
Gary, Lorraine, 222
Gary, Romain, 102
Gaynor, Janet, 45
Gaynor, Mitzi, 83
Gentle (Zanuck), Lili, 103–104, 105, 118–120,
    187, 222, 225, 260
Gentleman's Agreement, 21, 71–72
Georges V Hotel, 137
Gerber, David, 121–122
Gill, Keith, 268, 276
Gillaizeau (Gilles), Genevieve:
    appearance of, 117, 136, 139, 268
    background of, 117–118, 138–139
    career of, 139, 140, 141, 167, 241, 285
    Darryl Zanuck's animosity toward, 281
    Darryl Zanuck's bequests to, 203, 207–208
    Darryl Zanuck's estate contested by, 9,
        241–247, 262–273, 282–289, 293
    Darryl Zanuck's gifts to, 142–143, 162, 166,
        271, 272
    Darryl Zanuck's health and, 2, 3–4, 146,
        164, 165–166, 168–170, 174–175, 204,
        271–272
    Darryl Zanuck's retirement and, 160–162,
        166–167
    fidelity and, 197, 271–272
    film appearances by, 128–129, 131,
        147–153, 164
    Hollander book and, 202–203
    lawsuits against, 286–287, 289
    litigation by, 137, 138, 279
    on marriage, 143–144
    P. Savineau on, 214–215
    at Ric-Su-Dar, 2, 4–7, 171–174, 205
    self-image of, 137–138

studio politics and, 152–155, 199
testimony by, 271–272
Zanuck children and, 145–146, 148, 149,
    151, 153–154, 160, 172–175, 199
Girl from Petrovka, The, 222
Girls' Dormitory, 57
Glyn, Elinor, 22
Goetz, Edith, 51, 69–70
Goetz, William, 40–41, 51, 69, 70
Goldberg, Arthur, 144
Goldfarb, Gerald, 282, 285, 286
Goldwyn, Samuel, 44
Gone with the Wind, 114
Goodman, Ezra, 86–87, 190
Gossett, William, 159–160
Grable, Betty, 176, 209
Graham, Sheilah, 148
Grapes of Wrath, The, 65
Grauman, Sid, 37, 40
Greco, Juliette, 110, 166, 185
    autobiography of, 107–108
    background of, 99–100
    as film actress, 103, 106, 136, 147
Greer, Gloria, 218–219
Griffith, Raymond, 21, 22, 23, 36, 41, 45
Grudet, Fernande (Madame Claude), 116–117,
    139, 213, 262, 263
Guide for the Married Man, A, 123
Gussow, Mel, 31, 142

Haber, Joyce, 134
Habit (Zanuck), 23, 26
Hakim, André, Jr.:
    bequests to, 248, 288
    birth of, 192
    childhood of, 217, 248–249, 250
    drug problems of, 235, 238, 252–253, 294
    estate claims of, 277, 278, 280, 294
    family deaths and, 254, 256, 257, 258–259
    father's escape aided by, 216–217
    financial interests of, 252, 255, 256, 257,
        286, 287, 288, 293–294
    with grandparents, 2, 170, 172, 204,
        251–252
    mother's marriage and, 228, 229, 230
    at Susan Savineau's funeral, 239–240
Hakim, André, Sr.:
    background of, 85, 191
    black money scheme and, 131–132, 143,
        147–148, 216–217
    career of, 86, 122, 135, 191, 238, 250
    death of, 254
    ex-wife's death and, 237–238, 239
    on finances, 237–238
    marriage of, 85–86, 189, 191, 192, 193,
        213
    Paris nightlife and, 116–117, 118, 139
    sons and, 250, 251
    studio politics and, 199–200
    yacht owned by, 150

Hakim, Raymond Edwin (Dino):
  birth of, 192–193
  childhood of, 217, 248–249, 250
  death of, 255–256
  domestic quarrels and, 229
  drug involvement of, 219, 231, 235, 238, 253, 254–255
  financial interests of, 252, 253–254, 255, 256
  with grandparents, 230–231, 250–251
  misbehavior by, 220, 229
  sexuality of, 249–250
Hakim, Sharon Marie (Sherry):
  bequests to, 253–254, 278, 283–284, 287, 288, 289, 293, 294
  birth of, 193
  brothers and, 253, 257
  childhood of, 230, 248, 249
  domestic quarrels and, 217, 228, 229, 255
  education of, 252
  at grandfather's funeral, 232
  health problems of, 284, 294–295
  mother's death and, 235–237, 238–239, 240
  mother's jewelry and, 234, 277, 278
Happy Hooker, The (Hollander), 201–203
Hardie, Glenn, 286
Harding, Ann, 53
Harris, John, 275
Harrison, Linda:
  background of, 118–119
  children of, 222
  at family gatherings, 129, 146, 199, 200, 212
  film career of, 135, 163
  guru sued by, 261–262, 295
  marriage of, 121–123, 220, 222, 224–225
  religious interest of, 222–225
Harrison, Rex, 77, 125
Hart, Moss, 2, 74, 78–79
Harvard School, 95, 179
Hawks, Howard, 75
Hays, Will H., 66
Hayworth, Rita, 63, 77
Hell and High Water, 82
Hello, Dolly!, 115, 125, 127, 157
Hello—Goodbye, 128, 134–135, 148–151, 154, 157, 161, 163
Hemingway, Ernest, 58, 99, 101
Hepburn, Katharine, 60
historical dramas, 43
Hitler, Adolf, 100
Hobson, Laura Z., 71–72
Hollander, Xaviera, 201–203
Hollywood, 12–13, 20–21
Hollywood Redheads, 55
homosexuality, 81
Houghton, William, 195
House of Rothschild, The, 43
How Green Was My Valley, 64
Hudkins Ranch, 36

Hughes, Howard, 99, 101, 181, 189
hypospadias, 249

Internal Revenue Commission (IRC), 65–66
International Productions, 69
International Real Estate Corporation, 285
intertitles, 19
Island in the Sun, 98, 99, 100

Jacks, Diane, 93, 95, 181–182, 195, 265–266, 291, 292
Jacks, Helena, 181, 195, 211, 291
Jacks, Lindolyn, 181, 281
Jacks, Robert Darryl, 181, 195, 280, 281
Jacks, Robert Livingston:
  appearance of, 72–73, 95
  career of, 100, 101, 122, 181, 182, 185, 210
  children of, 181–182, 194, 195, 210–211
  Darrylin Pineda's lawsuit against, 210–211
  death of, 292
  on location, 102, 103
  marriages of, 72–73, 95, 180–181, 183–185, 291
  novelistic account of, 264
  Pineda Carranza vs., 186
Jacks, Robin Lyn, 181, 200, 211, 219, 281
Jacks, Steven, 181, 195, 211, 291
Jacks, Wendalyn, 182, 281
Jackson, Glenda, 149
Janios, Nick, 94
Jaws, 2, 212, 222, 223
Jaws II, 225
Jazz Singer, The, 31
Je Suis Comme Je Suis (Greco), 107–108
Jews, Hollywood power structure and, 21, 39
Johnson, Alva, 42
Johnson, Nunnally, 45, 48, 49, 82
Jolson, Al, 31, 37
Jones, Jennifer, 74, 75
Jourdan, Louis, 74, 76
Jurgens, Curt, 149
Justine, 157

Kaplan, George, 268, 270
Kazan, Elia, 64, 71, 137
Keaton, Buster, 24, 25, 40, 53
Keeler, Ruby, 53
Kennedy, Edward, 144
Kent, Sidney R., 44, 45
Kerr, Deborah, 149
Khan, Aly, 77
Koo, Choon Sil, 237, 238
Krantz, Judith, 271
Kunhardt, Philip, 83–84
Kurnitz, Harry, 108

La Barba, Fidel, 46–47
Laemmle, Carl, 21, 37, 40
Landis, Carole, 77–78
Lang, Fritz, 19
Lang, Otto, 47, 59

Laufer, Robert, 168, 208
Laug, Andre, 142
League of Nations, 71
Leavitt's, 243
Lee, Mary, 74
legal malpractice, 273, 282–283
Leggewie, Edward, 169
  on European trip, 167
  in film industry, 117
  as French tutor, 59, 62, 108
  on Gillaizeau, 140
  on Richard Zanuck, 295
Lehman, Ernest, 114
Lehman, Robert, 112
Leith, Mrs., 17
LeMaire, Charles, 83, 188, 189
Lennon, John, 241
Leopold and Loeb murder, 105, 106
LeRoy, Mervyn, 32
Levin, Meyer, 105
"Lie Detector," 274–276, 288
Lights of New York, The, 31
Little Caesar, 32
Lloyd, Mildred, 27
Lloyds of London, 57
Lomelin, Ricardo, 200
Longest Day, The, 110–111, 113, 126, 161, 197
Los Angeles, 110
Los Angeles Athletic Club, 21–22, 23, 28, 55–56
Loy, Myrna, 34, 56, 67, 78
Lubitsch, Ernst, 19, 29
Lucky Baldwin, 48

MacArthur, Douglas, 70
McCarthy, Neal, 37
McHarry, Charles, 208
McIntyre, Henry, 127, 128, 129, 130, 131, 132, 159, 160, 218
McLaglen, Victor, 45
MacLaine, Shirley, 149
McLean, Barbara, 48
"Mad Desire" (Zanuck), 19
Mahon, Rita, 174, 206–207, 270
Mandeville, Molly, 77
Mangione, Chuck, 198
Man Who Broke the Bank at Monte Carlo, The, 46
March of Time, 100
Marlborough School, 63, 178, 179
Martinez, Angel, 186, 195, 196, 198, 199, 200
Marvin, Lee, 241, 242
Marx, Chico, 66
M*A*S*H, 134
Mattison, Graham, 144
Maugham, W. Somerset, 22
Maxwell, Elsa, 2, 179
Mayer, Louis B., 36, 40–41, 51, 61
Meena, Ed:
  background of, 200

Darryl Zanuck's contested will and, 246, 263–264, 269
  financial issues and, 209, 226, 227
  at Ric-Su-Dar, 3, 5, 6, 205, 206, 207
  Shirley's disappearance and, 277, 288
Meredyth, Bess, 29, 45
Merrick, David, 125, 155, 162
Merrill, Mrs. Merrill, 52
Metropolitan, 46
Meyer, Russ, 127–128
MGM, 40, 41, 155
Midwick Country Club, 36, 63
Millay, Edna St. Vincent, 53–54
Miller, Vee, 182
Misérables, Les, 11, 43
Mitchelson, Marvin, 241, 242–243, 244, 267, 272–273, 274
  late petition filed by, 246–247, 267, 273, 277, 282–283
Mohlis, William, 268
Monroe, Marilyn, 84
Moore, Colleen, 53–54
Moore, Frank, 246, 273, 282, 284, 287, 289, 294
Moore, Terry, 81, 83, 179, 187, 188, 189–190, 212
Mountbatten, Louis, Lord, 67
movie musicals, 124–125
Movietone City, 45
Mr. Belvedere Rings the Bell, 191
Murder, 75–76
Murdoch, Rupert, 282
Mussolini, Benito, 47, 165
Myra Breckinridge, 128, 129, 135

Naff, Captain, 62
Napoleon I, Emperor of France, 45, 71
National Guard, 17–18
Neame, Ronald, 148, 149, 150
Nebraska, University of, 291
nepotism, 131
Never Wear Black for Me (Pineda), 291–292
Newman, Alfred, 48, 87–88, 179, 198, 200
Newman, Paul, 134
New Yorker, 42
New York Herald Tribune, 42
New York Times, 49–50, 151
Niven, David, 2, 74, 149
Niven, Hjordis, 74
Noah's Ark, 31–32, 56
Noonan, Tommy, 83, 88, 122, 188, 189
North Woods, 55
Norton, C. C., 15–16
Norton, Louise Torpin Zanuck, 15–16
Nugent, Frank, 12–13, 43

Oberon, Merle, 77, 176, 198, 209
Oberstein, Norman, 267, 272
O'Grady, John:
  background of, 209
  on Darrylin Pineda, 177, 178
  on Darryl Zanuck's health, 127, 147

O'Grady, John (cont.)
  estate battles and, 261, 278, 286
  on Hollywood gossip, 77
  jewelry theft investigated by, 209–210
  on Shirley, 227
  on Susan Savineau, 231, 238–239
  on Zanuck grandchildren, 251
Oland, Warner, 45
Oldfield, Barney, 291–292
Oliver, Mike, 212
Oliver, Rita, 197
Only Game in Town, The, 125, 157
Our Club, 53
Ox-Bow Incident, The, 70

pain experiment, 213
Paley, William, 144
Palmer, Lilli, 176
Palm Springs Life, 179–180
Panic in Needle Park, The, 157
Parsons, Louella, 107
Patton, 134, 157
Paul, Richard, 170, 208, 276
Pickford, Jack, 21
Pickford, Mary, 27, 52, 53, 61
Pictorial Service, U.S., 97
Pineda, Darrylin Zanuck Jacks:
  in Acapulco, 186–187, 194–196, 198
  alleged forgery by, 243, 244–245, 264, 266–
    267, 269, 274, 275–276, 283, 287
  appearance of, 177, 179, 183, 197–198, 232
  bequests to, 162, 290
  birth of, 34
  brother and, 104, 281–282
  in business, 185–186, 187, 194, 195, 197
  California return of, 212, 217
  charity work of, 177, 182, 196, 198–199
  childhood of, 61–64, 176–180
  estate litigation and, 7, 139
  on family history, 281–282, 290–292
  family social activities and, 75, 129, 130
  father's illness and, 2, 170–172, 203–205,
    206, 207
  father's influence on, 8, 14, 95, 177–178,
    182, 197
  finances of, 197–198, 208–209, 211–212,
    226–227, 259
  at funeral, 258, 259
  Gillaizeau and, 146, 281, 286–287
  grandchild of, 209, 211
  jewelry stolen from, 209–210, 274
  lawsuits filed by, 210–211, 286–287, 288,
    289
  marriages of, 72–73, 81, 95, 180–182, 183–
    185, 189, 194
  at memorial service, 232, 233
  motherhood and, 181–182, 195, 196–197,
    281
  mother's estate and, 259, 260, 277–281, 290
  parental reunion and, 3–4, 5, 6
  sister and, 227–228, 240
  studio politics and, 199–200

Pineda Carranza, Julio, 186, 194, 195–196,
  209
Pinky, 72, 78
Pitts, ZaSu, 27
Planet of the Apes, 123
Playhouse, The, 24
Poe, Seymour, 123–124, 163
polo, 36, 46
POOIE (People's Organization of Intelligent
  Educatees), 114
Portnoy's Complaint (Roth), 128, 129
Pour la Contessa, 186
Powell, Dick, 46
Powell, William, 74, 75
Power, Tyrone, 57, 63, 74, 83, 91, 99, 176,
  209
Prime of Miss Jean Brodie, The, 149
producers, screen credits for, 31
Prudence and the Pill, 149
psychiatry, 86–87
Public Enemy, 12, 32–33
Purdom, Edmund, 82

Racer, The, 85
Radio City Music Hall, 46
Radziwill, Prince John, 167, 271
Raft, George, 45
Ragland, Martha Newman:
  on Darrylin Pineda, 181
  on Darryl Zanuck's infidelities, 48
  on plastic surgery, 197–198
  social life of, 200
  on studio politics, 87–88
  on Virginia Zanuck's friendship, 85
  on Zanuck children, 72, 73, 179
Ratoff, Gregory, 74, 181
Redford, Robert, 134
Reuben, Tim, 288
Reynal, Juan, 36
Rhoden, Harold, 243, 244, 247,
  272–273
Ric-Su-Dar, 2, 74–77, 145, 290
Rin Tin Tin, 27–28, 55
Risen Christ Temple Light of Translation
  Foundation, 222–223
Rivkin, Betty, 68
Roarke, Aidan, 36, 46
Robe, The, 96
Robinson, Edward G., 32
Rockefeller, Nelson, 144, 166
Rodgers, Richard, 75
Rogers, Will, 36, 45
Romanoff, Michael, 59
Romero, Cesar, 89
Roosevelt, Franklin D., 38, 69
Roots of Heaven, The, 102–103, 104
Rope of Sand, 187
Rosenman, Samuel, 111–112
Roth, Philip, 128
Russell, William, 22
Russian Revolution, 53

Sacco, Nicola, 37
St. Clair, Mal, 23, 25, 26, 27–28
St. Laurent, Yves, 142
Sanctuary, 106
Sands, Tommy, 103–104
Santa Anita racetrack, 37–38
Saroyan, William, 108
Saturday Evening Post, 91
Savineau, Craig:
  bequests to, 162, 248, 292–293
  birth of, 214
  custody of, 229, 230
  mother's alcoholism and, 229, 230, 235–236
  in Oklahoma, 234, 252, 292–293
Savineau, Pierre:
  background of, 212–213
  on black money scheme, 216–217
  on Darvi, 84–85, 190–191
  at family gatherings, 129, 200
  as father, 229, 230
  finances of, 217, 219, 220, 292–293
  on Gentle, 118
  on Gillaizeau, 143, 214–215
  on jewelry theft, 274
  marriages of, 213–214, 215–216, 228–230, 234, 292
  on Paris nightlife, 116–117
  on Pineda Carranza, 195–196
  at Ric-Su-Dar, 218
  son's bequest sent to, 248, 292–293
  stepsons and, 193, 249–250, 252
Savineau, Susan Zanuck Hakim:
  alcohol and, 179, 215, 219, 220, 229, 230, 231, 233, 234–235
  appearance of, 177, 179, 232, 234–235
  birth of, 39, 59
  California return of, 217–218
  childhood of, 61–64, 72, 176–180
  Darryl Zanuck's bequest to, 162
  Darryl Zanuck's contested will and, 269
  death of, 236–240
  estate of, 238, 248, 277–278
  at family gatherings, 129, 200
  father's illness and, 2, 170–172, 204
  father's influence on, 8, 177, 178
  finances of, 220–221, 238, 252
  friends of, 75, 81
  on Gillaizeau, 143
  Hollywood friends of, 187–188
  jewelry of, 234, 277–278
  marriages of, 85–86, 187, 191, 192–193, 213, 214, 215–216, 228–230, 234
  as mother, 104, 150, 192–193, 213, 214, 215, 229, 230, 253
  mother and, 178
  parental reunion and, 2, 4, 6
  parents' liaisons and, 84–85, 188, 190–192
  in Paris, 116
  as performer, 83, 188, 189–190
  romantic involvements of, 189, 192, 193, 212–213
  sister and, 227–228, 240

Scheider, Roy, 222
Schenck, Joseph:
  background of, 40
  gifts from, 209
  Palm Springs estate of, 74
  at poker games, 37
  tax problems of, 65–66
  at Twentieth Century-Fox, 45, 69
  United Artists organization and, 12, 40, 43, 44
Schenck, Nicholas, 40
Schrock, Raymond, 30
Scola, Kathryn, 33
Scott, Walter, 188
  column by, 148, 154
  on Darrylin Pineda, 181, 185, 186, 197
  on Darryl Zanuck's office, 47
  as decorator, 110, 123
  on family structure, 62
  on Virginia Zanuck, 89, 119, 259
  on Zanuck homes, 60, 61, 110
screen credits, 31
Screen Producers Guild, 14
screenwriting, 19
Securities and Exchange Commission (SEC), 159, 162
Seeger, Pocahontas (Pokie) Crowfoot Noonan:
  background of, 83, 122
  on Darryl Zanuck's health, 218
  on Darvi, 85
  daughter of, 235
  on Savineau household, 229
  on Susan Savineau, 86, 188
  Twentieth Century-Fox, 122, 132, 135
  on Virginia Zanuck, 88–89
  on Zanuck social life, 75–76, 84
Selznick, David, 51, 74, 75
Selznick, Irene Mayer, 51
senile dementia, 208
Sennett, Mack, 21, 23, 24, 53, 201
Shakespeare, William, 42
Shands, Margaret:
  background of, 200
  on Darrylin Pineda, 183, 185, 197
  Darryl Zanuck's contested will and, 246
  on Darryl Zanuck's health, 218
  on Darvi, 99
  on financial adviser, 226–227, 274
  on Gillaizeau, 145
  on Hollander book, 201–203
  on marital separation, 109, 145
  on Richard Zanuck's divorce, 119
  on Zanuck children, 61–62
Sharon Marie, 150
Sharp, Floyd, 120
Shaw, Irwin, 108
Shaw, Robert, 212
Shearer, Norma, 52–53
Sheinberg, Sidney, 222
Shirley, Thomas L.:
  background of, 200

Shirley, Thomas L. (cont.)
  contested wills and, 243, 244–246, 247–248,
    263–264, 267, 269, 283
  disappearance of, 277, 288
  as financial adviser, 208–209, 226–227
  litigation and, 210
  novel by, 264–266
  at Ric-Su-Dar, 3, 6, 206
  television appearance by, 274–275, 276–277,
    288
Shock Treatment, 113
Short Cut, The, 165
Show Them No Mercy, 46
Siegel, Lee, 146
Signal Corps, U.S., 97
Silver, Sam, 73, 94
Sinatra, Frank, 144
Sing, Boy, Sing, 104
"60 Minutes," 288
skiing, 59
Skoff, Mona:
  André Hakim helped by, 287, 294
  on Dino Hakim's death, 255–256
  at funerals, 239, 240, 258
  on Hakim marriage, 192
  Jacks children identified by, 210
  on Jacks marriage, 184, 292
  in Palm Springs, 219
  on stock sale, 220
  on Zanuck sisters, 177, 228
Skouras, Spyros, 69, 74, 75, 87, 100, 102,
  111
Smasher, 102
Smith, Maggie, 149
Snake Pit, The, 78
Snows of Kilimanjaro, The, 96
Social Highwayman, The, 30
Song to Remember, A, 77
sound movies, 31
Sound of Music, The, 113, 114–115,
  124
Sousa, John Philip, 27
Sperling, Milton, 38, 47–48
Spiegel, Sam, 108
Spielberg, Steven, 212, 221
Staircase, 125–126, 157
Stanfill, Dennis, 131, 156, 157, 159
Stanford Research Institute (SRI), 130
Star!, 115, 124–125
Stark, Ray, 134
Star Wars, 220, 221
Stevens, George, 111
Stevens, Larraine, 121
Sting, The, 2, 90, 221, 223
Storm, The, 22
Studio Club, 25, 52
Sugarland Express, 221
Sullivan, Ed, 154, 198
Sun Also Rises, The, 99, 101
Susann, Jacqueline, 78, 127, 128
Swearingen, Ronald, 278

Sylvia, Elizabeth, 270
Sylvia, Henry, 270

Take Her, She's Mine, 113
Take Two (Dunne), 111
Talmadge, Constance, 40
Talmadge, Norma, 40
taxes, 12–13, 65–66
Taylor, Elizabeth, 61, 111, 114, 144, 151
teenagers, movies for, 105
television, 113, 114, 123
Temple, Shirley, 45, 63, 64, 176, 177
Tenderloin, 56
Irving Thalberg awards, 11
Thanks a Million, 46
Tibbett, Lawrence, 45, 46
Time, 78
Tora! Tora! Tora!, 126, 134–135, 157, 161
Torpin, Henry, 15, 16, 17, 21
Triola, Michelle, 241
Tri-Star Pictures, 296
Trotti, Lamar, 49
Truman, Henry, 69
Tunis Expedition, The (Zanuck), 68
Turriziani, Maha Genii Vincentii, 222–225,
  261–262
Twentieth Century-Fox:
  Darryl Zanuck's departure from, 87–88, 100,
    159–160
  DFZ and, 100, 101, 103, 110–111
  establishment of, 44–46
  estate contests and, 279–281, 287, 293
  finances of, 154, 156–157, 220
  management of, 69, 100, 111–113,
    123–124, 126–127, 130–132, 152–154,
    156
  personnel of, 1, 45, 46–47, 57, 59, 63
  Richard Zanuck's ouster from, 132–135,
    153–154, 163, 199
  scripts at, 48
  shareholders' suit against, 162–163, 167–168
  stock battles at, 155–160
  takeover threat at, 96
  teenage audience of, 105
  television programs from, 113, 114, 123
Twentieth Century Productions:
  establishment of, 40–41
  films released by, 43
  Fox Film merged with, 44–45
  second anniversary of, 12

Uer, Paris M., 144
unions, 66
United Artists (UA), 12, 40, 41, 43–44
Universal Pictures, 22, 121, 221
USO, 67, 74, 83

Valentino, 142
Valley of the Dolls (Susann), 78, 128
Van de Kamp, John, 281
Vanzetti, Bartolomeo, 37
Verdict, The, 90, 269

Vicale, Carmine T., 168, 203, 269
Villa, Pancho, 17
Vitaphone, 31
Vreeland, Diana, 144

Wagner, Irven, 16–17
Wagner, Robert, 187
Wahl, Philippe, 116
Wakeman, Frederic, 101
Wald, Jerry, 111
Walkabout, 157
Wallis, Hal, 30–31, 38–39
"Waltons, The," 210
Warner, Harry, 38–40
Warner, Jack, 27–28, 30–34, 37, 39, 55, 107
Warner Brothers, 29, 36, 38–39, 107, 221
Washington Post, 154
Waters, Sharon, 269
Watt, Douglas, 148
Webb, Clifton, 74, 176, 179, 180, 209
Wegier, Bella, *see* Darvi, Bella
Welles, Orson, 105–106, 108, 232
Wellman, William, 33, 35–36
Welmas, Leon, 96
What Price Glory?, 187
When Willie Comes Marching Home, 187
will contests, grounds for, 242
Williams, Mary, 245
Will Success Spoil Rock Hunter?, 104
Wilson, 71, 72
Wilson, Earl, 105, 151, 155
Wilson, Woodrow, 70–71
Winter, Chantal, 262
Wise, Robert, 114, 115
Witwer, H. C., 23, 54
World of Fashion, The, 147–148
World War II, 66–68
wrestling matches, 94–95
Wuthering Heights, 77

Yeshiva University, 285–286, 287, 288, 289, 293
Young, Loretta, 41, 42, 45, 53
Young and Dangerous, 103
Yuccatone, 20, 23, 32

Zanuck, Darryl Francis:
  appearance of, 11, 12, 24, 27–28, 136, 164
  athleticism of, 21, 34–36, 46–47, 59, 83–84
  black money scheme and, 131–132, 143, 147–148, 216–217
  career of, 1, 50, 152
  childhood of, 14–18, 87
  competitiveness of, 106, 124, 126, 127, 128–130, 132–133, 135
  contested will of, 241–247, 262–273, 274–276, 282–289, 293
  daily routine of, 73
  death of, 231–233
  dogs of, 161, 165, 166, 167, 172, 206, 208
  early jobs of, 18–24
  estate of, 7, 9–10, 162, 169, 203, 207–208, 241–248, 279–281
  as father, 34, 43, 50, 60, 61, 62–64, 72–73, 90–96, 104, 177–178, 180–181, 185, 197
  financial concerns of, 13, 65–66, 98–99, 166, 207, 210
  French call girls and, 116–117, 139
  as grandfather, 9, 182, 249, 251
  health of, 1–2, 7, 125, 127, 146–147, 163–171, 174–175, 200, 203–204, 206–208, 210, 218–219
  Hollander book and, 201–203
  Hollywood memorabilia of, 279–280, 291
  as independent producer, 87–88, 97, 100–103, 110–111
  infidelities of, 2, 8, 14, 34, 47–48, 56–57, 77–78, 80, 82–83, 84–85, 86, 116–117, 144, 187–188, 192; *see also* Darvi, Bella; Demick, Irina; Gillaizeau, Genevieve; Greco, Juliette
  marriage of, 25–27, 28–29, 34, 55, 78–79, 88, 98, 109, 115–116, 143–144, 145
  office of, 47
  Palm Springs return of, 1–6, 9, 171–175, 204–205
  personal influence of, 8–9, 11, 176
  political beliefs of, 65, 66–67, 71–72
  practical jokes and, 22, 29, 37, 48, 76
  professional flaws of, 100–101
  pseudonyms of, 29
  publicity on, 12, 41–43, 49–50
  retirement of, 161–162
  self-image of, 13–14, 58, 166
  social life of, 21–22, 24, 28, 34–37, 69–70, 74–77, 190
  son's dismissal and, 14, 90, 133–134, 135, 153–154, 199
  stockholders' suit and, 162–163, 167–168
  tax problems of, 65–66
  travel by, 59–60, 101–102, 167, 199
  Twentieth Century Pictures and, 40–41
  Twentieth Century-Fox and, 44–50, 64–65, 70–72, 87–88, 112–115, 124–129, 130–132, 156–161, 162–163, 165, 199–200, 208
  at Warner Brothers, 27–28, 29–33, 34, 38–39, 55–56, 114
  wealth of, 13, 60
  as writer, 19, 22–23, 27–28, 29–30, 60, 97
Zanuck, Darrylin, *see* Pineda, Darrylin Zanuck Jacks
Zanuck, Dean, 222, 259
Zanuck, Donald, 15
Zanuck, Frank, 15
Zanuck, Harrison, 222, 259
Zanuck, Janet Beverly, 232, 295
  bequests to, 169, 260, 278
  birth of, 110
  childhood of, 222, 224, 225–226
Zanuck, Lili Fini, 226, 232, 259, 261
  as film producer, 281, 295–296

Zanuck, Lili Gentle, *see* Gentle, Lili
Zanuck, Linda Harrison, *see* Harrison, Linda
Zanuck, Michelle Linda, 144
Zanuck, Richard Darryl:
  anger of, 93–94, 118, 120–122, 224, 245
  appearance of, 104, 105, 124
  birth of, 43, 60
  career of, 2, 8, 90, 104–105, 254, 295, 296
  childhood of, 61–63, 72, 90–96
  college years of, 96–97
  Darryl Zanuck's bequest to, 162
  Darryl Zanuck's contested will and, 242, 244, 245, 246, 266–267, 268, 270, 272
  as DFZ liaison, 100, 101, 102, 103, 110
  at DFZ Productions, 98, 99, 100
  dismissal of, 132–135, 153–154, 163, 199
  education of, 81, 95, 96, 97
  estate litigation and, 7, 125, 279–281
  ex-wife's litigation aided by, 261–262
  family criticism of, 222, 281–282, 291
  as father, 110, 225–226, 295, 296
  father's competition with, 106, 124, 126, 127, 128–130, 132–133, 135
  father's illness and, 170–172, 204
  father's influence on, 8, 11, 14, 90–96
  films produced by, 105–107, 212, 269, 281
  finances of, 220–221, 222, 226
  Gillaizeau and, 146, 148, 149, 151, 153–154, 160, 172, 173, 263
  marriages of, 103–104, 105, 118–120, 122–123, 187, 222–225, 232
  mother's estate and, 259–261, 277, 278
  parental reunion and, 3, 4–5, 6, 205
  parental separation and, 98, 110
  as production chief, 112–113, 114, 115, 121, 149
  proxy battle and, 155–156, 157–158, 159, 160, 199–200
  sister's estate handled by, 248
  stockholders' suits and, 162, 163
  as Twentieth Century-Fox executive, 123, 126–128, 130, 131, 132, 152
  at Universal, 221–222, 224
Zanuck, Susan, *see* Savineau, Susan Zanuck Hakim
Zanuck, Virginia Fox:
  appearance of, 24, 25, 201, 239
  cable code name for, 102

  contested estate of, 7, 259–261, 273–274, 277–281, 287
  courtship of, 14, 25–26
  Darrylin Pineda and, 197, 198, 200, 291
  Darvi and, 79–85, 96, 182, 190–191, 215
  daughter's death and, 236–240
  detectives hired by, 110, 127, 209–210
  executive dismissals and, 133, 135, 154–155
  family background of, 52
  family crises and, 219, 225, 226, 228, 229, 230, 237–238
  film career of, 24, 27, 51, 52–53
  financial issues and, 169, 212, 220, 279
  funeral of, 258–259
  with grandchildren, 250–252
  health of, 231
  on Hollander book, 201–203
  husband's career and, 71, 157–158, 160
  husband's health and, 206, 218
  husband's return to, 1–6, 172, 173–174, 206
  infidelity tolerated by, 8, 77, 78, 86, 145, 201–203
  kindness of, 58–59
  marital separation of, 2, 3, 4, 88–89, 98, 109, 113, 115–116, 144
  marriage of, 28–29, 34, 51, 54–58, 64, 78–79, 109, 183
  memorial service arranged by, 232–233
  as mother, 62, 63, 72–73, 92, 93, 178, 180–181, 185, 193
  penthouse of, 123
  political beliefs of, 65
  pregnancies of, 41, 59–60
  professional opinions of, 33–34, 57–58, 64
  proxy battle and, 155–156, 157–158
  social life of, 62, 69–70, 75–77, 200
  son's marriage and, 104, 119
  wedding of, 26–27
  will forgery and, 245, 246, 264, 267, 269, 274, 275
  World War II and, 67–69
Zanuck, Virginia Laurine, 232, 295
  bequests to, 260, 278
  birth of, 110
  childhood of, 222, 223, 225–226
Virginia Zanuck Charitable Foundation, 278, 280–281, 291
Zukor, Adolph, 21